UNCTAD/DITE/3(Vol. X)

United Nations Conference on Trade and Development
Division on Investment, Technology and Enterprise Development

International Investment Instruments: A Compendium

Volume X

United Nations
New York and Geneva, 2002

Note

UNCTAD serves as the focal point within the United Nations Secretariat for all matters related to foreign direct investment and transnational corporations. In the past, the Programme on Transnational Corporations was carried out by the United Nations Centre on Transnational Corporations (1975-1992) and the Transnational Corporations and Management Division of the United Nations Department of Economic and Social Development (1992-1993). In 1993, the Programme was transferred to the United Nations Conference on Trade and Development. UNCTAD seeks to further the understanding of the nature of transnational corporations and their contribution to development and to create an enabling environment for international investment and enterprise development. UNCTAD's work is carried out through intergovernmental deliberations, technical assistance activities, seminars, workshops and conferences.

The term "country", as used in the boxes added by the UNCTAD secretariat at the beginning of the instruments reproduced in this volume, also refers, as appropriate, to territories or areas; the designations employed and the presentation of the material do not imply the expression of any opinion whatsoever on the part of the Secretariat of the United Nations concerning the legal status of any country, territory, city or area or of its authorities, or concerning the delimitation of its frontiers or boundaries. Moreover, the country or geographical terminology used in the boxes may occasionally depart from standard United Nations practice when this is made necessary by the nomenclature used at the time of negotiation, signature, ratification or accession of a given international instrument.

To preserve the integrity of the texts of the instruments reproduced in this volume, references to the sources of the instruments that are not contained in their original text are identified as "note added by the editor".

The texts of the instruments included in this volume are reproduced as they were written in one of their original languages or as an official translation thereof. When an obvious linguistic mistake has been found, the word "sic" has been added in brackets.

The materials contained in this volume have been reprinted with special permission of the relevant institutions. For those materials under copyright protection, all rights are reserved by the copyright holders.

It should be further noted that this collection of instruments has been prepared for documentation purposes only, and its contents do not engage the responsibility of UNCTAD.

UNCTAD/DITE/3 Vol. X

UNITED NATIONS PUBLICATION

Sales No. E.02.II.D.21

ISBN 92-1-112570-7

PREFACE

International Investment Instruments: A Compendium contains a collection of international instruments relating to foreign direct investment (FDI) and transnational corporations (TNCs). The collection is presented in ten volumes. The first three volumes were published in 1996. *Volumes IV* and *V* were published in 2000 followed by *Volume VI* in 2001. Four volumes were published in 2002, *Volumes VII, VIII, and IX* in June, followed by *Volume X* in August, bringing the collection up to date.

The collection has been prepared to make the texts of international investment instruments conveniently available to interested policy-makers, scholars and business executives. The need for such a collection has increased in recent years as bilateral, regional, interregional and multilateral instruments dealing with various aspects of FDI have proliferated, and as new investment instruments are being negotiated or discussed at all levels.

While by necessity selective, the present collection seeks to provide a faithful record of the evolution and present status of intergovernmental cooperation concerning FDI and TNCs. Although the emphasis of the collection is on relatively recent documents (the majority of the instruments reproduced date from after 1990), it was deemed useful to include important older instruments as well, with a view towards providing some indications of the historical development of international concerns over FDI in the decades since the end of the Second World War.

The core of this collection consists of legally binding international instruments, mainly multilateral conventions, regional agreements, and bilateral treaties that have entered into force. In addition, a number of "soft law" documents, such as guidelines, declarations and resolutions adopted by intergovernmental bodies, have been included since these instruments also play a role in the elaboration of an international framework for FDI. In an effort to enhance the understanding of the efforts behind the elaboration of this framework, certain draft instruments that never entered into force, or texts of instruments on which the negotiations were not concluded, are also included; prototypes of bilateral investment treaties are reproduced as well. Included also are a number of influential documents prepared by business, consumer and labour organizations, as well as by other non-governmental organizations. It is clear from the foregoing that no implications concerning the legal status or the legal effect of an instrument can be drawn from its inclusion in this collection.

In view of the great diversity of the instruments in this *Compendium* -- in terms of subject matter, approach, legal form and extent of participation of States -- the simplest possible method of presentation was deemed the most appropriate. Thus, the relevant instruments are distributed among the *ten volumes of the Compendium* as follows:

- *Volume I* is devoted to multilateral instruments, that is to say, multilateral conventions as well as resolutions and other documents issued by multilateral organizations.

- *Volume II* covers interregional and regional instruments, including agreements, resolutions and other texts from regional organizations with an inclusive geographical context.

- *Volume III* is divided into three annexes covering three types of instruments that differ in their context or their origin from those included in the first two volumes:

  - Annex A reproduces investment-related provisions in free trade and regional integration agreements. The specific function and, therefore, the effect of such provisions is largely determined by the economic integration process which they are intended to promote and in the context of which they operate.

  - Annex B (the only section that departs from the chronological pattern) offers the texts of prototype bilateral treaties for the promotion and protection of foreign investments (BITs) of several developed and developing countries, as well as a list of these treaties concluded up to July 1995. The bilateral character of these treaties differentiates them from the bulk of the instruments included in this *Compendium*. Over 900 such treaties had been adopted by July 1995.

  - Annex C supplies the texts of documents prepared by non-governmental organizations; these give an indication of the broader environment in which the instruments collected here are prepared.

- *Volume IV*, divided into two parts, covers additional multilateral (Part One) and regional instruments (Part Two) not covered in *Volumes I* and *II*, including, but not limited to, those adopted between 1996 and the end of 1999.

- *Volume V* is divided into four parts, as follows:

  - Part One reproduces investment-related provisions in a number of additional free trade and economic integration agreements not covered in *Volume III*.

  - Part Two includes for the first time investment-related provisions in association agreements as well as bilateral and interregional cooperation agreements. These are divided into three annexes. Annex A is devoted to agreements signed between the countries members of the European Free Trade Association (EFTA) and third countries. Annex B covers investment-related provisions in agreements signed between the countries members of the European Community (EC) and third countries as well as other regional groups. Annex C includes types of bilateral agreements related to investment that differ from those covered in other parts.

  - Part Three contains the texts of a number of additional prototype BITs of several developed and developing countries, as well as a list of these treaties concluded between July 1995 and the end of 1998, when the total number of BITs concluded since 1959 reached over 1,730.

  - Part Four reproduces additional texts of recent documents prepared by non-governmental organizations.

- *Volume VI* is divided into the following six parts:

  - Part One contains an additional multilateral instrument.

  - Part Two covers additional interregional and regional instruments, including agreements, resolutions and other texts from regional organizations with an inclusive geographical context.

  - Part Three reproduces investment-related provisions in a number of additional free trade and economic integration agreements not covered in previous volumes.

  - Part Four includes investment-related provisions in association agreements as well as bilateral and interregional cooperation agreements not covered in previous volumes.

  - Part Five contains the texts of a number of additional prototype BITs of several developed and developing countries not covered in previous volumes.

  - Part Six includes for the first time prototype double taxation treaties (DTTs).

- *Volume VII* is divided into the following three parts:

  - Part One contains an additional multilateral instrument.

  - Part Two reproduces investment-related provisions in a number of additional free trade and cooperation agreements signed between countries members of the European Free Trade Association (EFTA) and countries members of the European Community (EC) with third countries not covered in previous volumes.

  - Part Three contains the texts of a number of additional prototype BITs not covered in previous volumes.

- *Volume VIII* is divided into the following three parts:

  - Part One covers additional interregional and regional instruments, including agreements and other texts from regional organizations with an inclusive geographical context.

  - Part Two reproduces investment-related provisions in a number of additional free trade, economic integration and cooperation agreements not covered in previous volumes.

  - Part Three contains the texts of a number of additional prototype BITs not covered in previous volumes.

- *Volume IX* is divided into the following three parts:

  - Part One covers additional interregional and regional instruments, including agreements and other texts from regional organizations with an inclusive geographical context.

  - Part Two reproduces investment-related provisions in a number of additional free trade, economic integration and cooperation agreements not covered in previous volumes.

  - Part Three contains the texts of a number of additional prototype BITs not covered in previous volumes.

- *Volume X* is divided into the following two parts:

  - Part One reproduces investment-related provisions in a number of additional free trade, economic integration and cooperation agreements not covered in previous volumes.

  - Part Two contains texts of additional prototype BITs and a prototype double taxation treaty not included in previous volumes.

Within each of these subdivisions, instruments are reproduced in chronological order, except for the sections dedicated to prototypes instruments.

The multilateral and regional instruments covered are widely differing in scope and coverage. Some are designed to provide an overall, general framework for FDI and cover many, although rarely all, aspects of investment operations. Most instruments deal with particular aspects and issues concerning FDI. A significant number address core FDI issues, such as the promotion and protection of investment, investment liberalization, dispute settlement and insurance and guarantees. Others cover specific issues, of direct but not exclusive relevance to FDI and TNCs, such as transfer of technology, intellectual property, avoidance of double taxation, competition and the protection of consumers and the environment. A relatively small number of instruments of this last category has been reproduced, since each of these specific issues often constitutes an entire system of legal regulation of its own, whose proper coverage would require an extended exposition of many kinds of instruments and arrangements.[a]

The *Compendium* is meant to be a collection of instruments, not an anthology of relevant provisions. Indeed, to understand a particular instrument, it is normally necessary to take its entire text into consideration. An effort has been made, therefore, to reproduce complete instruments, even though, in a number of cases, reasons of space and relevance have dictated the inclusion of excerpts.

The UNCTAD secretariat has deliberately refrained from adding its own commentary to the texts reproduced in the *Compendium*. The only exception to this rule is the boxes added to

---

[a] For a collection of instruments (or excerpts therefrom) dealing with transfer of technology, see UNCTAD, *Compendium of International Arrangements on Transfer of Technology: Selected Instruments* (Geneva: United Nations), United Nations publication, Sales No. E.01.II.D.28.

each instrument. They provide some basic facts, such as its date of adoption and date of entry into force and, where appropriate, signatory countries. Also, a list of agreements containing investment-related provisions signed by the EFTA countries and by the EC countries with third countries or regional groups are reproduced in the *Compendium*. Moreover, to facilitate the identification of each instrument in the table of contents, additional information has been added, in brackets, next to each title, on the year of its signature and the name of the relevant institution involved.

Rubens Ricupero
Secretary-General of UNCTAD

Geneva, June 2002

ACKNOWLEDGEMENTS

Volume X of the *Compendium* was prepared by Abraham Negash under the overall direction of Karl P. Sauvant. Comments were received from Victoria Aranda, Americo Beviglia Zampetti, Anna Joubin-Bret and Anh-Nga Tran-Nguyen. The cooperation of the relevant countries and organizations from which the relevant instruments originate is acknowledged with gratitude.

CONTENTS

VOLUME X

PART ONE

BILATERAL INSTRUMENTS

PART TWO

PROTOTYPE INSTRUMENTS

CONTENTS OF OTHER VOLUMES

VOLUME I

MULTILATERAL INSTRUMENTS

VOLUME II

REGIONAL INSTRUMENTS

REGIONAL INSTRUMENTS

VOLUME III

REGIONAL INTEGRATION, BILATERAL AND NON-GOVERNMENTAL INSTRUMENTS

ANNEX C. NON-GOVERNMENTAL INSTRUMENTS

VOLUME IV

MULTILATERAL AND REGIONAL INSTRUMENTS

PART ONE

MULTILATERAL INSTRUMENTS

PART TWO

REGIONAL INSTRUMENTS

VOLUME V

REGIONAL INTEGRATION, BILATERAL AND NON-GOVERNMENTAL INSTRUMENTS

PART ONE

INVESTMENT-RELATED PROVISIONS IN FREE TRADE AND ECONOMIC INTEGRATION AGREEMENTS

PART TWO

INVESTMENT-RELATED PROVISIONS IN ASSOCIATION AGREEMENTS, BILATERAL AND INTERREGIONAL COOPERATION AGREEMENTS

ANNEX C. OTHER BILATERAL INVESTMENT-RELATED AGREEMENTS

PART THREE

PROTOTYPE BILATERAL INVESTMENT TREATIES
AND LIST OF BILATERAL INVESTMENT TREATIES
(MID-1995 — END-1998)

PART FOUR

NON-GOVERNMENTAL INSTRUMENTS

VOLUME VI

PART ONE

MULTILATERAL INSTRUMENTS

PART TWO

INTERREGIONAL AND REGIONAL INSTRUMENTS

PART THREE

INVESTMENT-RELATED PROVISIONS IN FREE TRADE AND ECONOMIC INTEGRATION AGREEMENTS

PART FOUR

INVESTMENT-RELATED PROVISIONS IN ASSOCIATION AGREEMENTS, BILATERAL AND INTERREGIONAL COOPERATION AGREEMENTS

PART FIVE

PROTOTYPE BILATERAL INVESTMENT TREATIES

PART SIX

PROTOTYPE BILATERAL DOUBLE TAXATION TREATIES

CONTENTS

VOLUME VII

PART ONE

MULTILATERAL INSTRUMENTS

PART TWO

BILATERAL INSTRUMENTS

PART THREE

PROTOTYPE INSTRUMENTS

VOLUME VIII

PART ONE

INTERREGIONAL AND REGIONAL INSTRUMENTS

PART TWO

BILATERAL INSTRUMENTS

PART THREE

PROTOTYPE INSTRUMENTS

CONTENTS

VOLUME IX

PART ONE

INTERREGIONAL AND REGIONAL INSTRUMENTS

PART TWO

BILATERAL INSTRUMENTS

PART THREE

PROTOTYPE INSTRUMENTS

PART ONE

BILATERAL INSTRUMENTS

AGREEMENT BETWEEN THE EUROPEAN ECONOMIC COMMUNITY AND THE REPUBLIC OF ALBANIA, ON TRADE AND COMMERCIAL AND ECONOMIC COOPERATION*
[excerpts]

> The Agreement between the European Economic Community and the Republic of Albania, on Trade and Commercial and Economic Cooperation was signed on 11 May 1992. It entered in to force on 1 December 1992. The member States of the European Communities are: Austria, Belgium, Denmark, Finland, France, Germany, Greece, Ireland, Italy, Luxembourg, the Netherlands, Portugal, Spain, Sweden and the United Kingdom.

TITLE II

Trade and commercial cooperation

Article 13

1.   The Contracting Parties shall make every effort to promote, expand and diversify their trade on the basis of non-discrimination and reciprocity. In the spirit of this Article, the Joint Committee established under Title V of this Agreement will attach special importance to examining ways of encouraging the reciprocal and harmonious expansion of trade.

2.   In furtherance of the aims of this Article and within the limits of their respective powers, the Contracting Parties agree on the necessity to improve favourable business regulations and facilities for each other's firms or companies on their respective markets, inter alia by taking steps:

   - to ensure the publication and facilitate exchanges of commercial and economic information on all matters which would assist the development of commercial and economic cooperation, for example:

   - economic development plans or forecasts,

   - general and sectoral import arrangements,

   - economic and commercial law, including regulations on markets, companies and investment,

   - macro-economic information and statistics, including production, consumption and foreign trade statistics,

---

* *Source*: European Communities (1992). "Agreement between the European Economic Community and the Republic of Albania, on Trade and Commercial and Economic Cooperation", *Official Journal of the European Communities*, L 343, 25 November 1992, pp. 2 – 9; available on the Internet (http://europa.eu.int). [Note added by the editor.]

- to facilitate the establishment and operation of each other's companies,

- to encourage trade promotion activities,

- to provide natural and legal persons of the other Party with guarantees of their individual and property rights, such as non-discriminatory access for that purpose to courts and appropriate administrative bodies of the Community and Albania.

3.   Albania will take measures guaranteeing an effective and adequate protection of intellectual, industrial and commercial property, at a level similar to that which exists in the Community, and will adhere to International Conventions on intellectual, industrial and commercial property.

4.   The Contracting Parties undertake to facilitate, within the limits of their respective powers, administrative cooperation between the appropriate authorities in matters relating to customs, in particular in the following areas:

- vocational training,

- simplification of customs documentation and procedures, and

- prevention and detection of infringements of the rules on customs matters, including the rules governing import quotas.

5.   The Contracting Parties recognize that counter-trade practices may create distortions in international trade and that they should be regarded as temporary and exceptional.

For this reason they agree not to impose countertrade requirements on companies established in Albania or the Community, or to compel them to engage in such trade practices.

Nevertheless, where firms or companies decide to resort to counter-trade operations, the Contracting Parties shall encourage them to furnish all relevant information to facilitate the transaction.

Article 14

Within the limits of their respective powers, the Contracting Parties:

- shall encourage the adoption of arbitration for the settlement of disputes arising out of commercial and cooperation transactions concluded by companies, enterprises or economic organizations of the Community and those of Albania,

- agree that when a dispute is submitted to arbitration, each party to the dispute may freely choose its own arbitrator, irrespective of nationality, and that the presiding third arbitrator or the sole arbitrator may be a citizen of a third State,

- shall encourage recourse to the arbitration rules developed by the United Nations Commission on International Trade Law (Uncitral) and to arbitration by any centre of a State signatory to the Convention on Recognition and Enforcement of Foreign Arbitral Awards concluded in New York on 10 June 1958.

TITLE III
Economic Cooperation

Article 15

1.   In the light of their respective economic policies and objectives, the Contracting Parties, within the limits of their respective powers, shall foster economic cooperation on as broad a base as possible in all fields deemed to be in their mutual interest.

The objectives of such cooperation shall be, inter alia:

  - to reinforce and diversify economic links between the Contracting Parties,

  - to contribute to the development of their respective economies and standards of living,

  - to open up new sources of supply and new markets,

  - to encourage cooperation between economic operators with a view to promoting joint ventures, licensing agreements, and other forms of industrial cooperation to develop their respective industries,

  - to encourage scientific and technological progress,

  - to support structural changes in the Albanian economy which will increase and diversify trade in goods and services with the Community,

  - to encourage the participation of small and medium-sized enterprises in trade and industrial cooperation.

2.   In order to achieve these objectives, the Contracting Parties shall make efforts to encourage and promote economic cooperation in areas of mutual interest, in particular in the following sectors:

  - industry, including light industry and craft industries,
  - mining,
  - agriculture, including agro-industry, and cooperation in animal and plant health,
  - fisheries,
  - construction and housing,
  - science and technology in areas in which the Contracting Parties are active and which they consider to be of mutual interest,
  - telecommunications,
  - energy, including the development of new sources of energy,
  - environmental protection, including protection from water and air pollution and industrial accidents, and the management of natural resources,
  - transport, communications and the running of ports,
  - tourism and other service activities,
  - economic, monetary, banking, insurance and financial services,
  - development of human resources, vocational and management training,
  - health,
  - economic policy,

- standards,
- statistics.

3.   To give effect to the objectives of economic cooperation and within the limits of their respective powers, the Contracting Parties shall encourage the adoption of measures aimed at creating favourable conditions for economic and industrial cooperation, including:

-          the facilitation of exchanges of commercial and economic information,

-          the development of a favourable climate for investment, notably by the extension by the Member States of the Community and Albania of arrangements for investment promotion and protection, in particular for the transfer of profits and the repatriation of invested capital, on the basis of non-discrimination and reciprocity, and also of agreements on the avoidance of double taxation,

-          exchanges and contacts between persons and delegations representing commercial or other appropriate organizations,

-          the organization of seminars, fairs or exhibitions, symposia and business weeks,

-          the encouragement of activities involving the provision of technical competence in specific fields, notably commercialization.

TITLE V
Joint Committee

Article 18

1.   (a)   A Joint Committee shall be set up, comprising representatives of the Community, on the one hand, and representatives of Albania, on the other.

        (b)   The Joint Committee shall formulate recommendations by mutual agreement between the Contracting Parties.

        (c)   The Joint Committee shall, as necessary, adopt its own rules of procedure and programme of work.

        (d)   The Joint Committee shall meet once a year in Brussels and Tirana alternately. Special meetings may be convened by mutual agreement, at the request of either Contracting Party. The Joint Committee shall be chaired alternately by each of the Contracting Parties. Wherever possible, the agenda for meetings of the Joint Committee shall be agreed beforehand.

        (e)   The Joint Committee may decide to set up working parties to assist it in carrying out its duties.

2.   (a)   The Joint Committee shall ensure the proper functioning of this Agreement and shall devise and recommend practical measures for achieving its objectives, keeping in view the economic and social policies of the Contracting Parties.

(b)   The Joint Committee shall endeavour to find ways of encouraging the development of trade and commercial and economic cooperation between the Contracting Parties. In particular, it shall:

-        examine the various aspects of trade between the Parties, notably its overall pattern, rate of growth, structure and diversification, the trade balance and the various forms of trade and trade promotion,

-        make recommendations on any trade or economic cooperation problem of mutual concern,

-        seek appropriate means of avoiding possible difficulties in the fields of trade and cooperation and encourage various forms of commercial and economic cooperation in areas of mutual interest,

-        consider measures likely to develop and diversify trade and economic cooperation, notably by improving import opportunities in the Community and in Albania,

-        exchange information on macro-economic plans and forecasts for the economies of the two Parties which have an impact on trade and cooperation and, by extension, on the scope for developing complementarity between their respective economies and also on proposed economic development programmes,

-        exchange information on amendments to and developments in the laws, regulations and formalities of the Contracting Parties in the areas covered by this Agreement,

-        seek methods of arranging and encouraging the exchange of information and contacts in matters relating to economic cooperation between the Contracting Parties on a mutually advantageous basis, and work towards the creation of favourable conditions for such cooperation,

-        examine the situation concerning procedures for the award of contracts for supplying goods and services following an international invitation to tender,

-        examine favourably ways of improving conditions for the development of direct contacts between firms established in the Community and those established in Albania,

-        formulate and submit to the authorities of both Contracting Parties recommendations for resolving any problems that arise, where appropriate by means of the conclusion of arrangements or agreements.

*

AGREEMENT ON TRADE AND ECONOMIC COOPERATION BETWEEN THE EUROPEAN ECONOMIC COMMUNITY AND MONGOLIA *
[excerpts]

The Agreement on Trade and Economic Cooperation between the European Economic Community and Mongolia was signed on 16 June 1992. It entered in to force on 1 March 1993. The member States of the European Communities are: Austria, Belgium, Denmark, Finland, France, Germany, Greece, Ireland, Italy, Luxembourg, the Netherlands, Portugal, Spain, Sweden and the United Kingdom.

CHAPTER II

Economic cooperation

Article 9

Within the limits of their competence respectively, and with the main aims of encouraging the development of industry and agriculture in the Community and in Mongolia, of diversifying their economic links, encouraging scientific and technological progress, opening up new sources of supply and new markets and helping to develop their economies and raise their respective standards of living, the two Contracting Parties agree to develop economic cooperation based on the principle of mutual interest, in all the areas within the framework of their respective policies, and in particular:

- industry and mining,
- agriculture and forestry,
- science and technology,
- energy,
- telecommunications,
- environmental protection,
- tourism,
- intellectual and industrial property, norms and standards,
- statistics.

Article 10

According to their needs, and within the means at their disposal, the two Contracting Parties shall encourage the application of the various forms of industrial and technical cooperation, for the benefit of their undertakings or organizations.

In order to attain the objectives of this Agreement, the two Contracting Parties shall endeavour to facilitate and promote, among other activities:

---

* *Source*: European Communities (1993). "Agreement on Trade and Economic Cooperation between the European Economic Community and Mongolia", *Official Journal of the European Communities*, L 041, 18 February 1993, pp. 46 - 49; available also on the Internet (http://europa.eu.int). [Note added by the editor.]

- joint production and joint ventures,
- common exploitation of resources,
- the transfer of technology,
- cooperation between financial institutions,
- actions such as visits, contacts and promotional activities designed to enhance cooperation between individuals and delegations representing enterprises or economic organizations,
- the organization of seminars and symposia,
- consultancy services.

Article 11

1.   In order to attain the objectives of this Agreement, the two Contracting Parties agree, within the framework of their respective laws, rules and policies, to promote and encourage greater and mutually beneficial investment.

2. In addition, the Parties undertake to improve further the investment climate, particularly through encouraging the extension, by and to the Member States of the Community and by and to Mongolia, of investment promotion and protection arrangements, based on the principles of reciprocity and equitable treament.

Article 12

In view of the difference in the two Contracting Parties' levels of development, the Community will extend its financial and technical cooperation activities to the development of Mongolia, within the framework of its aid programmes in favour of non-associated developing countries.

*

COOPERATION AGREEMENT BETWEEN THE EUROPEAN COMMUNITY AND THE REPUBLIC OF INDIA ON PARTNERSHIP AND DEVELOPMENT*
[excerpts]

The Cooperation Agreement between the European Community and the Republic of India on Partnership and Development was signed on 20 December 1993. It entered in to force 1 August 1994. The member States of the European Communities are: Austria, Belgium, Denmark, Finland, France, Germany, Greece, Ireland, Italy, Luxembourg, the Netherlands, Portugal, Spain, Sweden and the United Kingdom.

Article 4
Economic cooperation

1.   The Contracting Parties undertake, in their mutual interests and in accordance with their respective policies and objectives, to foster economic cooperation of the widest possible scope in order to contribute to the expansion of their respective economies and their developmental needs.

2.   The Contracting Parties agree that economic cooperation will involve three broad fields of action:

   (a)   improving the economic environment in India by facilitating access to Community know-how and technology;

   (b)   facilitating contacts between economic operators and other measures designed to promote commercial exchanges and investments;

   (c)   reinforcing mutual understanding of their respective economic, social and cultural environment as a basis for effective cooperation.

3.   In the broad fields described above, the aims shall be in particular to:

   - improve the economic environment and business climate,
   - cooperate in the protection of the environment and natural resources,
   - cooperate in the field of energy and energy efficiency,
   - cooperate in the field of telecommunications, information technology, and related matters,
   - cooperate in all aspects of industrial standards and intellectual property,
   - encourage technology transfer in other sectors of mutual benefit,
   - exchange information on monetary matters and the macro-economic environment,
   - reinforce and diversify economic links between them,
   - encourage the two-way flow of Community-Indian trade and investments,
   - activate industrial cooperation including agro-industry,

---

* *Source*: European Communities (1994). "Cooperation Agreement between the European Community and the Republic of India on Partnership and Development", *Official Journal of the European Communities*, L 223, 27 July 1994, pp. 24 - 34; available also on the Internet (http://europa.eu.int). [Note added by the editor.]

- promote cooperation in order to develop agriculture, fisheries, mining, transport and communication, health, banking and insurance, tourism and other services,
- encourage close cooperation between the private sectors of both regions,
- promote cooperation in industrial and urban ecology,
- promote support of undertaking by means of trade promotion and market development,
- promote scientific and technological development,
- promote training and specific training programmes,
- cooperate in the fields of information and culture.

Cooperation in a number of the abovementioned sectors is set out in more detail in Articles 5 to 15 included which follow.

4.   The Contracting Parties shall consider in particular the following means to achieve these aims:

- exchange of information and ideas,
- preparation of studies,
- provision of technical assistance,
- training programmes,
- establishment of links between research and training centres, specialized agencies and business organizations,
- promotion of investment and joint ventures,
- institutional development of public and private agencies and administrations,
- access to each other's existing data bases and creation of new ones,
- workshops and seminars,
- exchanges of experts.

5.   The Contracting Parties will determine together and to their mutual advantage the areas and priorities to be covered by concrete actions of economic cooperation, in conformity with their long-term objectives. In view of the importance of long-term enhancement of cooperation between the Community and India, no sector shall be excluded a priori from the field of economic cooperation.

Article 5
Industry and services

1.   The Contracting Parties shall:

(a)   identify sectors of industry on which cooperation will centre and the means to promote industrial cooperation with a heavy technological bias;

(b)   promote the expansion and diversification of India's production base in the industrial and service sectors, including modernization and reform of the public sector, directing their cooperation activities at small and medium-sized enterprises in particular and taking steps to facilitate their access to sources of capital, markets and technology directed especially towards promoting trade between the Contracting Parties as well as at third country markets.

2.   The Contracting Parties shall facilitate, within the relevant existing rules, access to available information and capital facilities in order to encourage projects and operations

promoting cooperation between firms, such as joint ventures, sub-contracting, transfer of technology, licences, applied research and franchises.

Article 6
Private sector

The Contracting Parties agree to promote the involvement of the private sector in their cooperation programmes in order to strengthen economic and industrial cooperation between themselves.

The Contracting Parties shall take measures to:

(a)   encourage the private sectors of both geographical regions to find effective ways of joint consultations, results of which could then be transmitted to the Joint Commission, referred to in Article 22 of this Agreement, for the required follow-up action;

(b)   involve the private sectors of the Contracting Parties in activities developed within the framework of this Agreement.

Article 8
Telecommunications, electronics, and information and satellite technologies

The Contracting Parties recognize the importance of cooperation in the fields of telecommunications, electronics, and information technologies which contribute to increased economic development and trade. Such cooperation may include:

(a)   standardization, testing and certification;
(b)   earth and space-based telecommunications;
(c)   electronics and micro-electronics;
(d)   information and automation;
(e)   high definition television;
(f)   research and development in new information technologies and telecommunications;
(g)   promotion of investment and joint investment.

Article 10
Intellectual property

The Contracting Parties undertake to ensure as far as their laws, regulations and policies allow that suitable and effective protection is provided for intellectual property rights, including patents, trade or service marks, copyright and similar rights, geographical designations (including marks of origin), industrial designs and integrated circuit topographics, reinforcing this protection where desirable. They also undertake, wherever possible, to facilitate access to the data bases of intellectual property organizations.

Article 11
Investment

1.   The Contracting Parties shall encourage an increase in mutually beneficial investment by establishing a favourable climate for private investments including better conditions for the transfer of capital and exchange of information on investment opportunities.

2.   Taking into account work done in this area in relevant international fora, and recognizing in particular the recent signing by India of the Multilateral Investments Guarantee Agency (MIGA) Convention, the Contracting Parties agree to support the promotion and protection of investments between the Member States of the Community and India on the basis of the principles of non-discrimination and reciprocity.

3.   The Contracting Parties undertake to encourage cooperation between their respective financial institutions.

Article 13
Tourism

The Contracting Parties agree to contribute to cooperation on tourism, to be achieved through specific measures, including:

(a)   interchange of information and the carrying out of studies;

(b)   training programmes;

(c)   promotion of investment and joint ventures.

Article 22
Joint Commission

1.   The Contracting Parties agree to retain the Joint Commission set up under Article 10 of the 1981 Agreement for Commercial and Economic Cooperation.

2.   The Joint Commission is in particular required to:

(a)   ensure the proper functioning and implementation of the Agreement;

(b)   make suitable recommendations for promoting the objectives of the Agreement;

(c)   establish priorities in relation to the aims of the Agreement;

(d)   examine ways and means of enhancing the partnership and development cooperation in the areas covered by the Agreement.

The Joint Commission shall be composed of representatives of both sides, at an appropriately high level. The Joint Commission shall normally meet every year, alternately in Brussels and New Delhi, on a date fixed by mutual agreement. Extraordinary meetings may be convened by agreement between the Contracting Parties.

The Joint Commission may set up specialized sub-groups to assist in the performance of its tasks and to coordinate the formulation and implementation of projects and programmes within the framework of the Agreement.

The agenda for meetings of the Joint Commission shall be determined by agreement between the Contracting Parties.

The Contracting Parties agree that it shall also be the task of the Joint Commission to ensure the proper functioning of any sectoral agreements concluded or which may be concluded between the Community and India.

*

TRATADO DE LIBRE COMERCIO ENTRE LOS ESTADOS UNIDOS MEXICANOS Y LA REPÚBLICA DE BOLIVIA*
[excerpts]

The Free Trade Agreement between Mexico and Bolivia was signed on 10 September 1994. It entered into force 1 January 1995.

Capítulo IX

Principios generales sobre el comercio de servicios

Artículo 9-01: Definiciones.

Para efectos de este capítulo, se entenderá por:

ejercicio profesional: la realización habitual de todo acto profesional o la prestación de cualquier servicio propio de cada profesión que requiera autorización gubernamental;

empresa de una Parte: una empresa constituida u organizada de conformidad con la legislación de una Parte, incluidas las sucursales localizadas en el territorio de una Parte que realiza actividades económicas en ese territorio;

prestador de servicios de una Parte: una persona de una Parte que preste o pretenda prestar un servicio;

restricción cuantitativa: una medida no discriminatoria que imponga limitaciones sobre:

a)   el número de prestadores de servicios, ya sea a través de una cuota, monopolio o una prueba de necesidad económica o por cualquier otro medio cuantitativo; o

b)   las operaciones de cualquier prestador de servicios, ya sea a través de una cuota o de una prueba de necesidad económica, o por cualquier otro medio cuantitativo;

servicios profesionales: los servicios que, para su prestación, requieren educación media superior, superior especializada, o adiestramiento o experiencia equivalentes y cuyo ejercicio es autorizado o restringido por una Parte, pero no incluye los servicios prestados por personas que practican un oficio ni los prestados por tripulantes de barcos mercantes o aeronaves.

---

*   Source*: The Government of Bolivia and the Government of Mexico (1995). "Tratado de Libre Comercio entre los Estados Unidos Mexicanos y la República de Bolivia", available on the Internet (http://www.economia-snci.gob.mx/nueva-snci/tratados/tlcbol/frame3.htm) and (http://www.oas.org). [Note added by the editor.]

Artículo 9-02: Ambito de aplicación.

1.   Este capítulo se aplica a las medidas que una Parte adopte o mantenga sobre el comercio de servicios que realicen los prestadores de servicios de la otra Parte, incluidas las relativas a:

   a)   la producción, distribución, comercialización, venta y prestación de un servicio;

   b)   la compra, el uso o el pago de un servicio;

   c)   el acceso a sistemas de distribución y transporte relacionados con la prestación de un servicio y el uso de los mismos;

   d)   el acceso a redes y servicios públicos de telecomunicaciones y el uso de los mismos;

   e)   la presencia, en su territorio, de un prestador de servicios de la otra Parte; y

   f)   el otorgamiento de una fianza u otra forma de garantía financiera, como condición para la prestación de un servicio.

2.   Este capítulo no se aplica a:

   a)   los servicios de transporte aéreo nacional o internacional, con y sin itinerario fijo, así como las actividades auxiliares de apoyo a los servicios aéreos, salvo:

      i)   los servicios de reparación y mantenimiento de aeronaves durante el periodo en que se retira una aeronave de servicio;

      ii)   los servicios aéreos especializados; y

      iii)   los sistemas computarizados de reservación;

   b)   los servicios financieros;

   c)   los subsidios o donaciones otorgados por una Parte o por una empresa del Estado, incluidos los préstamos, garantías y seguros apoyados por entidades gubernamentales; ni

   d)   los servicios o funciones gubernamentales tales como la ejecución de las leyes, los servicios de readaptación social, el seguro sobre el ingreso, la seguridad o el seguro social, el bienestar social, la educación pública, la capacitación pública, la salud y la atención a la niñez.

3.   Para efectos de este capítulo, cualquier referencia a los gobiernos federal o central y estatales o departamentales, incluye a los organismos no gubernamentales que ejerzan facultades reglamentarias, administrativas u otras de carácter gubernamental que le hayan sido delegadas por esos gobiernos.

4.   Para efectos de este Tratado, comercio de servicios significa el suministro de un servicio:

a) del territorio de una Parte al territorio de la otra Parte;

b) en el territorio de una Parte a un consumidor de la otra Parte;

c) por conducto de la presencia de prestadores de servicios de una Parte en el territorio de la otra Parte;

d) por personas físicas de una Parte en el territorio de la otra Parte.

5. Ninguna disposición de este capítulo se interpretará en el sentido de:

a) imponer a una Parte obligación alguna respecto a un nacional de la otra Parte que pretenda ingresar a su mercado de trabajo o que tenga empleo permanente en su territorio, ni de conferir derecho alguno a ese nacional, respecto a ese acceso o empleo; ni

b) imponer obligación o derecho alguno a una Parte, respecto a las compras gubernamentales hechas por otra Parte o empresa del Estado.

Artículo 9-03: Trato nacional.

Cada Parte otorgará a los servicios y a los prestadores de servicios de la otra Parte un trato no menos favorable que el concedido, en circunstancias similares, a sus servicios y a sus prestadores de servicios.

Artículo 9-04: Trato de nación más favorecida.

1. Cada Parte otorgará a los servicios y a los prestadores de servicios de la otra Parte un trato no menos favorable que el concedido, en circunstancias similares, a los servicios y a los prestadores de servicios de la otra Parte o de cualquier país que no sea Parte.

2. Las disposiciones de este capítulo no se interpretarán en el sentido de impedir que una Parte confiera o conceda ventajas a países limítrofes con el fin de facilitar intercambios en las zonas fronterizas contiguas, de servicios que se produzcan y consuman localmente.

Artículo 9-05: Presencia local.

1. Ninguna Parte exigirá a un prestador de servicios de la otra Parte que establezca o mantenga una oficina de representación u otro tipo de empresa, o que resida en su territorio, como condición para la prestación de un servicio.

2. Sin perjuicio de lo dispuesto en el párrafo 1, todo prestador de servicios de una Parte que elija establecerse en territorio de la otra Parte, deberá cumplir con el ordenamiento legal de esa Parte.

Artículo 9-06: Consolidación de medidas.

1. Ninguna Parte incrementará el grado de disconformidad de sus medidas a la entrada en vigor de este Tratado respecto a los artículos 9-03 al 9-05. Ninguna reforma de alguna de esas

medidas disminuirá el grado de conformidad de las mismas tal como estaba en vigor inmediatamente antes de la reforma.

2.   En un plazo de un año contado a partir de la entrada en vigor de este Tratado, las Partes inscribirán en el anexo 1 a este artículo las medidas a que se refiere el párrafo 1.

3.   Las disposiciones de los artículos 9-03 al 9-05 no se aplicarán a cualquier medida disconforme que adopte o mantenga una Parte respecto de las actividades que hayan sido listadas en el anexo 2 a este artículo a la firma de este Tratado. Transcurrido un periodo de dos años posteriores a la entrada en vigor de este Tratado cualquier medida que adopte una Parte no podrá ser más restrictiva que aquellas existentes al final del mismo. Las Partes, en la adopción o mantenimiento de las medidas disconformes referidas, buscarán alcanzar un equilibrio global en sus obligaciones.

4.   Para las medidas estatales y departamentales disconformes con los artículos 9-03 al 9-05, el plazo para listarlas en el anexo 1 a este artículo no será mayor a dos años contados a partir de la entrada en vigor de este Tratado.

5.   Las Partes no tienen la obligación de inscribir las medidas locales ni municipales.

Artículo 9-07: Restricciones cuantitativas.

1.   Las Partes procurarán negociar, al menos cada dos años, la liberalización o eliminación de restricciones cuantitativas existentes a la entrada en vigor de este Tratado o las que se adopten posteriormente a nivel federal o central y estatal o departamental.

2.   En un plazo de un año contado a partir de la entrada en vigor de este Tratado, las Partes inscribirán en el anexo a este artículo las restricciones cuantitativas a que se refiere el párrafo 1.

3.   Cada Parte notificará a la otra Parte cualquier restricción cuantitativa, diferente a las de nivel de gobierno local o municipal, que adopte después de la entrada en vigor de este Tratado, e inscribirá la restricción en el anexo a este artículo.

Artículo 9-08: Liberalización futura.

A través de las negociaciones futuras que convoque la Comisión, las Partes profundizarán la liberalización alcanzada en los diferentes sectores de servicios, con miras a lograr la eliminación de las medidas inscritas en los anexos 1 y 2 al artículo 9-06 de conformidad con los párrafos 2 al 4 de ese artículo para un equilibrio global en los compromisos.

Artículo 9-09: Liberalización de medidas no discriminatorias.

Cada Parte podrá negociar la liberalización de restricciones cuantitativas, requisitos para el otorgamiento de licencias y otras medidas no discriminatorias. Las Partes inscribirán los compromisos adquiridos en el anexo a este artículo.

Articulo 9-10: Procedimientos.

Las Partes establecerán procedimientos para:

a)   que una Parte notifique a la otra Parte e incluya en el anexo correspondiente:

      i)   las medidas federales o centrales, de conformidad con los párrafos 2 y 3 del artículo 9-06;

      ii)   las medidas estatales o departamentales, de conformidad con el párrafo 4 del artículo 9-06;

      iii)   las restricciones cuantitativas no discriminatorias, de conformidad con el artículo 9-07;

      iv)   los compromisos referentes al artículo 9-09; y

      v)   las modificaciones a las medidas a que se hace referencia en el artículo 9-06; y

b)   la celebración de negociaciones futuras tendientes a perfeccionar la liberalización global de los servicios entre las Partes, de conformidad con el artículo 9-08.

Artículo 9-11: Cooperación técnica.

A partir de la entrada en vigor de este Tratado, las Partes establecerán un sistema para facilitar a los prestadores de servicios información referente a sus mercados en relación con:

a)   los aspectos comerciales y técnicos del suministro de servicios;

b)   la posibilidad de obtener tecnología en materia de servicios; y

c)   aquellos aspectos que la Comisión considere pertinente sobre este tema.

Artículo 9-12: Reconocimiento de títulos profesionales y otorgamiento de licencias.

1.   Con objeto de garantizar que toda medida que una Parte adopte o mantenga en relación con los requisitos y procedimientos para el otorgamiento de licencias y el reconocimiento de títulos a los nacionales de la otra Parte no constituya una barrera innecesaria al comercio, cada Parte procurará garantizar que esas medidas:

a)   se sustenten en criterios objetivos y transparentes, tales como la capacidad y la aptitud para prestar un servicio;

b)   no sean más gravosas de lo necesario para asegurar la calidad de un servicio; y

c)   no constituyan una restricción encubierta a la prestación transfronteriza de un servicio.

2.   Cuando una Parte revalide, de manera unilateral o por acuerdo con otro país, las licencias o los títulos profesionales obtenidos en el territorio de la otra Parte o de cualquier país que no sea Parte:

a)   nada de lo dispuesto en el artículo 9-04 se interpretará en el sentido de exigir a esa Parte que revalide los estudios, las licencias o los títulos profesionales obtenidos en el territorio de la otra Parte; y

b)   esa Parte proporcionará a la otra Parte oportunidad adecuada para demostrar que los estudios, las licencias o los títulos profesionales obtenidos en territorio de esa otra Parte también deberán ser revalidados, o para negociar o celebrar un acuerdo que tenga efectos equivalentes.

3.   Cada Parte, en un plazo de dos años contados a partir de la entrada en vigor de este Tratado, eliminará todo requisito de nacionalidad o de residencia permanente que mantenga para el otorgamiento de licencias a los prestadores de servicios profesionales de la otra Parte. Cuando una Parte no cumpla con esta obligación con respecto a un sector en particular, la otra Parte podrá mantener, en el mismo sector y durante el mismo tiempo que la Parte en incumplimiento mantenga su requisito, como único recurso, un requisito equivalente al indicado en su lista del anexo a este artículo o restablecer:

a)   cualquiera de esos requisitos a nivel federal o central que hubiere eliminado conforme a este artículo; o

b)   cualquiera de esos requisitos a nivel estatal o departamental que hubieren estado vigentes a la entrada en vigor de este Tratado, mediante notificación a la Parte en incumplimiento.

4.   En el anexo a este artículo se establecen procedimientos para el reconocimiento de la educación, experiencia y otras normas y requisitos que rigen para los prestadores de servicios profesionales.

Artículo 9-13: Denegación de beneficios.

Una Parte podrá denegar los beneficios derivados de este capítulo a un prestador de servicios de la otra Parte, previa notificación y realización de consultas, cuando la Parte determine que el servicio está siendo prestado por una empresa de propiedad o bajo control de personas de un país que no es Parte; y

a)   la empresa no realice actividades de negocios importantes en territorio de cualquier Parte; o

b)   la Parte que deniegue los beneficios:

i)   no mantenga relaciones diplomáticas con el país que no sea Parte; y

ii)   adopte o mantenga medidas en relación con el país que no es Parte, que prohíban transacciones con esa empresa, o que serían violadas o eludidas si los beneficios de este capítulo se otorgan a esa empresa.

Artículo 9-14: Otras disciplinas.

1.   La Comisión determinará los procedimientos para el establecimiento de disciplinas necesarias para regular:

a) las medidas de salvaguardia; y

b) la imposición de cuotas compensatorias.

2. Para efectos del párrafo 1, la Comisión hará un seguimiento de los trabajos realizados por los organismos internacionales pertinentes y, en su caso, los tomará en cuenta.

Artículo 9-15: Relación con acuerdos multilaterales sobre servicios.

1. Las Partes se comprometen a aplicar entre sí las disposiciones contenidas en los acuerdos multilaterales sobre servicios de los cuales las Partes sean parte.

2. No obstante lo dispuesto en el párrafo 1, en caso de incompatibilidad entre las disposiciones de esos acuerdos y las de este Tratado, estas últimas prevalecerán en la medida de la incompatibilidad.

Anexo 1 al artículo 9-06
Consolidación de medidas

Las Partes listarán en este anexo las medidas incompatibles con los artículos 9-03 al 9-05, de conformidad con lo establecido en el párrafo 2 del artículo 9-06.

Anexo 2 al artículo 9-06

Lista de actividades

Bolivia:

1. Servicios de consultoría en:

a) derecho

b) contabilidad y administración

c) ingeniería y arquitectura; y

d) economía.

2. Servicios de investigación de mercados y encuestas a las empresas.

3. Servicios de ensayos y análisis técnicos.

4. Servicios relacionados con la distribucuón de energía.

5. Servicios de colocación y suministro de personal.

6. Servicios de investigación y seguridad.

7. Servicios de mantenimiento y reparación de equipo.

8.   Servicios de limpieza de edificios.

9.   Servicios fotográficos.

10.   Servicios de empaque.

11.   Servicios de editoriales y de imprenta.

12.   Servicios prestados con ocasión de asambleas o convenciones.

13.   Servicios postales.

14.   Servicios de correo.

15.   Servicios de telecomunicación (excepto los servicios de telecomunicaciones de valor agregado.

16.   Servicios de transporte marítimo.

17.   Transporte por vías navegables superiores.

18.   Transporte por el espacio.

19.   Servicios de construcción y servicios de ingeniería conexos.

20.   Trabajos generales de construcción para la edificación.

21.   Trabajos generales de construcción para la ingeniería civil.

22.   Armado de construcciones prefabricadas y trabas de instalación.

23.   Trabajos de terminación de edificios.

Anexo al artículo 9-12
Servicios profesionales

1.   Definiciones.

Para efectos de este anexo, se entenderá por ejercicio profesional, la realización habitual de todo acto profesional o la prestación de cualquier servicio propio de cada profesión que requiera autorización gubernamental.

2.   Objetivo.

Este anexo tiene como objetivo establecer las reglas que habrán de observar las Partes para la reducción y eliminación, en su territorio, de las barreras a la prestación de servicios profesionales.

3.   Ambito de aplicación.

Este anexo se aplica a todas las medidas relacionadas con los criterios para el mutuo reconocimiento de títulos profesionales y para el otorgamiento de licencias para el ejercicio profesional.

4.   Elaboración de disposiciones y criterios profesionales.

      a)   Las Partes acuerdan que el proceso de reconocimiento mutuo de títulos y otorgamiento de licencias para el ejercicio profesional, en su territorio, se hará sobre la base de elevar la calidad de los servicios profesionales, a través del establecimiento de disposiciones y criterios que protejan a los consumidores y salvaguarden el interés público.

      b)   Las Partes alentarán a los organismos pertinentes, entre otros, a las universidades, a las asociaciones y colegios profesionales y a las dependencias gubernamentales competentes, para:

            i)   elaborar tales criterios y disposiciones; y

            ii)   formular y presentar recomendaciones sobre el reconocimiento mutuo a las Partes.

      c)   La elaboración de criterios y disposiciones a los que se refieren los literales a) y b) podrá considerar los elementos siguientes: educación, exámenes, experiencia, conducta y ética, desarrollo y actualización profesionales, renovación o actualización de licencias, campo de acción, conocimiento local y protección al consumidor.

      d)   Para poner en práctica lo dispuesto en los literales a) al c), las Partes se comprometen a proporcionar la información detallada y necesaria para el reconocimiento mutuo de títulos y para el otorgamiento de licencias, incluyendo la correspondiente a: cursos académicos, guías y materiales de estudio, derechos, fechas de exámenes, horarios, ubicaciones, afiliación a sociedades o colegios profesionales. Esta información incluye la legislación, las directrices administrativas y las medidas de aplicación general de carácter central o federal y las elaboradas por organismos gubernamentales y no gubernamentales.

5.   Revisión.

      a)   Con base en la revisión de las recomendaciones recibidas por las Partes, si son congruentes con las disposiciones de este Tratado, cada Parte alentará a la autoridad competente para que adopte esas recomendaciones.

      b)   Las Partes revisarán, al menos una vez cada tres años, la aplicación de las disposiciones de este anexo.

Capítulo X
Telecomunicaciones

Artículo 10-01: Definiciones.

Para efectos de este capítulo, se entenderá por:

comunicaciones intracorporativas: las telecomunicaciones mediante las cuales una empresa se comunica:

a)   internamente o con sus subsidiarias, sucursales y filiales según las defina cada Parte, o entre las mismas; o

b)   de una manera no comercial, con todas las personas de importancia fundamental para la actividad económica de la empresa, y que sostienen una relación contractual continua con ella, pero no incluye a los servicios de telecomunicaciones que se suministren a terceras personas distintas a las descritas;

equipo autorizado: el equipo terminal o de otra clase que ha sido aprobado para conectarse a la red pública de telecomunicaciones de acuerdo con los procedimientos de evaluación de la conformidad de una Parte;

equipo terminal: cualquier dispositivo digital o analógico capaz de procesar, recibir, conmutar, señalizar o transmitir señales a través de medios electromagnéticos y que se conecta a la red pública de telecomunicaciones en un punto terminal;

medida de normalización: una "medida de normalización", tal como se define en el capítulo XIII (Medidas de normalización);

procedimiento de evaluación de la conformidad: un "procedimiento de evaluación de la conformidad", tal como se define en el capítulo XIII (Medidas de normalización);

protocolo: un conjunto de reglas y formatos que rigen el intercambio de información entre dos entidades pares, para efectos de la transferencia de información de señales o datos;

punto terminal de la red: la demarcación final de la red pública de telecomunicaciones en las instalaciones del usuario;

red privada: una red de telecomunicaciones que establece una persona con su propia infraestructura o mediante arrendamiento de canales o circuitos de redes públicas de telecomunicaciones para uso de sus comunicaciones internas o aquellas vinculadas sustancialmente con su proceso productivo o de servicios;

red pública de telecomunicaciones: la infraestructura física que permite la prestación de servicios públicos de telecomunicaciones;

servicios de radiodifusión: los servicios de transmisión al aire de programas de radio y televisión;

servicios de valor agregado: los servicios de telecomunicaciones que emplean sistemas de procesamiento computarizado que:

a)　actúan sobre el formato, contenido, código, protocolo o aspectos similares de la información transmitida del usuario;

b)　proporcionan al cliente información adicional, diferente o reestructurada; o

c)　implican la interacción del usuario con información almacenada;

servicio público de telecomunicaciones: cualquier servicio de telecomunicaciones fijo o móvil que una Parte obligue explícitamente o de hecho, a que se ofrezca al público en general y que, por lo regular, conlleva la transmisión en tiempo real de información suministrada por el cliente entre dos o más puntos, sin cambio "de punto a punto" en la forma o contenido de la información del usuario;

tasa fija: la fijación de precio sobre la base de una cantidad fija por periodo, independientemente de la cantidad de uso;

telecomunicaciones: la transmisión y recepción de señales por cualquier medio electromagnético.

Artículo 10-02: Ambito de aplicación.

1.　Reconociendo el doble papel de los servicios de telecomunicaciones, como sector específico de actividad económica y como medio de prestación de servicios para otras actividades económicas, este capítulo se aplica a:

a)　las medidas que adopte o mantenga una Parte, relacionadas con la prestación de servicios públicos de telecomunicaciones;

b)　las medidas que adopte o mantenga una Parte, relacionadas con el acceso a redes o servicios públicos de telecomunicaciones y su uso continuo por personas de la otra Parte, incluyendo su acceso y uso cuando operen redes privadas para llevar a cabo las comunicaciones intracorporativas;

c)　las medidas que adopte o mantenga una Parte sobre la prestación de servicios de valor agregado por personas de la otra Parte en el territorio de la primera o a través de sus fronteras;

d)　las medidas relativas a normalización respecto de conexión de equipo terminal u otro equipo a las redes públicas de telecomunicaciones.

2.　Ninguna disposición de este capítulo se interpretará en el sentido de:

a)　obligar a cualquier Parte a autorizar a una persona de la otra Parte a que establezca, construya, adquiera, arriende, opere o suministre redes o servicios de telecomunicaciones;

b)   obligar a cualquier Parte a que establezca, construya, adquiera, arriende, opere o suministre redes o servicios públicos de telecomunicaciones que no se ofrezcan al público en general;

c)   permitir que una Parte exija a una persona que establezca, construya, adquiera, arriende, opere o suministre redes o servicios públicos de telecomunicaciones que no se ofrezcan al público en general;

d)   impedir a cualquier Parte que prohiba a las personas que operen redes privadas el uso de esas redes para suministrar redes o servicios públicos de telecomunicaciones a terceras personas; o

e)   obligar a una Parte a exigir a cualquier persona que radiodifunda o distribuya por cable programas de radio o de televisión, a ofrecer sus instalaciones de radiodifusión o de cable como red pública de telecomunicaciones.

3.   No obstante lo dispuesto en el párrafo 2, en caso de emergencia, los operadores de los servicios de telecomunicaciones de las Partes, deberán colaborar con las autoridades en la transmisión de las comunicaciones que aquéllas requieran, durante un tiempo prudencial.

Artículo 10-03: Acceso a redes y servicios públicos de telecomunicaciones y su uso.

1.   Cada Parte garantizará que cualquier persona de la otra Parte tenga acceso a cualquier red o servicio público de telecomunicaciones y pueda hacer uso de los mismos, incluyendo los circuitos privados arrendados, ofrecidos en su territorio o de manera transfronteriza en términos y condiciones razonables y no discriminatorios, para la conducción de sus negocios, según se especifica en los párrafos 2 al 8.

2.   Sujeto a lo dispuesto en los párrafos 7 y 8, cada Parte garantizará que a las personas de la otra Parte se les permita:

a)   comprar o arrendar y conectar el equipo terminal u otro equipo que haga interfaz, con la red pública de telecomunicaciones, que no afecte técnicamente a esa red o la degrade;

b)   interconectar redes privadas, arrendadas o propias, con las redes públicas de telecomunicaciones en territorio de esa Parte o a través de sus fronteras, incluido el acceso mediante marcado directo a sus usuarios o clientes y desde los mismos, o con circuitos arrendados o propios de otra persona, en términos y condiciones mutuamente aceptadas por esas personas, de conformidad con las disposiciones vigentes en cada Parte;

c)   realizar funciones de conmutación, señalización y procesamiento; y

d)   utilizar los protocolos de operación que ellos elijan.

3.   Cada Parte procurará que:

a) la fijación de precios para los servicios públicos de telecomunicaciones refleje los costos económicos directamente relacionados con la prestación de esos servicios; y

b) los circuitos privados arrendados estén disponibles sobre la base de una tarifa fija o descrita por el mecanismo tarifario vigente en cada Parte.

4. Ninguna disposición del párrafo 3 se interpretará en el sentido de impedir subsidios cruzados entre los servicios públicos de telecomunicaciones.

5. Cada Parte garantizará que las personas de la otra Parte puedan emplear las redes o los servicios públicos de telecomunicaciones para transmitir la información en su territorio o a través de sus fronteras, incluso para las comunicaciones intracorporativas y para el acceso a la información contenida en bases de datos o almacenada en cualquier otra forma que sea legible por una máquina en territorio de cualquier Parte.

6. Las Partes podrán adoptar cualquier medida necesaria para asegurar la confidencialidad y seguridad de los mensajes y la protección de la intimidad de los suscriptores de redes o servicios públicos de telecomunicaciones.

7. Cada Parte garantizará que no se impongan más condiciones al acceso a redes o servicios públicos de telecomunicaciones y a su uso, que las necesarias para:

a) salvaguardar las responsabilidades del servicio público de los proveedores de redes o servicios públicos de telecomunicaciones, en particular su capacidad para poner sus redes o servicios a disposición del público en general; o

b) proteger la integridad técnica de las redes o los servicios públicos de telecomunicaciones.

8. Siempre que las condiciones para el acceso a redes o servicios públicos de telecomunicaciones y su uso cumplan los lineamientos establecidos en el párrafo 7, esas condiciones podrán incluir:

a) restricciones a la reventa o al uso compartido de tales servicios;

b) requisitos para utilizar interfaces técnicas determinadas, inclusive protocolos de interfaz para la interconexión con las redes o los servicios mencionados;

c) restricciones en la interconexión de circuitos privados, arrendados o propios, con las redes o los servicios mencionados, o con circuitos arrendados o propios de otra persona, que sean utilizados para el suministro de redes o servicios públicos de telecomunicaciones;

d) procedimientos para otorgar concesiones, licencias, permisos o registros que, de adoptarse o mantenerse, sean transparentes y cuyo trámite de solicitudes se resuelva de manera expedita; y

e) restricciones a la utilización en caso de situaciones que pongan en peligro la seguridad nacional por efecto de actividades relacionadas con el tráfico de drogas u otras actividades ilícitas.

Artículo 10-04: Condiciones para la prestación de servicios de valor agregado.

1. Considerando el papel estratégico de los servicios de valor agregado para elevar la competitividad de todas las actividades económicas, las Partes establecen las condiciones necesarias para su prestación, tomando en cuenta para ello los procedimientos y la información requerida para tal efecto.

2. Cada Parte garantizará que:

a) cualquier procedimiento que adopte o mantenga para otorgar permisos o registros referentes a la prestación de servicios de valor agregado sea transparente y no discriminatorio y que las solicitudes se tramiten de manera expedita; y

b) la información requerida conforme a esos procedimientos se limite a la necesaria para acreditar que el solicitante tiene la solvencia financiera y técnica para iniciar la prestación del servicio, o que los servicios o el equipo terminal u otro equipo del solicitante cumplen con las medidas de normalización aplicables de la Parte.

3. Ninguna Parte podrá exigir que un prestador de servicios de valor agregado:

a) preste esos servicios al público en general, cuando éstos han sido contratados por usuarios específicos u orientados a los mismos en condiciones técnicas definidas;

b) justifique sus tarifas de acuerdo con sus costos;

c) interconecte sus redes con cualquier cliente o red en particular; o

d) satisfaga alguna medida de normalización en particular, para una interconexión distinta a la interconexión con una red pública de telecomunicaciones.

4. Cada Parte podrá requerir el registro de tarifas a:

a) un prestador de servicios, con el fin de corregir una práctica de este prestador que la Parte, de conformidad con su legislación, haya considerado, en un caso particular, como contraria a la competencia; o

b) un monopolio al que se aplique las disposiciones del artículo 10-06.

Artículo 10-05: Medidas de normalización.

1. Cada Parte garantizará que sus medidas de normalización que se refieran a la conexión del equipo terminal u otro equipo a las redes públicas de telecomunicaciones, incluso aquellas medidas que se refieran al uso del equipo de prueba y medición para el procedimiento de evaluación de la conformidad, se adopten o mantengan solamente en la medida que sean necesarias para:

a)   evitar daños técnicos a las redes públicas de telecomunicaciones;

b)   evitar la interferencia técnica con los servicios públicos de telecomunicaciones o su deterioro;

c)   evitar la interferencia electromagnética y asegurar la compatibilidad con otros usos del espectro electromagnético;

d)   evitar el mal funcionamiento del equipo de facturación; o

e)   garantizar la seguridad del usuario y su acceso a las redes o servicios públicos de telecomunicaciones.

2.   Las Partes podrán establecer el requisito de aprobación para la conexión del equipo terminal u otro equipo que no esté autorizado, a la red pública de telecomunicaciones, siempre que los criterios de aprobación sean compatibles con lo dispuesto en el párrafo 1.

3.   Cada Parte garantizará que los puntos terminales de las redes públicas de telecomunicaciones se definan a partir de una base razonable y transparente.

4.   Una vez autorizado el equipo empleado como dispositivo de protección a las redes públicas de telecomunicaciones, con base en los criterios establecidos en el párrafo 1, ninguna Parte exigirá autorización adicional para el equipo que se conecte del lado del consumidor.

5.   Cada Parte:

a)   asegurará que sus procedimientos de evaluación de la conformidad sean transparentes y no discriminatorios y que las solicitudes que se presenten al efecto se tramiten de manera expedita;

b)   permitirá que cualquier entidad técnicamente calificada y registrada en alguna Parte realice la prueba requerida al equipo terminal o a otro equipo que vaya a ser conectado a las redes públicas de telecomunicaciones, de acuerdo con los procedimientos de evaluación de la conformidad de la Parte, a reserva del derecho de la misma a revisar la exactitud y la integridad de los resultados de las pruebas; y

c)   garantizará que no sean discriminatorias las medidas que adopte o mantenga para autorizar a las personas que actúan como agentes de proveedores de equipo de telecomunicaciones ante los organismos competentes de evaluación de la conformidad de la Parte.

6.   A más tardar dos años contados a partir de la entrada en vigor de este Tratado, cada Parte adoptará, como parte de sus procedimientos de evaluación de la conformidad, las disposiciones necesarias para aceptar los resultados de las pruebas que, con base en sus medidas y procedimientos, realicen los laboratorios que se encuentran en territorio de la otra Parte.

7.   El Subgrupo de Trabajo de Telecomunicaciones establecido de conformidad con el numeral iii) del literal a) del artículo 13-17 (Grupo de Trabajo de Medidas de Normalización)

estará encargado de implementar los lineamientos contenidos en este capítulo, de manera congruente con las disposiciones correspondientes del capítulo XIII (Medidas de normalización).

Artículo 10-06: Monopolios.

1.   Cuando una Parte mantenga o establezca un monopolio para proveer redes y servicios públicos de telecomunicaciones y el monopolio compita, directamente o a través de filiales, en la fabricación o venta de bienes de telecomunicaciones, en la prestación de servicios de valor agregado u otros servicios de telecomunicaciones, la Parte asegurará que el monopolio no utilice su posición monopólica para incurrir en prácticas contrarias a la competencia en esos mercados, ya sea de manera directa o a través de los tratos con sus filiales, de modo tal que afecte desventajosamente a una persona de la otra Parte. Esas prácticas pueden incluir subsidios cruzados, conducta predatoria y acceso discriminatorio a las redes y a los servicios públicos de telecomunicaciones.

2.   Cada Parte introducirá o mantendrá medidas eficaces para impedir la conducta contraria a la competencia a que se refiere el párrafo 1, tales como:

   a)   requisitos de contabilidad;

   b)   requisitos de separación estructural;

   c)   reglas para asegurar que el monopolio otorgue a sus competidores acceso a sus redes o sus servicios de telecomunicaciones y uso de los mismos, en términos y condiciones no menos favorables que los que se conceda a sí mismo o a sus filiales; o

   d)   reglas para asegurar la divulgación oportuna de los cambios técnicos de las redes públicas de telecomunicaciones y sus interfaces.

3.   Las Partes intercambiarán oportunamente información sobre las medidas a que se refiere el párrafo 2.

Artículo 10-07: Relación con organizaciones y acuerdos internacionales.

1.   Las Partes se esforzarán por estimular el papel de los organismos regionales y subregionales e impulsarlos como foros para promover el desarrollo de las telecomunicaciones de la región.

2.   Las Partes, reconociendo la importancia de las normas internacionales para lograr la compatibilidad e interoperabilidad global de las redes o servicios de telecomunicaciones, se comprometen a aplicar esas normas mediante la labor de los organismos internacionales competentes, tales como la Unión Internacional de Telecomunicaciones y la Organización Internacional de Normalización.

Artículo 10-08: Cooperación técnica y otras consultas.

Con el fin de estimular el desarrollo de la infraestructura y de los servicios de telecomunicaciones interoperables, las Partes cooperarán en el intercambio de información técnica, en el desarrollo de los recursos humanos del sector, y en la creación e implementación de programas de intercambios empresariales, académicos e intergubernamentales. Las Partes establecen el Grupo Técnico de Alto Nivel, constituido por representantes de las entidades pertinentes y encargado de implementar las obligaciones que se desprenden de este párrafo. Este Grupo se instalará, a más tardar, seis meses después de la entrada en vigor de este Tratado.

Artículo 10-09: Transparencia.

Además de lo dispuesto en el artículo 17-02 (Publicación), cada Parte pondrá a disposición del público y de la otra Parte las medidas relativas al acceso a redes o servicios públicos de telecomunicaciones y su uso, incluyendo las medidas referentes a:

a)   tarifas y otros términos y condiciones del servicio;

b)   especificaciones de las interfaces técnicas con esos servicios y redes;

c)   información sobre los órganos responsables de la elaboración y adopción de medidas de normalización que afecten ese acceso y uso;

d)   condiciones aplicables a la conexión de equipo terminal o de otra clase, a la red pública de telecomunicaciones; y

e)   requisitos de concesión, permiso, registro o licencia.

Artículo 10-10: Relación con otros capítulos.

En caso de incompatibilidad entre una disposición de este capítulo y otro capítulo, la de este capítulo prevalecerá en la medida de la incompatibilidad.

Capítulo XI

Entrada Temporal de Personas de Negocios

Artículo 11-01: Definiciones.

Para efectos de este capítulo, se entenderá por:

entrada temporal: la entrada de una persona de negocios de una Parte a territorio de la otra Parte, sin la intención de establecer residencia permanente;

nacional: tal como se define en el anexo a este artículo para las Partes señaladas en el mismo;

persona de negocios: el nacional de una Parte que participa en el comercio de bienes o prestación de servicios, o en actividades de inversión;

vigente: la calidad de obligatoriedad de los preceptos legales de las Partes en el momento de entrada en vigor de este Tratado.

Artículo 11-02: Principios generales.

Las disposiciones de este capítulo reflejan la relación comercial preferente entre las Partes, la conveniencia de facilitar la entrada temporal de personas de negocios conforme al principio de reciprocidad y la necesidad de establecer criterios y procedimientos transparentes para tal efecto. Asimismo, reflejan la necesidad de garantizar la seguridad de las fronteras y de proteger el trabajo de sus nacionales y el empleo permanente en sus respectivos territorios.

Artículo 11-03: Obligaciones generales.

1.   Cada Parte aplicará las medidas relativas a este capítulo de conformidad con el artículo 11-02 y de manera expedita para evitar demoras o perjuicios indebidos en el comercio de bienes y de servicios, o en las actividades de inversión comprendidas en este Tratado.

2.   Las Partes procurarán desarrollar y adoptar criterios, definiciones e interpretaciones comunes para la aplicación de este capítulo.

Artículo 11-04: Autorización de entrada temporal.

1.   Cada Parte autorizará, de conformidad con las disposiciones de este capítulo, la entrada temporal a personas de negocios que cumplan con las demás medidas aplicables relativas a la salud, seguridad pública y seguridad nacional.

2.   Una Parte podrá negar la expedición de un documento migratorio que autorice empleo a una persona de negocios, cuando su entrada temporal afecte desfavorablemente:

   a)   la solución de cualquier conflicto laboral que exista en el lugar donde esté empleada o vaya a emplearse; o

   b)   el empleo de cualquier persona que intervenga en ese conflicto.

3.   Cuando, de conformidad con el párrafo 2, una Parte niegue la expedición de un documento migratorio que autorice empleo, esa Parte:

   a)   informará por escrito a la persona de negocios afectada las razones de la negativa; y

   b)   notificará sin demora y por escrito las razones de la negativa a la Parte a cuyo nacional se niega la entrada.

4.   Cada Parte limitará el importe de los derechos que cause el trámite de solicitud de entrada temporal al costo aproximado de los servicios de tramitación que se presten.

Artículo 11-05: Disponibilidad de información.

1.   Además de lo dispuesto en el artículo 17-02 (Publicación), cada Parte:

   a)   proporcionará a la otra Parte los materiales que le permitan conocer las medidas relativas a este capítulo; y

b)   a más tardar un año contado a partir de la entrada en vigor de este Tratado, preparará, publicará y pondrá a disposición de los interesados, tanto en su territorio como en el de la otra Parte, un documento consolidado con material que explique los requisitos para la entrada temporal conforme a este capítulo, de manera que puedan conocerlos las personas de negocios de la otra Parte.

2.   Cada Parte recopilará, mantendrá y pondrá a disposición de la otra Parte, de conformidad con su legislación, la información relativa al otorgamiento de autorizaciones de entrada temporal, de acuerdo con este capítulo. Esta recopilación incluirá información específica para cada ocupación, profesión o actividad.

Artículo 11-06: Grupo de Trabajo.

1.   Las Partes establecen un Grupo de Trabajo sobre Entrada Temporal, integrado por representantes de cada una de ellas, que incluya funcionarios de migración.

2.   El Grupo de Trabajo se reunirá cuando menos una vez al año para examinar:

a)   la aplicación y administración de este capítulo;

b)   la elaboración de medidas que faciliten aún más la entrada temporal de personas de negocios conforme al principio de reciprocidad;

c)   la exención de pruebas de certificación laboral o de procedimientos de efecto similar para el cónyuge de la persona a la que se haya autorizado la entrada temporal por más de un año conforme a las secciones B o C del anexo al artículo 11-04; y

d)   las propuestas de modificaciones o adiciones a este capítulo.

Artículo 11-07: Solución de Controversias.

1.   Las Partes no podrán iniciar los procedimientos previstos en el artículo 19-05 (Intervención de la Comisión - buenos oficios, conciliación y mediación), respecto de una negativa de autorización de entrada temporal conforme a este capítulo, ni de algún caso particular relativo a la aplicación de las disposiciones del artículo 11-03, salvo que:

a)   el asunto se refiera a una práctica recurrente; y

b)   la persona afectada haya agotado los recursos administrativos a su alcance relativos a ese asunto en particular.

2.   Los recursos mencionados en el literal b) del párrafo 1 se considerarán agotados cuando la autoridad competente no haya emitido una resolución definitiva dentro de un año contado a partir del inicio del procedimiento administrativo y la resolución no se haya demorado por causas imputables a la persona de negocios afectada.

Artículo 11-08: Relación con otros capítulos.

Salvo lo dispuesto en este capítulo y en los capítulos I (Disposiciones iniciales), XVII (Trasparencia) y XIX (Solución de controversias), ninguna disposición de este Tratado impondrá obligación alguna a las Partes respecto a sus medidas migratorias.

Anexo al artículo 11-01

Definiciones específicas por país

Para los efectos de este capítulo, se entenderá por:

nacional:

a)   respecto a Bolivia, un nacional, de acuerdo con las disposiciones de los artículos 36 al 39 de la Constitución Política del Estado; y

b)   respecto a México, un nacional, de acuerdo con las disposiciones vigentes del artículo 30 de la Constitución Política de los Estados Unidos Mexicanos.

Anexo al artículo 11-04
Categorías de personas de negocios

Sección A - Visitantes de negocios

1.   Cada Parte autorizará la entrada temporal de la persona de negocios que, a petición de una empresa inscrita en el padrón bilateral señalado en el párrafo 7, pretenda llevar a cabo alguna actividad mencionada en el apéndice 1 de esta sección, sin exigirle autorización de empleo, siempre que, además de cumplir con las medidas migratorias vigentes, exhiba:

      a)   prueba de nacionalidad de una Parte;

      b)   documentación que acredite la petición de una empresa establecida en el territorio de una Parte;

      c)   documentación que acredite que emprenderá esas actividades y señale el propósito de su entrada; y

      d)   prueba del carácter internacional de la actividad de negocios que se propone realizar y de que la persona no pretende ingresar en el mercado local de trabajo.

2.   Cada Parte estipulará que una persona de negocios puede cumplir con los requisitos señalados en el literal d) del párrafo 1 cuando demuestre que:

      a)   la fuente principal de remuneración correspondiente a esa actividad se encuentra fuera del territorio de la Parte que autoriza la entrada temporal; y

      b)   el lugar principal del negocio y donde se obtiene la mayor parte de las ganancias se encuentra fuera de este territorio.

3.   La Parte que autorice la entrada temporal aceptará normalmente una declaración verbal sobre el lugar principal del negocio y el de obtención de ganancias. Cuando esa Parte requiera comprobación adicional, por lo regular considerará prueba suficiente una carta de la empresa registrada en el padrón bilateral de empresas señalado en el párrafo 7, donde consten estas circunstancias.

4.   Cada Parte autorizará la entrada temporal a la persona de negocios que pretenda llevar a cabo alguna actividad distinta de las señaladas en el apéndice 1 de esta sección, en términos no menos favorables que los previstos en las disposiciones vigentes de las medidas señaladas en el apéndice 2 de esta sección, siempre que esa persona de negocios cumpla además con las medidas migratorias vigentes.

5.   Ninguna Parte podrá:

   a)   exigir como condición para autorizar la entrada temporal conforme al párrafo 1 ó 4, procedimientos previos de aprobación, peticiones, pruebas de certificación laboral u otros procedimientos de efecto similar; o

   b)   imponer ni mantener restricción numérica alguna a la entrada temporal, de conformidad con el párrafo 1 ó 4.

6.   No obstante lo dispuesto en el párrafo 5, una Parte podrá requerir de la persona de negocios que solicite entrada temporal conforme a esta sección, que obtenga previamente a la entrada una visa o documento equivalente. Cuando en una Parte exista el requisito de visa y, a petición de la Parte cuyas personas de negocios estén sujetas a él, consultarán entre ellos con miras a eliminarlo.

7.   Para efectos de esta sección, las Partes establecerán un padrón bilateral de empresas para visitantes de negocios.

Sección B - Comerciantes e inversionistas

1.   Cada Parte autorizará la entrada temporal y otorgará la documentación correspondiente a la persona de negocios que pretenda:

   a)   llevar a cabo un intercambio comercial cuantioso de bienes o servicios, principalmente entre el territorio de la Parte de la cual es nacional y el territorio de la Parte a la que se solicita la entrada; o

   b)   establecer, desarrollar, administrar o prestar asesoría o servicios técnicos clave, en funciones de supervisión, ejecutivas o que conlleven habilidades esenciales, para llevar a cabo o administrar una inversión en la cual la persona o su empresa hayan comprometido un monto importante de capital o estén en vías de comprometerlo, siempre que la persona cumpla además con las medidas migratorias vigentes.

2.   Ninguna Parte podrá:

   a)   exigir pruebas de certificación laboral u otros procedimientos de efecto similar, como condición para autorizar la entrada temporal conforme al párrafo 1; ni

b)   imponer ni mantener restricciones numéricas en relación con la entrada temporal conforme al párrafo 1.

3.   No obstante lo dispuesto en el párrafo 2, una Parte podrá examinar, en un tiempo perentorio, la propuesta de inversión de una persona de negocios para evaluar si la inversión cumple con las disposiciones legales aplicables.

4.   No obstante lo dispuesto en el párrafo 2, una Parte podrá requerir de la persona de negocios que solicite entrada temporal conforme a esta sección que obtenga, previamente a la entrada, una visa o documento equivalente.

Sección C - Transferencias de personal dentro de una empresa

1.   Cada Parte autorizará la entrada temporal y expedirá documentación comprobatoria a la persona de negocios empleada por una empresa listada en el padrón bilateral de empresas señalado en el párrafo 4 que pretenda desempeñar funciones gerenciales, ejecutivas o que conlleven conocimientos especializados en esa empresa o en una de sus subsidiarias o filiales, siempre que cumpla con las medidas migratorias vigentes aplicables. La Parte que autorice la entrada temporal podrá exigir que la persona de negocios haya sido empleada por la empresa de manera continua durante un año, dentro de los tres años inmediatamente anteriores a la fecha de presentación de la solicitud.

2.   Ninguna Parte podrá:

a)   exigir pruebas de certificación laboral u otros procedimientos de efecto similar como condición para autorizar la entrada temporal conforme al párrafo 1; ni

b)   imponer ni mantener restricciones numéricas en relación con la entrada temporal conforme al párrafo 1.

3.   No obstante lo dispuesto en el párrafo 2, una Parte podrá requerir de la persona de negocios que solicite entrada temporal conforme a esta sección, que obtenga previamente a la entrada una visa o documento equivalente. Cuando en una Parte exista el requisito de visa y, a petición de la Parte cuyas personas de negocios estén sujetas a él, consultarán entre ellas con miras a eliminarlo.

4.   Para efectos de esta sección, las Partes establecerán un padrón bilateral de empresas para transferencia de personal.

Apéndice 1 de la sección A del anexo al artículo 11-04
Actividades

I.   Investigación y diseño

- Investigadores técnicos, científicos y estadísticos que realicen investigaciones de manera independiente o para una empresa ubicada en territorio de la otra Parte.

II.   Cultivo, manufactura y producción

- Propietarios de máquinas cosechadoras que supervisen a un grupo de operarios, admitido de conformidad con las disposiciones aplicables.

- Personal de compras y de producción a nivel gerencial, que lleve a cabo operaciones comerciales para una empresa ubicada en territorio de la otra Parte.

III. Comercialización

- Investigadores y analistas de mercado que efectúen investigaciones o análisis de manera independiente o para una empresa ubicada en territorio de la otra Parte.

- Personal de ferias y de promoción que asista a convenciones comerciales.

IV. Ventas

- Representantes y agentes de ventas que levanten pedidos o negocien contratos sobre bienes o servicios para una empresa ubicada en territorio de la otra Parte, pero que no entreguen los bienes ni presten los servicios.

- Compradores que hagan adquisiciones para una empresa ubicada en territorio de la otra Parte.

V. Distribución

- Agentes aduanales que brinden servicios de asesoría para facilitar la importación o exportación de bienes.

VI. Servicios posteriores a la venta

- Personal de instalación, reparación, mantenimiento y supervisión que cuente con los conocimientos técnicos especializados esenciales para cumplir con la obligación contractual del vendedor y que preste servicios, o capacite a trabajadores para que presten esos servicios, de conformidad con una garantía u otro contrato de servicios conexo a la venta de equipo o maquinaria comercial o industrial, incluidos los programas de computación comprados a una empresa ubicada fuera del territorio de la Parte a la cual se solicita entrada temporal, durante la vigencia del contrato de garantía o de servicio.

VII. Servicios generales

- Personal gerencial y de supervisión que intervenga en operaciones comerciales para una empresa ubicada en territorio de la otra Parte.

- Personal de servicios financieros (agentes de seguros, personal bancario o corredores de inversiones) que intervenga en operaciones comerciales para una empresa ubicada en territorio de la otra Parte.

- Personal de relaciones públicas y de publicidad que brinde asesoría a clientes o que asista o participe en convenciones.

- Personal de turismo (agentes de excursiones y de viajes, guías de turistas u operadores de viajes) que asista o participe en convenciones o conduzca alguna excursión que se haya iniciado en territorio de la otra Parte.

- Traductores o intérpretes que presten servicios como empleados de una empresa ubicada en territorio de la otra Parte.

Apéndice 2 a la sección A del anexo al artículo 11-04
Medidas migratorias vigentes

1.   En el caso de Bolivia:

- Ley de Residencia del 18 de enero de 1911.

- Ley de Prohibición de Ingreso del 12 de enero de 1924.

- Ley de Inmigración del 27 de diciembre de 1926.

- Decreto Ley del 2 de agosto de 1937, Clasificación oficial de extranjeros en Bolivia.

- Decreto Ley del 17 de diciembre de 1937, Clasificación oficial de turistas.

- Decreto Supremo del 28 de enero de 1937, Reglamento de permisos de ingreso a Bolivia.

- Decreto Supremo del 26 de abril de 1937.

- Decreto Supremo del 20 de mayo de 1937, Reglamento de pasaportes al extranjero.

- Decreto Supremo del 30 de septiembre de 1937.

- Decreto Supremo del 5 de octubre de 1937, Control de emigración de braceros nacionales al exterior.

- Decreto Supremo del 30 de julio de 1938, Reglamento de emigración.

- Decreto Supremo del 18 de diciembre de 1938, Trámite de nacionalización.

- Decreto Supremo del 15 de febrero de 1939, Normas de aplicación de la ley de residencia a extranjeros indeseables.

- Decreto Supremo del 28 de junio de 1939, Reglamento para el ingreso de agricultores extranjeros.

- Decreto Supremo del 10 de enero de 1940.

- Decreto Supremo del 18 de enero de 1940, Trámite de radicatoria definitiva en el país.

- Decreto Supremo del 22 de agosto de 1940.

- Decreto Supremo del 18 de septiembre de 1940, Obligación de los inmigrantes llegados al país para recabar el carnet sanitario en el Ministerio de Higiene y Salubridad.

- Decreto Supremo del 8 de abril de 1942, Requisitos para autorizar el ingreso al país de familiares de los extranjeros residentes.

- Decreto Supremo del 13 de febrero de 1950, Procedimientos que deben seguir los inmigrantes que desean radicarse en el país.

- Decreto Supremo del 12 de junio de 1958, Plazo mínimo de permanencia obligada en el país para extranjeros que han obtenido su naturalización.

- Resolución Suprema del 31 de julio de 1937.

2.   En el caso de México, el Capítulo III de la Ley General de Población, 1974, con sus enmiendas.

Capítulo XII

Servicios financieros

Artículo 12-01: Definiciones.

Para efectos de este capítulo, se entenderá por:

autoridades reguladoras: cualquier entidad gubernamental que ejerza autoridad de supervisión sobre prestadores de servicios financieros o instituciones financieras;

entidad pública: un banco central o autoridad monetaria de una Parte, o cualquier institución financiera de naturaleza pública, propiedad de una Parte o bajo su control;

institución financiera: cualquier empresa o intermediario financiero que esté autorizado para hacer negocios y esté regulado o supervisado como una institución financiera conforme a la legislación de la Parte en cuyo territorio se encuentre ubicada;

institución financiera de la otra Parte: una institución financiera, incluso una sucursal, constituida de acuerdo con la legislación vigente, ubicada en territorio de una Parte que sea controlada por personas de la otra Parte;

inversión:

a)   una empresa;

b)   acciones de una empresa;

c)   instrumentos de deuda de una empresa:

  i)   cuando la empresa es una filial del inversionista; o

      ii)   cuando la fecha de vencimiento original del instrumento de deuda sea por lo menos de tres años, pero no incluye un instrumento de deuda de una empresa del Estado, independientemente de la fecha original de vencimiento;

d)   un préstamo a una empresa:

      i)   cuando la empresa es una filial del inversionista; o

      ii)   cuando la fecha de vencimiento original del préstamo sea por lo menos de tres años, pero no incluye un préstamo a una empresa del Estado, independientemente de la fecha original del vencimiento;

e)   una participación en una empresa, que le permita al propietario participar en los ingresos o en las utilidades de la empresa;

f)   una participación en una empresa, que otorgue derecho al propietario para participar del haber de esa empresa en una liquidación, siempre que ésta no derive de una obligación o de un préstamo excluidos conforme a los literales c) y d);

g)   bienes raíces u otra propiedad, tangibles o intangibles, adquiridos o utilizados con el propósito de obtener un beneficio económico o para otros fines empresariales;

h)   beneficios provenientes de destinar capital en otros recursos para el desarrollo de una actividad económica en territorio de la otra Parte, entre otros, conforme a:

      i)   contratos que involucran la presencia de la propiedad de un inversionista en territorio de la otra Parte, incluidos las concesiones, los contratos de construcción y de llave en mano; o

      ii)   contratos donde la remuneración dependa sustancialmente de la producción, ingresos o ganancias de una empresa; e

i)   un préstamo otorgado por un prestador de servicios financieros transfronterizos o un valor de deuda propiedad del mismo, excepto un préstamo a una institución financiera o un valor de deuda emitido por la misma;

inversión no significa:

j)   reclamaciones pecuniarias que no conlleven los tipos de derechos dispuestos en los literales a) al i), derivadas exclusivamente de:

      i)   contratos comerciales para la venta de bienes o servicios por un nacional o empresa en territorio de una Parte a una empresa en territorio de la otra Parte; o

      ii)   el otorgamiento de crédito en relación con una transacción comercial, como el financiamiento al comercio, salvo un préstamo cubierto por las disposiciones del literal d);

k)   cualquier otra reclamación pecuniaria que no conlleve los tipos de derechos dispuestos en los literales a) al i);

l)   un préstamo otorgado a una institución financiera o un valor de deuda propiedad de una institución financiera, salvo que se trate de un préstamo a una institución financiera que sea tratado como capital para efectos regulatorios, por cualquier Parte en cuyo territorio esté ubicada la institución financiera; ni

m)   un préstamo a una Parte o a una empresa del Estado de esa Parte, o un valor de deuda emitido por éstas;

inversión de un inversionista de una Parte: la inversión propiedad de un inversionista de una Parte o bajo el control directo o indirecto de éste;

inversionista de una Parte: una Parte o una empresa del Estado de la misma, o una persona de esa Parte que pretenda realizar, realice o haya realizado una inversión;

inversionista contendiente: un inversionista que someta a arbitraje una reclamación en los términos de este capítulo y de la sección B del capítulo XV (Inversión);

nuevo servicio financiero: un servicio financiero no prestado en territorio de una Parte que sea prestado en territorio de la otra Parte incluyendo cualquier forma nueva de distribución de un servicio financiero o de venta de un producto financiero que no sea vendido en el territorio de la Parte;

organismos autoregulados: una entidad no gubernamental, incluso una bolsa o mercado de valores o de futuros, cámara de compensación o cualquier otra asociación u organización que ejerza una autoridad, propia o delegada, de regulación o de supervisión, sobre prestadores de servicios financieros o instituciones financieras;

persona de una Parte: un nacional o una empresa de una Parte y, para mayor certidumbre, no incluye una sucursal de una empresa de un país no Parte;

prestación transfronteriza de servicios financieros o comercio transfronterizo de servicios financieros: la prestación de un servicio financiero:

a)   del territorio de una Parte hacia el territorio de la otra Parte;

b)   en territorio de una Parte, por una persona de esa Parte a una persona de la otra Parte; o

c)   por una persona de una Parte en territorio de la otra Parte;

prestador de servicios financieros de una Parte: una persona de una Parte que se dedica al negocio de prestar algún servicio financiero en territorio de la otra Parte;

prestador de servicios financieros transfronterizos de una Parte: una persona de una Parte que se dedica al negocio de prestar servicios financieros en su territorio y que pretenda realizar o realice la prestación transfronteriza de servicios financieros;

servicio financiero: un servicio de naturaleza financiera y cualquier servicio conexo o auxiliar, incluidos:

a)   todos los servicios de seguros y relaciones con seguros, entre otros:

i)   los seguros directos, incluido el coaseguro;

ii)   los seguros de vida, de daños y de enfermedades;

iii)   los reaseguros y retrocesión;

iv)   las actividades de intermediación de seguros, tales como las de los corredores y agentes de seguros; y

v)   los servicios auxiliares de los seguros, tales como los prestados por consultores y actuarios, la evaluación de riesgos e indemnización de siniestros;

b)   todos los servicios bancarios y demás servicios financieros, entre otros:

i)   la aceptación de depósitos y otros fondos reembolsables del público;

ii)   préstamos de todo tipo, con inclusión de créditos personales, créditos hipotecarios, factoraje financiero y financiamiento de transacciones comerciales;

iii)   servicios financieros de arrendamiento con opción de compra;

iv)   todos los servicios de pago y transferencia monetaria, con inclusión de tarjetas de crédito, de débito y similares, cheques de viajero y giros bancarios;

v)   garantías y compromisos;

vi)   el intercambio comercial por cuenta propia o de clientes, ya sea en bolsa, en un mercado extra bursátil o de otro modo a través de:

- instrumentos del mercado monetario, incluidos cheques, letras y certificados de depósito;

- divisas;

- productos derivados, incluidos futuros y opciones;

- instrumentos de los mercados cambiario y monetario, tales como "swaps" y acuerdos de tipo de interés a plazo;

- valores transferibles; u

- otros instrumentos y activos financieros negociables, incluyendo metales;

vii)   participación en emisiones de toda clase de valores, con inclusión de la suscripción y colocación como agentes y la prestación de servicios relacionados con esas emisiones;

viii) corretaje de cambios;

ix) administración de activos incluyendo la administración de fondos en efectivo o de cartera de valores, la gestión de inversiones colectivas en todas sus formas, la administración de fondos de pensiones, los servicios de depósito y custodia de servicios fiduciarios;

x) servicios de pago y compensación respecto de activos financieros, con inclusión de valores, productos derivados y otros instrumentos negociables;

xi) suministro y transferencia de información financiera y procesamiento de datos financieros y soporte lógico relacionado con ellos, por proveedores de otros servicios financieros;

xii) servicios de asesoramiento e intermediación y otros servicios financieros auxiliares respecto de cualesquiera de las actividades enumeradas en los literales i) al xi), con inclusión de informes y análisis de crédito, estudios y asesoramiento sobre inversiones y carteras de valores, y asesoramiento sobre adquisiciones, reestructuración y estrategia de empresas.

Artículo 12-02: Ambito de aplicación.

1. Este capítulo se aplica a las medidas que adopte o mantenga una Parte relativas a:

a) instituciones financieras de la otra Parte;

b) inversionistas de una Parte e inversiones de esos inversionistas en instituciones financieras en territorio de la otra Parte; y

c) el comercio transfronterizo de servicios financieros.

2. Nada de lo dispuesto en este capítulo se interpretará en el sentido de impedir a una Parte, o a sus entidades públicas, que conduzcan o presten en forma exclusiva en su territorio:

a) las actividades realizadas por las autoridades monetarias o por cualquier otra institución pública, dirigidas a la consecución de políticas monetarias o cambiarias;

b) las actividades y servicios que formen parte de planes públicos de retiro o de sistemas obligatorios de seguridad social; o

c) otras actividades o servicios por cuenta de la Parte, con su garantía, o que usen los recursos financieros de la misma o de sus entidades públicas.

3. Las Partes se comprometen a liberalizar entre sí, progresiva y gradualmente, toda restricción o reserva financiera con el propósito de hacer efectiva la complementación económica entre ellas.

4. Las disposiciones de este capítulo prevalecerán sobre las de otros capítulos, salvo en los casos en que se haga remisión expresa a esos capítulos.

Artículo 12-03: Organismos autoregulados.

Cuando una Parte requiera que una institución financiera o un prestador de servicios financieros transfronterizos de la otra Parte sea miembro, participe, o tenga acceso a un organismo autoregulado para ofrecer un servicio financiero en su territorio o hacia éste, la Parte hará todo lo que esté a su alcance para que ese organismo cumpla con las obligaciones de este capítulo.

Artículo 12-04: Derecho de establecimiento.

1.   Las Partes reconocen el principio de que a los inversionistas de una Parte, dedicados al negocio de prestar servicios financieros en su territorio, se les debe permitir establecer una institución financiera en el territorio de la otra Parte, mediante cualesquiera de las modalidades de establecimiento y de operación que ésta permita.

2.   Cada Parte podrá imponer, en el momento del establecimiento, términos y condiciones que sean compatibles con el artículo 12-06.

Artículo 12-05: Comercio transfronterizo.

1.   Ninguna Parte incrementará las restricciones de sus medidas relativas al comercio transfronterizo de servicios financieros que realicen los prestadores de servicios financieros transfronterizos de la otra Parte, entrada en vigor de este Tratado.

2.   Cada Parte permitirá a personas ubicadas en su territorio y a sus nacionales, donde quiera que se encuentren, adquirir servicios financieros de prestadores de servicios financieros transfronterizos de la otra Parte ubicados en territorio de esa otra Parte. Esto no obliga a una Parte a permitir que estos prestadores hagan negocios o se anuncien en su territorio. Ajustándose a lo dispuesto por el párrafo 1, cada Parte podrá definir lo que es "hacer negocios" y "anunciarse" para efectos de esta obligación.

3.   Sin perjuicio de otros medios de regulación prudencial al comercio transfronterizo de servicios financieros, cualquier Parte podrá exigir el registro de prestadores de servicios financieros transfronterizos de la otra Parte y de instrumentos financieros.

Artículo 12-06: Trato nacional.

1.   En circunstancias similares, cada Parte otorgará a los inversionistas de la otra Parte trato no menos favorable del que otorga a sus propios inversionistas respecto al establecimiento, adquisición, expansión, administración, conducción, operación, venta, así como otras formas de enajenación de instituciones financieras e inversiones en instituciones financieras en su territorio.

2.   En circunstancias similares, cada Parte otorgará a las instituciones financieras de la otra Parte y a las inversiones de los inversionistas de la otra Parte en instituciones financieras, trato no menos favorable del que otorga a sus propias instituciones financieras y a las inversiones de sus propios inversionistas en instituciones financieras respecto al establecimiento, adquisición, expansión, administración, conducción, operación, venta y otras formas de enajenación de instituciones financieras e inversiones.

3.   En circunstancias similares, conforme al artículo 12-05, cuando una Parte permita la prestación transfronteriza de un servicio financiero, otorgará a prestadores de servicios

financieros de la otra Parte, un trato no menos favorable del que otorga a sus propios prestadores de servicios financieros, respecto a la prestación de ese servicio.

4.   El trato que una Parte otorgue a instituciones financieras y a prestadores de servicios financieros transfronterizos de la otra Parte, ya sea idéntico o diferente al otorgado a sus propias instituciones o prestadores de servicios en circunstancias similares, es congruente con los párrafos 1 al 3, si ofrece igualdad en las oportunidades para competir.

5.   El tratamiento de una Parte no ofrece igualdad en las oportunidades para competir si, en circunstancias similares, sitúa en una posición desventajosa a las instituciones financieras y prestadores de servicios financieros transfronterizos de la otra Parte en su capacidad de prestar servicios financieros, comparada con la capacidad de las propias instituciones financieras y prestadores de servicios de la Parte para prestar esos servicios.

Artículo 12-07: Trato de nación más favorecida.

Cada Parte otorgará a los inversionistas de la otra Parte, a las instituciones financieras de la otra Parte, a las inversiones de los inversionistas en instituciones financieras y a los prestadores de servicios financieros transfronterizos de la otra Parte, un tratamiento no menos favorable que el otorgado a los inversionistas, a las instituciones financieras, a las inversiones de los inversionistas, las instituciones financieras y a los prestadores de servicios financieros transfronterizos de la otra Parte o de un país que no sea Parte, en circunstancias similares.

Artículo 12-08: Reconocimiento y armonización.

1.   Al aplicar las medidas comprendidas en este capítulo, cada Parte podrá reconocer las medidas prudenciales de la otra Parte o de un país que no sea Parte. Tal reconocimiento podrá ser:

   a)   otorgado unilateralmente;

   b)   alcanzado a través de la armonización u otros medios; o

   c)   con base en un acuerdo con la otra Parte o con un país no Parte.

2.   La Parte que otorgue reconocimiento de medidas prudenciales de conformidad con el párrafo 1, brindará oportunidades apropiadas a la otra Parte para demostrar que hay circunstancias por las cuales existen o existirán regulaciones equivalentes, supervisión y puesta en práctica de la regulación y, de ser conveniente, procedimientos para compartir información entre las Partes.

3.   Cuando una Parte otorgue reconocimiento a las medidas prudenciales de conformidad con el párrafo 1 y las circunstancias dispuestas en el párrafo 2 existan, esa Parte brindará oportunidades adecuadas a la otra Parte para negociar la adhesión al acuerdo, o para negociar un acuerdo similar.

Artículo 12-09: Excepciones.

1.   Nada de lo dispuesto en este capítulo, se interpretará como impedimento para que una Parte adopte o mantenga medidas razonables por motivos prudenciales, tales como:

a)   proteger a inversionistas, depositantes, participantes en el mercado financiero, tenedores o beneficiarios de pólizas, o personas acreedoras de obligaciones fiduciarias a cargo de una institución financiera o de un prestador de servicios financieros transfronterizos;

b)   mantener la seguridad, solidez, integridad o responsabilidad financiera de instituciones financieras o de prestadores de servicios financieros transfronterizos; y

c)   asegurar la integridad y estabilidad del sistema financiero de una Parte.

2.   Nada de lo dispuesto en este capítulo se aplica a medidas no discriminatorias de aplicación general adoptadas por una entidad pública en la conducción de políticas monetarias o de políticas de crédito conexas, o bien de políticas cambiarias. Este párrafo no afectará las obligaciones de cualquier Parte derivadas de requisitos de desempeño en inversión respecto a las medidas cubiertas por el capítulo XV (Inversión) o del artículo 12-17.

3.   El artículo 12-06, no se aplicará al otorgamiento de derechos de exclusividad que haga una Parte a una institución financiera, para prestar uno de los servicios financieros a que se refiere el literal a) del párrafo 2 del artículo 12-02.

4.   No obstante lo dispuesto en los párrafos 1 al 3 del artículo 12-17, una Parte podrá evitar o limitar las transferencias de una institución financiera o de un prestador de servicios financieros transfronterizos, o en beneficio de una filial o una persona relacionada con esa institución o con ese prestador de servicios, por medio de la aplicación justa y no discriminatoria de medidas relacionadas con el mantenimiento de la seguridad, solidez, integridad o responsabilidad financiera de instituciones financieras o de prestadores de servicios financieros transfronterizos. Lo establecido en este párrafo se aplicará sin perjuicio de cualquier otra disposición de este Tratado que permita a una Parte restringir transferencias.

Artículo 12-10: Transparencia.

1.   En adición a lo dispuesto en el artículo 17-02 (Publicación), cada Parte se asegurará de que cualquier medida que adopte sobre asuntos relacionados con este capítulo se publique oficialmente o se dé a conocer con oportunidad a los destinatarios de la misma por algún otro medio escrito.

2.   Las autoridades reguladoras de cada Parte pondrán a disposición de los interesados los requisitos para llenar una solicitud para la prestación de servicios financieros.

3.   A petición del solicitante, la autoridad reguladora le informará sobre la situación de su solicitud. Cuando esa autoridad requiera del solicitante información adicional, se lo notificará sin demora injustificada.

4.   Cada una de las autoridades reguladoras dictará en un plazo no mayor de 180 días, una medida administrativa respecto a una solicitud completa relacionada con la prestación de un servicio financiero, presentada por un inversionista en una institución financiera, por una institución financiera o por un prestador de servicios financieros transfronterizos de la otra Parte. La autoridad notificará al interesado, sin demora, la medida. No se considerará completa la solicitud hasta que se celebren todas las audiencias pertinentes y se reciba toda la información

necesaria. Cuando no sea viable dictar una resolución en el plazo de 180 días, la autoridad reguladora lo comunicará al interesado sin demora injustificada y posteriormente procurará emitir la resolución en un plazo razonable.

5.   Ninguna disposición de este capítulo obliga a una Parte a divulgar ni a permitir acceso a:

a)   información relativa a los asuntos financieros y cuentas de clientes individuales de instituciones financieras o de prestadores de servicios financieros transfronterizos; ni

b)   cualquier información confidencial cuya divulgación pudiera contravenir la aplicación de la ley, o, de algún otro modo, ser contraria al interés público o dañar intereses comerciales legítimos de empresas determinadas.

6.   Cada Parte mantendrá o establecerá uno o más centros de consulta, a más tardar 120 días después de la entrada en vigor de este Tratado, para responder por escrito a la brevedad posible todas las preguntas razonables de personas interesadas respecto a las medidas de aplicación general que adopte esa Parte en relación con este capítulo.

Artículo 12-11: Grupo de Trabajo de Servicios Financieros.

1.   Las Partes establecen el Grupo de Trabajo de Servicios Financieros integrado por funcionarios de las autoridades competentes señaladas en el anexo a este artículo.

2.   El Grupo de Trabajo:

a)   supervisará la aplicación de este capítulo y su desarrollo posterior;

b)   considerará aspectos relativos a servicios financieros que le sean presentados por una Parte;

c)   participará en los procedimientos de solución de controversias de conformidad con el artículo 12-19; y

d)   facilitará el intercambio de información entre autoridades de supervisión y cooperará en materia de asesoría sobre regulación prudencial, procurando la armonización de los marcos normativos de regulación así como de las otras políticas, cuando se considere conveniente.

3.   El Grupo de Trabajo se reunirá al menos una vez al año para evaluar la aplicación de este capítulo.

Artículo 12-12: Consultas.

1.   Cualquier Parte podrá solicitar consultas con la otra Parte, respecto a cualquier asunto relacionado con este Tratado que afecte los servicios financieros. La otra Parte considerará favorablemente esa solicitud. La Parte consultante dará a conocer al Grupo de Trabajo los resultados de sus consultas, durante las reuniones que éste celebre.

2. En las consultas previstas en este artículo participarán funcionarios de las autoridades competentes señaladas en el anexo al artículo 12-11.

3. Una Parte podrá solicitar que las autoridades reguladoras de la otra Parte intervengan en las consultas realizadas de conformidad con este artículo, para discutir las medidas de aplicación general de esa otra Parte que puedan afectar las operaciones de las instituciones financieras o de los prestadores de servicios financieros transfronterizos en el territorio de la Parte que solicitó la consulta.

4. Nada de lo dispuesto en este artículo será interpretado en el sentido de obligar a las autoridades reguladoras que intervengan en las consultas conforme al párrafo 3, a divulgar información o a actuar de manera que pudiera interferir en asuntos particulares en materia de regulación, supervisión, administración o aplicación de medidas.

5. En los casos en que, para efectos de supervisión, una Parte necesite información sobre una institución financiera en territorio de la otra Parte o sobre prestadores de servicios financieros transfronterizos en territorio de la otra Parte, la Parte podrá acudir a la autoridad reguladora responsable en territorio de esa otra Parte para solicitar la información.

Artículo 12-13: Nuevos servicios financieros y procesamiento de datos.

1. Cada Parte permitirá que, en circunstancias similares, una institución financiera de la otra Parte preste cualquier nuevo servicio financiero de tipo similar a aquellos que esa Parte permita prestar a sus instituciones financieras, conforme a su legislación. La Parte podrá decidir la modalidad institucional y jurídica a través de la cual se ofrezca ese servicio y podrá exigir autorización para la prestación del mismo. Cuando esa autorización se requiera, la resolución respectiva se dictará en un plazo razonable y solamente podrá ser denegada por razones prudenciales.

2. Cada Parte permitirá a las instituciones financieras de la otra Parte transferir, para su procesamiento, información hacia el interior o el exterior del territorio de la Parte, utilizando cualquiera de los medios autorizados en ella, cuando sea necesario para llevar a cabo las actividades ordinarias de negocios de esas instituciones.

Artículo 12-14: Alta dirección empresarial y consejos de administración.

1. Ninguna Parte podrá obligar a las instituciones financieras de la otra Parte a que contraten personal de una nacionalidad en particular, para ocupar puestos de alta dirección empresarial u otros cargos esenciales.

2. Ninguna Parte podrá exigir que el consejo de administración de una institución financiera de la otra Parte se integre por una mayoría superior a la simple de nacionales de esa Parte, de residentes en su territorio o de una combinación de ambos.

Artículo 12-15: Reservas y compromisos específicos.

1. Los artículos 12-04, al 12-07, 12-13 y 12-14 no se aplican a:

   a) cualquier medida disconforme que cada Parte incluya en el anexo a este artículo en un plazo de un año contado a partir de la entrada en vigor de este Tratado;

b)   la continuación o pronta renovación de cualquier medida disconforme a que se refiere el literal a); o

c)   cualquier modificación a una medida disconforme a que se refiere el literal a), en tanto esa modificación no reduzca el grado de conformidad de la medida con los artículos 12-04, al 12-07, 12-13 y 12-14, tal y como estaba en vigor inmediatamente antes de la modificación.

2.   Cuando una Parte haya establecido en la tercera parte (Comercio de servicios) y la sexta parte (Inversión) una reserva relativa al derecho de establecimiento, comercio transfronterizo de servicios, trato nacional, trato de nación más favorecida, nuevos servicios financieros y procesamiento de datos y alta dirección empresarial y consejos de administración, la reserva se entenderá hecha a los artículos 12-04, al 12-07, 12-13 y 12-14, según sea el caso, en el grado que la medida, sector, subsector o actividad especificados en la reserva estén cubiertos por este capítulo.

Artículo 12-16: Denegación de beneficios.

1.   Una Parte podrá denegar, parcial o totalmente, los beneficios derivados de este capítulo a un prestador de servicios financieros de la otra Parte o a un prestador de servicios financieros transfronterizos de la otra Parte, previa notificación y realización de consultas, de conformidad con los artículos 12-10 y 12-12, cuando la Parte determine que el servicio está siendo prestado por una empresa que no realiza actividades de negocios importantes en territorio de cualquier Parte o que es propiedad de personas de un país que no es Parte o está bajo el control de las mismas.

Artículo 12-17: Transferencias.

1.   Cada Parte permitirá que todas las transferencias relacionadas con la inversión en su territorio de un inversionista de la otra Parte, se hagan libremente y sin demora. Esas transferencias incluyen:

a)   ganancias, dividendos, intereses, ganancias de capital, pagos por regalías, gastos por administración, asistencia técnica y otros cargos, ganancias en especie y otros montos derivados de la inversión;

b)   productos derivados de la venta o liquidación, total o parcial, de la inversión;

c)   pagos realizados conforme a un contrato del que sea parte un inversionista o su inversión;

d)   pagos efectuados de conformidad con el artículo 15-09; y

e)   pagos que resulten de un procedimiento de solución de controversias entre una Parte y un inversionista de la otra Parte conforme a este capítulo y a la sección B del capítulo XV (Inversión).

2.   Cada Parte permitirá que las transferencias se realicen en divisa de libre convertibilidad, al tipo de cambio vigente en el mercado en la fecha de la transferencia para transacciones al contado de la divisa que vaya a transferirse, sin perjuicio de lo dispuesto en el artículo 12-18.

3.   Ninguna Parte podrá exigir a sus inversionistas que efectúen transferencias de sus ingresos, ganancias, o utilidades u otros montos derivados de inversiones llevadas a cabo en territorio de la otra Parte o atribuibles a las mismas.

4.   No obstante lo dispuesto en los párrafos 1 y 2, cada Parte podrá impedir la realización de transferencias, mediante la aplicación equitativa y no discriminatoria de su legislación, en los siguientes casos:

  a)   quiebra, insolvencia o protección de los derechos de los acreedores;

  b)   emisión, comercio, y operaciones de valores;

  c)   infracciones penales o administrativas;

  d)   reportes de transferencias de divisas u otros instrumentos monetarios; o

  e)   garantía del cumplimiento de las sentencias o laudos en un procedimiento contencioso.

5.   El párrafo 3 no se interpretará como un impedimento para que una Parte, a través de la aplicación de su legislación de manera equitativa, no discriminatoria y de buena fe, imponga cualquier medida relacionada con los literales a) y e) del párrafo 4.

Artículo 12-18: Balanza de pagos y salvaguardia.

1.   Cada Parte podrá adoptar o mantener una medida para suspender, por tiempo razonable, todos o sólo algunos de los beneficios contenidos en este capítulo y en el artículo 15-08 (Transferencias), cuando:

  a)   la aplicación de alguna disposición de este capítulo o del artículo 15-08 (Transferencias) resulte en un grave trastorno económico y financiero en territorio de la Parte, que no sea posible solucionar adecuadamente mediante alguna otra medida alternativa; o

  b)   la balanza de pagos de una Parte, incluyendo el estado de sus reservas monetarias, se vea gravemente amenazada o enfrente serias dificultades.

2.   La Parte que suspenda o pretenda suspender los beneficios de este capítulo, deberá notificar a la otra Parte lo antes posible:

  a)   en qué consiste el grave trastorno económico y financiero ocasionado por la aplicación de este capítulo o del artículo 15-08 (Transferencias), según corresponda, la naturaleza y el alcance de las dificultades que amenacen o enfrente su balanza de pagos;

  b)   la situación de la economía y del comercio exterior de la Parte;

  c)   las medidas alternativas que tenga disponibles para corregir el problema; y

d)   las políticas económicas que adopte para enfrentar los problemas mencionados en el párrafo 1, así como la relación directa que exista entre aquéllas y la solución de éstas.

3.   La medida adoptada o mantenida por la Parte, en todo tiempo:

a)   evitará daños innecesarios a los intereses económicos, comerciales y financieros de la otra Parte;

b)   no impondrá mayores cargas que las necesarias para enfrentar las dificultades que originen que la medida se adopte o mantenga;

c)   será temporal, liberalizándose progresivamente en la medida en que la balanza de pagos, o la situación económica y financiera de la Parte, según sea el caso, mejore;

d)   será aplicada procurando en todo tiempo que esa medida evite la discriminación entre las Partes; y

e)   procurará ser compatible con los criterios internacionalmente aceptados.

4.   Cualquier Parte que adopte una medida para suspender beneficios contenidos en este capítulo o en artículo 15-08 (Transferencias), informará a la otra Parte sobre la evolución de los eventos que dieron origen a la adopción de la medida.

5.   Para efectos de este artículo, tiempo razonable significa aquél durante el cual persistan los eventos descritos en el párrafo 1.

Artículo 12-19: Solución de controversias entre las Partes.

1.   En los términos en que lo modifica este artículo, el capítulo XIX (Solución de controversias) se aplica a la solución de controversias que surjan entre las Partes respecto a este capítulo.

2.   El Grupo de Trabajo de Servicios Financieros integrará por consenso una lista de hasta diez individuos que incluya hasta cinco individuos de cada Parte, que cuenten con las aptitudes y disposiciones necesarias para actuar como árbitros en controversias relacionadas con este capítulo. Los integrantes de esta lista deberán, además de satisfacer los requisitos establecidos en el capítulo XIX (Solución de controversias), tener conocimientos especializados en materia financiera, amplia experiencia derivada del ejercicio de responsabilidades en el sector financiero o en su regulación.

3.   Para los fines de la constitución del tribunal arbitral, se utilizará la lista a que se refiere el párrafo 2, excepto que las Partes contendientes acuerden que pueden formar parte del tribunal arbitral individuos no incluidos en esa lista, siempre que cumplan con los requisitos establecidos en el párrafo 2. El presidente siempre será escogido de esa lista.

4.   En cualquier controversia en que el tribunal arbitral haya encontrado que una medida es incompatible con las obligaciones de este capítulo cuando proceda la suspensión de beneficios a que se refiere el capítulo XIX (Solución de controversias) y la medida afecte:

a) sólo al sector de los servicios financieros, la Parte reclamante podrá suspender sólo beneficios en ese sector;

b) al sector de servicios financieros y a cualquier otro sector, la Parte reclamante podrá suspender beneficios en el sector de los servicios financieros que tengan un efecto equivalente al efecto de esa medida en el sector de servicios financieros; o

c) cualquier otro sector que no sea el de servicios financieros, la Parte reclamante no podrá suspender beneficios en el sector de los servicios financieros.

Artículo 12-20: Controversia sobre inversión en materia de servicios financieros.

1. La sección B del capítulo XV (Inversión) se incorpora a este capítulo y es parte integrante del mismo.

2. Cuando un inversionista de la otra Parte, de conformidad con el artículo 15-19 (Demanda del Inversionista de una Parte, por cuenta propia o en representación de una empresa) y al amparo de la sección B del capítulo XV (Inversión) someta a arbitraje una controversia en contra de una Parte, y esa Parte demandada invoque el artículo 12-09 a solicitud de ella misma, el tribunal remitirá por escrito el asunto al Grupo de Trabajo para su decisión. El tribunal no podrá proceder hasta que haya recibido una decisión o un informe según los términos de este artículo.

3. En la remisión del asunto conforme al párrafo 1, el Grupo de Trabajo decidirá si el artículo 12-09 es una defensa válida contra la reclamación del inversionista y en qué grado lo es. El Grupo de Trabajo transmitirá copia de su decisión al tribunal arbitral y a la Comisión. Esa decisión será obligatoria para el tribunal.

4. Cuando el Grupo de Trabajo no haya tomado una decisión en un plazo de 60 días a partir de que reciba la remisión conforme al párrafo 1, la Parte contendiente o la Parte del inversionista contendiente podrán solicitar que se establezca un panel arbitral de conformidad con el artículo 15-26 (Consentimiento para la designación de árbitros) el panel estará constituido conforme al artículo 12-19 y enviará al Grupo de Trabajo y al tribunal arbitral su determinación definitiva, que será obligatoria para el tribunal.

5. Cuando no se haya solicitado la instalación de un panel en los términos del párrafo 3 dentro de un lapso de diez días a partir del vencimiento del plazo de 60 días a que se refiere ese párrafo, el tribunal podrá proceder a resolver el caso.

Anexo al artículo 12-11
Autoridades competentes

1. El Grupo de Trabajo de Servicios Financieros estará integrado por los funcionarios que designe:

a) para el caso de Bolivia la Superintendencia de Bancos e Instituciones Financieras, de manera transitoria, mientras Bolivia no notifique una autoridad distinta; y

b) para el caso de México, la Secretaría de Hacienda y Crédito Público.

2.   El representante principal de cada Parte será el que esa autoridad designe para tal efecto.

Capítulo XV

Inversión

Sección A – Inversión

Artículo 15-01: Definiciones.

Para efectos de este capítulo, se entenderá por:

CIADI: el Centro Internacional de Arreglo de Diferencias Relativas a Inversiones;

Convenio de CIADI: el Convenio sobre arreglo de diferencias relativas a inversiones entre Estados y nacionales de otros Estados, celebrado en Washington, D.C. el 18 de marzo de 1965;

Convención Interamericana: la Convención interamericana sobre arbitraje comercial internacional, celebrada en Panamá, el 30 de enero de 1975;

Convención de Nueva York: la Convención de las Naciones Unidas sobre el reconocimiento y ejecución de laudos arbitrales extranjeros, celebrada en Nueva York, el 10 de junio de 1958;

demanda: la reclamación hecha por el inversionista contendiente contra una Parte, cuyo fundamento sea una presunta violación a las disposiciones contenidas en este capítulo;

empresa de una Parte: una empresa constituida u organizada de conformidad con la legislación de una Parte y una sucursal ubicada en territorio de una Parte que desempeñe actividades comerciales en la misma;

inversión:

a)   la aplicación o transferencia de recursos al territorio de una Parte por inversionistas de la otra Parte con propósito de lucro;

b)   la participación de inversionistas de una Parte, en cualquier proporción en el capital social, de las empresas de la otra Parte o en las actividades contempladas por la legislación en materia de inversión de esa otra Parte; o

c)   aquella realizada de conformidad con los literales a) y b) por una empresa de una Parte con mayoría de capital perteneciente a inversionistas de la otra Parte o que se encuentra bajo el control de los mismos;

inversión no incluye:

a)   una obligación de pago de un crédito a una empresa del Estado ni el otorgamiento del mismo;

b)   reclamaciones pecuniarias derivadas exclusivamente de:

i) contratos comerciales para la venta de bienes o servicios por un nacional o una empresa en territorio de una Parte a una empresa en territorio de la otra Parte; o

ii) el otorgamiento de un crédito en relación con una transacción comercial, cuya fecha de vencimiento sea menor a tres años, tal como el financiamiento al comercio;

inversión de un inversionista de una Parte: la inversión propiedad de un inversionista de una Parte o bajo el control directo o indirecto de éste;

inversionista de una Parte: una Parte o una empresa del Estado de la misma, o un nacional o empresa de esa Parte, que lleve a cabo los actos jurídicos tendientes a materializar una inversión, o que realice o haya realizado una inversión en el territorio de la otra Parte;

inversionista contendiente: un inversionista que someta a arbitraje una reclamación en los términos de la sección B;

nacional de una Parte: una persona física que sea nacional de una Parte de conformidad con su legislación;

Parte contendiente: la Parte contra la cual se hace una reclamación en los términos de la sección B;

parte contendiente: el inversionista contendiente o la Parte contendiente;

partes contendientes: el inversionista contendiente y la Parte contendiente;

Reglas de arbitraje de CNUDMI: las Reglas de arbitraje de la Comisión de las Naciones Unidas sobre Derecho Mercantil Internacional (CNUDMI), aprobadas por la Asamblea General de las Naciones Unidas, el 15 de diciembre de 1976;

Secretario General: el Secretario General de CIADI;

transferencias: las remisiones y pagos internacionales;

tribunal: un tribunal arbitral establecido conforme al artículo 15-21;

tribunal de acumulación: un tribunal arbitral establecido conforme al artículo 15-27.

Artículo 15-02: Ambito de aplicación.

1. Este capítulo se aplica a las medidas que adopte o mantenga una Parte relativas a:

   a) los inversionistas de la otra Parte;

   b) las inversiones de inversionistas de una Parte realizadas en territorio de la otra Parte; y

   c) en lo relativo al artículo 15-05, todas las inversiones en el territorio de la otra Parte.

2.	Este capítulo se aplica en el territorio de cada Parte, en cualquier nivel u orden de gobierno, a pesar de las medidas incompatibles que pudieran existir en sus legislaciones respectivas, salvo por lo dispuesto en el artículo 15-07.

3.	Este capítulo no se aplica a:

a)	las actividades económicas reservadas a cada Parte, de conformidad con su legislación vigente, las cuales se listarán en un plazo no mayor a un año contado a partir de la entrada en vigor de este Tratado;

b)	las medidas que adopte o mantenga una Parte en materia de servicios financieros; y

c)	las medidas que adopte una Parte para restringir la participación de las inversiones de inversionistas de la otra Parte en su territorio, por razones de seguridad nacional.

Artículo 15-03: Trato nacional.

1.	Cada Parte brindará a los inversionistas de la otra Parte y a las inversiones de los inversionistas de la otra Parte, un trato no menos favorable que el que otorgue, en circunstancias similares, a sus propios inversionistas.

2.	Cada Parte otorgará a los inversionistas de la otra Parte, respecto de las inversiones que sufran pérdidas en su territorio debidas a conflictos armados o contiendas civiles, o caso fortuito o fuerza mayor, trato no discriminatorio respecto de cualquier medida que adopte o mantenga en relación con esas pérdidas.

Artículo 15-04: Trato de nación más favorecida.

1.	Cada Parte brindará a los inversionistas de la otra Parte y a las inversiones de inversionistas de la otra Parte, un trato no menos favorable que el que otorgue, en circunstancias similares, a los inversionistas y a las inversiones de los inversionistas de la otra Parte o de un país que no sea Parte, salvo en lo dispuesto por el párrafo 2.

2.	Si una Parte hubiere otorgado o en lo sucesivo otorgare un tratamiento especial a los inversionistas o a las inversiones de éstos, provenientes de un país que no sea Parte, en virtud de convenios que establezcan disposiciones para evitar la doble tributación, zonas de libre comercio, uniones aduaneras, mercados comunes, uniones económicas o monetarias o instituciones similares, esa Parte no estará obligada a otorgar el tratamiento de que se trate a los inversionistas o a las inversiones de la otra Parte.

Artículo 15-05: Requisitos de desempeño.

1.	Ninguna Parte podrá imponer ni obligar al cumplimiento de los siguientes requisitos o compromisos, en relación con cualquier inversión en su territorio:

a)	exportar un determinado nivel o porcentaje de bienes o servicios;

b)	alcanzar un determinado grado o porcentaje de contenido nacional;

c) adquirir, utilizar u otorgar preferencia a bienes producidos o a servicios prestados en su territorio, o adquirir bienes de productores o servicios de prestadores de servicios en su territorio;

d) relacionar en cualquier forma el volumen o valor de las importaciones con el volumen o valor de las exportaciones, o con el monto de las entradas de divisas asociadas con esa inversión;

e) restringir las ventas en su territorio de los bienes o servicios que esa inversión produzca o preste, relacionando de cualquier manera esas ventas al volumen o valor de sus exportaciones o a ganancias en divisas que generen;

f) transferir a una persona en su territorio, tecnología, proceso productivo u otro conocimiento reservado, salvo cuando el requisito se imponga por un tribunal judicial o administrativo o autoridad competente para reparar una supuesta violación a las leyes en materia de competencia o para actuar de una manera que no sea incompatible con otras disposiciones de este Tratado; o

g) actuar como el proveedor exclusivo de los bienes que produzca o servicios que preste para un mercado específico, regional o mundial.

2. El párrafo 1 no se aplica a requisito alguno distinto a los señalados en el mismo.

3. Ninguna Parte podrá condicionar la recepción de un incentivo o que se continúe recibiendo el mismo, al cumplimiento de los siguientes requisitos, en relación con cualquier inversión en su territorio:

a) adquirir, utilizar u otorgar preferencia a bienes producidos en su territorio o a comprar bienes de productores en su territorio;

b) alcanzar un determinado grado o porcentaje de contenido nacional;

c) relacionar en cualquier forma el volumen o valor de las importaciones con el volumen o valor de las exportaciones, o con el monto de las entradas de divisas asociadas con esa inversión; o

d) restringir las ventas en su territorio de los bienes o servicios que esa inversión produzca o preste, relacionando de cualquier manera esas ventas al volumen o valor de sus exportaciones o a ganancias en divisas que generen.

4. El párrafo 3 no se aplica a un requisito distinto de los señalados en el mismo.

5. Nada de lo dispuesto en los párrafos 1 y 2 se interpretará como impedimento para que una Parte condicione la recepción de un incentivo o la continuación de su recepción, en relación con cualquier inversión en su territorio, a requisitos de localización geográfica de unidades productivas, de generación de empleo o capacitación de mano de obra o de realización de actividades en materia de investigación y desarrollo.

Artículo 15-06: Alta dirección empresarial y consejos de administración.

1.   Ninguna Parte podrá exigir que sus empresas, designen a individuos de alguna nacionalidad en particular para ocupar puestos de alta dirección.

2.   Una Parte podrá exigir que la mayoría de los miembros de los órganos de administración de una empresa sean de una nacionalidad en particular, siempre que el requisito no menoscabe materialmente la capacidad del inversionista para ejercer el control de su inversión.

Artículo 15-07: Reservas y excepciones.

1.   Los artículos 15-03 al 15-06 no se aplican a cualquier medida incompatible que mantenga una Parte de conformidad con su legislación vigente a la entrada en vigor de este Tratado, sea cual fuere el nivel u orden de gobierno. Cada Parte listará esas medidas en el anexo 1 a este artículo dentro de un plazo no mayor a un año, contado a partir de la entrada en vigor. Cualquier medida que en el futuro adoptare una Parte, no podrá ser más restrictiva que aquellas existentes a la entrada en vigor de este Tratado.

2.   Los artículos 15-03 al 15-06 no se aplicarán a cualquier medida incompatible que adopte o mantenga una Parte respecto de las actividades que hayan sido listadas en el anexo 2 a este artículo a la firma de este Tratado. Las Partes, en la adopción o mantenimiento de las medidas incompatibles referidas, buscarán alcanzar un equilibrio global en sus obligaciones. Transcurrido un periodo de dos años, contado a partir de la entrada en vigor de este Tratado, cualquier medida que adopte una Parte no podrá ser más restrictiva que aquellas existentes al final del mismo.

3.   El trato otorgado por una Parte de conformidad con el artículo 15-04, no se aplica a los tratados o sectores estipulados en su lista del anexo a este artículo.

4.   Los artículos, 15-03, 15-04 y 15-06 no se aplican a:

   a)   las adquisiciones realizadas por una Parte o por una empresa del Estado; o

   b)   los subsidios o subvenciones, incluyendo los préstamos, garantías y seguros gubernamentales otorgados por una Parte o por una empresa del Estado.

5.   Las disposiciones contenidas en:

   a)   los literales a) al c) del párrafo 1 y los literales a) y b) del párrafo 3 del artículo 15-05 no se aplican en lo relativo a los requisitos para calificación de los bienes y servicios con respecto a programas de promoción a las exportaciones;

   b)   los literales b), c), f) y g) del párrafo 1 y los literales a) y b) del párrafo 3 del artículo 15-05 no se aplican a la adquisición por una Parte o por una empresa del Estado; y

   c)   los literales a) y b) del párrafo 3 del artículo 15-05 no se aplican a los requisitos impuestos por una Parte importadora relacionados con el contenido necesario de bienes para calificar para aranceles o cuotas preferenciales.

Artículo 15-08: Transferencias.

1.   Cada Parte permitirá que todas las transferencias relacionadas con la inversión en su territorio de un inversionista de la otra Parte se hagan libremente y sin demora. Esas transferencias incluyen:

   a)   ganancias, dividendos, intereses, ganancias de capital, pagos por regalías, gastos por administración, asistencia técnica, ganancias en especie y otros montos derivados de la inversión;

   b)   productos derivados de la venta o liquidación, total o parcial, de la inversión;

   c)   pagos realizados conforme a un contrato del que sea parte un inversionista o su inversión, incluidos pagos efectuados conforme a un convenio de préstamo;

   d)   pagos derivados de compensaciones por concepto de expropiación; y

   e)   pagos que provengan de la aplicación de las disposiciones relativas al mecanismo de solución de controversias.

2.   Cada Parte permitirá que las transferencias se realicen en divisa de libre convertibilidad al tipo de cambio vigente en el mercado en la fecha de la transferencia.

3.   No obstante lo dispuesto en los párrafos 1 y 2, cada Parte podrá impedir la realización de transferencias, mediante la aplicación equitativa y no discriminatoria de su legislación, en los siguientes casos:

   a)   quiebra, insolvencia o protección de los derechos de los acreedores;

   b)   emisión, comercio y operaciones de valores;

   c)   infracciones penales o administrativas;

   d)   reportes de transferencias de divisas u otros instrumentos monetarios; o

   e)   garantía del cumplimiento de las sentencias o laudos en un procedimiento contencioso.

4.   No obstante lo dispuesto en este artículo, cada Parte podrá establecer controles temporales a las operaciones cambiarias, siempre y cuando la balanza de pagos de la Parte de que se trate presente un desequilibrio e instrumente un programa de acuerdo a los criterios internacionalmente aceptados.

Artículo 15-09: Expropiación e indemnización.

1.   Ninguna Parte podrá nacionalizar ni expropiar, directa o indirectamente, una inversión de un inversionista de la otra Parte en su territorio, ni adoptar una medida equivalente ("expropiación"), salvo que sea:

   a)   por causa de interés nacional o utilidad pública;

b)   sobre bases no discriminatorias;

c)   con apego al principio de legalidad; y

d)   mediante indemnización conforme a los párrafos 2 al 4.

2.   La indemnización será equivalente al valor justo de mercado que tenga la inversión expropiada inmediatamente antes de que la medida expropiatoria se haya llevado a cabo ("fecha de expropiación"), y no reflejará cambio alguno en el valor debido a que la intención de expropiar se haya conocido con antelación a la fecha de expropiación. Los criterios de valuación incluirán el valor fiscal declarado de bienes tangibles, así como otros criterios que resulten apropiados para determinar el valor justo de mercado.

3.   El pago de la indemnización se hará sin demora y será completamente liquidable.

4.   La cantidad pagada no será inferior a la cantidad equivalente que por indemnización se hubiera pagado en una divisa de libre convertibilidad en el mercado financiero internacional en la fecha de expropiación, y esta divisa se hubiese convertido a la cotización de mercado vigente en la fecha de valuación, más los intereses que hubiese generado a una tasa comercial razonable para esa divisa hasta el día del pago.

Artículo 15-10: Formalidades especiales y requisitos de información.

1.   Nada de lo dispuesto en el artículo 15-03 se interpretará en el sentido de impedir a una Parte adoptar o mantener una medida que prescriba formalidades especiales conexas al establecimiento de inversiones por inversionistas de la otra Parte, tales como que las inversiones se constituyan conforme a la legislación de la Parte, siempre que esas formalidades no menoscaben sustancialmente la protección otorgada por una Parte conforme a este capítulo.

2.   No obstante lo dispuesto en los artículos 15-03 y 15-04, cada Parte podrá exigir de un inversionista de la otra Parte o de su inversión, en su territorio, que proporcione información rutinaria, referente a esa inversión, exclusivamente con fines de información o estadística. La Parte protegerá la información que sea confidencial, de cualquier divulgación que pudiera afectar negativamente la situación competitiva de la inversión o del inversionista.

Artículo 15-11: Relación con otros capítulos.

En caso de incompatibilidad entre una disposición de este capítulo y la de otro capítulo, prevalecerá la de este último en la medida de la incompatibilidad.

Artículo 15-12: Denegación de beneficios.

Previa notificación y consulta con la otra Parte, una Parte podrá denegar los beneficios de este capítulo a un inversionista de la otra Parte que sea una empresa de esa Parte y a las inversiones de ese inversionista, cuando inversionistas de un país no Parte sean propietarios mayoritarios o controlen la empresa y ésta no tenga actividades empresariales sustanciales en el territorio de la Parte conforme a cuya legislación esté constituida u organizada.

Artículo 15-13: Aplicación extraterritorial de la legislación de una Parte.

1.   Una Parte, en relación con las inversiones de sus inversionistas constituidas y organizadas conforme a la legislación de la otra Parte, no podrá ejercer jurisdicción ni adoptar medida alguna que tenga por efecto la aplicación extraterritorial de su legislación o la obstaculización del comercio entre las Partes, o entre una Parte y un país no Parte.

2.   Si una Parte incumpliere lo dispuesto por el párrafo 1, la Parte donde la inversión se hubiere constituido podrá adoptar las medidas y ejercitar las acciones que considere necesarias, a fin de dejar sin efectos la legislación o la medida de que se trate y los obstáculos al comercio consecuencia de las mismas.

Artículo 15-14: Medidas relativas al ambiente, la salud y la seguridad.

1.   Nada de lo dispuesto en este capítulo se interpretará como impedimento para que una Parte adopte, mantenga o ponga en ejecución cualquier medida compatible con este capítulo, que considere apropiada para asegurar que las inversiones en su territorio observen la legislación en materia ambiental.

2.   Las Partes reconocen que es inadecuado alentar la inversión por medio de la atenuación de las medidas internas aplicables al ambiente, la salud y la seguridad. En consecuencia, ninguna Parte deberá eliminar, o comprometerse a eximir de la aplicación de esas medidas, a los inversionistas o a sus inversiones, como medio para inducir el establecimiento, la adquisición, la expansión o conservación de la inversión en su territorio. Si una Parte estima que la otra Parte ha alentado una inversión de tal manera, podrá solicitar consultas con esa otra Parte.

Artículo 15-15: Promoción de inversiones e intercambio de información.

1.   Con la intención de incrementar significativamente la participación recíproca de la inversión, cada Parte elaborará documentos de promoción de oportunidades de inversión y diseñará mecanismos para su difusión; asimismo, las Partes mantendrán y perfeccionarán mecanismos financieros que hagan viables las inversiones de un inversionista de una Parte en el territorio de la otra Parte.

2.   Cada Parte dará a conocer información detallada sobre oportunidades de:

   a)   inversión en su territorio, que puedan ser desarrolladas por inversionistas de la otra Parte;

   b)   alianzas estratégicas entre inversionistas de las Partes, mediante la investigación y recopilación de intereses y oportunidades de asociación; o

   c)   inversión en sectores económicos específicos que interesen a las Partes y a sus inversionistas, de acuerdo a la solicitud expresa que haga cualquiera de las Partes.

3.   Las Partes acuerdan mantenerse informadas y actualizadas respecto de:

   a)   las oportunidades de inversión de que trata el párrafo 2, incluyendo la difusión de los instrumentos financieros disponibles que coadyuven al incremento de la inversión en el territorio de cada Parte;

b)   la legislación o disposiciones que, directa o indirectamente, afecten a la inversión extranjera incluyendo, entre otros, regímenes cambiarios y de carácter fiscal; o

c)   el comportamiento de la inversión extranjera en el territorio de cada Parte.

Artículo 15-16: Doble tributación.

Las Partes, con el ánimo de promover las inversiones dentro de sus respectivos territorios mediante la eliminación de obstáculos de índole fiscal y la vigilancia en el cumplimiento de las obligaciones fiscales a través del intercambio de información tributaria, convienen en iniciar las negociaciones tendientes a la celebración de convenios para evitar la doble tributación, de acuerdo con el calendario que se establezca entre las autoridades competentes de las mismas.

Sección B - Solución de controversias entre una Parte y un inversionista de la otra Parte

Artículo 15-17: Objetivo.

Esta sección establece un mecanismo para la solución de controversias en materia de inversión que se susciten, a partir de la entrada en vigor de este Tratado, entre uno o más inversionistas de una y otra Parte, y cuyo fundamento sea el que esa otra Parte haya violado una obligación establecida en este capítulo, y que asegura, tanto el trato igual entre inversionistas de las Partes de acuerdo con el principio de reciprocidad internacional, como el debido ejercicio de la garantía de audiencia y defensa dentro de un proceso legal ante un tribunal imparcial.

Artículo 15-18: Solución de controversias mediante consulta y negociación.

Las partes contendientes intentarán primero dirimir la controversia por vía de consulta o negociación.

Artículo 15-19: Demanda del inversionista de una Parte, por cuenta propia o en representación de una empresa.

1.   De conformidad con esta sección, sólo el inversionista de una Parte podrá, por cuenta propia o en representación de una empresa de la otra Parte que sea una persona jurídica de su propiedad o bajo su control directo o indirecto, someter a arbitraje una demanda cuyo fundamento sea el que la otra Parte o una empresa controlada directa o indirectamente por esa Parte, haya violado una obligación establecida en este capítulo, siempre y cuando la empresa haya sufrido pérdidas o daños en virtud de la violación o a consecuencia de ella.

2.   El inversionista no podrá presentar una demanda conforme a esta sección, si han transcurrido más de tres años contados a partir de la fecha en la cual tuvo conocimiento o debió haber tenido conocimiento de la presunta violación cometida a su inversión, así como de las pérdidas o daños sufridos.

3.   Cuando un inversionista presente una demanda en representación de una empresa que sea una persona jurídica de su propiedad o bajo su control directo o indirecto, y de manera paralela un inversionista que no tenga el control de una empresa presente una demanda por cuenta propia como consecuencia de los mismos actos, o dos o más demandas se sometan a arbitraje en virtud de la misma medida adoptada por una Parte, el tribunal de acumulación establecido de

conformidad con el artículo 15-27 examinará conjuntamente esas demandas, salvo que ese tribunal determine que los intereses de una parte contendiente se verían perjudicados.

4.   Cuando una empresa de una Parte que sea una persona jurídica propiedad de uno o más inversionistas de la otra Parte o que esté bajo su control directo o indirecto, alegue en procedimientos ante un tribunal judicial, que otra Parte ha violado presuntamente una obligación de la sección A, el o los inversionistas no podrán alegar la presunta violación en un procedimiento arbitral conforme a esta sección.

5.   Una inversión o una empresa no podrá someter una demanda a arbitraje conforme a esta sección.

Artículo 15-20: Notificación de la intención de someter la reclamación a arbitraje.

El inversionista contendiente notificará por escrito a la Parte contendiente su intención de someter una reclamación a arbitraje, cuando menos 90 días antes de que se presente formalmente la demanda y la notificación señalará lo siguiente:

a)   el nombre y domicilio del inversionista contendiente y, cuando la demanda se haya realizado en representación de una empresa, la denominación o razón social y el domicilio de la misma;

b)   las disposiciones de este capítulo presuntamente incumplidas y cualquier otra disposición aplicable;

c)   los hechos en que se funde la demanda; y

d)   la reparación que se solicite y el monto aproximado de los daños reclamados.

Artículo 15-21: Sometimiento de la reclamación al arbitraje.

1.   Siempre que hayan transcurrido seis meses desde que tuvieron lugar las medidas que motivan la reclamación, un inversionista contendiente podrá someter la demanda a arbitraje de acuerdo con:

a)   el Convenio de CIADI, siempre que tanto la Parte contendiente como la Parte del inversionista, sean Estados parte del mismo;

b)   las Reglas del mecanismo complementario de CIADI, cuando la Parte contendiente o la Parte del inversionista, pero no ambas, sean Estados parte del Convenio de CIADI; o

c)   las Reglas de arbitraje de CNUDMI.

2.   Salvo lo dispuesto por el artículo 15-27 y siempre que, tanto la Parte contendiente como la Parte del inversionista contendiente sean Estados parte del Convenio de CIADI, toda controversia entre las mismas será sometida conforme al literal a) del párrafo 1.

3.   Las reglas que se elijan conforme a un procedimiento arbitral establecido en este capítulo, serán aplicables salvo en la medida de lo modificado por esta sección.

Artículo 15-22: Condiciones previas al sometimiento de una reclamación al procedimiento arbitral.

1.   Un inversionista contendiente por cuenta propia o en representación de una empresa, podrá someter una reclamación al procedimiento arbitral de conformidad con esta sección, sólo si:

a)   en el caso del inversionista contendiente por cuenta propia, éste consienta en someterse al arbitraje en los términos de los procedimientos establecidos en esta sección;

b)   en el caso del inversionista contendiente en representación de una empresa, tanto el inversionista contendiente como la empresa consientan en someterse al arbitraje en los términos de los procedimientos establecidos en esta sección; y

c)   tanto el inversionista contendiente como, en su caso, la empresa que represente, renuncien a su derecho de iniciar procedimientos ante cualquier tribunal judicial de cualquier Parte con respecto a la medida presuntamente violatoria de las disposiciones de este capítulo, salvo el desahogo de los recursos administrativos ante las propias autoridades ejecutoras de la medida presuntamente violatoria previstos en la legislación de la Parte contendiente.

2.   El consentimiento y la renuncia requeridos por este artículo se manifestarán por escrito, se entregarán a la Parte contendiente y se incluirán en el sometimiento de la reclamación a arbitraje.

Artículo 15-23: Consentimiento al arbitraje.

1.   Cada Parte consiente en someter reclamaciones a arbitraje con apego a los procedimientos y requisitos señalados en esta sección.

2.   El sometimiento de una reclamación a arbitraje por parte de un inversionista contendiente cumplirá con los requisitos señalados en:

a)   el capítulo II del Convenio de CIADI (Jurisdicción del centro) y las Reglas del mecanismo complementario de CIADI que exigen el consentimiento por escrito de las Partes;

b)   el artículo II de la Convención de Nueva York, que exige un acuerdo por escrito; y

c)   el artículo I de la Convención Interamericana, que requiere un acuerdo.

Artículo 15-24: Número de árbitros y método de nombramiento.

Con excepción de lo dispuesto por el artículo 15-27 y, sin perjuicio de que las partes contendientes acuerden algo distinto, el tribunal estará integrado por tres árbitros. Cada parte contendiente nombrará a un árbitro; el tercer árbitro, quien será el presidente del tribunal arbitral, será designado por las partes contendientes de común acuerdo.

Artículo 15-25: Integración del tribunal en caso de que una parte contendiente no designe árbitro o no se logre un acuerdo en la designación del presidente del tribunal arbitral.

1.   El Secretario General nombrará a los árbitros en los procedimientos de arbitraje, de conformidad con esta sección.

2.   Cuando un tribunal, que no sea el establecido de conformidad con el artículo 15-27, no se integre en un plazo de 90 días contados a partir de la fecha en que la reclamación se someta al arbitraje, el Secretario General, a petición de cualquiera de las partes contendientes, nombrará, a su discreción, al árbitro o árbitros no designados todavía, pero no al presidente del tribunal, quién será designado conforme a lo dispuesto en el párrafo 3.

3.   El Secretario General designará al presidente del tribunal de entre los árbitros de la lista a la que se refiere el párrafo 4, asegurándose que el presidente del tribunal no sea nacional de la Parte contendiente o nacional de la Parte del inversionista contendiente. En caso de que no se encuentre en la lista un árbitro disponible para presidir el tribunal, el Secretario General designará, del Panel de árbitros de CIADI, al presidente del tribunal, siempre que sea de nacionalidad distinta a la de la Parte contendiente o a la de la Parte del inversionista contendiente.

4.   A la entrada en vigor de este Tratado, las Partes establecerán y mantendrán una lista de 15 árbitros como posibles presidentes del tribunal arbitral, que reúnan las cualidades establecidas en el Convenio de CIADI y en las reglas contempladas en el artículo 15-21 y que cuenten con experiencia en derecho internacional y en asuntos en materia de inversiones. Los árbitros que conformen la lista serán designados por consenso sin importar su nacionalidad.

Artículo 15-26: Consentimiento para la designación de árbitros.

Para efectos del artículo 39 del Convenio de CIADI y del artículo 7 de la Parte C de las Reglas del mecanismo complementario de CIADI y, sin perjuicio de objetar a un árbitro de acuerdo con lo dispuesto por el párrafo 3 del artículo 15-25 o sobre una base distinta de la nacionalidad:

    a)   la Parte contendiente acepta la designación de cada uno de los miembros de un tribunal establecido de conformidad con el Convenio de CIADI o con las Reglas del mecanismo complementario del CIADI;

    b)   un inversionista contendiente, sea por cuenta propia o en representación de una empresa, podrá someter una reclamación a arbitraje o continuar el procedimiento conforme al Convenio de CIADI o las Reglas del mecanismo complementario de CIADI, únicamente a condición de que el inversionista contendiente y, en su caso, la empresa que representa, manifiesten su consentimiento por escrito sobre la designación de cada uno de los miembros del tribunal.

Artículo 15-27: Acumulación de procedimientos.

1.   Un tribunal de acumulación establecido conforme a este artículo se instalará con apego a las Reglas de arbitraje de CNUDMI y procederá de conformidad con lo contemplado en esas reglas, salvo lo que disponga esta sección.

2.   Cuando un tribunal de acumulación determine que las reclamaciones sometidas a arbitraje de acuerdo con el artículo 15-21 plantean cuestiones en común de hecho y de derecho, el tribunal de acumulación, en interés de su resolución justa y eficiente, y habiendo escuchado a las Partes contendientes, podrá asumir jurisdicción, dar trámite y resolver:

a)   todas o parte de las reclamaciones, de manera conjunta; o

b)   una o más de las reclamaciones sobre la base de que ello contribuirá a la resolución de las otras.

3.   Una parte contendiente que pretenda que se determine la acumulación en los términos del párrafo 2, solicitará al Secretario General que instale un tribunal de acumulación y especificará en su solicitud:

a)   el nombre de la Parte contendiente o de los inversionistas contendientes contra los cuales se pretenda obtener el acuerdo de acumulación;

b)   la naturaleza del acuerdo de acumulación solicitado; y

c)   el fundamento en que se apoya la petición solicitada.

4.   En un plazo de 60 días contados a partir de la fecha de la petición, el Secretario General instalará un tribunal de acumulación integrado por tres árbitros. El Secretario General nombrará al presidente del tribunal de acumulación de la lista de árbitros a que se refiere el párrafo 4 del artículo 15-25. En caso de que no se encuentre en la lista un árbitro disponible para presidir el tribunal de acumulación, el Secretario General designará, del Panel de árbitros de CIADI, al presidente de ese tribunal, quien no será nacional de la Parte contendiente o nacional de la Parte del inversionista contendiente. El Secretario General designará a los otros dos integrantes del tribunal de acumulación de la lista a la que se refiere el párrafo 4 del artículo 15-25 y, cuando no estén disponibles, los seleccionará del Panel de árbitros de CIADI. De no haber disponibilidad de árbitros en ese Panel, el Secretario General hará discrecionalmente los nombramientos faltantes. Uno de los miembros será nacional de la Parte contendiente y el otro miembro del tribunal de acumulación será nacional de la Parte del inversionista contendiente.

5.   Cuando se haya establecido un tribunal de acumulación, el inversionista contendiente que haya sometido una reclamación a arbitraje y no haya sido mencionado en la petición de acumulación hecha de acuerdo con el párrafo 3, podrá solicitar por escrito al tribunal de acumulación que se le incluya en ella y especificará en esa solicitud:

a)   el nombre y domicilio del inversionista contendiente y, en su caso, la denominación o razón social y el domicilio de la empresa;

b)   la naturaleza del acuerdo de acumulación solicitado; y

c)   los fundamentos en que se apoya la solicitud.

6.   El tribunal de acumulación proporcionará, a costa del inversionista interesado, copia de la petición de acumulación a los inversionistas contendientes contra quienes se pretende obtener el acuerdo de acumulación.

7. Un tribunal establecido conforme al artículo 15-21 no tendrá jurisdicción para resolver una demanda o parte de ella, respecto de la cual haya asumido jurisdicción un tribunal de acumulación.

8. A solicitud de una parte contendiente, un tribunal de acumulación podrá, en espera de su decisión conforme al párrafo 2, disponer que los procedimientos de un tribunal establecido de acuerdo con el artículo 15-21 se suspendan hasta que se resuelva sobre la procedencia de la acumulación.

9. Una Parte contendiente entregará a su sección nacional del Secretariado, en un plazo de 15 días contados a partir de la fecha en que la Parte contendiente reciba:

   a) una solicitud de arbitraje hecha conforme al párrafo 1 del artículo 36 del Convenio de CIADI;

   b) una notificación de arbitraje en los términos del artículo 2 de la Parte C de las Reglas del mecanismo complementario del CIADI; o

   c) una notificación de arbitraje en los términos previstos por las Reglas de arbitraje de CNUDMI.

10. Una Parte contendiente entregará a su sección nacional del Secretariado copia de la solicitud formulada en los términos del párrafo 3:

   a) en un plazo de 15 días contados a partir de la recepción de la solicitud, en el caso de una petición hecha por el inversionista contendiente; o

   b) en un plazo de 15 días contados a partir de la fecha de la solicitud, en el caso de una petición hecha por la Parte contendiente.

11. Una Parte contendiente entregará a su sección nacional del Secretariado copia de la solicitud formulada en los términos del párrafo 6 en un plazo de 15 días contados a partir de la fecha de recepción de la solicitud.

12. El Secretariado conservará un registro público de los documentos a los que se refieren los párrafos 9 al 11.

Artículo 15-28: Notificación.

La Parte contendiente entregará a la otra Parte:

a) notificación escrita de la reclamación que se haya sometido a arbitraje a más tardar 30 días después de la fecha de sometimiento de la reclamación a arbitraje; y

b) copias de todas las comunicaciones presentadas en el procedimiento arbitral.

Artículo 15-29: Participación de una Parte.

Previa notificación escrita a las partes contendientes, una Parte podrá presentar comunicaciones a cualquier tribunal establecido conforme a esta sección sobre una cuestión de interpretación de este capítulo.

Artículo 15-30: Documentación.

1.   Una Parte tendrá, a su costa, derecho a recibir de la Parte contendiente una copia de:

   a)   las pruebas ofrecidas a cualquier tribunal establecido conforme a esta sección; y

   b)   las comunicaciones escritas presentadas por las partes contendientes.

2.   Una Parte que reciba información conforme a lo dispuesto en el párrafo 1, dará tratamiento a la información como si fuera una Parte contendiente.

Artículo 15-31: Sede del procedimiento arbitral.

Salvo que las partes contendientes acuerden algo distinto, cualquier tribunal establecido conforme a esta sección llevará a cabo el procedimiento arbitral en el territorio de una Parte que sea Estado parte de la Convención de Nueva York, el cual será elegido de conformidad con:

a)   las Reglas del mecanismo complementario de CIADI, si el arbitraje se rige por esas reglas o por el Convenio de CIADI; o

b)   las Reglas de arbitraje de CNUDMI, si el arbitraje se rige por esas reglas.

Artículo 15-32: Derecho aplicable.

1.   Cualquier tribunal establecido conforme a esta sección decidirá las controversias que se sometan a su consideración de conformidad con este Tratado y con las reglas aplicables del derecho internacional.

2.   La interpretación que formule la Comisión sobre una disposición de este Tratado, será obligatoria para cualquier tribunal establecido de conformidad con esta sección en la medida en que esa interpretación le sea aplicable a este capítulo.

Artículo 15-33: Interpretación de los anexos.

1.   Cuando una Parte alegue como defensa que una medida presuntamente violatoria cae en el ámbito de una reserva o excepción consignada en cualquiera de los anexos, a petición de la Parte contendiente, cualquier tribunal establecido de conformidad con esta sección solicitará a la Comisión una interpretación sobre ese asunto. La Comisión, en un plazo de 60 días contados a partir de la entrega de la solicitud, presentará por escrito a ese tribunal su interpretación.

2.   La interpretación de la Comisión sometida conforme al párrafo 1 será obligatoria para cualquier tribunal establecido de conformidad con esta sección. Si la Comisión no somete una interpretación dentro de un plazo de 60 días, ese tribunal decidirá sobre el asunto.

Artículo 15-34: Medidas provisionales o precautorias.

Un tribunal establecido conforme a esta sección podrá ordenar una medida provisional de protección para preservar los derechos de la parte contendiente o para asegurar que la jurisdicción del tribunal surta plenos efectos. Ese tribunal no podrá ordenar el apego a la medida presuntamente violatoria a la que se refiere el artículo 15-19 o la suspensión de la aplicación de la misma.

Artículo 15-35: Alcance de laudo.

1.   Cuando un tribunal establecido conforme a esta sección dicte un laudo desfavorable a una Parte, ese tribunal sólo podrá otorgar:

   a)   el resarcimiento por los daños pecuniarios y los intereses correspondientes; o

   b)   la restitución de la propiedad, en cuyo caso el laudo dispondrá que la Parte contendiente pueda pagar por los daños pecuniarios, más los intereses que procedan, en lugar de la restitución.

2.   Cuando la reclamación la haga un inversionista en representación de una empresa con base en el artículo 15-19:

   a)   el laudo que prevea la restitución de la propiedad dispondrá que la restitución se otorgue a la empresa;

   b)   el laudo que conceda el pago por daños pecuniarios e intereses correspondientes dispondrá que la suma de dinero se pague a la empresa; y

   c)   el laudo se dictará sin perjuicio de los derechos que cualquier persona con interés jurídico tenga sobre la reparación de los daños que haya sufrido, conforme a la legislación aplicable.

Artículo 15-36: Definitividad, obligatoriedad y ejecución del laudo.

1.   El laudo dictado por cualquier tribunal establecido conforme a esta sección será obligatorio sólo para las partes contendientes y únicamente respecto del caso concreto.

2.   Conforme a lo dispuesto en el párrafo 3 y al procedimiento de revisión aplicable a un laudo provisional, una parte contendiente acatará y cumplirá con el laudo sin demora.

3.   Una parte contendiente podrá solicitar la ejecución de un laudo definitivo siempre que:

   a)   en el caso de un laudo definitivo dictado conforme al Convenio de CIADI:

   i)   hayan transcurrido 120 días contados desde la fecha en que se dictó el laudo sin que alguna parte contendiente haya solicitado la revisión o anulación del mismo; o

   ii)   hayan concluido los procedimientos de revisión o anulación; y

b)   en el caso de un laudo definitivo conforme a las Reglas del mecanismo complementario de CIADI o las Reglas de arbitraje de CNUDMI:

    i)   hayan transcurrido tres meses contados desde la fecha en que se dictó el laudo sin que alguna parte contendiente haya iniciado un procedimiento para revisarlo, desecharlo o anularlo; o

    ii)   un tribunal haya desechado o admitido una solicitud de reconsideración, desechamiento o anulación del laudo y esta resolución no pueda recurrirse.

4.   Cada Parte dispondrá la debida ejecución de un laudo en su territorio.

5.   Cuando una Parte contendiente incumpla o no acate un laudo definitivo, la Comisión, a la recepción de una solicitud de una Parte cuyo inversionista fue parte en el procedimiento de arbitraje, integrará un panel conforme al capítulo XIX (Solución de controversias). La Parte solicitante podrá invocar esos procedimientos para obtener:

a)   una determinación en el sentido de que el incumplimiento o desacato de los términos del laudo definitivo es contrario a las obligaciones de este Tratado; y

b)   una recomendación en el sentido de que la Parte se ajuste y observe el laudo definitivo.

6.   El inversionista contendiente podrá recurrir a la ejecución de un laudo arbitral conforme al Convenio de CIADI, la Convención de Nueva York o la Convención Interamericana, independientemente de que se hayan iniciado o no los procedimientos contemplados en el párrafo 5.

7.   Para efectos del artículo I de la Convención de Nueva York y del artículo I de la Convención Interamericana, se considerará que la reclamación que se somete a arbitraje conforme a esta sección, surge de una relación u operación comercial.

Artículo 15-37: Disposiciones generales.
Momento en que la reclamación se considera sometida al procedimiento arbitral

1.   Una reclamación se considera sometida a arbitraje en los términos de esta sección cuando:

a)   la solicitud para un arbitraje conforme al párrafo 1 del artículo 36 de CIADI ha sido recibida por el Secretario General;

b)   la notificación de arbitraje, de conformidad con el artículo 2 de la Parte C de las Reglas del mecanismo complementario de CIADI, ha sido recibida por el Secretario General; o

c)   la notificación de arbitraje contemplada en las Reglas de arbitraje de CNUDMI, se ha recibido por la Parte contendiente.

Entrega de documentos

2.   La entrega de la notificación y otros documentos a una Parte se hará en el lugar designado por ella a la entrada en vigor de este Tratado.

Pagos conforme a contratos de seguro o garantía

3.   En un procedimiento arbitral conforme a lo previsto en esta sección, una Parte no aducirá como defensa, contrademanda, derecho de compensación, u otros, que el inversionista contendiente recibió o recibirá, de acuerdo con un contrato de seguro o garantía, indemnización u otra compensación por todos o parte de los presuntos daños cuya restitución solicita.

Publicación de laudos

4.   Los laudos definitivos se publicarán únicamente en el caso de que exista acuerdo por escrito entre las Partes.

Artículo 15-38: Exclusiones.

Las disposiciones de solución de controversias de esta sección y las del capítulo XIX (Solución de controversias) no se aplican a los supuestos contenidos en el anexo a este artículo.

Anexo 1 al artículo 15-07
Reservas y excepciones

Las Partes listarán en este anexo las medidas incompatibles con los artículos 15-03 al 15-06, de conformidad con lo establecido en el párrafo 1 del artículo 15-07.

Anexo 2 al artículo 15-07
Lista de actividades

Bolivia:

1.   Energía e Hidrocarburos.

2.   Fundiciones.

3.   Telecomunicaciones (excepto los servicios de valor agregado).

4.   Transporte:

    a)   transporte marítimo

    b)   transporte aéreo

    c)   transporte por ferrocarril

    d)   transporte por carretera

    e)   transporte por tuberías

f)   servicios auxiliares a los medios de transporte mencionados en los literales a) al e)

Anexo al artículo 15-38
Exclusiones de México

No estarán sujetas a los mecanismos de solución de controversias previstos en la sección B, ni a las del capítulo XIX (Solución de controversias), las resoluciones que adopte la Comisión Nacional de Inversiones Extranjeras, ya sea en virtud del literal c) del párrafo 3 del artículo 15-02, o en virtud de la resolución que prohiba o restrinja la adquisición de una inversión en el territorio de los Estados Unidos Mexicanos que sea propiedad o esté controlada por sus nacionales, o por parte de uno o más inversionistas de la otra Parte.

Capítulo XVI

Propiedad intelectual

Sección A - Disposiciones generales y principios básicos

Artículo 16-01: Definiciones.

Para efectos de este capítulo, se entenderá por:

derechos de propiedad intelectual: todas las categorías de propiedad intelectual que son objeto de protección en este capítulo, en los términos que se indican;

nacionales de la otra Parte: respecto del derecho de propiedad intelectual pertinente, las personas que cumplirían con los criterios de elegibilidad para la protección previstos por el Arreglo de Lisboa para la protección de las denominaciones de origen y su registro internacional, 1967 (Arreglo de Lisboa); la Convención internacional sobre la protección de los artistas intérpretes o ejecutantes, los productores de fonogramas y los organismos de radiodifusión, 1961 (Convención de Roma); la Convención relativa a la distribución de señales portadoras de programas transmitidas por satélite, 1974 (Convención de Bruselas); el Convenio de Berna para la protección de la obras literarias y artísticas, 1971 (Convenio de Berna); el Convenio de Ginebra para la protección de los productores de fonogramas contra la reproducción no autorizada de sus fonogramas, 1971 (Convenio de Ginebra); el Convenio de París para la protección de la propiedad industrial, 1967 (Convenio de París); y el Convenio internacional para la protección de las obtenciones vegetales, 1978 ó 1991 (Convenio UPOV); como si cada Parte fuera parte de esos convenios;

público: para efectos de los derechos de autor y de los derechos conexos en relación con los derechos de comunicación y ejecución de las obras previstos en los artículos 11, 11bis.1 y 14.1.2º del Convenio de Berna, con respecto, por lo menos, a las obras dramáticas, dramático-musicales, musicales, literarias, artísticas o cinematográficas, incluye toda agrupación de individuos a quienes se pretenda dirigir y sean capaces de percibir comunicaciones o ejecuciones de obras, sin importar si lo pueden hacer al mismo tiempo y en el mismo lugar o en diferentes tiempos y lugares, siempre que esa agrupación sea más grande que una familia y su círculo inmediato de conocidos o que no sea un grupo formado por un número limitado de individuos que tengan el mismo tipo de relaciones cercanas, que no se haya formado con el propósito principal de recibir esas ejecuciones y comunicaciones de obras;

señal de satélite cifrada portadora de programas: aquella que se transmite de forma tal que las características auditivas o visuales, o ambas, se modifican o alteran para impedir la recepción no autorizada por personas que carezcan del equipo autorizado que está diseñado para eliminar los efectos de esa modificación o alteración del programa portado en esa señal.

Artículo 16-02: Protección de los derechos de propiedad intelectual.

1.   Cada Parte otorgará en su territorio a los nacionales de la otra Parte, protección y defensa adecuada y eficaz para los derechos de propiedad intelectual y asegurará que las medidas destinadas a defender esos derechos no se conviertan, a su vez, en obstáculos al comercio legítimo.

2.   Cada Parte podrá otorgar en su legislación una protección más amplia a los derechos de propiedad intelectual que la requerida en este capítulo, siempre que esa protección no sea incompatible con el mismo.

Artículo 16-03: Principios básicos.

1.   Con objeto de otorgar protección y defensa adecuada y eficaz a los derechos de propiedad intelectual las Partes aplicarán, cuando menos, las disposiciones contenidas en este capítulo y las disposiciones sustantivas de: el Arreglo de Lisboa, la Convención de Bruselas, la Convención de Roma, el Convenio de Berna, el Convenio de Ginebra y el Convenio de París.

2.   Cada Parte hará todo lo posible para adherirse a los convenios a que se refiere el párrafo 1, si aún no son parte de ellos a la entrada en vigor de este Tratado.

Artículo 16-04: Trato nacional.

1.   Cada Parte otorgará a los nacionales de la otra Parte, trato no menos favorable del que conceda a sus nacionales en materia de protección y defensa de todos los derechos de propiedad intelectual, a reserva de las excepciones ya previstas en la Convención de Roma, el Convenio de Berna y el Convenio de París.

2.   Ninguna Parte podrá exigir a los titulares de derechos de propiedad intelectual, que cumplan con formalidad o condición alguna para adquirir derechos de autor y derechos conexos, como condición para el otorgamiento de trato nacional conforme a este artículo.

Artículo 16-05: Trato de nación más favorecida.

Con respecto a la protección de los derechos de propiedad intelectual, toda ventaja, favor, privilegio o inmunidad que conceda un Parte a los nacionales de cualquier otro país, se otorgará inmediatamente y sin condiciones a los nacionales de la otra Parte. Quedan exentos de esta obligación toda ventaja, favor, privilegio o inmunidad concedidos por una Parte que:

a)   se deriven de acuerdos internacionales de carácter general sobre asistencia judicial y observancia de la ley y no limitados, en particular, a la protección de los derechos de propiedad intelectual;

b)   se hayan otorgado de conformidad con las disposiciones del Convenio de Berna o de la Convención de Roma que autorizan que el trato concedido no esté en función del trato nacional sino del trato dado en el otro país; y

c)   se refieran a los derechos de los artistas intérpretes o ejecutantes, los productores de fonogramas y los organismos de radiodifusión, que no estén previstos en este capítulo.

Artículo 16-06: Excepciones.

Cada Parte podrá recurrir a las excepciones señaladas en el artículo 16-04, en relación con los procedimientos administrativos y judiciales para la protección y defensa de los derechos de propiedad intelectual, inclusive cualquier procedimiento que requiera que un nacional de la otra Parte señale un domicilio legal o designe un agente en territorio de esa Parte, siempre que esa excepción:

a)   sea necesaria para asegurar el cumplimiento de medidas que no sean incompatibles con este capítulo; y

b)   no se aplique en forma tal que constituya una restricción encubierta al comercio.

Artículo 16-07: Control de prácticas y condiciones abusivas o contrarias a la competencia.

Ninguna disposición de este capítulo impedirá que cada Parte contemple en su legislación prácticas o condiciones relativas a la concesión de licencias que, en casos particulares, puedan constituir un abuso de los derechos de propiedad intelectual con efecto negativo sobre la competencia en el mercado correspondiente. Cada Parte podrá adoptar o mantener, de conformidad con otras disposiciones de este Tratado, las medidas adecuadas para impedir o controlar esas prácticas o condiciones.

Artículo 16-08: Cooperación para eliminar el comercio de bienes objeto de infracciones.

Las Partes cooperarán con miras a eliminar el comercio de bienes objeto de infracciones a los derechos de propiedad intelectual. Con ese fin, cada Parte designará una oficina competente, a efecto de intercambiar información relativa al comercio de esos bienes.

Artículo 16-09: Promoción de la innovación y la transferencia de tecnología.

Las Partes contribuirán a la promoción de la innovación tecnológica y a la transferencia y difusión de la tecnología, mediante regulaciones gubernamentales favorables para la industria y el comercio, que no sean contrarias a la libre competencia.

Sección B - Derechos de autor y derechos conexos

Artículo 16-10: Derechos de autor.

1.   Cada Parte protegerá las obras comprendidas en el artículo 2 del Convenio de Berna, incluyendo cualesquiera otras que incorporen una expresión original en el sentido que confiere a este término ese convenio, tales como los programas de cómputo o las compilaciones de datos que, por razones de compendio, selección, arreglo o disposición de su contenido constituyan creaciones de carácter intelectual. La protección conferida a las compilaciones de datos no se

extenderá a los datos o materiales en sí mismos, ni se otorgará en perjuicio de derecho de autor alguno que exista sobre esos datos o materiales.

2.   Cada Parte otorgará a los autores o a sus causahabientes los derechos que se enuncian en el Convenio de Berna con respecto a las obras contempladas en el párrafo 1, incluyendo el derecho de autorizar o prohibir:

    a)   la importación a su territorio de copias de la obra hechas sin autorización del titular del derecho;

    b)   la primera distribución pública del original y de cada copia de la obra mediante venta, arrendamiento o cualquier otro medio;

    c)   la comunicación de la obra al público; y

    d)   el arrendamiento del original o de una copia de un programa de cómputo.

3.   El literal d) del párrafo 2 no se aplica cuando la copia del programa de cómputo no constituya en sí misma un objeto esencial del arrendamiento. Cada Parte dispondrá que la introducción del original o de una copia del programa de cómputo en el mercado, con el consentimiento del titular del derecho, no agote el derecho de arrendamiento.

4.   Cada Parte dispondrá que para los derechos de autor y derechos conexos:

    a)   cualquier persona que adquiera o detente derechos económicos pueda, libremente y por separado, transferirlos mediante contrato para efectos de explotación y goce por el cesionario; y

    b)   cualquier persona que adquiera y detente esos derechos económicos, en virtud de un contrato, incluidos los contratos de fonograma y los de empleo que impliquen la creación de cualquier tipo de obra, tenga la capacidad de ejercitar esos derechos en nombre propio y de disfrutar plenamente los beneficios derivados de los mismos.

5.   Cada Parte circunscribirá las limitaciones o excepciones a los derechos que establece este artículo a casos especiales determinados que no impidan la explotación normal de la obra ni ocasionen perjuicios injustificados a los legítimos intereses del titular del derecho.

6.   Ninguna Parte concederá licencias para la reproducción y traducción permitidas conforme al Apéndice del Convenio de Berna, cuando las necesidades legítimas de copias o traducciones de la obra en el territorio de esa Parte pudieran cubrirse mediante acciones voluntarias del titular del derecho, de no ser por obstáculos creados por las medidas de la Parte.

7.   Los derechos de autor son permanentes durante toda la vida de éste. Después de su fallecimiento, quienes hayan adquirido legítimamente esos derechos, los disfrutarán por el término de 50 años como mínimo. Cuando la duración de la protección de una obra se calcule sobre una base distinta de la vida de una persona física, esa duración será de:

    a)   no menos de 50 años contados a partir del final del año de la publicación o divulgación autorizada de la obra; o

b) 50 años a partir del final del año de la realización de la obra, a falta de su publicación o divulgación autorizada dentro de un plazo de 50 años contado a partir de su realización.

Artículo 16-11: Artistas intérpretes o ejecutantes.

1. Cada Parte otorgará a los artistas intérpretes o ejecutantes el derecho de autorizar o prohibir:

a) la fijación de sus interpretaciones o ejecuciones no fijadas y la reproducción de esa fijación;

b) la comunicación al público, la transmisión y la retransmisión por medios inalámbricos; y

c) cualquier otra forma de uso de sus interpretaciones o ejecuciones.

2. El párrafo 1 no será aplicable una vez que un artista intérprete o ejecutante haya consentido que se incorpore su actuación en una fijación visual o audiovisual.

Artículo 16-12: Productores de fonogramas.

1. Cada Parte otorgará al productor de un fonograma el derecho de autorizar o prohibir:

a) la reproducción directa o indirecta del fonograma;

b) la importación a su territorio de copias del fonograma hechas sin la autorización del productor;

c) la primera distribución pública del original y de cada copia del fonograma mediante venta, arrendamiento o cualquier otro medio; y

d) el arrendamiento del original o de una copia del fonograma, excepto cuando exista estipulación expresa en otro sentido en un contrato celebrado entre el productor del fonograma y los autores de las obras fijadas en el mismo.

2. Cada Parte dispondrá que la introducción del original o de una copia de un fonograma en el mercado, con el consentimiento del titular del derecho, no agote el derecho de arrendamiento.

3. Cada Parte establecerá un periodo de protección para los fonogramas de por lo menos 50 años, contado a partir del final del año en que se haya hecho la primera fijación.

4. Cada Parte circunscribirá las limitaciones o excepciones a los derechos que establece este artículo a casos especiales determinados que no impidan la explotación normal del fonograma ni ocasionen perjuicios injustificados a los legítimos intereses del titular del derecho.

Artículo 16-13: Protección de señales de satélite portadoras de programas.

1. Dentro del año siguiente a la entrada en vigor de este Tratado, cada Parte:

a) tipificará como delito la fabricación, importación, venta, arrendamiento o cualquier acto comercial que permita tener un dispositivo o sistema que sea de ayuda primordial para descifrar una señal de satélite cifrada portadora de programas, sin autorización del distribuidor legítimo de esa señal; y

b) establecerá como causa de responsabilidad civil la recepción, en relación con actividades comerciales, o la ulterior distribución de una señal de satélite cifrada portadora de programas, que ha sido recibida sin autorización del distribuidor legítimo de la señal, o la participación en cualquier actividad prohibida conforme al literal a).

2.   Cada Parte dispondrá que cualquier persona que posea un interés en el contenido de esa señal podrá ejercer acción respecto de cualquier ilícito civil establecido conforme al literal b) del párrafo 1.

Artículo 16-14: Protección a otros derechos.

1.   Cada Parte podrá conceder protección a los derechos sobre:

a) títulos o cabezas de periódicos, revistas, noticiarios cinematográficos y, en general, sobre toda publicación o difusión periódica;

b) personajes ficticios o simbólicos en obras literarias, historietas gráficas o en cualquier publicación periódica, cuando los mismos tengan una originalidad señalada y sean utilizados habitual o periódicamente;

c) personajes humanos de caracterización empleados en actuaciones artísticas, los nombres artísticos, así como las denominaciones artísticas;

d) características gráficas originales, distintivas de la obra o colección en su uso; y

e) características de promociones publicitarias, cuando presenten una originalidad señalada, excepto los avisos comerciales.

2.   La duración de la protección de los derechos a que se refiere el párrafo 1, será determinada por la legislación de cada Parte.

Sección C - Propiedad industrial

Marcas

Artículo 16-15: Materia objeto de protección.

1.   Podrá constituir una marca cualquier signo o combinación de signos que permita distinguir los bienes o servicios de una persona de los de otra, inclusive nombres de personas, diseños, letras, números, colores, elementos figurativos, o la forma de los bienes o la de su empaque. Las marcas incluirán las de servicio y las colectivas. Cada Parte podrá establecer como condición para el registro de las marcas que los signos sean visibles.

2.   La naturaleza de los bienes y servicios a los que se aplica una marca no será, en ningún caso, obstáculo para su registro.

3.   Las Partes ofrecerán a las personas interesadas una oportunidad razonable para oponerse al registro de una marca o para solicitar la cancelación del mismo.

Artículo 16-16: Derechos conferidos.

El titular de una marca registrada tendrá el derecho de impedir a cualquier tercero que no cuente con el consentimiento del titular, usar en el comercio signos idénticos o similares para bienes o servicios que sean idénticos o similares a aquéllos para los que se ha registrado la marca del titular, cuando ese uso genere una probabilidad de confusión. Se presumirá que existe probabilidad de confusión cuando se use un signo idéntico o similar para bienes o servicios idénticos o similares. Los derechos antes mencionados se otorgarán sin perjuicio de derechos existentes con anterioridad y no afectarán la posibilidad de cada Parte para reconocer derechos sobre la base del uso.

Artículo 16-17: Marcas notoriamente conocidas.

1.   Cada Parte aplicará el artículo 6bis del Convenio de París, con las modificaciones que corresponda, a las marcas de servicio. Se entenderá que una marca es notoriamente conocida en una Parte cuando un sector determinado del público o de los círculos comerciales de la Parte conozca la marca como consecuencia de las actividades comerciales desarrolladas en una Parte o fuera de ésta, por una persona que emplea esa marca en relación con sus bienes o servicios. A efecto de demostrar la notoriedad de la marca, podrá emplearse todos los medios probatorios admitidos en la Parte de que se trate.

2.   Ninguna Parte registrará como marca aquellos signos o figuras iguales o similares a una marca notoriamente conocida, para ser aplicada a cualquier bien o servicio, en cualquier caso en que el uso de la marca, por quien solicita su registro, pudiese crear confusión o un riesgo de asociación con la persona referida en el párrafo 1, o constituyese un aprovechamiento injusto del prestigio de la marca. Esta prohibición no será aplicable cuando el solicitante del registro sea la persona referida en el párrafo 1.

3.   La persona que inicie una acción de nulidad de un registro de marca concedido en contravención del párrafo 2, deberá acreditar haber solicitado, en una Parte, el registro de la marca notoriamente conocida, cuya titularidad reivindica.

Articulo 16-18: Marcas registradas.

1.   Cuando en las Partes existan registros sobre una marca idéntica o similar a nombre de titulares diferentes, para distinguir bienes o servicios idénticos o similares, se prohibirá la comercialización de los bienes o servicios identificados con esa marca en el territorio de la otra Parte donde se encuentre también registrada, salvo que los titulares de esas marcas suscriban acuerdos que permitan esa comercialización.

2.   Los titulares de las marcas que suscriban los acuerdos mencionados en el párrafo 1, deberán adoptar las provisiones necesarias para evitar la confusión del público respecto del origen de los bienes o servicios de que se trate, incluyendo lo relativo a la identificación del origen de los bienes o servicios en cuestión, con caracteres destacados y proporcionales a los

mismos para la debida información al público consumidor. Esos acuerdos deberán respetar las normas sobre prácticas comerciales y promoción de la libre competencia e inscribirse en las oficinas nacionales competentes.

3.   En cualquier caso, no se prohibirá la importación de un bien o servicio que se encuentre en la situación descrita en el párrafo 2, cuando la marca no esté siendo utilizada por su titular en el territorio de la Parte importadora, salvo que el titular de esa marca presente razones válidas apoyadas en la existencia de obstáculos para el uso. Cada Parte reconocerá como razones válidas para la falta de uso, las circunstancias ajenas a la voluntad del titular de la marca que constituyan un obstáculo para el uso de la misma, tales como restricciones a la importación u otros requisitos gubernamentales aplicables a bienes o servicios identificados por la marca.

4.   Se entenderá que una marca se encuentra en uso, cuando los bienes o servicios que ella distingue han sido puestos en el comercio o se encuentran disponibles en el mercado bajo esa marca, en la cantidad y del modo que normalmente corresponde, teniendo en cuenta la naturaleza de los bienes o servicios y las modalidades bajo las cuales se efectúa su comercialización en el mercado.

Artículo 16-19: Excepciones.

Cada Parte podrá establecer excepciones limitadas a los derechos conferidos por una marca, tal como el uso correcto de términos descriptivos, a condición de que, en las excepciones, se tomen en cuenta los intereses legítimos del titular de la marca y de terceros.

Artículo 16-20: Duración de la protección.

El registro inicial de una marca tendrá, por lo menos, una duración de diez años contados, de conformidad con la legislación de cada Parte, a partir de la fecha de la presentación de la solicitud o de la fecha de su concesión, y podrá renovarse indefinidamente por periodos sucesivos no menores de diez años, siempre que se satisfagan las condiciones para su renovación.

Artículo 16-21: Uso de la marca.

1.   Cada Parte exigirá el uso de una marca para mantener el registro. El registro podrá cancelarse por falta de uso únicamente después de que transcurra, como mínimo, un periodo ininterrumpido de falta de uso de dos años, a menos de que el titular de la marca demuestre razones válidas apoyadas en la existencia de obstáculos para el uso. Cada Parte reconocerá como razones válidas para la falta de uso, las circunstancias referidas en el párrafo 3 del artículo 16-18.

2.   Para fines de mantener el registro, se reconocerá el uso de una marca por una persona distinta del titular de la marca, cuando ese uso esté sujeto al control del titular.

Artículo 16-22: Otros requisitos.

No se dificultará en el comercio el uso de una marca mediante requisitos especiales, tales como un uso que disminuya la función de la marca como indicación de procedencia, o un uso con otra marca.

Artículo 16-23: Licencias y cesión.

Cada Parte podrá establecer condiciones para el licenciamiento y cesión de marcas, quedando entendido que no se permitirán las licencias obligatorias de marcas y que el titular de una marca registrada tendrá derecho a cederla con o sin la transferencia de la empresa a que pertenezca la marca.

Artículo 16-24: Franquicias.

Cada Parte protegerá y facilitará el establecimiento de franquicias permitiendo la celebración de contratos que incluyan la licencia de uso de una marca, la transmisión de conocimientos técnicos o de asistencia técnica, para que la persona a quien se le concede esa franquicia pueda producir o vender bienes o prestar servicios de manera uniforme y con los métodos operativos, comerciales y administrativos establecidos por el titular de la marca, tendientes a mantener la calidad, prestigio e imagen de los bienes o servicios a los que ésta distingue.

Indicaciones geográficas y denominaciones de origen

Artículo 16-25: Protección de las indicaciones geográficas y de las denominaciones de origen.

1.   Cada Parte protegerá las denominaciones de origen y las indicaciones geográficas, en los términos de su legislación.

2.   Cada Parte podrá declarar la protección de denominaciones de origen o, en su caso, de indicaciones geográficas, según lo prevea su legislación, a solicitud de las autoridades competentes de la Parte donde la denominación de origen esté protegida.

3.   Las denominaciones de origen o las indicaciones geográficas protegidas en una Parte no serán consideradas comunes o genéricas para distinguir el bien, mientras subsista su protección en el país de origen.

4.   En relación con las denominaciones de origen y las indicaciones geográficas, cada Parte establecerá los medios legales para que las personas interesadas puedan impedir:

    a)   el uso de cualquier medio que, en la designación o presentación del bien, indique o sugiera que el bien de que se trate proviene de un territorio, región o localidad distinto del verdadero lugar de origen, de modo que induzca al público a error en cuanto al origen geográfico del bien; y

    b)   cualquier otra utilización que constituya un acto de competencia desleal en el sentido del artículo 10bis del Convenio de París.

5.   Cada Parte, de oficio si su legislación lo permite, o a petición de persona interesada, negará o anulará el registro de una marca que contenga o consista en una indicación geográfica o denominación de origen respecto a bienes que no se originen en el territorio, región o localidad indicado, si el uso de esa indicación en la marca para esos bienes es de naturaleza tal que induzca al público a error en cuanto al verdadero lugar de origen de los bienes.

6.   Los párrafos 4 y 5 se aplican a toda denominación de origen o indicación geográfica que, aunque indique de manera correcta el territorio, región o localidad en que se originan los bienes, proporcione al público una idea falsa de que éstos se originan en otro territorio, región o localidad.

Diseños industriales

Artículo 16-26: Condiciones para la protección.

1.   Cada Parte otorgará protección a los diseños industriales nuevos u originales que sean de creación independiente. Cada Parte podrá establecer que los diseños no se consideren nuevos u originales si no difieren en grado significativo de diseños conocidos o de combinaciones de características de diseños conocidos. Cada Parte podrá establecer que esa protección no se extienda a los diseños basados esencialmente en consideraciones funcionales o técnicas.

2.   Cada Parte garantizará que los requisitos para obtener la protección de diseños industriales, particularmente en lo que se refiere a cualquier costo, examen o publicación, no menoscaben injustificadamente la oportunidad de una persona para solicitar y obtener esa protección.

Artículo 16-27: Duración de la protección.

Cada Parte otorgará un periodo de protección para los diseños industriales de por lo menos diez años, contados a partir de la fecha de la presentación de la solicitud.

Artículo 16-28: Derechos conferidos.

1.   El titular de un diseño industrial tendrá el derecho de impedir que terceros que no cuenten con el consentimiento del titular, fabriquen o vendan bienes que ostenten o incorporen su diseño o que fundamentalmente copien el mismo, cuando esos actos se realicen con fines comerciales.

2.   Cada Parte podrá prever excepciones limitadas a la protección de los diseños industriales, a condición de que esas excepciones no interfieran la explotación normal de los diseños industriales de manera indebida, ni ocasionen un perjuicio injustificado a los legítimos intereses del titular del diseño, tomando en cuenta los intereses legítimos de terceros.

Patentes

Artículo 16-29: Materia patentable.

1.   Sujeto a lo dispuesto en los párrafos 2 y 3, las patentes se otorgarán para invenciones, ya sean de bienes o de procesos, en aquellas áreas tecnológicas que permita la legislación de cada Parte, siempre que sean nuevas, resulten de una actividad inventiva y sean susceptibles de aplicación industrial.

2.   Sujeto a lo dispuesto en el párrafo 3, no habrá discriminación en el otorgamiento de las patentes, ni en el goce de los derechos respectivos, en función del campo de la tecnología, del territorio del país en que la invención fue realizada o de si los bienes son importados o producidos localmente.

3.   Cada Parte podrá excluir de la patentabilidad las invenciones cuya explotación comercial en su territorio deba impedirse para proteger el orden público o la moral, inclusive para proteger la salud o la vida humana, animal o vegetal, o para evitar daño grave a la naturaleza o al ambiente, siempre que esa exclusión no se fundamente únicamente en que la Parte prohiba en su territorio la explotación comercial de la materia que sea objeto de la patente.

4.   De conformidad con su legislación, cada Parte otorgará protección a las variedades vegetales. Cada Parte procurará, en la medida en que sus sistemas sean compatibles, atender las disposiciones sustantivas vigentes del Convenio UPOV.

Artículo 16-30: Derechos conferidos.

1.   Una patente conferirá a su titular los siguientes derechos exclusivos:

    a)   cuando la materia de una patente sea un bien, el de impedir que terceros, sin su consentimiento, fabriquen, usen o vendan la materia objeto de la patente; y

    b)   cuando la materia de la patente sea un proceso, el de impedir que terceros, sin su consentimiento, utilicen el proceso y usen, vendan o importen por lo menos el bien obtenido directamente de ese proceso.

2.   Los titulares de las patentes tendrán asimismo el derecho de ceder o transferir por cualquier medio la patente y de concertar contratos de licencia.

Artículo 16-31: Excepciones.

Cada Parte podrá prever excepciones limitadas a los derechos exclusivos conferidos por una patente, a condición de que esas excepciones no impidan la explotación normal de la patente de manera indebida, ni ocasionen un perjuicio injustificado a los intereses legítimos de terceros.

Artículo 16-32: Otros usos sin autorización del titular del derecho.

1.   Cuando la legislación de una Parte permita otros usos de la materia objeto de una patente, distintos a los permitidos conforme al artículo 16-31, sin autorización del titular del derecho, incluido el uso por el gobierno o por terceros autorizados por el gobierno, se observarán las siguientes disposiciones:

    a)   la autorización de esos usos se considerará en función del fondo del asunto del que se trate;

    b)   sólo podrá permitirse esos usos cuando, con anterioridad a los mismos, el usuario potencial hubiera hecho esfuerzos por obtener la autorización del titular del derecho en términos y condiciones comerciales razonables y esos esfuerzos no hubiesen tenido éxito en un plazo razonable. Cada Parte podrá soslayar requisitos en casos de emergencia nacional o en circunstancias de extrema urgencia, o en casos de uso público sin fines comerciales. No obstante, en situaciones de emergencia nacional o en circunstancias de extrema urgencia, se notificará al titular del derecho tan pronto como sea razonablemente posible. En el caso de uso público sin fines comerciales, cuando el gobierno o el contratista, sin hacer una búsqueda de patentes, sepa o tenga bases comprobables para saber que una patente válida es o será utilizada por o para el gobierno, se informará con prontitud al titular del derecho;

c)   el alcance y duración de esos usos se limitarán a los fines para los que hayan sido autorizados;

d)   esos usos no serán exclusivos;

e)   esos usos no podrán cederse, excepto junto con la parte de la empresa que goce esos usos;

f)   se autorizarán esos usos principalmente para abastecer el mercado interno de la Parte que los autorice;

g)   a reserva de la protección adecuada de los intereses legítimos de las personas que han recibido autorización para esos usos, podrá revocarse su autorización, si las circunstancias que la motivaron dejan de existir y sea improbable que se susciten nuevamente. La autoridad competente estará facultada para revisar, previa petición fundada, si esas circunstancias siguen existiendo;

h)   al titular del derecho se le pagará una remuneración adecuada según las circunstancias de cada caso, habida cuenta del valor económico de la autorización;

i)   la validez jurídica de cualquier resolución relativa a la autorización de esos usos estará sujeta a revisión judicial o a una revisión independiente por una autoridad superior diferente;

j)   cualquier resolución relativa a la remuneración otorgada para esos usos estará sujeta a revisión judicial o a una revisión independiente por una autoridad superior diferente;

k)   ninguna Parte estará obligada a aplicar las condiciones establecidas en los literales b) y f) cuando esos usos se permitan para corregir una práctica que, en virtud de un procedimiento judicial o administrativo, se haya encontrado contraria a la libre competencia. La autoridad competente estará facultada para rechazar la revocación de la autorización si resulta probable que las condiciones que la motivaron se repitan; y

l)   ninguna Parte autorizará el uso de la materia objeto de una patente para permitir la explotación de otra patente, salvo para corregir una infracción que hubiere sido sancionada en un procedimiento sobre prácticas contrarias a la libre competencia de conformidad con su legislación.

Artículo 16-33: Revocación.

Cada Parte podrá revocar una patente solamente cuando:

a)   existan motivos que habrían justificado la negativa de otorgarla; o

b)   el otorgamiento de una licencia obligatoria no haya corregido su falta de explotación.

Artículo 16-34: Pruebas en casos de infracción de procesos patentados.

1.   Cuando la materia de una patente es un proceso para la obtención de un bien, cada Parte dispondrá que, en cualquier procedimiento de infracción, el demandado tenga la carga de probar que el bien objeto de la presunta infracción fue hecho por un proceso diferente al patentado, en el caso de que:

a)   el bien obtenido por el proceso patentado sea nuevo; o

b)   exista una probabilidad significativa de que el bien objeto de la presunta infracción haya sido fabricado mediante el proceso patentado y el titular de la patente no haya logrado, mediante esfuerzos razonables, determinar el proceso efectivamente utilizado.

2.   En la recopilación y valoración de las pruebas se tomará en cuenta el interés legítimo del demandado para la protección de su información no divulgada.

Artículo 16-35: Duración de la protección.

Cada Parte establecerá un periodo de protección para las patentes de por lo menos 20 años, contado a partir de la fecha de presentación de la solicitud.

Modelos de utilidad

Artículo 16-36: Protección a los modelos de utilidad.

1.   Cada Parte protegerá los modelos de utilidad, entendidos como objetos, utensilios, aparatos y herramientas que, como resultado de una modificación en su disposición, configuración, estructura o forma, presenten una función diferente respecto de las partes que los integran o ventajas en cuanto a su utilidad.

2.   El registro de los modelos de utilidad tendrá una vigencia de diez años improrrogables contados a partir de la fecha de presentación de la solicitud.

Protección a la información no divulgada

Artículo 16-37: Protección de los secretos industriales y de negocios.

1.   Cada Parte protegerá los secretos industriales y de negocios, entendidos éstos como aquellos que incorporan información de aplicación industrial o comercial que, guardada con carácter confidencial, permita a una persona obtener o mantener una ventaja competitiva frente a terceros en la realización de actividades económicas.

2.   Las personas tendrán los medios legales para impedir que los secretos industriales y de negocios se revelen, adquieran o usen por terceros sin el consentimiento de la persona que

legalmente tenga bajo control la información, de manera contraria a las prácticas leales del comercio, tales como el incumplimiento de contratos, el abuso de confianza, la instigación a la infracción y la adquisición de información no divulgada por terceros que supieran, o que no supieran por negligencia grave, que la adquisición implicaba esas prácticas, siempre que:

a)   la información sea secreta, en el sentido de que, como conjunto o en la configuración y composición precisas de sus elementos, no sea conocida en general ni fácilmente accesible a las personas integrantes de los círculos que normalmente manejan el tipo de información de que se trate;

b)   la información tenga un valor comercial efectivo o potencial por ser secreta; y

c)   en las circunstancias dadas, la persona que legalmente la tenga bajo control haya adoptado medidas razonables para mantenerla secreta.

3.   Para otorgar la protección a que se refiere este artículo, cada Parte exigirá que un secreto industrial y de negocios conste en documentos, medios electrónicos o magnéticos, discos ópticos, microfilmes, películas u otros instrumentos similares.

4.   Ninguna Parte podrá limitar la duración de la protección para los secretos industriales y de negocios, en tanto existan las condiciones descritas en los literales a), b) y c) del párrafo 2.

5.   Ninguna Parte desalentará ni impedirá el licenciamiento voluntario de secretos industriales y de negocios imponiendo condiciones excesivas o discriminatorias a esas licencias, o condiciones que diluyan el valor de los secretos industriales y de negocios.

Artículo 16-38: Protección de datos de bienes farmoquímicos o agroquímicos.

1.   Si como condición para aprobar la comercialización de bienes farmoquímicos o de bienes agroquímicos que utilicen nuevos componentes químicos, una Parte exige la presentación de datos sobre experimentos o de otro tipo que no se hayan publicado y que sean necesarios para determinar su seguridad y eficacia, esa Parte protegerá los datos referidos, siempre que su generación implique un esfuerzo considerable, salvo cuando la publicación de esos datos sea necesaria para proteger al público o cuando se adopten medidas para garantizar la protección de los datos contra todo uso comercial desleal.

2.   Cada Parte dispondrá, respecto de los datos mencionados en el párrafo 1 que le sean presentados después de la entrada en vigor de este Tratado, que ninguna persona distinta a la que los haya presentado pueda, sin autorización de esta última, contar con esos datos en apoyo a una solicitud para la aprobación de un bien durante un periodo razonable después de su presentación. Para este fin, por periodo razonable se entenderá normalmente un lapso no menor a cinco años contado a partir de la fecha en que la Parte haya concedido a la persona que produjo los datos, la aprobación para poner en el mercado su bien, tomando en cuenta la naturaleza de los datos y los esfuerzos y gastos de la persona para generarlos. Sujeto a esta disposición, nada impedirá que una Parte lleve a cabo procedimientos sumarios de aprobación para esos bienes sobre la base de estudios de bioequivalencia o biodisponibilidad.

Sección D - Observancia de los derechos de propiedad intelectual

Artículo 16-39: Disposiciones generales.

1.   Cada Parte garantizará que en su legislación se establezcan procedimientos de observancia de los derechos de propiedad intelectual conforme a lo previsto en este artículo y en los artículos 16-40 al 16-43, que permitan la adopción de medidas eficaces contra cualquier acción infractora de los derechos de propiedad intelectual a que se refiere este capítulo, incluyendo recursos ágiles para prevenir las infracciones y recursos que constituyan un medio eficaz de disuasión de nuevas infracciones. Estos procedimientos se aplicarán de forma que se evite la creación de obstáculos al comercio legítimo y preverán salvaguardias contra su abuso.

2.   Los procedimientos relativos a la observancia de los derechos de propiedad intelectual serán justos y equitativos, y no serán innecesariamente complicados o gravosos ni comportarán plazos injustificados o retrasos indebidos.

3.   Las decisiones sobre el fondo de un caso se formularán por escrito y contendrán las razones en que se fundan. Esas decisiones se pondrán a disposición al menos de las partes en litigio, sin retrasos indebidos, y sólo se basarán en pruebas acerca de las cuales se haya dado a las partes la oportunidad de ser oídas.

4.   Se dará a las partes en litigio la oportunidad de una revisión por una autoridad judicial de las decisiones administrativas finales y de al menos los aspectos jurídicos de todas las decisiones judiciales de primera instancia sobre el fondo del caso, con sujeción a las disposiciones en materia de competencia jurisdiccional de las leyes relativas a la importancia de un caso. Sin embargo, no será obligatorio darles la oportunidad de revisión de las sentencias absolutorias dictadas en casos penales.

5.   Queda entendido que esta sección no impone ninguna obligación de instaurar un sistema judicial para la observancia de los derechos de propiedad intelectual distinto del ya existente para la aplicación de la legislación en general. Asimismo, la aplicación de esos derechos no crea obligación alguna con respecto a la distribución de los recursos entre los medios destinados a lograr la observancia de los derechos de propiedad intelectual y los destinados a la observancia de las leyes en general.

Artículo 16-40: Aspectos procesales específicos y recursos en los procedimientos civiles y administrativos.

1.   Cada Parte pondrá al alcance de los titulares de derechos los procedimientos judiciales civiles para la defensa de cualquier derecho de propiedad intelectual comprendido en este capítulo y preverá que:

   a)   los demandados tengan derecho a recibir una notificación oportuna por escrito en la que conste con suficiente detalle el fundamento de la reclamación;

   b)   se autorice a las partes en un procedimiento a estar representadas por un abogado independiente;

   c)   los procedimientos no impongan requisitos excesivos de comparecencias personales obligatorias;

d) todas las partes en un procedimiento estén debidamente facultadas para sustanciar sus pretensiones y presentar pruebas pertinentes; y

e) los procedimientos incluyan medios para identificar y proteger la información confidencial.

2. Cada Parte preverá que sus autoridades judiciales tengan la facultad de:

a) ordenar que, cuando una parte en un procedimiento haya presentado las pruebas suficientes a las que razonablemente tenga acceso como base de sus alegatos y haya identificado alguna prueba pertinente para sustanciar sus alegatos que se encuentre bajo el control de la contraparte, esta última aporte esa prueba, con sujeción, en su caso, a las condiciones que garanticen la protección de la información confidencial;

b) dictar resoluciones preliminares y definitivas, de naturaleza positiva o negativa, en caso de que una de las partes en un procedimiento, voluntariamente y sin motivo válido, niegue el acceso a pruebas o no proporcione pruebas pertinentes bajo su control en un plazo razonable u obstaculice de manera significativa un procedimiento relativo a un caso de defensa de derechos de propiedad intelectual. Esas resoluciones se dictarán con base en las pruebas presentadas, incluyendo la demanda o los alegatos presentados por la parte que afecte desfavorablemente la denegación del acceso a las pruebas, a condición de que se conceda a las partes la oportunidad de ser oídas respecto de los alegatos o las pruebas;

c) ordenar a una parte en un procedimiento que desista de la presunta infracción hasta la resolución final del caso, incluso para impedir que los bienes importados que impliquen la infracción de un derecho de propiedad intelectual entren en los circuitos comerciales de su jurisdicción. Esta orden se pondrá en práctica al menos inmediatamente después del despacho aduanal de esos bienes;

d) ordenar al infractor de un derecho de propiedad intelectual que pague al titular del derecho un resarcimiento adecuado como compensación por el daño que el titular del derecho haya sufrido como consecuencia de la infracción, cuando el infractor sabía que estaba involucrado en una actividad infractora o tenía fundamentos razonables para saberlo;

e) ordenar al infractor de un derecho de propiedad intelectual que cubra los gastos del titular del derecho, que podrán incluir los honorarios apropiados de abogado; y

f) ordenar a una parte en un procedimiento, a cuya solicitud se hubieran adoptado medidas y que hubiera abusado de los procedimientos de defensa, que proporcione una adecuada compensación a cualquier parte erróneamente sometida o restringida en el procedimiento, por concepto de daño sufrido a causa de ese abuso y para pagar los gastos de esa parte, que podrán incluir honorarios apropiados de abogado.

3. Con relación a la facultad señalada en el literal c) del párrafo 2, ninguna Parte estará obligada a otorgar esa facultad respecto a la materia objeto de protección que hubiera sido

adquirida u ordenada por una persona antes que esa persona supiera que el tratar con esa materia implicaría la infracción de un derecho de propiedad intelectual o tuviera fundamentos razonables para saberlo.

4.   Con respecto a la facultad indicada en el literal d) del párrafo 2, cada Parte podrá, al menos en lo relativo a las obras protegidas por derechos de autor y a los fonogramas, prever en favor de las autoridades judiciales la facultad de ordenar la recuperación de ganancias o el pago de daños previamente determinados, o ambos, aun cuando el infractor no supiera que estaba involucrado en una actividad infractora o no tuviera fundamentos razonables para saberlo.

5.   Cada Parte preverá, con objeto de disuadir eficazmente que se cometan infracciones, que sus autoridades judiciales tengan la facultad de ordenar que:

a)   los bienes que éstas hayan determinado que infringen los derechos de propiedad intelectual sean, sin indemnización de ningún tipo, retirados de los circuitos comerciales de modo tal que se evite cualquier daño al titular del derecho, o bien se destruyan, siempre que no sea contrario a las disposiciones constitucionales vigentes; y

b)   los materiales e instrumentos que se hayan utilizado predominantemente para la producción de bienes objeto de infracciones sean, sin indemnización de ningún tipo, retirados de los circuitos comerciales de modo tal que se reduzcan al mínimo los riesgos de infracciones subsecuentes.

6.   Al considerar la emisión de las órdenes a que se refiere el párrafo 5, las autoridades judiciales de cada Parte tomarán en cuenta la necesidad de proporcionalidad entre la gravedad de la infracción y las medidas ordenadas, así como los intereses de otras personas, incluidos los del titular del derecho. En cuanto a los bienes falsificados, la simple remoción de la marca ilícitamente adherida no será suficiente para permitir el despacho de aduanas de los bienes, salvo en casos excepcionales tales como aquellos en que la autoridad disponga su donación a instituciones de beneficencia.

7.   Con respecto a la administración de cualquier ley relativa a la protección o defensa de los derechos de propiedad intelectual, cada Parte sólo eximirá a las autoridades y funcionarios públicos de la responsabilidad a que den lugar las medidas correctoras apropiadas, cuando las acciones se hayan adoptado o dispuesto de buena fe durante la administración de esas leyes.

8.   Sin perjuicio de las disposiciones de los artículos 16-39 al 16-43, cuando una Parte sea demandada por la infracción de un derecho de propiedad intelectual como resultado del uso, por ésta o por su cuenta, de ese derecho, esa Parte podrá establecer como único recurso disponible contra ella, el pago de una compensación adecuada al titular del derecho, según las circunstancias del caso, tomando en consideración el valor económico del uso.

9.   Cada Parte preverá que cuando pueda ordenarse una reparación de naturaleza civil como resultado de procedimientos administrativos sobre el fondo de un asunto, esos procedimientos se ajusten a los principios que sean esencialmente equivalentes a los enunciados en este artículo.

Artículo 16-41: Medidas precautorias.

1.   Cada Parte preverá que sus autoridades judiciales tengan la facultad de ordenar medidas precautorias rápidas y eficaces para:

   a)   evitar una infracción de cualquier derecho de propiedad intelectual y, en particular, evitar la introducción de bienes objeto de la presunta infracción en el comercio dentro de su jurisdicción, incluyendo medidas para evitar la entrada de bienes importados al menos inmediatamente después del despacho aduanal; y

   b)   conservar las pruebas pertinentes relacionadas con la presunta infracción.

2.   Cada Parte preverá que sus autoridades judiciales tengan la facultad de ordenar a un solicitante de medidas precautorias que presente cualquier prueba a la que razonablemente tenga acceso y que esas autoridades consideren necesaria para determinar con un grado suficiente de certidumbre si:

   a)   el solicitante es el titular del derecho;

   b)   el derecho del solicitante está siendo infringido o si esa infracción es inminente; y

   c)   cualquier demora en la emisión de esas medidas tiene la probabilidad de llegar a causar un daño irreparable al titular del derecho o si existe un riesgo comprobable de que se destruyan las pruebas.

3.   Para efectos del párrafo 2, cada Parte preverá que sus autoridades judiciales tengan la facultad de ordenar al solicitante que aporte una fianza o garantía equivalente que sea suficiente para proteger los intereses del demandado y para evitar abusos.

4.   Cada Parte preverá que sus autoridades competentes tengan la facultad de ordenar a un solicitante de medidas precautorias que proporcione cualquier información necesaria para la identificación de los bienes relevantes por parte de la autoridad que ejecute las medidas precautorias.

5.   Cada Parte preverá que sus autoridades judiciales tengan la facultad de ordenar medidas precautorias en las que no se dé audiencia a la contraparte, en particular cuando haya probabilidad de que cualquier retraso cause daño irreparable al titular del derecho o cuando haya un riesgo comprobable de que se destruyan las pruebas.

6.   Cada Parte preverá que cuando se adopten medidas precautorias por las autoridades judiciales de esa Parte en las que no se dé audiencia a la contraparte:

   a)   la persona afectada sea notificada de esas medidas sin demora y en ningún caso a más tardar inmediatamente después de la ejecución de las medidas; y

   b)   el demandado, a partir de que lo solicite, obtenga la revisión judicial de las medidas por parte de las autoridades judiciales de esa Parte, para efecto de decidir, dentro de un plazo razonable después de la notificación de esas medidas, si éstas serán modificadas, revocadas o confirmadas.

7.   Sin perjuicio de lo dispuesto en el párrafo 6, cada Parte preverá que, a solicitud del demandado, las autoridades judiciales de la Parte revoquen o dejen de alguna manera sin efecto las medidas precautorias tomadas con fundamento en los párrafos 1 al 5, si los procedimientos conducentes a una decisión sobre el fondo del asunto no se inician:

a)   dentro de un periodo razonable que determine la autoridad judicial que ordena las medidas, cuando la legislación de esa Parte lo permita; o

b)   a falta de esa determinación, dentro de un plazo no mayor de 20 días hábiles o 31 días, aplicándose el que sea más extenso.

8.   Cada Parte preverá que, cuando las medidas precautorias sean revocadas, cuando caduquen por acción u omisión del solicitante o cuando la autoridad judicial determine posteriormente que no hubo infracción ni amenaza de infracción de un derecho de propiedad intelectual, las autoridades judiciales tengan la facultad de ordenar al solicitante, a petición del demandado, que proporcione a éste último una compensación adecuada por cualquier daño causado por estas medidas.

9.   Cada Parte preverá que, cuando pueda ordenarse una medida precautoria como resultado de procedimientos administrativos, esos procedimientos se ajusten a los principios que sean esencialmente equivalentes a los establecidos en este artículo.

Artículo 16-42: Procedimientos y sanciones penales.

1.   Cada Parte preverá procedimientos y sanciones penales que se apliquen cuando menos en los casos de falsificación dolosa de marcas o de ejemplares protegidos por derechos de autor a escala comercial. Cada Parte dispondrá que las sanciones aplicables incluyan pena de prisión o multas, o ambas, que sean suficientes como medio de disuasión y compatibles con el nivel de las sanciones aplicadas a delitos de gravedad equiparable.

2.   Cada Parte preverá que sus autoridades judiciales puedan ordenar el decomiso y la destrucción de los bienes objeto de infracciones y de cualquiera de los materiales e instrumentos que se hayan utilizado predominantemente para la comisión del ilícito.

3.   Para efectos del párrafo 2, las autoridades judiciales tomarán en cuenta, al considerar la emisión de esas órdenes, la necesidad de proporcionalidad entre la gravedad de la infracción y las medidas ordenadas, así como los intereses de otras personas incluidos los del titular del derecho. En cuanto a los bienes falsificados, la simple remoción de la marca ilícitamente adherida no será suficiente para permitir el despacho de aduanas de los bienes, salvo en casos excepcionales, tales como aquellos en que la autoridad disponga su donación a instituciones de beneficencia.

4.   Cada Parte podrá prever la aplicación de procedimientos y sanciones penales en casos de infracción de derechos de propiedad intelectual distintos de aquéllos a que se refiere el párrafo 1, cuando se cometan con dolo y a escala comercial.

Artículo 16-43: Defensa de los derechos de propiedad intelectual en la frontera.

1.   Cada Parte adoptará, de conformidad con este artículo, los procedimientos que permitan al titular de un derecho que tenga motivos válidos para sospechar que puede producirse la

importación de bienes falsificados o pirateados relacionados con marcas o derechos de autor, presentar una solicitud por escrito ante las autoridades competentes, sean administrativas o judiciales, para que la autoridad aduanera suspenda la libre circulación de esos bienes. Ninguna Parte estará obligada a aplicar esos procedimientos a los bienes en tránsito. Cada Parte podrá autorizar la presentación de una solicitud de esta naturaleza respecto de los bienes que impliquen otras infracciones de derechos de propiedad intelectual, siempre que se cumplan los requisitos de este artículo. Cada Parte podrá establecer también procedimientos análogos para la suspensión por las autoridades aduaneras del despacho de aduanas de los bienes destinados a la exportación desde su territorio.

2.   Cada Parte preverá que sus autoridades competentes tengan la facultad de ordenar a cualquier solicitante que inicie un procedimiento de conformidad con el párrafo 1, que presente pruebas adecuadas para:

   a)   que las autoridades competentes de la Parte importadora se cercioren de que puede presumirse una infracción a los derechos de propiedad intelectual conforme a su legislación; y

   b)   para brindar una descripción suficientemente detallada de los bienes que los haga fácilmente reconocibles para las autoridades aduaneras.

3.   Cada Parte preverá que sus autoridades competentes comuniquen al actor, dentro de un plazo razonable, si han aceptado la demanda y, cuando sean esas autoridades competentes quienes lo establezcan, el plazo de actuación de las autoridades aduaneras.

4.   Cada Parte preverá que sus autoridades competentes tengan la facultad de ordenar a un solicitante conforme al párrafo 1, que aporte una fianza o garantía equivalente que sea suficiente para proteger al demandado y a las autoridades competentes y para impedir abusos. Esa fianza o garantía equivalente no deberá disuadir de manera indebida al solicitante para recurrir a esos procedimientos.

5.   Cada Parte preverá que, el propietario, el importador o el consignatario de bienes que conlleven diseños industriales, patentes o secretos industriales y de negocios, tenga el derecho a obtener que se proceda al despacho de aduanas de los mismos, previo depósito de una fianza por un importe suficiente para proteger al titular del derecho contra cualquier infracción, siempre que:

   a)   como consecuencia de una demanda presentada de conformidad con los procedimientos de este artículo, las autoridades aduaneras hayan suspendido el despacho para la libre circulación de esos bienes, con fundamento en una resolución no dictada por una autoridad judicial o por otra autoridad independiente;

   b)   el plazo estipulado en los párrafos 8, 9, 10 y 11 haya vencido sin que la autoridad competente hubiere dictado una medida de suspensión provisional; y

   c)   se hayan cumplido con las demás condiciones para la importación.

6.   El pago de la fianza a que se refiere el párrafo 5, se entenderá sin perjuicio de cualquier otro recurso que esté a disposición del titular del derecho, y se devolverá si el titular del derecho no ejerce su acción en un plazo razonable.

7.   Cada Parte preverá que su autoridad competente notifique con prontitud al importador y al solicitante sobre la suspensión del despacho de aduanas de los bienes a que se refiere el párrafo 1.

8.   Cada Parte preverá que su autoridad aduanera proceda al despacho de aduanas de los bienes siempre que se hayan cumplido todas las demás condiciones para la importación o exportación de éstos, si en un plazo que no exceda de diez días hábiles contado a partir de que se haya notificado mediante aviso la suspensión al solicitante, las autoridades aduaneras no han sido informadas de que:

   a)   una parte que no sea el demandado ha iniciado el procedimiento conducente a la obtención de una decisión sobre el fondo del asunto; o

   b)   la autoridad competente facultada al efecto ha adoptado medidas provisionales que prolongue la suspensión del despacho de aduanas de los bienes.

9.   Para efectos del párrafo 8, cada Parte preverá que sus autoridades aduaneras tengan la facultad de prorrogar, en los casos que proceda, la suspensión del despacho de aduanas de los bienes por otros diez días hábiles.

10.   Si se ha iniciado el procedimiento conducente a la obtención de una decisión sobre el fondo del asunto, a petición del demandado se procederá, en un plazo razonable, a una revisión. Esa revisión incluirá el derecho del demandado a ser oído, con objeto de decidir si esas medidas deben modificarse, revocarse o confirmarse.

11.   Sin perjuicio de lo dispuesto en los párrafos 8, 9 y 10, cuando la suspensión del despacho de aduana se efectúe o se continúe de conformidad con una medida judicial precautoria, se aplicarán las disposiciones del párrafo 7 del artículo 16-41.

12.   Cada Parte preverá que sus autoridades competentes tengan la facultad de ordenar al solicitante, de conformidad con el párrafo 1, que pague al importador, al consignatario y al propietario de los bienes una indemnización adecuada por cualquier daño que hayan sufrido a causa de la retención indebida de los bienes o por la retención de los bienes que se hayan liberado de conformidad con lo dispuesto en los párrafos 8 y 9.

13.   Sin perjuicio de la protección a la información confidencial, cada Parte preverá que sus autoridades competentes tengan facultad de conceder:

   a)   oportunidad suficiente al titular del derecho para hacer inspeccionar cualquier bien retenido por las autoridades aduaneras con el fin de sustanciar su reclamación; y

   b)   una oportunidad equivalente al importador de hacer inspeccionar esos bienes.

14.   Cuando las autoridades competentes hayan dictado una resolución favorable sobre el fondo del asunto, cada Parte podrá conferir a esas autoridades la facultad de proporcionar al

titular del derecho los nombres y domicilios del consignador, del importador y del consignatario, así como la cantidad de los bienes en cuestión.

15.   Cuando una Parte requiera a sus autoridades competentes actuar por iniciativa propia y suspender el despacho de aduanas de los bienes respecto de los cuales tengan pruebas que, a primera vista, hagan presumir que infringen un derecho de propiedad intelectual:

a)   las autoridades competentes podrán requerir en cualquier momento al titular del derecho cualquier información que pueda auxiliarles en el ejercicio de esa facultad;

b)   el importador y el titular del derecho serán notificados de la suspensión, con prontitud, por las autoridades competentes de la Parte. Cuando el importador haya solicitado una reconsideración de la suspensión ante las autoridades competentes, esa suspensión estará sujeta, con las modificaciones conducentes, a lo dispuesto en los párrafos 8, 9, 10 y 11; y

c)   la Parte eximirá únicamente a las autoridades y funcionarios públicos de la responsabilidad a que den lugar las medidas correctivas adecuadas, tratándose de actos ejecutados o dispuestos de buena fe.

16.   Sin perjuicio de las demás acciones que correspondan al titular del derecho y a reserva del derecho del demandado de solicitar una revisión ante una autoridad judicial, cada Parte preverá que sus autoridades competentes tengan la facultad de ordenar la destrucción o eliminación de los bienes objeto de infracciones de conformidad con los principios establecidos en los párrafos 5 y 6 del artículo 16-40. En cuanto a los bienes falsificados, las autoridades no permitirán, salvo en circunstancias excepcionales, que éstos se reexporten en el mismo estado ni los someterán a un procedimiento aduanal distinto.

17.   Cada Parte podrá excluir de la aplicación de los párrafos 1 al 16, las cantidades pequeñas de bienes que no tengan carácter comercial y formen parte del equipaje personal de los viajeros o se envíen en pequeñas partidas no reiteradas.

18.   Cada Parte realizará su mayor esfuerzo para cumplir tan pronto como sea posible con las obligaciones establecidas en este artículo, y lo hará en un plazo que no exceda de tres años contado a partir de la entrada en vigor de este Tratado.

Anexo
Asistencia técnica

1.   Con el fin de facilitar la aplicación de este capítulo, México, en coordinación con otros programas de cooperación internacional, prestará, previa petición, y en los términos y condiciones mutuamente acordados, asistencia técnica a Bolivia. Esa asistencia comprenderá:

a)   apoyo en la adecuación de procedimientos y reglamentos para la aplicación del Convenio de París y del Arreglo de Lisboa;

b)   capacitación para el uso de la Clasificación Internacional de Patentes;

c)   intercambio de documentos de patentes;

d)   capacitación en materia de registros de diseños industriales y en el tratamiento de los modelos de utilidad;

e)   asesoría sobre la búsqueda automatizada y el registro de marcas figurativas;

f)   intercambio de información sobre la experiencia de México en el establecimiento del Instituto Mexicano de la Propiedad Industrial;

g)   intercambio de información sobre la actualización del marco legislativo en materia de derechos de propiedad intelectual; y

h)   asesoría en materia de derechos de autor y derechos conexos.

2.   La asistencia técnica a que se refiere el párrafo 1 no implicará ningún compromiso de apoyo financiero por parte de México.

*

COOPERATION AGREEMENT BETWEEN THE EUROPEAN COMMUNITY AND THE DEMOCRATIC SOCIALIST REPUBLIC OF SRI LANKA ON PARTNERSHIP AND DEVELOPMENT[*]
[excerpts]

The Cooperation Agreement between the European Community and the Democratic Socialist Republic of Sri Lanka on Partnership and Development was signed on 18 July 1994. It entered in to force in the 2nd trimestre of 1995. The member States of the European Communities are: Austria, Belgium, Denmark, Finland, France, Germany, Greece, Ireland, Italy, Luxembourg, the Netherlands, Portugal, Spain, Sweden and the United Kingdom.

Article 4
Economic Cooperation

1.   The Contracting Parties undertake, in accordance with their respective polices and objectives and within their financial means available, to foster economic cooperation for mutual benefit.

2.   The Contracting Parties agree that economic cooperation will involve three broad fields of action:

    (a)   improving the economic environment in Sri Lanka by facilitating access to Community know-how, technology and capital;

    (b)   facilitating contracts between economic operators and other measures designed to promote commercial exchanges and investments;

    (c)   reinforcing mutual understanding of their respective economic, social and cultural environment as a basis for effective cooperation.

3.   In the broad fields described above, and without excluding any area from the outset, the aims of the Contracting Parties shall be in particular to:

- improve the economic environment and business climate,
- cooperate in the protection of the environment and natural resources,
- cooperate in the field of energy, including non conventional sources and energy efficiency,
- cooperate in the field of telecommunications, information technology, and related matters,
- cooperate in the field of metrology and industrial standards,

---

[*]   *Source*: European Communities (1995). "Cooperation Agreement between the European Community and the Democratic Socialist Republic of Sri Lanka on Partnership and Development", *Official Journal of the European Communities*, L 085, 19 April 1995, pp. 33 - 42; available also on the Internet (http://europa.eu.int). [Note added by the editor.]

- cooperate in the field of intellectual property,
- cooperate in the area of regional integration, through transfer of experience,
- encourage technology transfer in other sectors of mutual benefit,
- exchange information on monetary matters and the macroeconomic environment,
- reinforce and diversify economic links between them,
- encourage, by means of a favourable climate, the two-way flow of Community-Sri Lanka trade and investment,
- promote cooperation in order to develop agriculture, fisheries, mining, transport and communication, health, drug abuse control, banking and insurance, tourism and other services,
- facilitate the establishment of conditions conducive to job creation,
- encourage close cooperation between their private sectors,
- promote cooperation between small and medium-sized enterprises,
- activate cooperation in the industrial sector, including agro-industry and industry with a heavy technological bias,
- promote cooperation in industrial and urban ecology,
- support Sri Lankan efforts in the field of trade promotion and market development,
- promote cooperation between education and training institutions,
- promote scientific and technological cooperation,
- encourage cooperation in the field of privatization in Sri Lanka,
- cooperate in the fields of information and culture.

Cooperation in certain of the abovementioned sectors is set out in more detail in Articles 5 to 12 of this Agreement.

4.   The Contracting Parties shall consider, each in their mutual interests and in accordance with their respective polices and objectives, the following means to achieve these aims:

- exchange of information and ideas,
- preparation of studies,
- provision of technical assistance,
- training programmes including vocational training,
- establishment of links between research and training centres, specialized agencies, business organizations,
- promotion of investment and joint ventures,
- institutional development of public and private agencies and administrations,
- access to each other's existing databases and creation of new ones,
- workshops and seminars,
- exchanges of experts.

5.   The Contracting Parties will determine together and to their mutual advantage the areas and priorities to be covered by concrete actions of economic cooperation, in conformity with their long-term objectives.

Article 5
Investment

1.   The Contracting Parties shall encourage an increase in mutually beneficial investment by establishing a more favourable climate for private investments including better conditions for the transfer of capital and exchange of information on investment opportunities.

2.   Taking into account work done in this area in relevant international fora, recognizing the bilateral investment treaties concluded between Sri Lanka and a number of Member States of the Community, that Sri Lanka is a contracting party to the Multilateral Investment Guarantee Agency (MIGA) Convention, and a signatory to the International Convention for the Settlement of Investment Disputes (ICSID), the Contracting Parties will support further agreements on the promotion and protection of investments between the Member States of the Community and Sri Lanka on the basis of the principles of non-discrimination and reciprocity.

3.   The Contracting Parties undertake to encourage cooperation between their respective financial institutions.

Article 6
Private Sector

1.   Contracting Parties agree to promote the involvement of the private sector in their cooperation programmes in order to strengthen economic and industrial cooperation between themselves.

The Contracting Parties shall take measures to:

(a)   encourage the private sectors of both geographical regions to find effective ways of joint consultations, results of which could then be transmitted to the Joint Commission, referred to in Article 20 of this Agreement, for the required follow-up action;

(b)   involve the private sectors of the Contracting Parties in activities developed within the framework of this Agreement.

2.   The Contracting Parties shall facilitate within the relevant rules, access to available information and capital facilities in order to encourage projects and operations promoting cooperation between firms, such as joint ventures, sub-contracting transfer of technology, licences, applied research and franchises.

Article 8
Intellectual Property

1.   In so far as their competences, regulations and policies permit, the Contracting Parties will:

(a)   aim to improve the conditions for adequate and effective protection and reinforcement of intellectual, industrial and commercial property rights in conformity with the highest international standards;

(b)   cooperate to secure these objectives.

2.   The Contracting Parties agree that they shall avoid discriminatory treatment in relation to intellectual property rights and to engage, if necessary, in consultations if intellectual property problems affecting trading relations arise.

Article 9
Science and Technology

1.   The Contracting Parties will, in accordance with their mutual interest and the aims of their development strategy in this area, promote scientific and technological cooperation with a view to:

   (a)   fostering the transfer of know-how and stimulating innovation;

   (b)   disseminating information and expertise in science and technology;

   (c)   opening up opportunities for future economic, industrial and trade cooperation.

2.   The Contracting Parties undertake to establish appropriate procedures to facilitate the greatest possible degree of participation by their scientists and research centres in cooperation between them.

Article 11
Tourism

The Contracting Parties agree to cooperate on tourism, through measures, which will take account of environmental issues and which will include interchange of information undertaking studies, training and promotion of investment including joint ventures.

Article 20

Joint Commission

1.   The Contracting Parties agree to maintain the Joint Commission set up under Article 8 of the Commercial Cooperation Agreement between the Community and Sri Lanka of 1975.

2.   The Joint Commission is in particular required to:

   (a)   ensure the proper functioning and implementation of the Agreement;

   (b)   make suitable recommendations for promoting the objectives of the Agreement;

   (c)   establish priorities in relation to the aims of the Agreement;

   (d)   examine ways and means of enhancing the cooperation in the areas covered under the provisions of this Agreement.

3.   The Joint Commission shall be composed of representatives of both Contracting Parties, at an appropriately high level. The Joint Commission shall normally meet every year, alternately in Brussels and Colombo, on a date fixed by mutual agreement. Extraordinary meetings may be convened by agreement between the Contracting Parties.

4.   The Joint Commission may set up specialized sub-groups to assist in the performance of its tasks and to coordinate the formulation and implementation of projects and programmes within the framework of this Agreement.

5.   The agenda for meetings of the Joint Commission shall be determined by agreement between the Contracting Parties.

6.   The Contracting Parties agree that it shall be the task of the Joint Commission to ensure the proper functioning of any sectoral agreements concluded or which may be concluded between the Community and Sri Lanka.

7.   Consultations in the fields covered by the Agreement may be held if any problem arises in the intervals between the meetings of the Joint Commission. These consultations shall be dealt with by the specialized sub-groups according to their responsibilities or be the subject of ad hoc consultations.

ANNEX

Declarations of the Community and Sri Lanka

1.   In the course of the negotiations on the Cooperation Agreement between the European Community and Sri Lanka on Partnership and Development, the Contracting Parties declared that the provisions of the Agreement should be without prejudice to their rights and obligations under the GATT, and that, in accordance with Article 30 (4) of the Vienna Convention on the Law of Treaties of 1969, any subsequent agreements which form part of the final outcome of the Uruguay Round of Multilateral Trade Negotiations and to which they both become parties shall prevail in the event of any inconsistency.

2.   The Contracting Parties agree that for the purpose of this Agreement 'intellectual, industrial and commercial property` includes in particular protection of copyright (including computer software) and related rights; trade and service marks; geographical indications, including indications of origin; industrial designs; patents; layout designs of integrated circuits as well as protection of undisclosed information and protection against unfair competition.

*

AGREEMENT BETWEEN UKRAINE AND CANADA ON ECONOMIC COOPERATION*

The Agreement between Ukraine and Canada on Economic Cooperation was signed on 24 October 1994.

The Government of Ukraine and the Government of Canada hereinafter referred to collectively as "Parties" and individually as "Party",

Desiring to strengthen the traditional links of warm friendship and the cordial relations that exist between the two countries, as reflected in the Declaration on Special Partnership signed on March 31, 1994;

Taking into Consideration the Agreement between the Government of Canada and the Government of Ukraine on Trade and Commerce, signed at Kyiv on March 31, 1994, and their Agreement for the Promotion and Protection of Investments, signed on October 24, 1994;

Recognizing that broader and more diversified links between their public and private sectors would be of mutual benefit;

Conscious of the importance of an open international trading system based on market principles and a liberalized regime for foreign investment;

Desiring to develop, promote and expand trade and investment, including through financial, industrial, scientific and technological cooperation between the two countries; and

Resolving to undertake new and energetic efforts to develop and expand this cooperation to their mutual benefit;

Have agreed as follows:

ARTICLE I
OBJECTIVES

The objectives of this Agreement are to promote economic cooperation, trade and investment between the Parties, and to foster financial, industrial, scientific and technological cooperations between the companies, enterprises, Government agencies and other organizations of the Parties. The Parties will seek to attain these objectives through the expansion of two-way trade, the facilitation of reciprocal market access, and the identification of mutually beneficial commercial and investment opportunities.

---

* *Source*: The Government of Canada and the Government of Ukraine (1994). "Agreement between Ukraine and Canada on Economic Cooperation", *Canada-Ukraine Monitor, vol. 3, no. 1, Winter, 1994-95;* available on the Internet (http://www.infoukes.com/ukremb/agreem-941024e.shtml). [Note added by the editor.]

ARTICLE II

1.   The Parties share a commitment to market principles with respect to international trade and foreign investment.

2.   The Parties shall encourage and facilitate, and on the basis of fair and equitable treatment, direct contact and broader cooperation between their business and academic communities, associations, organizations, and Government agencies, as set out in paragraphs 3 through 5 of this Article.

3.   The Parties shall exchange information on economic development priorities, national economic plans and forecasts, and other significant policies and developments that have an impact on economic relations between the two countries.

4.   Each Party shall:

   (a)   promote and support trade and investment missions, market analyses, links between business communities and institutions, and other initiatives that bring together potential business partners;

   (b)   provide appropriate trade, investment and market information to the other Party;

   (c)   provide appropriate information to the other Party at an early stage on significant forthcoming public sector industrial projects;

   (d)   identify and facilitate trade and investment opportunities by:

      (i)   ensuring that its laws, regulations, procedures and administrative rulings of general application respecting any matter covered by this Agreement are promptly published or otherwise made available to interested persons;

      (ii)   identifying specific projects and sectors of potential interest for cooperation;

      (iii)   informing its business communities of investment opportunities in the territory of the other Party;

      (iv)   encouraging the expansion of financial and banking cooperation;

      (v)   assisting in identifying appropriate sources of possible project financing;

      (vi)   ensuring the foreign investment and registration procedures are not unnecessarily burdensome;

      (vii)   facilitating, where appropriate, the staging of industrial fairs, exhibitions and other promotional activities;

      (viii)   encouraging business communities, particularly small and medium-sized enterprises, in their efforts to develop joint enterprises and other cooperative business activities;

(ix)   facilitating, on the basis of reciprocity, the entry and exit of public and private sector experts, investors, business representatives, scientists, and technicians, as well as material and equipment necessary for the fulfilment of activities falling within the scope of this Agreement;

(x)   encouraging joint activities between the companies, enterprises, and other organizations of the Parties, in exporting to third countries; and

(xi)   reviewing impediments to trade and investment that might hinder achievement of the objectives of this Agreement, with the aim of eliminating such impediments.

5.   The Parties shall encourage, support and facilitate:

(a)   the exchange of information on technologies and know-how;

(b)   the conclusion of licensing arrangements and industrial consulting agreements;

(c)   the industrial application of research and development results and the transfer of technology in order to promote the application, adaptation and improvement of existing and new high technology products, processes and management skills;

(d)   initiatives to improve quality control and standards for products, notably those for export;

(e)   joint projects or other collaborative ventures involving scientific and technological communities in the public and private sectors.

ARTICLE III

The principal sectors of cooperation between the Parties may include the following:

(i)   energy, particularly related to oil and gas exploration, and safety issues related to the generation of nuclear power;

(ii)   agriculture, and food processing, including the storage, handling, distribution and manufacture of equipment;

(iii)   conversion of the Ukrainian defence industry to civilian industries;

(iv)   natural resources, including resource management in forestry and related industries, fisheries, livestock and mining, including geological exploration, mine development and metallurgy;

(v)   telecommunications and information technology;

(vi)   construction, particularly urban dwellings and building materials;

(vii)   aerospace industry;

(viii)   development of transport infrastructure, distribution services and manufacture of means of transportation and associated equipment;

(ix)   environmental protection;

(x)   professional business services, particularly in finance and privatization;

(xi)   health care services and consumer health products;

(xii)   petrochemicals;

and any other fields of cooperation as may be agreed.

ARTICLE IV
FINANCIAL SUPPORT FOR COOPERATION

The Parties reaffirm:

(a)   the significance of credit and financial support, on mutually beneficial terms and conditions, for purposes of the stable and effective development of economic and commercial cooperation; and

(b)   their continued readiness to cooperate within the framework of international financial institutions.

ARTICLE V
INTERGOVERNMENTAL ECONOMIC COMMISSION

1.   The Parties hereby establish an Intergovernmental Economic Commission, comprising Ministerial-level representatives of the Parties or their designees.

2.   The Commission shall:

(a)   supervise the implementation of this Agreement;

(b)   supervise the work of any committees and working groups established under this Agreement; and

(c)   consider any other matter that may affect the eration of this Agreement.

3.   The Commission may:

(a)   establish, and delegate responsibilities to, ad hoc or standing committees, working groups or expert groups;

(b)   invite business representatives of either Party to participate in its activities, or the activities of any committees, working groups or expert groups;

(c)   consider issues related to the Agreement on Trade and Commerce; and

(d)   take such other action in the exercise of its functions as the Parties may agree.

4.   The Commission shall convene at periodic intervals in regular session, with meetings alternating between Canada and Ukraine. Regular sessions of the Commission shall be chaired successively by each Party.

*

PARTNERSHIP AND COOPERATION AGREEMENT BETWEEN THE EUROPEAN COMMUNITIES AND THEIR MEMBER STATES, OF THE ONE PART, AND THE REPUBLIC OF AZERBAIJAN, OF THE OTHER PART*
[excerpts]

The Partnership and Cooperation Agreement between the European Communities and Their Member States, of the One Part, and the Republic of Azerbaijan, of the Other Part was signed on 22 April 1996. It entered in to force on 1 July 1999. The member States of the European Communities are: Austria, Belgium, Denmark, Finland, France, Germany, Greece, Ireland, Italy, Luxembourg, the Netherlands, Portugal, Spain, Sweden and the United Kingdom.

TITLE IV

PROVISIONS AFFECTING BUSINESS AND INVESTMENT

CHAPTER I

LABOUR CONDITIONS

Article 20

1.   Subject to the laws, conditions and procedures applicable in each Member State, the Community and the Member States shall endeavour to ensure that the treatment accorded to Azerbaijani nationals legally employed in the territory of a Member State shall be free from any discrimination based on nationality, as regards working conditions, remuneration or dismissal, as compared to its own nationals.

2.   Subject to the laws, conditions and procedures applicable in the Republic of Azerbaijan, the Republic of Azerbaijan shall ensure that the treatment accorded to nationals of a Member State, legally employed in the territory of the Republic of Azerbaijan, shall be free from any discrimination based on nationality, as regards working conditions, remuneration or dismissal, as compared to its own nationals.

Article 21

The Cooperation Council shall examine which improvements can be made in working conditions for business people consistent with the international commitments of the Parties, including those set out in the document of the CSCE Bonn Conference.

---

*   *Source*: European Communities (1999). "Partnership and Cooperation Agreement between the European Communities and Their Member States, of the One Part, and the Republic of Azerbaijan, of the Other Part", *Official Journal of the European Communities*, L 246, 17 August 1999, pp. 3 - 51; available also on the Internet (http://europa.eu.int). [Note added by the editor.]

Article 22

The Cooperation Council shall make recommendations for the implementation of Articles 20 and 21.

CHAPTER II

CONDITIONS AFFECTING THE ESTABLISHMENT AND OPERATION OF COMPANIES

Article 23

1. The Community and its Member States shall grant treatment no less favourable than that accorded to any third country for the establishment of Azerbaijani companies as defined in Article 25(d).

2. Without prejudice to the reservations listed in Annex IV, the Community and its Member States shall grant to subsidiaries of Azerbaijani companies established in their territories a treatment no less favourable than that granted to any Community companies, in respect of their operation.

3. The Community and its Member States shall grant to branches of Azerbaijani companies established in their territories treatment no less favourable than that accorded to branches of companies of any third country, in respect of their operation.

4. Without prejudice to the reservations listed in Annex V, the Republic of Azerbaijan shall grant for the establishment of Community companies as defined in Article 25(d) treatment no less favourable than that accorded to Azerbaijani companies or to any third-country companies, whichever is the better, and shall grant to subsidiaries and branches of Community companies established in its territory treatment no less favourable than that accorded to its own companies or branches or to any third-country company or branch, whichever is the better, in respect of their operations.

Article 24

1. Without prejudice to the provisions of Article 100, the provisions of Article 23 shall not apply to air transport, inland waterways transport and maritime transport.

2. However, in respect of activities, as indicated below, undertaken by shipping agencies for the provision of services to international maritime transport, including intermodal transport operations involving a sea-leg, each Party shall permit the companies of the other Party to have a commercial presence in its territory in the form of subsidiaries or branches, under conditions of establishment and operation no less favourable than those accorded to its own companies or to subsidiaries or branches of companies of any third country, whichever are the better, and this in conformity with the legislation and regulations applicable in each Party.

3. Such activities include but are not limited to:

(a)   marketing and sales of maritime transport and related services through direct contact with customers, from quotation to invoicing, whether these services are operated or offered by the service supplier itself or by service suppliers with which the service seller has established standing business arrangements;

(b)   purchase and use, on their own account or on behalf of their customers (and the resale to their customers) of any transport and related services, including inward transport services by any mode, particularly inland waterways, road and rail, necessary for the supply of an integrated service;

(c)   preparation of documentation concerning transport documents, customs documents, or other documents related to the origin and character of the goods transported;

(d)   provision of business information by any means, including computerised information systems and electronic data interchange (subject to any non-discriminatory restrictions concerning telecommunications);

(e)   setting up of any business arrangement, including participation in the company's stock and the appointment of personnel recruited locally (or, in the case of foreign personnel, subject to the relevant provisions of this Agreement), with any locally established shipping agency;

(f)   acting on behalf of the companies, inter alia in organising the call of the vessel or taking over cargoes when required.

Article 25

For the purpose of this Agreement:

(a)   a "Community Company" or an "Azerbaijani company" respectively shall mean a company set up in accordance with the laws of a Member State or of the Republic of Azerbaijan respectively and having its registered office or central administration, or principal place of business in the territory of the Community or the Republic of Azerbaijan respectively. However, should the company, set up in accordance with the laws of a Member State or the Republic of Azerbaijan respectively, have only its registered office in the territory of the Community or the Republic of Azerbaijan respectively, the company shall be considered a Community or Azerbaijani company respectively if its operations possess a real and continuous link with the economy of one of the Member States or the Republic of Azerbaijan respectively;

(b)   "subsidiary" of a company shall mean a company which is effectively controlled by the first company;

(c)   "branch" of a company shall mean a place of business not having legal personality which has the appearance of permanency, such as the extension of a parent body, has a management and is materially equipped to negotiate business with third parties so that the latter, although knowing that there will if necessary be a legal link with the parent body, the head office of which is abroad, do not have to deal directly with such parent body but may transact business at the place of business constituting the extension;

(d)   "establishment" shall mean the right of Community or Azerbaijani companies, as referred to in point (a), to take up economic activities by means of the setting up of subsidiaries and branches in the Republic of Azerbaijan or in the Community respectively;

(e)   "operation" shall mean the pursuit of economic activities;

(f)   "economic activities" shall mean activities of an industrial, commercial and professional character.

With regard to international maritime transport, including intermodal operations involving a sea-leg, nationals of the Member States or of the Republic of Azerbaijan established outside the Community or the Republic of Azerbaijan respectively, and shipping companies established outside the Community or the Republic of Azerbaijan and controlled by nationals of a Member State or Azerbaijani nationals respectively, shall also be beneficiaries of the provisions of this chapter and Chapter III if their vessels are registered in that Member State or in the Republic of Azerbaijan respectively in accordance with their respective legislation.

Article 26

1.   Notwithstanding any other provisions of this Agreement, a Party shall not be prevented from taking measures for prudential reasons, including for the protection of investors, depositors, policy holders or persons to whom a fiduciary duty is owed by a financial service supplier, or to ensure the integrity and stability of the financial system. Where such measures do not conform with the provisions of this Agreement, they shall not be used as a means of avoiding the obligations of a Party under this Agreement.

2.   Nothing in this Agreement shall be construed as requiring a Party to disclose information relating to the affairs and accounts of individual customers or any confidential or proprietary information in the possession of public entities.

3.   For the purpose of this Agreement, "financial services" shall mean those activities described in Annex III.

Article 27

The provisions of this Agreement shall not prejudice the application by each Party of any measure necessary to prevent the circumvention of its measures concerning third-country access to its market, through the provisions of this Agreement.

Article 28

1.   Notwithstanding the provisions of Chapter I of this Title, a Community company or an Azerbaijani company established in the territory of the Republic of Azerbaijan or the Community respectively shall be entitled to employ, or have employed by one of its subsidiaries or branches, in accordance with the legislation in force in the host country of establishment, in the territory of the Republic of Azerbaijan and the Community respectively, employees who are nationals of Community Member States and the Republic of Azerbaijan respectively, provided that such employees are key personnel as defined in paragraph 2, and that they are employed exclusively by companies, or branches. The residence and work permits of such employees shall only cover the period of such employment.

2.   Key personnel of the abovementioned companies, herein referred to as "organisations" are "intra-corporate transferees" as defined in (c) in the following categories, provided that the organisation is a legal person and that the persons concerned have been employed by it or have been partners in it (other than majority shareholders), for at least the year immediately preceding such movement:

(a)   persons working in a senior position with an organisation, who primarily direct the management of the establishment, receiving general supervision or direction principally from the board of directors or stockholders of the business or their equivalent, including:

- directing the establishment or a department or subdivision of the establishment,

- supervising and controlling the work of other supervisory, professional or managerial employees,

- having the authority personally to hire and fire or recommend hiring, firing or other personnel actions;

(b)   persons working within an organisation who possess uncommon knowledge essential to the establishment's service, research equipment, techniques or management. The assessment of such knowledge may reflect, apart from knowledge specific to the establishment, a high level of qualification referring to a type of work or trade requiring specific technical knowledge, including membership of an accredited profession;

(c)   an "intra-corporate transferee" is defined as a natural person working within an organisation in the territory of a Party, and being temporarily transferred in the context of pursuit of economic activities in the territory of the other Party; the organisation concerned must have its principal place of business in the territory of a Party and the transfer be to an establishment (branch, subsidiary) of that organisation, effectively pursuing like economic activities in the territory of the other Party.

Article 29

1.   The Parties shall use their best endeavours to avoid taking any measures or actions which render the conditions for the establishment and operation of each other's companies more restrictive than the situation existing on the day preceding the date of signature of this Agreement.

2.   The provisions of this Article are without prejudice to those of Article 37: the situations covered by such Article 37 shall be solely governed by its provisions to the exclusion of any other.

3.   Acting in the spirit of partnership and cooperation and in the light of the provisions of Article 43 the Government of the Republic of Azerbaijan shall inform the Community of its intentions to submit new legislation or adopt new regulations which may render the conditions for the establishment or operation in the Republic of Azerbaijan of subsidiaries and branches of Community companies more restrictive than the situation existing on the day preceding the date

of signature of this Agreement. The Community may request the Republic of Azerbaijan to communicate the drafts of such legislation or regulations and to enter into consultations about those drafts.

4.   Where new legislation or regulations introduced in the Republic of Azerbaijan would result in rendering the conditions for operation of subsidiaries and branches of Community companies established in the Republic of Azerbaijan more restrictive than the situation existing on the day of signature of this Agreement, such respective legislation or regulations shall not apply during three years following the entry into force of the relevant act to those subsidiaries and branches already established in the Republic of Azerbaijan at the time of entry into force of the relevant act.

CHAPTER III

CROSS-BORDER SUPPLY OF SERVICES BETWEEN THE COMMUNITY AND THE REPUBLIC OF AZERBAIJAN

Article 30

1.   The Parties undertake in accordance with the provisions of this chapter to take the necessary steps to allow progressively the supply of services by Community or Azerbaijani companies which are established in a Party other than that of the person for whom the services are intended taking into account the development of the service sectors in the Parties.

2.   The Cooperation Council shall make recommendations for the implementation of paragraph 1.

Article 31

The Parties shall cooperate with the aim of developing a market-oriented service sector in the Republic of Azerbaijan.

Article 32

1.   The Parties undertake to apply effectively the principle of unrestricted access to the international maritime market and traffic on a commercial basis:

(a)   the above provision does not prejudice the rights and obligations arising from the United Nations Convention on a Code of Conduct for Liner Conferences, as applicable to one or other Contracting Party to this Agreement. Non-conference lines will be free to operate in competition with a conference as long as they adhere to the principle of fair competition on a commercial basis;

(b)   the Parties affirm their commitment to a freely competitive environment as being an essential feature of the dry and liquid bulk trade.

2.   In applying the principles of paragraph 1, the Parties shall:

(a) not apply, as from the entry into force of this Agreement, any cargo sharing provisions of bilateral agreements between any Member States of the Community and the former Soviet Union;

(b) not introduce cargo-sharing clauses into future bilateral agreements with third countries, other than in those exceptional circumstances where liner shipping companies from one or other Party to this Agreement would not otherwise have an effective opportunity to ply for trade to and from the third country concerned;

(c) prohibit cargo sharing arrangements in future bilateral agreements concerning dry and liquid bulk trade;

(d) abolish upon entry into force of this Agreement, all unilateral measures, administrative, technical and other obstacles which could have restrictive or discriminatory effects on the free supply of services in international maritime transport.

3. Each party shall grant, inter alia, no less favourable treatment, for the ships operated by nationals or companies of the other Party, than that accorded to a Party's own ships, with regard to access to ports open to international trade, the use of infrastructure and auxiliary maritime services of the ports, as well as related fees and charges, customs facilities and the assignment of berths and facilities for loading and unloading.

4. Nationals and companies of the Community providing international maritime transport services shall be free to provide international sea-river services in the inland waterways of the Republic of Azerbaijan and vice versa.

Article 33

With a view to assuring a coordinated development of transport between the Parties, adapted to their commercial needs, the conditions of mutual market access and provision of services in transport by road, rail and inland waterways and, if applicable, in air transport may be dealt with by specific agreements where appropriate negotiated between the Parties after entry into force of this Agreement.

CHAPTER IV

GENERAL PROVISIONS

Article 34

1. The provisions of this Title shall be applied subject to limitations justified on grounds of public policy, public security or public health.

2. They shall not apply to activities which in the territory of either Party are connected, even occasionally, with the exercise of official authority.

Article 35

For the purpose of this Title, nothing in this Agreement shall prevent the Parties from applying their laws and regulations regarding entry and stay, work, labour conditions and establishment of natural persons and supply of services, provided that, in so doing, they do not apply them in a manner as to nullify or impair the benefits accruing to any Party under the terms of a specific provision of this Agreement. The above provision does not prejudice the application of Article 34.

Article 36

Companies which are controlled and exclusively owned by Azerbaijani companies and Community companies jointly shall also be beneficiaries of the provisions of Chapters II, III and IV.

Article 37

Treatment granted by either Party to the other thereunder shall, as from the day one month prior to the date of entry into force of the relevant obligations of the General Agreement on Trade in Services (GATS), in respect of sectors or measures covered by the GATS, in no case be more favourable than that accorded by such first Party under the provisions of GATS and this in respect of each service sector, subsector and mode of supply.

Article 38

For the purposes of Chapters II, III and IV, no account shall be taken of treatment accorded by the Community, its Member States or the Republic of Azerbaijan pursuant to commitments entered into in economic integration agreements in accordance with the principles of Article V of the GATS.

Article 39

1.   The most-favoured-nation treatment granted in accordance with the provisions of this Title shall not apply to the tax advantages which the Parties are providing or will provide in the future on the basis of agreements to avoid double taxation, or other tax arrangements.

2.   Nothing in this Title shall be construed to prevent the adoption or enforcement by the Parties of any measures aimed at preventing the avoidance or evasion of taxes pursuant to the tax provisions of agreements to avoid double taxation and other tax arrangements, or domestic fiscal legislation.

3.   Nothing in this Title shall be construed to prevent Member States or the Republic of Azerbaijan from distinguishing, in the application of the relevant provisions of their fiscal legislation, between tax payers who are not in identical situations, in particular as regards their place of residence.

Article 40

Without prejudice to Article 28, no provision of Chapters II, III and IV shall be interpreted as giving the right to:

- nationals of the Member States or of the Republic of Azerbaijan respectively to enter, or stay in, the territory of the Republic of Azerbaijan or the Community respectively in any capacity whatsoever, and in particular as a shareholder or partner in a company or manager or employee thereof or supplier or recipient of services,

- Community subsidiaries or branches of Azerbaijani companies to employ or have employed in the territory of the Community nationals of the Republic of Azerbaijan,

- Azerbaijani subsidiaries or branches of Community companies to employ or have employed in the territory of the Republic of Azerbaijan nationals of the Member States,

- Azerbaijani companies or Community subsidiaries or branches of Azerbaijani companies to supply Azerbaijani persons to act for and under the control of other persons by temporary employment contracts,

- Community companies or Azerbaijani subsidiaries or branches of Community companies to supply workers who are nationals of the Member States by temporary employment contracts.

CHAPTER V

CURRENT PAYMENTS AND CAPITAL

Article 41

1.   The Parties undertake to authorise in freely convertible currency, any current payments between residents of the Community and of the Republic of Azerbaijan connected with the movement of goods, services or persons made in accordance with the provisions of this Agreement.

2.   With regard to transactions on the capital account of balance of payments, from entry into force of this Agreement, the free movement of capital relating to direct investments made in companies formed in accordance with the laws of the host country and investments made in accordance with the provisions of Chapter II, and the liquidation or repatriation of these investments and of any profit stemming therefrom shall be ensured.

3.   The provisions of paragraph 2 shall not prevent the Republic of Azerbaijan from applying restrictions on outward direct investment by Azerbaijani residents. Such restrictions shall not apply to subsidiaries and branches of Community companies. Five years after the entry into force of this Agreement, the Parties agree to consult over the maintenance of these restrictions, taking into account all the relevant monetary, fiscal and financial considerations.

4.   Without prejudice to paragraph 2 or to paragraph 6, as from the entry into force of this Agreement, no new foreign exchange restrictions on the movement of capital and current payments connected therewith between residents of the Community and the Republic of Azerbaijan shall be introduced and the existing arrangements shall not become more restrictive.

5.   The Parties shall consult each other with a view to facilitating the movement of forms of capital other than those referred to in paragraph 2 above between the Community and the Republic of Azerbaijan in order to promote the objectives of this Agreement.

6.   With reference to the provisions of this Article, until a full convertibility of the Azerbaijani currency within the meaning of Article VIII of the Articles of Agreement of the International Monetary Fund (IMF) is introduced, the Republic of Azerbaijan may in exceptional circumstances apply exchange restrictions connected with the granting or taking up of short and medium-term financial credits to the extent that such restrictions are imposed on the Republic of Azerbaijan for the granting of such credits and are permitted according to the Republic of Azerbaijan's status under the IMF. The Republic of Azerbaijan shall apply these restrictions in a non-discriminatory manner. They shall be applied in such a manner as to cause the least possible disruption to this Agreement. The Republic of Azerbaijan shall inform the Cooperation Council promptly of the introduction of such measures and of any changes therein.

7.   Without prejudice to paragraphs 1 and 2, where, in exceptional circumstances, movement of capital between the Community and the Republic of Azerbaijan cause, or threaten to cause, serious difficulties for the operation of exchange rate policy or monetary policy in the Community or the Republic of Azerbaijan, the Community and the Republic of Azerbaijan, respectively, may take safeguard measures with regard to movements of capital between the Community and the Republic of Azerbaijan for a period not exceeding six months if such measures are strictly necessary.

CHAPTER VI

INTELLECTUAL, INDUSTRIAL AND COMMERCIAL PROPERTY PROTECTION

Article 42

1.   Pursuant to the provisions of this Article and of Annex II, the Republic of Azerbaijan shall continue to improve the protection of intellectual, industrial and commercial property rights in order to provide, by the end of the fifth year after the entry into force of this Agreement, for a level of protection similar to that existing in the Community, including effective means of enforcing such rights.

2.   By the end of the fifth year after entry into force of this Agreement, the Republic of Azerbaijan shall accede to the multilateral conventions on intellectual, industrial and commercial property rights referred to in paragraph 1 of Annex II to which Member States are parties or which are de facto applied by Member States, according to the relevant provisions contained in these conventions.

TITLE V

LEGISLATIVE COOPERATION

Article 43

1.   The Parties recognise that an important condition for strengthening the economic links between the Republic of Azerbaijan and the Community is the approximation of the Republic of Azerbaijan's existing and future legislation to that of the Community. The Republic of Azerbaijan shall endeavour to ensure that its legislation will be gradually made compatible with that of the Community.

2.   The approximation of laws shall extend to the following areas in particular: customs law, company law, banking law, company accounts and taxes, intellectual property, protection of workers at the workplace, financial services, rules on competition, public procurement, protection of health and life of humans, animals and plants, the environment and legislation regarding the exploitation and utilisation of natural resources, consumer protection, indirect taxation, technical rules and standards, nuclear laws and regulations and transport.

3.   The Community shall provide the Republic of Azerbaijan with technical assistance for the implementation of these measures, which may include inter alia:

- the exchange of experts,
- the provision of early information especially on relevant legislation,
- organisation of seminars,
- training activities,
- aid for translation of Community legislation in the relevant sectors.

4.   The Parties agree to examine ways to apply their respective competition laws on a concerted basis in such cases where trade between them is affected.

TITLE VI

ECONOMIC COOPERATION

Article 44

1.   The Community and the Republic of Azerbaijan shall establish economic cooperation aimed at contributing to the process of economic reform and recovery and sustainable development of the Republic of Azerbaijan. Such cooperation shall strengthen existing economic links, to the benefit of both parties.

2.   Policies and other measures will be designed to bring about economic and social reforms and restructuring of the economic and trading systems in the Republic of Azerbaijan and will be guided by the requirements of sustainability and harmonious social development; they will also fully incorporate environmental considerations.

3.   To this end, cooperation will concentrate, in particular, on economic and social development, human resources development, support for enterprises (including privatisation,

investment and development of financial services), agriculture and food, energy, transport, tourism, environmental protection, regional cooperation and monetary policy.

4.   Special attention shall be devoted to measures, as in conformity with the legislation in force in the Republic of Azerbaijan capable of fostering cooperation among the Independent States of the Transcaucasus region, and with other neighbouring states, with a view to stimulating a harmonious development of the region.

5.   Where appropriate, economic cooperation and other forms of cooperation provided for in this Agreement may be supported by technical assistance from the Community, taking into account the Community's relevant Council regulation applicable to technical assistance in the Independent States, the priorities agreed upon in the indicative programme related to Community technical assistance to the Republic of Azerbaijan and its established coordination and implementation procedures.

Article 45
Cooperation in the field of trade in goods and services

The Parties will cooperate with a view to ensuring that the Republic of Azerbaijan's international trade is conducted in conformity with the rules of the WTO.

Such cooperation shall include specific issues directly relevant to trade facilitation, including:

- formulation of policy on trade and trade-related questions, including payments, and clearing mechanisms,

- drafting of relevant legislation,

- assistance to prepare for the Republic of Azerbaijan's eventual accession to the WTO.

Article 46
Industrial Cooperation

1.   Cooperation shall aim at promoting the following in particular:

- the development of business links between economic operators of both sides,

- Community participation in the Republic of Azerbaijan's efforts to restructure its industry,

- the improvement of management,

- the development of appropriate market-based commercial rules and practices, as well as the transfer of know-how,

- environmental protection.

2.   The provisions of this Article shall not affect the enforcement of Community competition rules applicable to undertakings.

Article 48
Investment promotion and protection

1. Bearing in mind the respective powers and competences of the Community and the Member States, cooperation shall aim to establish a favourable climate for private investment, both domestic and foreign, especially through better conditions for investment protection, the transfer of capital and the exchange of information on investment opportunities.

2. The aims of cooperation shall be in particular:

   - the conclusion, where appropriate, between the Member States and the Republic of Azerbaijan of agreements for the promotion and protection of investment,

   - the conclusion, where appropriate, between the Member States and the Republic of Azerbaijan of agreements to avoid double taxation,

   - the creation of favourable conditions for attracting foreign investments into the Azerbaijani economy,

   - to establish stable and adequate business law and conditions, and to exchange information on laws, regulations and administrative practices in the field of investment,

   - to exchange information on investment opportunities in the form of, inter alia, trade fairs, exhibitions, trade weeks and other events.

Article 49
Public procurement

The Parties shall cooperate to develop conditions for open and competitive award of contracts for goods and services in particular through calls for tenders.

Article 51
Mining and raw materials

1. The Parties shall aim at increasing investment and trade in mining and raw materials.

2. The cooperation shall focus in particular on the following areas:

   - exchange of information on the prospects of the mining and non-ferrous metals sectors,
   - the establishment of a legal framework for cooperation,
   - trade matters,
   - the adoption and implementation of environmental legislation,
   - training,
    safety in the mining industry.

Article 52
Cooperation in science and technology

1. The Parties shall promote cooperation in civil scientific research and technological development (RTD) on the basis of mutual benefit and, taking into account the availability of

resources, adequate access to their respective programmes and subject to appropriate levels of effective protection of intellectual, industrial and commercial property rights (IPR).

2.   Science and technology cooperation shall cover:

- the exchange of scientific and technical information,

- joint RTD activities,

- training activities and mobility programmes for scientists, researchers and technicians engaged in RTD on both sides.

Where such cooperation takes the form of activities involving education and/or training, it should be carried out in accordance with the provisions of Article 53.

The Parties, on the basis of mutual agreement, can engage in other forms of cooperation in science and technology.

3.   The cooperation covered by this Article shall implemented according to specific arrangements to be negotiated and concluded in accordance with the procedures adopted by each Party, and which shall set out, inter alia, appropriate IPR provisions.

Article 54
Agriculture and the agro-industrial sector

The purpose of cooperation in this area shall be the pursuance of agrarian reform, the modernisation, privatisation and restructuring of agriculture, the agro-industrial and service sectors in the Republic of Azerbaijan, development of domestic and foreign markets for Azerbaijani products, in conditions that ensure the protection of the environment, taking into account the necessity to improve security of food supply as well as the development of agribusiness, the processing and distribution of agricultural products. The Parties shall also aim at the gradual approximation of Azerbaijani standards to Community technical regulations concerning industrial and agricultural food products including sanitary and phytosanitary standards.

Article 55
Energy

1.   Cooperation shall take place within the principles of the market economy and the European Energy Charter and bearing in mind the Energy Charter Treaty and the Protocol on energy efficiency and related environmental aspects, against a background of progressive integration of the energy markets in Europe.

2.   The cooperation shall include among others the following areas:

- formulation and development of energy policy,

- improvement in management and regulation of the energy sector in line with a market economy,

- improvement of energy supply, including security of supply, in an economic and environmentally sound manner,

- promotion of energy saving and energy efficiency and implementation of the Energy Charter Protocol on energy efficiency and related environmental aspects,

- modernisation of energy infrastructures,

- improvement of energy technologies in supply and end-use across the range of energy types,

- management and technical training in the energy sector,

- transportation and transit of energy materials and products,

- the introduction of the range of institutional, legal, fiscal and other conditions necessary to encourage increased energy trade and investment,

- development of hydroelectric and other renewable energy resources.

3.   The Parties shall exchange relevant information relating to investment projects in the energy sector, in particular concerning the construction and refurbishing of oil and gas pipelines or other means of transporting energy products. They shall cooperate with a view to implementing as efficaciously as possible the provisions of Title IV and of Article 48, in respect of investments in the energy sector.

Article 58
Postal services and telecommunications

Within their respective powers and competences the Parties shall expand and strengthen cooperation in the following areas:

- the establishment of policies and guidelines for the development of the telecommunications sector and postal services,

- development of principles of a tariff policy and marketing in telecommunications and postal services,

- carry out transfer of technology and know-how, including on European technical standards and certification systems,

- encouraging the development of projects for telecommunications and postal services and attracting investment,

- enhancing efficiency and quality of the provision of telecommunications and postal services, amongst others through liberalisation of activities of subsectors,

- advanced application of telecommunications, notably in the area of electronic funds transfer,

- management of telecommunications networks and their "optimisation",

- an appropriate regulatory basis for the provision of telecommunications and postal services and for the use of the radio frequency spectrum,

- training in the field of telecommunications and postal services for operations in market conditions.

Article 59
Financial services

Cooperation shall in particular aim at facilitating the involvement of the Republic of Azerbaijan in universally accepted systems of mutual settlements. Technical assistance shall focus on:

- the development of a modern system of private and, in particular, commercial banking and financial services, the development of a common market of credit resources, the involvement of the Republic of Azerbaijan in a universally accepted system of mutual settlements,

- the development of a fiscal system and its institutions in the Republic of Azerbaijan, exchange of experience and personnel training,

- the development of insurance services, which would, inter alia, create a favourable framework for Community companies participation in the establishment of joint ventures in the insurance sector in the Republic of Azerbaijan, as well as the development of export credit insurance.

This cooperation shall in particular contribute to foster the development of relations between the Republic of Azerbaijan and the Member States in the financial services sector.

Article 60
Enterprise restructuring and privatisation

Recognising that privatisation is of fundamental importance to a sustainable economic recovery, the Parties agree to cooperate in the development of the necessary institutional, legal and methodological framework. To this end, technical assistance shall be given to implement the privatisation programme adopted by the Parliament of Azerbaijan. Particular Attention will be paid to the orderly and transparent nature of the privatisation process.
Technical assistance shall focus on, inter alia:

- the development of an institutional base within the government of Azerbaijan capable of defining and managing the privatisation process,

- the establishment of a database of enterprises,

- the corporatisation of enterprises,

- the development of a system of mass privatisation, which will aim to transfer property to the population, based on a system of vouchers,

- the development of a system for the registration of share holdings,

- the development of a system for the sale by tender of particular enterprises deemed not suitable for participation in the mass privatisation programme,

- the restructuring of those enterprises not yet ready for privatisation,

- the development of private enterprise, particularly in the small and medium-sized enterprise sector.

The objective of this cooperation is to contribute to the revitalisation of the economy of Azerbaijan, the promotion of foreign investment and the development of relations between Azerbaijan and the Member States.

Article 64
Small and medium-sized enterprises

1.   The Parties shall aim to develop and strengthen small and medium-sized enterprises and their associations and cooperation between SMEs in the Community and the Republic of Azerbaijan.

2.   Cooperation shall include technical assistance, in particular in the following areas:

- the development of a legislative framework for SMEs,

- the development of an appropriate infrastructure (an agency to support SMEs, communications, assistance to the creation of a fund for SMEs),

- the development of technology parks,

- training in the areas of marketing, accounting and control of the quality of products.

ANNEX II

INTELLECTUAL, INDUSTRIAL AND COMMERCIAL PROPERTY CONVENTIONS REFERRED TO IN ARTICLE 42

1.   Paragraph 2 of Article 42 concerns the following multilateral conventions:

- Berne Convention for the Protection of Literary and Artistic Works (Paris Act, 1971),

- International Convention for the Protection of Performers, Producers of Phonograms and Broadcasting Organisations (Rome, 1961),

- Protocol relating to the Madrid Agreement concerning the International Registration of Marks (Madrid, 1989),

- Nice Agreement concerning the International Classification of Goods and Services for the purposes of the Registration of Marks (Geneva 1977 and amended in 1979),

- Budapest Treaty on the International Recognition of the Deposit of Micro-organisms for the purposes of Patent Procedures (1977, modified in 1980),

- International Convention for the Protection of New Varieties of Plants (UPOV) (Geneva Act, 1991).

2.	The Cooperation Council may recommend that paragraph 2 of Article 42 shall apply to other multilateral conventions. If problems in the area of intellectual, industrial and commercial property affecting trading conditions were to occur, urgent consultations will be undertaken, at the request of either party, with a view to reaching mutually satisfactory solutions.

3.	The Parties confirm the importance they attach to the obligations arising from the following multilateral conventions:

- Paris Convention for the Protection of Industrial Property (Stockholm Act, 1967 and amended in 1979),

- Madrid Agreement concerning the International Registration of Marks (Stockholm Act, 1967 and amended in 1979),

- Patent Cooperation Treaty (Washington, 1970, amended in 1979 and modified in 1984).

4.	From the entry into force of this Agreement, the Republic of Azerbaijan shall grant to Community companies and nationals, in respect of the recognition and protection of intellectual, industrial and commercial property, treatment no less favourable than that granted by it to any third country under bilateral agreements.

5.	The provisions of paragraph 4 shall not apply to advantages granted by the Republic of Azerbaijan to any third country on an effective reciprocal basis and to advantages granted by the Republic of Azerbaijan to another country of the former USSR.

ANNEX III

FINANCIAL SERVICES REFERRED TO IN ARTICLE 26(3)

A financial service is any service of a financial nature offered by a financial service provider of a Party. Financial services include the following activities:

A.	All insurance and insurance-related services

1.	Direct insurance (including co-insurance):

(i)	life;

(ii)	non-life.

2.	Reinsurance and retrocession.

3.	Insurance intermediation, such as brokerage and agency.

4. Services auxiliary to insurance, such as consultancy, actuarial, risk assessment and claim settlement services.

B. Banking and other financial services (excluding insurance)

1. Acceptance of deposits and other repayable funds from the public.

2. Lending of all types, including, inter alia, consumer credit, mortgage credit, factoring and financing of commercial transactions.

3. Financial leasing.

4. All payment and money transmission services, including credit charge and debit cards, travellers cheques and bankers drafts.

5. Guarantees and commitments.

6. Trading for own account or for the account of customers, whether on an exchange, in an over-the-counter market or otherwise, the following:

    (a) money market instruments (cheques, bills, certificates of deposits, etc.);

    (b) foreign exchange;

    (c) derivative products including, but not limited to, futures and options;

    (d) exchange rates and interest rate instruments, including products such as swaps, forward rate agreements, etc.;

    (e) transferable securities;

    (f) other negotiable instruments and financial assets, including bullion.

7. Participation in issues of all kinds of securities, including underwriting and placement as agent (whether publicly or privately) and provision of services related to such issues.

8. Money brokering.

9. Asset management, such as cash or portfolio management, all forms of collective investment management, pension fund management, custodial depository and trust services.

10. Settlement and clearing services for financial assets, including securities, derivative products, and other negotiable instruments.

11. Advisory intermediation and other auxiliary financial services on all the activities listed in points 1 to 10 above, including credit reference and analysis, investment and portfolio research and advice, advice on acquisitions and on corporate restructuring and strategy.

12.   Provision and transfer of financial information, and financial data processing and related software by providers of other financial services.

The following activities are excluded from the definition of financial services:

(a)   activities carried out by central banks or by any other public institutions in pursuit of monetary and exchange rate policies;

(b)   activities conducted by central banks, government agencies or departments, or public institutions, for the account or with the guarantee of the government, except when those activities may be carried out by financial service providers in competition with such public entities;

(c)   activities forming part of a statutory system of social security or public retirement plans, except when those activities may be carried out by financial service providers in competition with public entities or private institutions.

ANNEX IV

COMMUNITY RESERVATIONS IN ACCORDANCE WITH ARTICLE 23(2)

Mining
In some Member States, a concession may be required for mining and mineral rights for non-Community controlled companies.

Fishing
Access to and use of the biological resources and fishing grounds situated in the maritime waters coming under the sovereignty or within the jurisdiction of Member States of the Community is restricted to fishing vessels flying the flag of a Community Member State and registered in Community territory unless otherwise provided for.

Real estate purchase
In some Member States, the purchase of real estate by non-Community companies is subject to restrictions.

Audiovisual services including radio
National treatment concerning production and distribution, including broadcasting and other forms of transmission to the public, may be reserved to audiovisual works meeting certain origin criteria.

Telecommunications services including mobile and satellite services

Reserved services
In some Member States market access concerning complementary services and infrastructure is restricted.

Professional services
Services reserved to natural persons who are nationals of Member States. Under certain conditions those persons may create companies.

Agriculture

In some Member States national treatment is not applicable to non-Community controlled companies which wish to undertake an agricultural enterprise. The acquisition of vineyards by non-EC controlled companies is subject to notification, or, as necessary, authorisation.

News agency services

In some Member States limitations of foreign participation in publishing companies and broadcasting companies.

ANNEX V

RESERVATIONS OF THE REPUBLIC OF AZERBAIJAN IN ACCORDANCE WITH ARTICLE 23(4)

Utilization of subsoil and natural resources, including exploration and production, and mining

A concession may be required for foreign companies for exploration and production of hydrocarbon resources as well as for mining some ores and metals.

Fishing

Authorisation from the competent governmental body is necessary for fishing.

Hunting

Authorisation from the competent governmental body is necessary for hunting.

Real estate (immovable property) purchase

Foreign companies are not allowed to acquire plots of land. Those companies can, however, lease plots of land on a long-term basis.

Banking services

Total capital of foreign-owned banks may not exceed a given percentage of the total capital in the domestic banking system.

Azerbaijan undertakes not to reduce for Azerbaijani subsidiaries and branches of Community companies, the ceiling limiting the overall share of foreign capital in the Azerbaijani banking system which applies on the date of initialling of this Agreement unless so required under the framework of IMF programmes in Azerbaijan.

At the latest within five years from the date of signature of the Agreement, Azerbaijan will consider the possibility of increasing the ceiling, taking into consideration all relevant monetary, fiscal, financial and balance-of-payments considerations and the state of the banking system of Azerbaijan.

Telecommunications and mass media services

Some limitations may be applied to foreign participation.

Professional activities

Some activities are closed, limited, or subject to special requirements for natural persons who are not Azerbaijani nationals.

Historical buildings and monuments
Activities in this area are subject to restrictions.

The application of the reservations in this Annex can in no case result in treatment less favourable than that accorded to companies of any third country.

Joint Declaration concerning Article 15

Until the Republic of Azerbaijan accedes to the WTO, the Parties shall hold consultations in the Cooperation Committee on their import tariff policies, including changes in tariff protection. In particular, such consultations shall be offered prior to the increase of tariff protection.

Joint Declaration concerning the notion of "control" in Article 25(b) and Article 36

1.   The Parties confirm their mutual understanding that the question of control shall depend on the factual circumstances of the particular case.

2.   A company shall, for example, be considered as being "controlled" by another company, and thus a subsidiary of such other company if:

   - the other company holds directly or indirectly a majority of the voting rights, or

   - the other company has the right to appoint or dismiss a majority of the administrative organ, of the management organ or of the supervisory organ and is at the same time a shareholder or member of the subsidiary;

3.   Both Parties consider the criteria in paragraph 2 to be non-exhaustive.

Joint Declaration concerning Article 35

The sole fact of requiring a visa for natural persons of certain Parties and not for those of others shall not be regarded as nullifying or impairing benefits under a specific commitment.

Joint Declaration concerning Article 42

The Parties agree that for the purpose of the Agreement, intellectual, industrial and commercial property includes in particular copyright, including the copyright in computer programs, and neighbouring rights, the rights relating to patents, industrial designs, geographical indications, including appellations of origin, trademarks and service marks, topographies of integrated circuits as well as protection against unfair competition as referred to in Article 10bis of the Paris Convention for the Protection of Industrial Property and Protection of Undisclosed Information on Know-how.

Joint Declaration concerning Article 55

The provisions of Article 55(3) shall not require either of the Parties to provide information of a confidential nature.

*

FREE TRADE AGREEMENT BETWEEN THE REPUBLIC OF ESTONIA AND THE REPUBLIC OF SLOVENIA *
[excerpts]

The Free Trade Agreement between the Republic of Estonia and the Republic of Slovenia was signed on 26 November 1996. It entered into force on 1 January1997.

Article 24
Rules of competition concerning undertakings

1.   The following are incompatible with the proper functioning of this Agreement in so far as they may affect trade between the Parties:

(a)   all agreements between undertakings, decisions by associations of undertakings and concerted practices between undertakings which have as their object or effect the prevention, restriction or distortion of competition;

(b)   abuse by one or more undertakings of a dominant position in the territories of the Parties as a whole or in substantial part thereof.

2.   The provisions of paragraph 1 of this Article shall apply to the activities of all undertakings including public undertakings and undertakings to which the Parties grant special or exclusive rights. Undertakings entrusted with the operation of services of general economic interest or having the character of a revenue-producing monopoly, shall be subject to provisions of paragraph 1 in so far as the application of these provisions does not obstruct the performance, in law or in fact, of the particular public tasks assigned to them.

3.   With regard to products referred to in Chapter II the provisions stipulated in paragraph 1(a) of this Article shall not apply to such agreements, decisions and practices which form an integral part of a national market organization.

4.   If a Party considers that a given practice is incompatible with paragraphs 1, 2 and 3 of this Article and if such practice causes or threatens to cause serious prejudice to the interest of that Party or material injury to its domestic industry, it may take appropriate measures under the conditions and in accordance with the procedure laid down in Article 33.

Article 26
Public Procurement

1.   The Parties consider the liberalization of their respective public procurement markets as an objective of this Agreement.

---

*   *Source*: World Trade Organization (1997). "Free Trade Agreement between the Republic of Estonia and the Republic of Slovenia", World Trade Organization, WT/REG37/1, 7 March 1997; available on the Internet (http://www.wto.org). [Note added by the editor.]

2.   The Parties shall progressively develop their respective regulations for public procurement with a view to grant suppliers of the other Party, on 1 January 1999 at the latest, access to contract award procedures on their respective public procurement markets according to the provisions of the Agreement on Government Procurement in Annex IV to the Agreement Establishing the World Trade Organization.

3.   The Joint Committee shall examine developments related to the achievement of the objectives of this Article and may recommend practical modalities of implementing the provisions of paragraph 2 so as to ensure free access, transparency and full balance of rights and obligations.

4.   During the examination referred to in paragraph 3, the Joint Committee may consider, especially in the light of international developments and regulations in this area, the possibility of extending the coverage and/or the degree of the market opening provided for in paragraph 2.

5.   The Parties shall endeavour to accede to the relevant Agreements negotiated under the auspices of the General Agreement on Tariffs and Trade 1994 and the Agreement Establishing the World Trade Organization.

Article 27
Protection of intellectual property

1.   The Parties shall grant and ensure the protection of intellectual property rights on a non-discriminatory basis, including measures for granting the enforcing such rights. The protection shall be gradually improved on a level corresponding to the substantive standards of the multilateral agreements which are specified in Annex I by 1 January 1999 at the latest.

2.   For the purposes of this Agreement "intellectual property protection" includes, in particular, protection of copyright, comprising computer programs and databases, and neighbouring rights, trademarks for goods and services, geographical indications including appellation of origin, industrial designs, patents, topographies of integrated circuits, as well as undisclosed information.

3.   The Parties shall co-operate in matters of intellectual property. They shall hold, upon request of any Party, expert consultations on these matters, in particular, on activities relating to the existing or to future international conventions on harmonization, administration and enforcement of intellectual property and on activities in international organizations, such as the World Trade Organization and the World Intellectual Property Organization, as well as relations of the Parties with any third country on matters concerning intellectual property.

4.   The Parties may conclude further agreements exceeding the requirements of this Agreement which are not contrary to the TRIPS Agreement.

Article 39
Services and investments

1.   The Parties recognize the growing importance of certain areas, such as services and investments. In their efforts to gradually develop and broaden their co-operation, in particular in the context of the European integration, they will co-operate with the aim of achieving a

progressive liberalization and mutual opening of markets for investments and trade in services, taking into account relevant provisions of the General Agreement on Trade in Services.

2.   The Parties will discuss in the Joint Committee the possibilities to extend their trade relations to the fields of foreign direct investment and trade in services.

ANNEX I

PROTECTION OF INTELLECTUAL PROPERTY
(referred to in Article 27)

Paragraph 1 of Article 27 concerns the following multilateral conventions:

-     International Convention for the Protection of Performers, producers of Phonograms and Broadcasting Organisations (Rome, 1961);

-     Nice Agreement concerning the International Classification of Goods and Services for the purposes of the Registration of Marks (Geneva, 1977 and amended in 1979);

-     Protocol relating to the Madrid Agreement concerning the International Registration of Marks (Madrid, 1989);

-     Budapest Treaty of 28 April 1977 on the International Recognition of the Deposit of Micro-organisins for the Purposes of Patent Procedure;

-     International Convention for the Protection of new Varieties of Plants (UPOV) (Geneva Act, 1991);

-     TRIPS Agreement.

The Joint Committee may decide that the paragraph I of Article 27 shall apply to other multilateral conventions.

The Parties confirm the importance they attach to the Obligations arising from the following multilateral conventions:

-     Berne Convention for the Protection of Literary and Artistic Works (Paris Act, 1971);

-     Paris Convention for the Protection of Industrial Property (Stockholm Act, 1967 and amended in 1979);

-     Patent Co-operation Treaty (Washington, 1970, amended in 1979 and modified in 1984);

*

FRAMEWORK AGREEMENT FOR TRADE AND COOPERATION BETWEEN THE EUROPEAN COMMUNITY AND ITS MEMBER STATES, ON THE ONE HAND, AND THE REPUBLIC OF KOREA, ON THE OTHER HAND*
[excerpts]

The Framework Agreement for Trade and Cooperation between the European Community and its Member States, on the One Hand, and the Republic of Korea, on the Other Hand was signed on 28 October 1996. It entered in to force on on 1 April 2001. The member States of the European Communities are: Austria, Belgium, Denmark, Finland, France, Germany, Greece, Ireland, Italy, Luxembourg, the Netherlands, Portugal, Spain, Sweden and the United Kingdom.

...

BELIEVING that it will be advantageous to the Parties to institutionalise relations and to establish economic cooperation between them, as such cooperation would encourage further development of trade and investment,

MINDFUL of the importance of facilitating the involvement in cooperation of the individuals and entities directly concerned, in particular economic operators and the bodies representing them,

...

Article 2
Aims of cooperation

With a view to enhancing cooperation between them, the Parties undertake to promote further development of economic relations between them. Their efforts will in particular be aimed at:

(a)   stepping up, establishing cooperation in and diversifying trade to their mutual advantage;

(b)   establishing economic cooperation in fields of mutual interest, including scientific and technological cooperation and industrial cooperation;

(c)   facilitating cooperation between businesses by facilitating investment on both sides and by promoting better mutual understanding.

---

* *Source*: European Communities (2001)."Framework Agreement for Trade and Cooperation between the European Community and Its Member States, on the One Hand, and the Republic of Korea, on the Other Hand", *Official Journal of the European Communities*, L 090, 30 March 2001, pp. 46 - 61; available also on the Internet (http://europa.eu.int). [Note added by the editor.]

Article 4
Most-favoured-nation treatment

In accordance with their rights and obligations under the World Trade Organisation, the Parties undertake to accord each other most-favoured-nation treatment.

Article 5
Trade cooperation

1.   The Parties undertake to promote the development and diversification of their reciprocal commercial exchanges to the highest possible level and to their mutual benefit.

The Parties undertake to achieve improved market access conditions. They will ensure that applied, most-favoured-nation customs duties are set, taking into account various elements, including the domestic market situation of one Party and the export interests of the other Party. They undertake to work towards the elimination of barriers to trade, in particular through the timely removal of non-tariff barriers and by taking measures to improve transparency, having regard to the work carried out by international oganisations in this field.

2.   The Parties shall take steps to conduct a policy aimed at:

(a)   multilateral and bilateral cooperation to address issues relating to the development of trade which are of interest to both sides, including the future proceedings of the WTO. To that end they shall cooperate at the international level and bilaterally in the solution of commercial problems of common interest;

(b)   promoting exchanges of information between economic operators and industrial cooperation between enterprises in order to diversify and increase existing flows of trade;

(c)   studying and recommending trade-promotion measures suitable for fostering the development of trade;

(d)   facilitating cooperation between the competent customs authorities of the European Community, its Member States and Korea;

(e)   improving market access for industrial, agricultural and fisheries products;

(f)   improving market access for services, such as financial services and telecommunications services;

(g)   strengthening cooperation in the fields of standards and technical regulations;

(h)   effectively protecting intellectual, industrial and commercial property;

(i)   organising trade and investment visits;

(j)   organising general and single industry trade fairs.

3.	The Parties shall foster fair competition of economic activities through fully enforcing their relevant laws and regulations.

4.	In accordance with their obligations under the WTO Government Procurement Agreement, the Parties shall ensure participation in procurement contracts on a non-discriminatory and reciprocal basis.

They will continue their discussions aimed at further mutual opening of their respective procurement markets in other sectors such as telecommunications procurement.

Article 7
Maritime transport

1.	The Parties undertake to move towards the goal of unrestricted access to the international maritime market and traffic based on fair competition on a commercial basis, in accordance with the provisions of this Article.

    (a)	The above provision does not prejudice the rights and obligations arising from the United Nations Convention Code of Conduct for Liner Conferences as applicable to one or the other Party to this Agreement. Non-conference lines will be free to operate in competition with a conference as long as they adhere to the principle of fair competition on a commercial basis.

    (b)	The Parties affirm their commitment to build a fair and competitive environment for the dry and liquid bulk trade. In view of this commitment, the Republic of Korea will take necessary steps to phase out the existing cargo reservation of designated bulk commodities for Korean flag carriers over a transitional period, which will end on 31 December 1998.

2.	In pursuit of the goal of paragraph 1, the Parties shall:

    (a)	abstain from introducing cargo-sharing clauses into future bilateral agreements with non-member countries concerning dry and liquid bulk and liner trade, except where, in exceptional circumstances, with regard to liner trade, shipping companies from one or the other Party to this Agreement would not otherwise have an effective opportunity to engage in trade to and from the non-member country concerned;

    (b)	abstain from implementing, on entry into force of this Agreement, administrative and technical and legislative measures which could have the effect of discriminating between their own nationals or companies and those of the other Party in the supply of services in international maritime transport;

    (c)	grant no less favourable treatment for the ships operated by nationals or companies of the other Party, than that accorded to its own ships, with regard to access to ports open to international trade, the use of infrastructure and auxiliary maritime services of the ports, as well as related fees and charges, customs facilities and assignment of berths and facilities for loading and unloading.

3.   For the purpose of this Article, access to the international maritime market shall include, inter alia, the right for international maritime transport providers of each Party to arrange door-to-door transport services involving a sea leg, and to this effect to directly contract with local providers of transport modes other than maritime transport on the territory of the other Party without prejudice to applicable nationality restrictions concerning the carriage of goods and passengers by those other transport modes.

4.   The provisions of this Article shall apply to European Community companies and Korean companies. Beneficiaries of the provisions of this Article shall also be shipping companies established outside the European Community or the Republic of Korea and controlled by nationals of a Member State or the Republic of Korea, if their vessels are registered in that Member State or in the Republic of Korea in accordance with their respective legislations.

5.   The issue of the operations in the European Community and in the Republic of Korea of shipping agency activities shall be dealt with by specific agreements, where appropriate.

Article 8
Shipbuilding

1.   The Parties agree to cooperate in the field of shipbuilding with a view to promoting fair and competitive market conditions and note the severe structural disequilibrium between supply and demand and the market trends which depress the world shipbuilding industry. For these reasons, the Parties shall not adopt any measure or take any action to support their shipbuilding industry which would distort competition or allow their shipbuilding industry to escape from any future difficult situation, in accordance with the OECD Agreement on Shipbuilding.

2.   The Parties agree to enter into consultations on a request from either Party regarding the implementation of the OECD Agreement on Shipbuilding, exchange of information on the development of the world market for ships and shipbuilding and on any other problem arising in this sector.

The representatives of the shipbuilding industry may be invited as observers to such consultations, on agreement by the Parties.

Article 9
Intellectual, industrial and commercial property protection

1.   The Parties undertake to ensure that adequate and effective protection is provided for intellectual, industrial and commercial property rights, including effective means of enforcing such rights.

2.   The parties agree to implement the WTO Agreement on Trade-related Aspects of Intellectual Property Rights not later than 1 July 1996.[1]

3.   The Parties confirm the importance they attach to the obligations contained in multilateral conventions for the protection of intellectual property rights. The Parties shall make efforts to accede as soon as practicable to the conventions in the Annex to which they have not acceded.

---

[1]   For the Republic of Korea with the exception of the Agrochemical Management Law which will enter into force as from 1 January 1997 and the Seedlings Industry Law (and Law on Protection of Geographical Indications) by 1 July 1998, subject to its legislative procedure.

Article 12
Economic and industrial cooperation

1.   The Parties, taking into account their mutual interest and their respective economic policies and objectives, shall foster economic and industrial cooperation in all fields deemed suitable by them.

2.   The objectives of such cooperation shall be in particular:

- to promote exchanges of information between economic operators, and develop and improve existing networks, while ensuring that personal data are suitably protected,

- to bring about exchanges of information on the terms and conditions for cooperation in the field of all services as well as information infrastructures,

- to promote mutually beneficial investment and establish a climate which favours investment,

- to improve the economic environment and business climate.

3.   As means to such ends, the Parties shall endeavour, inter alia:

(a)   to diversify and strengthen economic links between them;

(b)   to establish industry specific channels of cooperation;   .

(c)   to promote industrial cooperation between enterprises, in particular between small and medium-sized enterprises;

(d)   to promote sustainable development of their economies;

(e)   to encourage ways of production which are not prejudicial to the environment;

(f)   to encourage the flow of investment and technology;

(g)   to increase mutual understanding and awareness of their respective business environments.

Article 14
Cooperation in science and technology

...

3.   The Parties agree that all cooperation and joint actions in the field of science and technology take place on the basis of reciprocity.

The Parties agree to protect effectively the information and the intellectual property resulting from cooperation against any abuse or unauthorised use by others than the legitimate owners thereof.

In case of participation by institutions, bodies and undertakings of one of the Parties in specific research and technological development programmes of the other Party, such as those set up under the European Community's general framework programme, this participation and the dissemination and exploitation of knowledge obtained as a result thereof shall take place in accordance with the general rules laid down by that other Party.

...

Article 19
Joint Committee

1.   The Parties shall establish under this Agreement a Joint Committee consisting of representatives of the members of the Council of the European Union and representatives of the European Commission, on the one hand, and representatives of the Republic of Korea, on the other. Consultations shall be held in the Committee in order to facilitate the implementation and to further the general aims of this Agreement.

2.   The Joint Committee shall:

- ensure that the Agreement operates properly,

- study the development of trade and cooperation between the two Parties,

- seek appropriate methods of forestalling problems which might arise in areas covered by the Agreement,

- seek ways of developing and diversifying trade,

- exchange opinions and make suggestions on any issue of common interest relating to trade and cooperation, including future action and the resources available to carry it out,

- make recommendations suitable for promoting the expansion of trade and cooperation, taking into account the need to coordinate the measures proposed.

3.   The Joint Committee will normally meet once a year in Brussels and Seoul alternately. Special meetings of the Committee shall be held at the request of either Party. The Joint Committee shall be chaired alternately by each of the Parties.

4.   The Joint Committee may set up specialised sub-committees in order to assist it in the performance of its tasks. These sub-committees shall make detailed reports of their activities to the Joint Committee at each of its meetings.

ANNEX
Intellectual, industrial and commercial property Conventions referred to in Article 9

- Berne Convention for the Protection of Literary and Artistic Works (Paris Act, 1971)

- International Convention for the Protection of Performers, Producers of Phonograms and Broadcasting Organisations (Rome, 1961)

- Paris Convention for the Protection of Industrial Property (Stockholm Act, 1967, as amended in 1979)

- Patent Cooperation Treaty (Washington, 1970, as amended in 1979, and modified in 1984)

- Madrid Agreement concerning the International Registration of Marks (Stockholm Act, 1967, and amended in 1979)

- Protocol relating to the Madrid Agreement concerning the International Registration of Marks (Madrid, 1989)

- Nice Agreement concerning the International Classification of Goods and Services for the Purposes of the Registration of Marks (Geneva, 1977, and amended in 1979)

- Budapest Treaty on the International Recognition of the Deposit of Microorganisms for the Purposes of Patent Procedure (1977, modified in 1980)

- International Convention for the Protection of New Varieties of Plants (UPOV) (Geneva Act, 1991)

Joint Declarations

JOINT DECLARATION CONCERNING ARTICLE 7

Each Party shall allow the shipping companies of the other Party to have their commercial presence in its territory for the purpose of carrying out shipping agency activities under conditions of establishment and operation no less favourable than those accorded to its own companies or to subsidiaries or branches of companies of any non-member country, whichever is the better.

JOINT DECLARATION CONCERNING ARTICLE 9

The Parties agree that for the purpose of the Agreement, intellectual, industrial and commercial property includes in particular copyright, including the copyright in computer programs, and neighbouring rights, the rights relating to patents, industrial designs, geographical indications, including designations of origin, trade marks and service marks, topographies of integrated circuits as well as protection against unfair competition as referred to in Article 10 bis of the Paris Convention for the Protection of Industrial Property and protection of undisclosed information on know-how.

*

FREE TRADE AGREEMENT BETWEEN LATVIA AND SLOVENIA *
[excerpts]

The Free Trade Agreement between Latvia And Slovenia was signed on 22 April 1996. It entered into force on 1 August 1996.

Article 14
Public Procurement

1.   The Parties consider the liberalization of their respective public procurement markets as an objective of this Agreement, as defined in Article 1 (Objectives).

2.   The Parties shall progressively develop their respective regulations for public procurement with a view to grant suppliers of the other Party upon the entry into force of this Agreement access to contract award procedures on their respective public procurement markets in accordance with the provisions of the Agreement on Government Procurement in Annex IV of the Agreement Establishing the World Trade Organization.

3.   The Joint Committee shall examine developments related to the achievement of the objectives of this Article and may recommend practical modalities for implementing the provisions of paragraph 2 of this Article so as to ensure free access, transparency and full balance of rights and obligations.

4.   During the examination referred to in paragraph 3 of this Article, the Joint Committee may consider, especially in the light of developments in this area in international relations, the possibility of extending the coverage and/or the degree of the market opening provided for in paragraph 2.

5.   The Parties shall endeavour to accede to the relevant Agreements negotiated under the auspices of the World Trade Organization.

Article 15
Protection of Intellectual Property

1.   The Parties shall grant and ensure adequate, effective and non-discriminatory protection of intellectual property rights, including measures for the enforcement of such rights against infringement thereof, counterfeiting and piracy. Particular obligations of the Parties are contained in Annex IV.

2.   In the field of intellectual property the Parties shall, from the entry into force of this Agreement, grant to each others nationals and companies treatment no less favourable than that accorded to nationals and companies of any other country under international agreements.

---

*   *Source*: World Trade Organization (1997). "Free Trade Agreement between Latvia and Slovenia", World Trade Organization, WT/REG34/1, 17 December 1997; available on the Internet (http://www.wto.org). [Note added by the editor.]

3.   The provisions of paragraph 2 shall not apply to advantages granted by the Parties before the entry into force of this Agreement to any third country on an effective reciprocal basis.

4.   The Parties agree, upon request of either Party, to review the provisions on the protection on intellectual property rights contained in this Article and in Annex IV, with a view to further improve levels of protection and to avoid or remedy trade distortions which may be caused by actual levels of protection of intellectual property rights.

Article 16
Rules of Competition Concerning Undertakings

1.   The following are incompatible with the proper functioning of this Agreement insofar as they may affect trade between the Parties:

(a)   all agreements between undertakings, decisions by associations of undertakings and concerted practices between undertakings which have as their object or effect the prevention, restriction or distortion of competition;

(b)   abuse by one or more undertakings of a dominant position in the territories of the Parties, as a whole or in a substantial part thereof.

2.   The provisions of paragraph 1 shall apply to the activities of all undertakings, including public undertakings and undertakings to which a Party grants special or exclusive rights. Undertakings entrusted with the operation of services of general economic interest or having the character of a revenue-producing monopoly shall be subject to the rules contained in this Article, insofar as the application of such rules does not obstruct the performance, in law or in fact, of the particular tasks assigned to them.

3.   If a Party considers that a given practice is incompatible with paragraphs 1 and 2, it may take measures it considers necessary to deal with serious difficulties resulting from the practices in question, under the conditions and in accordance with the procedures laid down in Article 24 (Procedures for the Application of Safeguard Measures).

Article 26
The Joint Committee

1.   The implementation and functioning of this Agreement shall be supervised and administered by a Joint Committee.

2.   The Joint Committee shall be comprised of the representatives of the Parties.

3.   For the purposes of the proper implementation of this Agreement, the Parties shall exchange information and, at the request of any Party, shall hold consultations within the Joint Committee. The Committee shall keep under review the possibility of further removal of the obstacles to trade between the Parties.

4.   The Joint Committee may take decisions in cases provided for in this Agreement. On other matters it may make recommendations.

Article 29
Services and Investment

1.   The Parties recognise the growing importance of certain areas, such as services and investments. In their efforts to gradually develop and broaden their cooperation, in particular in the context of European integration, they will cooperate with the aim of achieving a gradual liberalization and mutual opening of markets for investments and trade in services, taking into account the results of the Uruguay Round as well as any relevant future work under the auspices of the World Trade Organization.

2.   The Parties will discuss this cooperation in the Joint Committee with the aim of developing and deepening their relations under this Agreement.

ANNEX IV

CONCERNING ARTICLE 15
PROTECTION OF INTELLECTUAL PROPERTY

ARTICLE 1
Definition and Intellectual property

For the purposes of this Agreement " intellectual property shall, in particular include copyright and neighbouring rights, including computer programmes and databases, trademarks for goods and services, geographical indications, including appeliations of origin, industrial designs, patents, topographies of integrated circuits, as well as undisclosed information.

ARTICLE 2
International Agreements

1.   The Parties confirm the importance they attach to their obligations arising from the Eollowing multilateral aqreements:

-       Paris Convention of 20 March 1883 for the Protection of Industrial Property (Stockhoirp Act, 1967);

-       Berne Convention of 9 September 1886 for the Protection of Literary and Artistic Works (Paris Act, 1971);

-       Patent Co-operation Treaty (Washington, 1970, amended in 1979 and modified in 1984).

2.   The Parties agree to comply with the substantive standards of the following multilateral agreements:

-       WTO Agreement on Trade-Related Aspects of Intellectual Property Rights (Marrakech, 15 April 1994);

-       European Patent Convention (Munich, 5 October 1973).

3.   The Parties shall make best endeavours to adhere, as soon as possible, to the following multilateral agreements:

-     International Convention of 26 October 1961 for the Protection of Performers, Producers of Phonograms and Broadcasting Organisations (Rome Convention);
-     Protocol relating to the Madrid Agreement concerning the International Registration Marks (Madrid, 1989);

-     International Convention for the Protection of New Varieties of Plants (UPOV) (Geneva Act, 1991).

4.   The Parties agree to promptly hold expert consultations, upon request of either Party, on activities relating to the existing or to future international conventions on harmonisation, administration and enforcement of intellectual property rights and on activities in international organisations, such as the World Trade organisation (WTO), the World Intellectual Property Organisation (WI PO) ' the European Patent Organisation as well as relations of the Parties with third countries on matters concerning intellectual property.

ARTICLE 3
Acquisition and maintenance of intellectial property rights

Where the acquisition of an intellectual, property right is subject to the right being granted or registered, the Parties shall ensure that the procedures for grant and registration be of a high quality, non-discriminatory, fair and equitable. They shall not be unnecessarily complicated and costly, or entail unreasonable time limits or unwarranted delays.

ARTICLE 4
Enforcement of intellectual property rights

(1)   The Parties shall provide for enforcement provisions under their national laws that are adequate, effective and nondiscriminatory so as to guarantee full protection of intellectual property rights against infringement. Such provisions shall include civil and criminal sanctions against infringements of any intellectual property right covered by this Agreement, and in particular injunctions, damages adequate to compensate for the injury suffered by the right holder, as well as provisional measures, including inaudita alter parte ones.

(2)   Enforcement procedures shall be non-discriminatory, fair and equitable. They shall not be unnecessarily complicated and postly, or entail unreasonable time limits or unwarranted delays.

(3)   Final administrative decisions in the procedures referred to in this Article shall be subject to review by a judicial or quasi-judicial authority.

ARTICLE 5
Technical co-operation

The Parties shall agree upon appropriate modalities for technical assistance and co-operation of respective authorities of the Parties. To this end, they shall co-ordinate efforts with relevant international organisations.

*

COOPERATION AGREEMENT BETWEEN THE EUROPEAN COMMUNITY AND THE KINGDOM OF CAMBODIA *
[excerpts

The Cooperation Agreement between the European Community and the Kingdom of Cambodia was signed on 29 April 1997. It entered in to force on 1 November 1999. The member States of the European Communities are: Austria, Belgium, Denmark, Finland, France, Germany, Greece, Ireland, Italy, Luxembourg, the Netherlands, Portugal, Spain, Sweden and the United Kingdom.

...

RECOGNISING the desire of the Parties to create favourable conditions for the development of trade and investment between the Community and Cambodia, and the need to adhere to the principles of international trade, the purpose of which is to promote trade liberalisation in a stable, transparent and non-discriminatory manner;

...

Article 4
Trade cooperation

1.   The Parties confirm their determination:

   (a)   to take all appropriate measures to create favourable conditions for trade between them;

   (b)   to do their utmost to improve the structure of their trade in order to diversify it further;

   (c)   to work towards the elimination of barriers to trade, and towards measures to improve transparency, in particular through the removal at an appropriate time of non-tariff barriers, in accordance with work undertaken in this connection by other international bodies while ensuring that personal data are suitably protected.

2.   In their trade relations, the Parties shall accord each other most-favoured-nation treatment in all matters regarding:

   (a)   customs duties and charges of all kinds, including the procedures for their collection;

   (b)   the regulations, procedures and formalities governing customs clearance, transit, warehousing and transhipment;

---

*   *Source*: European Communities (1999). "Cooperation Agreement between the European Community and the Kingdom of Cambodia", *Official Journal of the European Communities*, L 269, 19 October 1999, pp. 18 – 28; available on the Internet (http://europa.eu.int). [Note added by the editor.]

(c)   taxes and other internal charges levied directly or indirectly on imports or exports;

(d)   administrative formalities for the issue of import or export licences.

3.   Within the areas of their respective areas of jurisdiction, the Parties shall undertake:

(a)   to seek ways of establishing cooperation in the field of maritime transport leading to market access on a commercial and non-discriminatory basis, taking into account the work done in this connection by other international bodies;

(b)   to improve customs cooperation between their respective authorities, especially with regard to vocational training, the simplification and harmonisation of customs procedures and administrative assistance in the matter of customs fraud;

(c)   to exchange information on mutually advantageous opportunities, in particular in the field of tourism and cooperation on statistical matters.

4.   Paragraphs 2 and 3(a) shall not apply to:

(a)   advantages accorded by either Party to States which are fellow members of a customs union or free trade area;

(b)   advantages accorded by either Party to neighbouring countries with a view to facilitating border trade;

(c)   measures which either Party may take in order to meet its obligations under international commodity agreements.

5.   Cambodia shall improve conditions for the adequate and effective protection and enforcement of intellectual, industrial and commercial property rights in conformity with the highest international standards. To this end, Cambodia shall accede to the relevant international conventions on intellectual, industrial and commercial property(1) to which it is not yet a party. In order to enable Cambodia to fulfil the abovementioned obligations, technical assistance could be envisaged.

6.   Within their respective areas of jurisdiction and insofar as their rules and regulations permit, the Parties shall agree to consult each other on all questions, problems or disputes which may arise in connection with trade.

Article 6
Economic cooperation

Within the limits of their respective areas of jurisdiction and the financial resources available, the Parties undertake to foster economic cooperation to their mutual advantage.

This cooperation will be aimed at:

(a)   developing the economic environment in Cambodia by facilitating access to Community know-how and technology;

(b)   facilitating contacts between economic operators and taking other measures to promote trade;

(c)   encouraging, in accordance with their legislation, rules and policies, public- and private-sector investment programmes in order to strengthen economic cooperation, including cooperation between enterprises, technology transfers, licences and subcontracting;

(d)   facilitating the exchange of information and the adoption of initiatives, fostering cooperation on enterprise policy, particularly with regard to improving the business environment and encouraging closer contacts;

(e)   reinforcing mutual understanding of the Parties' respective economic environments as a basis for effective cooperation.

In the above fields the principal objectives shall be:

- to assist Cambodia in its efforts to restructure its economy by creating the conditions for a suitable economic environment and business climate;

- to encourage synergies between the Parties' respective economic sectors, and in particular their private sectors;

- within the Parties' respective areas of jurisdiction, and in accordance with their legislation, rules and policies, to establish a climate conducive to private investment by improving conditions for the transfer of capital and, where appropriate, by supporting the conclusion of agreements between the Member States of the Community and Cambodia on the promotion and protection of investment.

The Parties will together determine, to their mutual advantage, the areas and priorities for economic cooperation programmes and activities.

Article 10
Science and technology

The Parties, according to their respective policies, their mutual interest and within their respective areas of jurisdiction, may promote scientific and technological cooperation.

Cooperation will involve:

- the exchange of information and experience at regional (Europe-South-East Asia) level, especially on the implementation of policies and programmes,

- the promotion of lasting ties between the Parties' scientific communities,

- the stepping-up of activities aimed at promoting innovation in industry, including technology transfers.

Cooperation may involve:

> - the joint implementation of regional (Europe-South-East Asia) research projects in areas of mutual interest, facilitating, where appropriate, the active involvement of enterprises,

> - the exchange of scientists to promote the preparation of research projects and high-level training,

> - joint scientific meetings to foster exchanges of information and interaction and to identify areas for joint research,

> - the dissemination of results and the development of links between the public and private sectors;

> - evaluation of the activities concerned.

The Parties' higher education institutions, research centres and industries will play an appropriate part in this cooperation.

Article 12
Physical infrastructure

The Parties recognise that the present state of Cambodia's physical infrastructure constitutes a serious constraint to private investment and to economic development in general. The Parties therefore agree to encourage specific programmes for the rehabilitation, reconstruction and development of Cambodia's infrastructure, including transport.

Article 14
Institutional aspects

1.   The Parties agree to establish a Joint Committee, whose tasks are:

    (a)   to guarantee the smooth working and proper implementation of this Agreement and of the dialogue between the Parties;

    (b)   to make suitable recommendations for promoting the objectives of this Agreement;

    (c)   to establish priorities for potential operations in pursuit of this Agreement's objectives.

2.   The Joint Committee shall be composed of representatives of sufficient seniority of both Parties. It shall normally meet every other year, alternately in Phnom Penh and in Brussels, on a date fixed by mutual agreement. Extraordinary meetings may also be convened by agreement between the Parties.

3.   The Joint Committee may set up specialised sub-groups to assist it in the performance of its tasks and to coordinate the formulation and implementation of projects and programmes under this Agreement.

4.   The agenda for meetings of the Joint Committee shall be determined by agreement between the Parties.

5.   The Parties agree that it shall also be the task of the Joint Committee to ensure the proper functioning of any sectoral agreements concluded, or which may be concluded, between the Community and Cambodia.

6.   The organisational structures and the rules of procedure of the Joint Committee shall be determined by the Parties.

ANNEX II

Joint Declaration on Intellectual, Industrial and Commercial Property

The Parties agree for the purposes of the Agreement that "intellectual, industrial and commercial property" includes in particular protection of copyright and related rights, patents, industrial designs, software, brands and trademarks, topographies of integrated circuits, geographical indications, as well as protection against unfair competition and the protection of undisclosed information.

Joint Declaration on the readmission of citizens

The European Community recalls the importance that its Member States attach to the establishment of effective cooperation with third countries in order to facilitate the readmission by the latter of its nationals unlawfully residing on the territory of a Member State.

The Kingdom of Cambodia undertakes to finalise readmission agreements with those Member States of the European Union which request it.

*

COOPERATION AGREEMENT BETWEEN THE EUROPEAN COMMUNITY AND THE LAO PEOPLE'S DEMOCRATIC REPUBLIC *
[excerpts

> The Cooperation Agreement between the European Community and the Lao People's Democratic Republic was signed on 29 April 1997. It entered in to force on 1 December 1997. The member States of the European Communities are: Austria, Belgium, Denmark, Finland, France, Germany, Greece, Ireland, Italy, Luxembourg, the Netherlands, Portugal, Spain, Sweden and the United Kingdom.

...

DESIROUS OF creating favourable conditions for the development of trade and investment between the Community and the Lao PDR, and the need to adhere to the principles of international trade, the purpose of which is to promote trade liberalization in a stable, transparent and non-discriminatory manner which takes account of the Parties' economic differences;

...

Article 4
Trade cooperation

1.   The Parties confirm their determination:

   (a)   to take all appropriate measures to create favourable conditions for trade between them;

   (b)   to do their utmost to improve the structure of their trade in order to diversify it further;

   (c)   to work towards the elimination of barriers to trade, and towards measures to improve transparency, in particular through the removal at an appropriate time of non-tariff barriers, in accordance with work undertaken in this connection by other international bodies while ensuring that personal data are suitably protected.

2.   In their trade relations, the Parties shall accord each other most-favoured-nation treatment in all matters regarding:

   (a)   customs duties and charges of all kinds, including the procedures for their collection;

---

* *Source*: European Communities (1997). "Cooperation Agreement between the European Community and the Lao People's Democratic Republic", *Official Journal of the European Communities*, L 334, 5 December 1997, pp. 15 – 23; available also on the Internet (http://europa.eu.int). [Note added by the editor.]

    (b)   the regulations, procedures and formalities governing customs clearance, transit, warehousing and transhipment;

    (c)   taxes and other internal charges levied directly or indirectly on imports or exports;

    (d)   administrative formalities for the issue of import or export licences.

3.   Paragraph 2 shall not apply to:

    (a)   advantages accorded by either Party to states which are fellow members of a customs union or free trade area;

    (b)   advantages accorded by either Party to neighbouring countries with a view to facilitating border trade;

    (c)   measures which either Party may take in order to meet its obligations under international commodity agreements.

4.   Within their respective spheres of competence; the Parties shall undertake:

    (a)   to improve cooperation between their authorities in customs matters, in fields including vocational training, the simplification and harmonization of customs procedures and administrative assistance to combat customs fraud;

    (b)   to exchange information on markets likely to provide mutual advantages, including public procurement, tourism and statistical cooperation.

5.   The Lao PDR shall improve conditions for the adequate and effective protection and enforcement of intellectual, industrial and commercial property rights in conformity with the highest international standards. To this end, the Lao PDR shall accede to the relevant international conventions on intellectual, industrial and commercial property (1) to which it is not yet a party. In order to enable the Lao PDR to fulfil the abovementioned obligations, technical assistance could be envisaged.

6.   Within their respective areas of jurisdiction and insofar as their rules and regulations permit, the Parties shall agree to consult each other on all questions, problems or disputes which may arise in connection with trade.

Article 6
Economic cooperation

Within the limits of their respective areas of jurisdiction and the financial resources available, the Parties undertake to foster economic cooperation to their mutual advantage.

This cooperation will be aimed at:

(a)   developing the economic environment in the Lao PDR by facilitating access to Community know-how and technology;

(b)   facilitating contacts between economic operators and taking other measures to promote trade;

(c)   encouraging, in accordance with their legislation, rules and policies, public- and private-sector investment programmes in order to strengthen economic cooperation, including cooperation between enterprises, technology transfers, licences and subcontracting;

(d)   facilitating the exchange of information and the adoption of initiatives, fostering cooperation on enterprise policy, particularly with regard to improving the business environment and encouraging closer contacts;

(e)   reinforcing mutual understanding of the Parties' respective economic environments as a basis for effective cooperation;

(f)   undertaking activities in the fields of standardization, quality assessment, metrology and quality-assurance in order to promote international standards and quality assessment procedures and to facilitate trade.

In the above fields the principal objectives shall be:

- to assist the Lao PDR in its efforts to restructure its economy by creating the conditions for a suitable economic environment and business climate,

- to encourage synergies between the Parties' respective economic sectors, and in particular their private sectors,

- within the Parties' respective areas of jurisdiction, and in accordance with their legislation, rules and policies, to establish a climate conducive to private investment by improving conditions for the transfer of capital and, where appropriate, by supporting the conclusion of agreements between the Member States of the Community and the Lao PDR on the promotion and protection of investment.

The Parties will together determine, to their mutual advantage, the areas and priorities for economic cooperation programmes and activities.

Article 12
Physical infrastructure

The Parties recognize that the present shortcomings of the Lao PDR's physical infrastructure constitute a serious constraint to private investment and to economic development in general. The Parties therefore agree to encourage specific programmes for the rehabilitation, reconstruction and development of the Lao PDR's infrastructure, including transport and communications.

ANNEX II

Joint Declaration on Intellectual, Industrial and Commercial Property

The Parties agree for the purposes of the Agreement that 'intellectual, industrial and commercial property` includes in particular protection of copyright and related rights, patents, industrial designs, software, brands and trademarks, topographies of integrated circuits, geographical indications, as well as protection against unfair competition and the protection of undisclosed information.

*

FREE TRADE AGREEMENT BETWEEN THE REPUBLIC OF SLOVENIA AND THE REPUBLIC OF LITHUANIA*
[excerpts

The Free Trade Agreement between the Republic of Slovenia and the Republic of Lithuania was signed on 1 March 1997. It entered into force on the date of signature.

CHAPTER III

GENERAL PROVISIONS

Article 22
Rules of Competition Concerning Undertakings

1.   The following are incompatible with the proper functioning of this Agreement insofar as they may affect trade between the Parties:

   (a)   all agreements between undertakings, decisions by associations of undertakings and concerted practices between undertakings, which have as their object or effect the prevention, restriction or distortion of competition;

   (b)   abuse by one or more undertakings of a dominant position in the territories of the Parties as a whole or in a substantial part thereof.

2.   The provisions of paragraph 1 shall apply to the activities of all undertakings including public undertakings and undertakings to which the Parties grant special or exclusive rights. Undertakings entrusted with the operation of services of general economic interest or having the character of a revenue-producing monopoly, shall be subject to provisions of paragraph 1 insofar as the application of these provisions does not obstruct the performance, in law or fact, of the particular public tasks assigned to them.

3.   With regard to products referred to in Chapter II the provisions stipulated in paragraph 1(a) shall not apply to such agreements, decisions and practices which form an integral part of a national market organization.

4.   If a Party considers that a given practice is incompatible with paragraphs 1, 2 and 3 of this Article, or if such practice causes or threatens to cause serious prejudice to the interest of that Party or material injury to its domestic industry, the Party concerned may take appropriate measures under the conditions and in accordance with the procedure laid down in Article 31.

---

* *Source*: World Trade Organization (1997). "Free Trade Agreement between the Republic of Slovenia and the Republic of Lithuania", World Trade Organization, WT/REG35/1, 18 December 1997; available on the Internet (http://www.wto.org). [Note added by the editor.]

Article 24
Government Procurement

1.   The Parties consider the liberalization of their respective government procurement markets as an objective of this Agreement.

2.   The Parties shall progressively develop their respective rules, conditions and practices concerning government procurement with a view to grant suppliers of the other Parties, at the latest by 1 January 1999, access to contract award procedures on their respective government procurement markets according to the provisions of the Agreement on Government Procurement in Annex IV to the Agreement Establishing the World Trade Organization.

3.   The Joint Committee shall examine developments related to the achievement of the objectives of this Article and may recommend practical modalities of implementing the provisions of paragraph 2 of this Article, so as to ensure free access, transparency and full balance of rights and obligations.

4.   During the examination, referred to in paragraph 3 of this Article, the Joint Committee may consider, especially in the light of international regulations in this area, the possibility of extending the coverage and/or the degree of the market opening provided for in paragraph 2.

5.   The Parties shall endeavour to accede to the relevant Agreements negotiated under the auspices of the General Agreement on Tariffs and Trade 1994 and the Agreement Establishing the World Trade Organization.

Article 25
Protection of Intellectual Property

1.   The Parties shall grant and ensure protection of intellectual property rights on a non-discriminatory basis, including measures for the grant and enforcement of such rights. The protection shall be gradually improved on a level corresponding to the substantive standards of the multilateral agreements which are specified in Annex IV by 1 January 2001 at the latest.

2.   For the purpose of this Agreement "intellectual property protection" includes in particular protection of copyright, neighbouring rights, trade marks, geographical indications, industrial designs, patents, topographies of integrated circuits, as well as undisclosed information (know-how).

3.   The Parties to this Agreement may conclude further agreements exceeding the requirements of this Agreement and is in conformity with the TRIPS Agreement.

4.   The Parties shall cooperate in matters of intellectual property. They shall hold, upon request of a Party, expert consultations on these matters, in particular on activities relating to the existing or to future international conventions on harmonization, administration and enforcement of intellectual property and on activities in international organizations, such as the World Trade Organization, WIPO, as well as on relations of Parties with third countries in matters concerning intellectual property.

Article 34
The Joint Committee

1.   The Parties agree to set up the Joint Committee composed of representatives of the Parties.

2.   The implementation of this Agreement shall be supervised and administered by the Joint Committee.

3.   For the purpose of the proper implementation of the Agreement, the Parties shall exchange information and, at the request of any Party, shall hold consultations within the Joint Committee. The Committee shall keep under review the possibility of further removal of the obstacles to trade between the Parties.

4.   The Joint Committee may take decisions in cases provided for in this Agreement. On other matters the Committee may make recommendations.

Article 36
Services and Investment

1.   The Parties to this Agreement recognise the growing importance of certain areas, such as services and investments. In their efforts to gradually develop and broaden their cooperation, in particular in the context of the European integration, they will co-operate with the aim of achieving a progressive liberalization and mutual opening of markets for investments and trade in services, taking into account relevant provisions of the General Agreement on Trade in Services.

2.   The Parties will discuss in the Joint Committee the possibilities to extend their trade relations to the fields of foreign direct investment and trade in services.

Annex IV
Intellectual, Industrial and Commercial Property Protections

(referred to in Article 25)

1.   Paragraph 1 of Article 25 concerns the following multilateral conventions:

- •   WTO Agreement on Trade Related Aspects of Intellectual Property Rights (TRIPS Agreement).

- •   International Convention for the Protection of Performers, Producers of Phonograms and Broadcasting Organisations (Rome, 1961);

- •   Nice Agreement concerning the International Classification of Goods and Services for the purposes of the Registration of Marks (Geneva, 1977 and amended in 1979);

- •   Protocol relating to the Madrid Agreement concerning the International Registration of Marks (Madrid, 1989);

- Budapest Treaty of the International Recognition of the Deposit of Microorganisms for the Purposes of Patent Procedures (1977, modified in 1980);

- International Convention for the Protection of New Varieties of Plants (UPOV) (Geneva Act, 1991).

The Joint Committee may decide that paragraph 1 of Article 25 shall apply to other multilateral conventions.

2. The Parties confirm the importance they attach to the obligations arising from the following multilateral conventions:

- Bern Convention for the Protection of Literary and Artistic Works (Paris Act, 1971);

- Paris Convention for the Protection of Industrial Property (Stockholm Act 1967 and amended in 1979);

- Patent Co-operation Treaty (Washington 1970, amended in 1979 and modified in 1984).

*

INTERIM AGREEMENT ON TRADE-RELATED MATTERS BETWEEN THE EUROPEAN COMMUNITY, OF THE ONE PART, AND THE FORMER YUGOSLAV REPUBLIC OF MACEDONIA, OF THE OTHER PART[*]
[excerpts]

The Interim Agreement on Trade-Related Matters between the European Community, of the One Part, and the Former Yugoslav Republic of Macedonia, of the Other Part was signed on 29 April 1997. It entered in to force on 1 January 1998. The member States of the European Communities are: Austria, Belgium, Denmark, Finland, France, Germany, Greece, Ireland, Italy, Luxembourg, the Netherlands, Portugal, Spain, Sweden and the United Kingdom.

CHAPTER III

TITLE III

Payments, Competition and other Economic Provisions

Article 31 (SAA 58)

The Parties undertake to authorise, in freely convertible currency, in accordance with the provisions of Article VIII of the Articles of Agreement of the International Monetary Fund, any payments and transfers on the current account of balance-of-payments between the Community and the Former Yugoslav Republic of Macedonia.

Article 32 (SAA 65)

1.   The Parties shall endeavour wherever possible to avoid the imposition of restrictive measures, including measures relating to imports, for balance of payments purposes. A Party adopting such measures shall present as soon as possible to the other Party a timetable for their removal.

2.   Where one or more Member States or the Former Yugoslav Republic of Macedonia is in serious balance of payments difficulties, or under imminent threat thereof, the Community or the Former Yugoslav Republic of Macedonia, as the case may be, may, in accordance with the conditions established under the WTO Agreement, adopt restrictive measures, including measures relating to imports, which shall be of limited duration and may not go beyond what is strictly necessary to remedy the balance of payments situation. The Community or the Former Yugoslav Republic of Macedonia, as the case may be, shall inform the other Party forthwith.

---

[*] *Source*: European Communities (2001). "Interim Agreement on Trade-Related Matters between the European Community, of the One Part, and the Former Yugoslav Republic of Macedonia, of the Other Part", *Official Journal of the European Communities*, L 124, 4 May 2001, pp. 2 – 196; available on the Internet (http://europa.eu.int). [Note added by the editor.]

3.   Any restrictive measures shall not apply to transfers related to investment and in particular to the repatriation of amounts invested or reinvested or any kind of revenues stemming there from.

Article 33 (SAA 69)

Competition and other Economic Provisions

1.   The following are incompatible with the proper functioning of the Agreement, in so far as they may affect trade between the Community and the Former Yugoslav Republic of Macedonia:

   (i)   all agreements between undertakings, decisions by associations of undertakings and concerted practices between undertakings which have as their object or effect the prevention, restriction or distortion of competition;

   (ii)   abuse by one or more undertakings of a dominant position in the territories of the Community or of the Former Yugoslav Republic of Macedonia as a whole or in a substantial part thereof;

   (iii)   any public aid which distorts or threatens to distort competition by favouring certain undertakings or certain products.

2.   Any practices contrary to this Article shall be assessed on the basis of criteria arising from the application of the rules of Articles 81, 82 and 87 of the Treaty establishing the European Community.

3.   (a)   For the purposes of applying the provisions of paragraph 1(iii), the Parties recognise that during the first four years after the entry into force of this Agreement, any public aid granted by the Former Yugoslav Republic of Macedonia shall be assessed taking into account the fact that the Former Yugoslav Republic of Macedonia shall be regarded as an area identical to those areas of the Community described in Article 87(3)(a) of the Treaty establishing the European Community.

   (b)   Each Party shall ensure transparency in the area of public aid, inter alia by reporting annually to the other Party on the total amount and the distribution of the aid given and by providing, upon request, information on aid schemes. Upon request by one Party, the other Party shall provide information on particular individual cases of public aid. Each Party shall ensure that the provisions of this Article are applied within five years of the Agreement's entry into force.

4.   With regard to products referred to in chapter II of Title II:

   -      paragraph 1(iii) shall not apply.

   -      any practices contrary to paragraph 1(i) shall be assessed according to the criteria established by the Community on the basis of Articles 36 and 37 of the Treaty establishing the European Community and specific Community instruments adopted on this basis.

5.   If the Community or the Former Yugoslav Republic of Macedonia considers that a particular practice is incompatible with the terms of paragraph 1, and:

-       if such practice causes or threatens to cause serious injury to the interests of the other Party or material injury to its domestic industry, including its services industry, it may take appropriate measures after consultation within the Cooperation Council or after 30 working days following referral for such consultation.

In the case of practices incompatible with paragraph 1(iii), such appropriate measures may, where the WTO Agreement applies thereto, only be adopted in accordance with the procedures and under the conditions laid down thereby or the relevant Community internal legislation.

6.   The Parties shall exchange information taking into account the limitations imposed by the requirements of professional and business confidentiality.

Article 34 (SAA 70)

With regard to public undertakings, and undertakings to which special or exclusive rights have been granted, each Party shall ensure that as from the third year following the date of entry into force of this Agreement, the principles of the Treaty establishing the European Community, in particular Article 86 thereof, are upheld.

Article 35 (SAA 71)
Intellectual, Industrial and Commercial Property

1.   Pursuant to the provisions of this Article and Annex VI, the Parties confirm the importance that they attach to ensure adequate and effective protection and enforcement of intellectual, industrial and commercial property rights.

2.   The Former Yugoslav Republic of Macedonia shall take the necessary measures in order to guarantee no later than five years after entry into force of this Agreement a level of protection of intellectual, industrial and commercial property rights similar to that existing in the Community, including effective means of enforcing such rights.

3.   The Former Yugoslav Republic of Macedonia undertakes to accede, within the period referred above, to the multilateral conventions on intellectual, industrial and commercial property rights referred to in Annex VI.

4.   If problems in the area of intellectual, industrial and commercial property affecting trading conditions occur, they shall be referred urgently to the Cooperation Council, at the request of either Party, with a view to reaching mutually satisfactory solutions.

ANNEX VI

INTELLECTUAL, INDUSTRIAL AND COMMERCIAL PROPERTY RIGHTS
(referred to in Article 35)

1.   Article 35(3) concerns the following Multilateral Conventions:

- Budapest Treaty on the International Recognition of the Deposit of Microorganisms for the purposes of Patent Procedures (1977, modified in 1980);

- Protocol relating to the Madrid Agreement concerning the International Registration of Marks (Madrid, 1989);

- International Convention for the Protection of New Varieties of Plants (UPOV Geneva Act, 1991).

The Cooperation Council may decide that Article 35(3) shall apply to other multilateral conventions.

2.   The Parties confirm the importance they attach to the obligations arising from the following multilateral conventions:

- International Convention for the Protection of Performers, Producers of Phonograms and Broadcasting Organisations (Rome, 1961);

- Paris Convention for the Protection of Industrial Property (Stockholm Act, 1967 and amended in 1979);

- Madrid Agreement concerning the International Registration of Marks (Stockholm Act, 1967 and amended in 1979);

- Patent Cooperation Treaty (Washington, 1970, amended in 1979 and modified in 1984);

- Convention for the Protection of Producers of Phonograms against Unauthorised Duplications of their Phonograms (Geneva 1971);

- Berne Convention for the Protection of Literary and Artistic Works (Paris Act, 1971);

- Nice Agreement concerning the International Classification of Goods and Services for the purposes of the Registration of Marks (Geneva, 1977 and amended in 1979).

3.   From entry into force of this Agreement, the former Yugoslav Republic of Macedonia shall grant to Community companies and nationals, in respect of the recognition and protection of intellectual, industrial and commercial property, treatment no less favourable than that granted by it to any third country under bilateral agreements.

*

EURO-MEDITERRANEAN INTERIM ASSOCIATION AGREEMENT ON TRADE AND COOPERATION BETWEEN THE EUROPEAN COMMUNITY, OF THE ONE PART, AND THE PALESTINE LIBERATION ORGANIZATION (PLO) FOR THE BENEFIT OF THE PALESTINIAN AUTHORITY OF THE WEST BANK AND THE GAZA STRIP, OF THE OTHER PART *

[excerpts]

The Euro-Mediterranean Interim Association Agreement on Trade and Cooperation between the European Community, of the One Part, and the Palestine Liberation Organization (PLO) for the Benefit of the Palestinian Authority of the West Bank and the Gaza Strip, of the Other Part was signed on 24 February 1997. It entered in to force on 1 July 1997. The member States of the European Communities are: Austria, Belgium, Denmark, Finland, France, Germany, Greece, Ireland, Italy, Luxembourg, the Netherlands, Portugal, Spain, Sweden and the United Kingdom.

TITLE II

PAYMENTS, CAPITAL, COMPETITION, INTELLECTUAL PROPERTY AND PUBLIC PROCUREMENT

CHAPTER 1

Current Payments and Movement of Capital

Article 27

Subject to the provisions of Article 29, the Parties undertake to impose no restrictions on any current transactions.

Article 28

1.   With regard to transactions on the capital account of balance of payments, the Parties undertake to impose no restrictions on the movement of capital relating to direct investments in the West Bank and the Gaza Strip in companies formed in accordance with current laws, nor on the liquidation and repatriation of the yield from such investments, or any profit stemming therefrom.

2.   The Parties shall consult each other with a view to facilitating the movement of capital between the Community and the West Bank and the Gaza Strip.

---

* *Source*: European Communities (1997)."Euro-Mediterranean Interim Association Agreement on Trade and Cooperation between the European Community, of the One Part, and the Palestine Liberation Organization (PLO) for the Benefit of the Palestinian Authority of the West Bank and the Gaza Strip, of the Other Part", *Official Journal of the European Communities*, L 187, 16 July 1997, pp. 3 - 135; available also on the Internet (http://europa.eu.int). [Note added by the editor.]

Article 29

Where one or more Member States of the Community, or the Palestinian Authority, is in serious balance of payments difficulties, or under threat thereof, the Community or the Palestinian Authority, as the case may be, may, in accordance with the conditions established under the GATT and Articles VII and XIV of the Articles of Agreement of the International Monetary Fund, adopt restrictions on current transactions which shall be of limited duration and may not go beyond what is necessary to remedy the balance of payments situation. The Community or the Palestinian Authority, as the case may be, shall inform the other Party forthwith and shall submit to it as soon as possible a timetable for the elimination of the measures concerned.

CHAPTER 2

Competition, Intellectual Property and Public Procurement

Article 30

1.   The following are incompatible with the proper functioning of this Agreement, insofar as they may affect trade between the Community and the Palestinian Authority:

(i)   all agreements between undertakings, decisions by associations of undertakings and concerted practices between undertakings which have as their object or effect the prevention, restriction or distortion of competition;

(ii)   abuse by one or more undertakings of a dominant position in the territories of the Community or the West Bank and the Gaza Strip as a whole or in a substantial part thereof;

(iii)   any public aid which distorts or threatens to distort competition by favouring certain undertakings or the production of certain goods.

2.   The Parties shall, as appropriate, assess any practice contrary to this Article on the basis of the criteria resulting from the application of Community competition rules.

3.   The Joint Committee shall, before 31 December 2001, adopt by decision the necessary rules for the implementation of paragraphs 1 and 2.

Until these rules are adopted, the provisions of the Agreement on Subsidies and Countervailing Measures shall be applied as the rules for the implementation of paragraph 1 (iii) and the relevant parts of paragraph 2.

4.   As regards the implementation of paragraph 1 (iii), the Parties recognize that the Palestinian Authority may wish to use, during the period until 31 December 2001, public aid to undertakings as an instrument to tackle its specific development problems.

5.   Each Party shall ensure transparency in the area of public aid, inter alia by reporting annually to the other Party on the total amount and the distribution of the aid given by providing, upon request, information on aid schemes. Upon request by one Party, the other Party shall provide information on particular individual cases of public aid.

6.   With regard to products referred to in Title I, Chapter 2:

-       paragraph 1(iii) does not apply;

-       any practices contrary to paragraph 1(i) shall be assessed according to the criteria established by the Community on the basis of Articles 42 and 43 of the Treaty establishing the European Community and in particular those established in Council Regulation No.26/62.

7.   If the Community or the Palestinian Authority considers that a particular practice is incompatible with the terms of paragraph 1 of this Article, and:

-        is not adequately dealt with under the implementing rules referred to in paragraph 3, or

-       in the absence of such rules, and if such practice causes or threatens to cause serious prejudice to the interests of the other Party or material injury to its domestic industry, including its services industry,

it may take appropriate measures after consultation within the Joint Committee or after thirty working days following referral for such consultation.

With reference to practices incompatible with paragraph 1 (iii) of this Article, such appropriate measures, when the GATT is applicable to them, may only be adopted in accordance with the procedures and under the conditions laid down by the GATT or by any other relevant instrument negotiated under its auspices and applicable between the Parties.

8.   Notwithstanding any provisions to the contrary adopted in accordance with paragraph 3, the Parties shall exchange information taking into account the limitations imposed by the requirements of professional and business secrecy.

Article 31

The Member States and the Palestinian Authority shall progressively adjust, without prejudice to their commitments to the GATT where appropriate, any State monopolies of a commercial character, so as to ensure that, by 31 December 2001, no discrimination regarding the conditions under which goods are procured and marketed exists between nationals of the Member Sates and the Palestinian people of the West Bank and the Gaza Strip. The Joint Committee will be informed about the measures adopted to implement this objective.

Article 32

With regard to pubic enterprises and enterprises to which special or exclusive rights have been granted, the Joint Committee shall ensure that by 31 December 2001 there is neither enacted nor maintained any measure distorting trade between the Community and the Palestinian Authority contrary to the Parties' interests. This provision should not obstruct the performance in law or in fact of the particular tasks assigned to those undertakings.

Article 33

1.   The Parties shall grant and ensure adequate and effective protection of intellectual, industrial and commercial property rights in accordance with the highest international standards, including effective means of enforcing such rights.

2.   The implementation of this Article shall be regularly reviewed by the Parties. If problems in the area of intellectual, industrial and commercial property affecting trading conditions occur, urgent consultations shall be undertaken within the framework of the Joint Committee, at the request of either Party, with a view to reaching mutually satisfactory solutions.

Article 34

1.   The Parties agree on the objective of reciprocal and gradual liberalization of public procurement contracts.

2.   The Joint Committee shall take the necessary measures to implement paragraph 1.

TITLE III

ECONOMIC COOPERATION AND SOCIAL DEVELOPMENT

Article 35
Objectives

1.   The Parties undertake to intensify economic cooperation in their mutual interest and in accordance with the overall objectives of this Agreement.

2.   The aim of cooperation shall be to support the Palestinian Authority's own efforts to achieve sustainable economic and social development.

Article 36
Scope

1.   Cooperation shall focus primarily on sectors suffering from internal difficulties or affected by the overall process of liberalization of the economy of the West Bank and the Gaza Strip, and in particular by the liberalization of trade between the West Bank and the Gaza Strip and the Community.

2.   Similarly, cooperation shall focus on areas likely to bring the economies of the Community and the West Bank and the Gaza Strip closer together, particularly those which will generate sustainable growth and employment.

3.   Cooperation shall encourage the implementation of measures designed to develop intra-regional cooperation.

4.   Conservation of the environment and ecological balance shall be taken into account in the implementation of the various sectors of economic cooperation to which it is relevant.

5.   The Parties may agree to extend economic cooperation to other sectors not covered by the provisions of this Title.

Article 37
Methods and Modalities

Economic cooperation shall be implemented in particular by:

(a)   a regular economic dialogue between the Parties, which covers all areas of macro-economic policy and in particular budgetary policy, the balance of payments and monetary policy;

(b)   regular exchange of information and ideas in every sector of cooperation including meetings of officials and experts;

(c)   transfer of advice, expertise and training;

(d)   implementation of joint actions such as seminars and workshops;

(e)   technical, administrative and regulatory assistance;

(f)   encouragement of joint ventures;

(g)   dissemination of information on cooperation.

Article 38
Industrial Cooperation

The aim will be to:

-    support the Palestinian Authority, in its efforts to modernize and diversify industry and, in particular, to create an environment favourable to private sector and industrial development;

-    foster cooperation between the two Parties' economic operators;

-    foster cooperation regarding industrial policy, competitiveness in an open economy and the modernization and development of industry;

-    support for policies to diversify production and exports and external outlets;

-    promote research and development, innovation and technology transfer as far as they benefit industry;

-    develop and enhance the human resources required by industry;

-    facilitate access to venture and risk financing facilities for the benefit of Palestinian industry.

Article 39
Investment promotion and investment

The objective of cooperation will be the creation of a favourable and stable environment for investment in the West Bank and the Gaza Strip.

Cooperation will take the form of promotion of investment. This will entail the development of:

- harmonized and simplified administrative procedures;

- co-investment machinery, especially for small and medium-sized enterprises (SMEs) of both Parties;

- information channels and means of identifying investment opportunities;

- an environment conducive to investment in the West Bank and the Gaza Strip.

Cooperation may also extend to the conception and implementation of projects demonstrating the effective acquisition and use of basic technologies, the use of standards, the development of human resources (e.g. in technologies and management) and the creation of jobs.

Article 41
Approximation of legislation

The objective of cooperation will be to approximate Palestinian Council legislation to that of the Community, in the areas covered by the Agreement.

Article 42
Small and Medium-sized Enterprises

The objective of cooperation will be the creation of an environment propitious to the development of SMEs on local and export markets through, inter alia:

- promotion of contacts between enterprises, in particular through recourse to the Community's networks and instruments for the promotion of industrial cooperation and partnership;

- easier access to investment finance;

- information and support services;

- enhancement of human resources with the aim of stimulating innovation and the setting-up of projects and business ventures.

Article 43
Financial Services

The objective of cooperation will be the improvement and development of financial services.

It will take the form of:

- encouraging the strengthening and restructuring of the Palestinian financial sector;

- improving Palestinian accounting, supervisory and regulatory systems of banking, insurance and other parts of the financial sector.

Article 51
Tourism

Priorities for cooperation shall be:

- promoting investments in tourism;

- improving the knowledge of the tourist industry and ensuring greater consistency of policies affecting tourism;

- making tourism more competitive through support for increased professionalism ensuring the balanced and sustainable development of tourism.

TITLE VI INSTITUTIONAL, GENERAL AND FINAL PROVISIONS

Article 63

1.   A Joint Committee for European Community-Palestinian Authority trade and cooperation, referred to in this Agreement as 'the Joint Committee`, is hereby established. It shall have the power to take decisions in the cases provided for in the Agreement as well as in other cases necessary for the purpose of attaining the objectives set out in the Agreement.

The decisions taken shall be binding on the Parties, which shall take such measures as are required to implement them.

2.   The Joint Committee may also formulate any resolutions, recommendations or opinions which it considers desirable for the attainment of the common objectives and the smooth functioning of the Agreement.

3.   The Joint Committee shall adopt its own rules of procedure.

*

FREE TRADE AREA AGREEMENT BETWEEN THE REPUBLIC OF TURKEY AND THE REPUBLIC OF LATVIA *
[excerpts]

The Free Trade Area Agreement between the Republic of Turkey and the Republic of Latvia was signed on 16 June 1998. It entered into force on 1 July 2000.

CHAPTER III

Right of Establishment and Supply of Services

Article 13

1. The Parties shall seek to widen the scope of the Agreement to cover the right of establishment of firms of one Party in the territory of the other Party and the liberalization of the provision of services by one Party's firms to consumers of services in the other.

2. The Parties will discuss this cooperation in the Joint Committee with the aim of developing and deepening their relations under this Article.

CHAPTER IV

Article 25
Rules of Competition Concerning Undertakings, Public Aid

1. The following are incompatible with the proper functioning of this Agreement, in so far as they affect trade between the Parties:

   (a) all agreements between undertakings, decisions by associations of undertakings and concerted practices between undertakings which have as their object or effect the prevention, restriction or distortion of competition;

   (b) abuse by one or more undertakings of a dominant position in the territories of the Parties as a whole or in a substantial part thereof;

   (c) any public aid which distorts or threatens to distort competition by favoring certain undertakings or the production of certain goods. The provisions of this paragraph shall not apply to products referred in Chapter II.

2. Each Party shall ensure transparency in the area of public aid inter alia by reporting annually to the other Party on the total amount and the distribution of the aid given and by

* *Source*: World Trade Organization (2001). "Free Trade Area Agreement between the Republic of Turkey and the Republic of Latvia", World Trade Organization, WT/REG116/1, 22 January 2001; available also on the Internet (http://www.wto.org). [Note added by the editor.]

providing, upon request, information on aid schemes. Upon request by one Party, the other Party shall provide information on particular individual cases of public aid.

3.   If Turkey or Latvia considers that a particular practice is incompatible with the terms of the first paragraph of this Article, and:

(a)   is not adequately dealt with under the implementing rules referred to in paragraph 3 of this Article, or

(b)   in the absence of such rules, and if such practice causes or threatens to cause serious prejudice to the interest of the other Party or material injury to its domestic industry,

it may take appropriate measures under the conditions and in accordance with the provisions laid down in Article 21 of this Agreement.

4.   In the case of practices incompatible with paragraph 1(c) of this Article, such appropriate measures may, where the WTO/GATT 1994 applies thereto, only be adopted in conformity with the procedures and under the conditions laid down by the WTO/GATT 1994 and any other relevant instrument negotiated under its auspices which are applicable between the Parties.

5.   Notwithstanding any provisions to the contrary adopted in conformity with paragraph 3 of this Article, the Parties shall exchange information taking into account the limitations imposed by the requirements of professional and business secrecy.

Article 27
Intellectual, Industrial and Commercial Property

1.   Pursuant to the provisions of this Article and of Annex IV, by 1.1.1999, the Parties shall ensure adequate and effective protection of intellectual, industrial and commercial property rights in accordance with the international standards, including effective means of enforcing such rights.

2.   If problems in the area of intellectual, industrial and commercial property affecting trading conditions were to occur, urgent consultations within the Joint Committee will be undertaken, at the request of either party, with a view to reaching mutually satisfactory solutions.

Article 28
Public Procurement

1.   The Parties consider the opening up of the award of public contracts on the basis of non-discrimination and reciprocity, to be a desirable objective.

2.   As of the entry into force of this Agreement, both Parties shall grant each other's companies access to contract award procedures a treatment no less favorable than that granted to companies of any other country according to the provisions of their internal legislation.

Article 29
Establishment of the Joint Committee

1.   A Joint Committee is hereby established in which each Party shall be represented. The Joint Committee shall be responsible for the administration of this Agreement and shall ensure its proper implementation.

2.   For the purpose of the proper implementation of this Agreement, the Parties shall exchange information and, at the request of any Party, shall hold consultations within the Joint Committee. The Joint Committee shall keep under review the possibility of further removal of the obstacles to trade between the Parties.

3.   The Joint Committee may, in accordance with the provisions of paragraph 3 of Article 30, take decisions in the cases provided for in this Agreement. On other matters the Joint Committee may make recommendations.

Annex IV referred to in Article 27

1.   Paragraph 1 of Article 27 concerns the following multilateral conventions:

- Bern Convention for the Protection of Literary and Artistic Works (Paris Act, 1971);

- International Convention for the Protection of Performers, Producers of Phonograms and Broadcasting Organisations (Rome, 1961);

- Nice Agreement concerning the International Classification of Goods and Services for the purposes of the Registration of Marks (Geneva, 1977 and amended in 1979);

- Protocol relating to the Madrid Agreement concerning the International Registration of Marks (Madrid, 1989);

- Budapest Treaty of the International Recognition of the Deposit of Microorganisms for the Purposes of Patent Procedures (1977, modified in 1980);

- International Convention for the Protection of New Varieties of Plants (UPOV) (Geneva Act, 1991).

The Joint Committee may decide that paragraph 1 of Article 27 shall apply to other multilateral conventions.

2.   The Parties confirm the importance they attach to the obligations arising from the following multilateral conventions:

- Madrid Agreement concerning the International Registration of Marks (Stockholm Act, 1967 and amended in 1979);

- Paris Convention for the Protection of Industrial Property (Stockholm Act 1967 and amended in 1979);

- Patent Co-operation Treaty (Washington 1970, amended in 1979 and modified in 1984).

*

FREE TRADE AGREEMENT BETWEEN THE REPUBLIC OF TURKEY AND THE REPUBLIC OF MACEDONIA *
[excerpts]

The Free Trade Agreement between the Republic of Turkey and the Republic of Macedonia was signed on 7 September 1999. It entered into force on 1 September 2000.

CHAPTER III

Right of Establishment and Supply of Services

Article 13

1.   The Parties to this Agreement recognize the growing importance of certain areas, such as services and investments. In their efforts to gradually develop and broaden their co-operation, in particular in the context of the European integration, they will co-operate with the aim of achieving a progressive liberalization and mutual opening of their markets for investments and trade in services, taking into account relevant provisions of the General Agreement on Trade and Services.

2.   The Parties will discuss in the Joint Committee this cooperation with the aim of developing and deepening of their relations governed in this Article.

CHAPTER IV

Article 23
Payments

Any settlement and payment arising from trade of goods, services and rights to non-material goods between both states shall be made in convertible currency, in accordance with the respective legislation of the Parties.

Article 24
Rules of Competition Concerning Undertakings, State Aid

1.   The following are incompatible with the proper functioning of this Agreement, in so far as they affect trade between the Parties:

   (a)   all agreements between undertakings, decisions by associations of undertakings and concerted practices between undertakings which have as their object or effect the prevention, restriction or distortion of competition;

---

* *Source*: World Trade Organization (2001). "Free Trade Agreement between the Republic of Turkey and the Republic of Macedonia", World Trade Organization, WT/REG115/1, 22 January 2001; available on the Internet (http://www.wto.org). [Note added by the editor.]

(b)   abuse by one or more undertakings of dominant position in the territories of the Parties as a whole or in a substantial part thereof;

(c)   any state aid which distorts or threatens to distort competition by favoring certain undertakings or the production of certain goods.

2.   Each Party shall ensure transparency in the area of state aid. Upon request by one Party, the other Party shall provide information on particular individual cases of state aid.

3.   For the purpose of applying the provisions of paragraph 1 of this Article, the Parties will take the measures in conformity with the procedures and under the conditions laid down in their respective Agreements with the European Communities.   In case of any change in those procedures and/or conditions these changes will be applicable between the Parties.

4.   If the Parties consider that a particular practice is incompatible with the terms of the first paragraph of this Article, and:

(a)   is not adequately dealt with under the implementing rules referred to in paragraph 3 of this Article, or;

(b)   in the absence of such rules, and if such practice causes or threatens to cause serious prejudice to the interest of the other Party or material injury to its domestic industry, including its services industry,

it may take appropriate measures after consultation within the Joint Committee or after thirty working days following referral for such consultation.

5.   In the case of practices incompatible with paragraph 1(c) of this Article, such appropriate measures may, where the WTO/GATT 1994 applies thereto, only be adopted in conformity with the procedures and under the conditions laid down by the WTO/GATT 1994 and any other relevant instrument negotiated under its auspices which are applicable between the Parties.

6.   Notwithstanding any provisions to the contrary adopted in conformity with paragraph 3 of this Article, the Parties shall exchange information taking into account the limitations imposed by the requirements of professional and business secrecy.

Article 25
Balance of Payments Difficulties

Where either Party is in a serious balance of payments difficulties or under threat thereof, the Party concerned may in accordance with the conditions laid down within the framework of WTO/GATT 1994 and with Article VIII of the Articles of Agreement of International Monetary Fund, adopt restrictive measures, which shall be of limited duration and may not go beyond what is necessary to remedy the balance of payments situation. The Party concerned shall inform the other Party forthwith of their introduction and present to the other Party, as soon as possible, of a time schedule of their removal.

Article 26
Intellectual, Industrial and Commercial Property

1.   The Parties shall provide suitable and effective protection of intellectual, industrial and commercial property rights in line with the highest international standards. This shall encompass effective means of enforcing such rights.

2.   Implementation of this Article shall be regularly assessed by the Parties. If difficulties which affect trade arise in connection with intellectual, industrial and commercial property rights, either Party may request urgent consultations to find mutually satisfactory solutions.

Article 27
Public Procurement

1.   The Parties consider the opening up of the award of public contracts on the basis of non-discrimination and reciprocity, to be a desirable objective.

2.   As of the entry into force of this Agreement, both Parties shall grant each other's companies access to contract award procedures a treatment no less favorable than that accorded to companies of any other country.

Article 28
Establishment of the Joint Committee

1.   A Joint Committee is hereby established in which each Party shall be represented. The Joint Committee shall be responsible for the administration of this Agreement and shall ensure its proper implementation.

2.   For the purpose of the proper implementation of this Agreement, the Parties shall exchange information and, at the request of either Party, shall hold consultations within the Joint Committee. The Joint Committee shall keep under review the possibility of further removal of the obstacles to trade between the Parties.

3.   The Joint Committee may, in accordance with the provisions of paragraph 3 of Article 29, take decisions in the cases provided for in this Agreement. On other matters the Joint Committee may make recommendations.

*

FREE TRADE AGREEMENT BETWEEN TURKEY AND THE REPUBLIC OF SLOVENIA[*]
[excerpts]

The Free Trade Agreement between Turkey and the Republic of Slovenia was signed on 5 May 1998. It entered into force on 1 June 2000.

The Republic of Turkey and the Republic of Slovenia (hereinafter "the Parties"),

…

Convinced that this Agreement will create a new climate for their economic relations and in particular for the development of trade, investment and economic and technological co-operation;

Have agreed as follows:

CHAPTER III

Article 26
Payments

1.   Payments in freely convertible currencies relating to commercial transactions within framework of this Agreement between the Parties and the transfer of such payments to the territory of the Party where the creditor resides shall be free from any restrictions.

2.   The Parties shall refrain from any exchange or administrative restrictions other than those existing in the current legislation of the Parties, on the grant, repayment or acceptance of short and medium term credits covering commercial transactions within framework of this Agreement in which resident participates.

3.   Notwithstanding the provisions of paragraph 2, any measures concerning current payments connected with the movement of goods shall be in conformity with the conditions laid down under Article VIII of the Articles of the Agreement of the International Monetary Fund.

Article 27
Rules of competition concerning undertakings, State aid

1.   The following are incompatible with the proper functioning of this Agreement in so far as they may affect trade between the Parties:

---

[*]   *Source*: World Trade Organization (2002). "Free Trade Agreement between Turkey and the Republic of Slovenia", World Trade Organization, WT/REG135/1, 5 March 2002; available also on the Internet (http://www.wto.org). [Note added by the editor.]

(a)   all agreements between undertakings, decisions by associations of undertakings and concerted practices between undertakings which have as their object or effect the prevention, restriction or distortion of competition;

(b)   abuse by one or more undertakings of a dominant position in the territories of the Parties as a whole or in a substantial part thereof;

(c)   any state aid which distorts or threatens to distort competition by favouring certain undertakings or certain products.

2.   The Parties shall ensure transparency in the area of state aid, in accordance with the provisions of the Agreement on Subsidies and Countervailing Measures and the WTO/GATT 1994 and each Party, upon request of the other Party, will provide information on aid schemes and on particular individual cases of state aid.

3.   With regard to products referred to in Chapter II the provisions in paragraph 1 (c) shall not apply.

4.   If a Party considers that a given practice is incompatible with this Article and if such practice causes or threatens to cause serious prejudice to the interest of that Party or material injury to its domestic industry, it may take appropriate measures under the conditions and in accordance with the procedure laid down in Article 23.

5.   Subject to its laws, regulations and policies, each Party will accord fair and equitable treatment to the individuals, companies, government agencies and other entities of the other Party engaged in the pursuit of activities under this Agreement.

Article 29
Protection of intellectual, industrial and commercial property

1.   Pursuant to the provisions of this Article and of Annex IV to this Agreement (hereinafter "Annex IV") the Parties shall grant and ensure adequate and effective protection of intellectual, industrial and commercial property rights in accordance with the highest international standards, including effective means of enforcing such rights.

2.   The implementation of this Article and of Annex IV shall be regularly reviewed by the Parties. If problems in the area of intellectual and commercial property affecting trading conditions were to occur, urgent consultation within the Joint Committee shall be undertaken, at the request of either Party, with a view to reaching mutually satisfactory solutions.

Article 30
Public procurement

1.   The Parties consider the liberalization of their respective public procurement markets as an objective of this Agreement.

2.   As of the entry into force of this Agreement the Parties shall grant each other's companies access to contract award procedures and treatment no less favourable than that accorded to companies of any other country.

3.   The Parties shall progressively develop their respective regulations for public procurement with the view to grant suppliers of the other Party by the end of the transitional period at the latest access to contract award procedures on their respective public procurement markets according to the provisions of the Agreement on Government Procurement concluded within the framework of the WTO and the Parties' undertakings therein.

4.   The Joint Committee shall examine developments related to the achievement of the objectives of this Article so as to ensure free access, transparency and mutual opening of their respective public procurement markets.

Article 31
The Joint Committee

1.   A Joint Committee is hereby established in which each Party shall be represented. The Joint Committee shall be responsible for the administration of this Agreement and shall ensure its proper implementation.

2.   For the purpose of the proper implementation of this Agreement, the Parties shall exchange information and, at the request of any Party, shall hold consultations within the Joint Committee. The Joint Committee shall keep under review the possibility of further removal of the obstacles to trade between the Parties.

3.   The Joint Committee may take decisions in the cases provided for in this Agreement. These decisions shall be implemented by the Parties in accordance with their legislation. The Joint Committee may also make recommendations on any other trade and economic matter of mutual interest to the Parties.

ANNEX IV
(referred to in paragraph I of Article 29)

ON INTELLECTUAL, INDUSTRIAL AND COMMERCIAL PROPERTY

1   By I January 2001 the Republic of Slovenia shall accede the following multilateral convention on intellectual, industrial and commercial property rights to which the Republic of Turkey shall accede or is Party.

-      International Convention for the Protection of New Varieties of Plants ((UPOV) Geneva Act, 1991).

2.   The Republic of Turkey shall also accede the following multilateral conventions by 1 January 2001 to which the Republic of Slovenia shall accede or is Party.

-      Protocol relating to the Madrid Agreement concerning the International Registration of Marks (Madrid, 1989);

-      Budapest Treaty on the International Recognition of the Deposit of Microorganisms for the purpose of Patent Procedures (1977, modified in 1980);

-      International Convention for the Protection of Performers, Producers of Phonograms and Broadcasting Organizations (Rome, 1961);

- International Convention for the Protection of New Varieties of Plants ((UPOV) Geneva Act, 199 1).

3. The Joint Committee may recommend that the Parties accede to other multilateral conventions in this field.

4. The Parties confirm the importance they attach to the obligations arising from the following multilateral conventions:

- Agreement Establishing the World Trade Organization - Agreement on Trade Related Aspects of the Intellectual Property Rights (TRIPs) (Marrakesh 1994),

- Paris Convention for the Protection of Industrial Property (Stockholm Act, 1967 and amended in 1979);

- Patent Co-operation Treaty (Washington, 1970, amended in 1979 and modified in 1984);

- Berne Convention for the Protection of Literary and Artistic Works (Paris Act, 1971).

*

INTERIM AGREEMENT BETWEEN THE EUROPEAN FREE TRADE ASSOCIATION (EFTA) STATES AND THE PALESTINE LIBERATION ORGANIZATION (PLO) FOR THE BENEFIT OF THE PALESTINIAN AUTHORITY *
[excerpts]

> The Interim Agreement between the European Free Trade Association (EFTA) States and the Palestine Liberation Organization (PLO) for the Benefit of the Palestinian Authority was signed on 30 November 1998. It entered in to force on 1 July 1999. The member States of the European Free Trade Association are: Iceland, Liechtenstein, Norway and Switzeland.

The Republic of Iceland, the Principality of Liechtenstein, the Kingdom of Norway, the Swiss Confederation (hereinafter referred to as the EFTA States)

and

the PLO for the benefit of the Palestinian Authority (hereinafter referred to as the Palestinian Authority),

…

14. **Convinced** that this Agreement provides an appropriate framework for exchange of information and views on economic developments and trade as well as related matters,

15. **Convinced** that this Agreement will create favourable conditions to strengthen both bilateral and multilateral relations between the Parties in the economic field, in particular concerning trade and investment,

17. **HAVE DECIDED**, in pursuit of the above, to conclude the following interim Agreement (hereinafter called this Agreement):

ARTICLE 13
Payments and Transfers

1.   Payments relating to trade between an EFTA State and the West Bank and the Gaza Strip and the transfer of such payments to the territory of the Party to this Agreement where the creditor resides, shall be free from any restrictions.

2.   The Parties to this Agreement shall refrain from any currency exchange or administrative restrictions on the grant, repayment or acceptance of short and medium-term credits covering commercial transactions in which a resident participates.

---

* *Source*: European Free Trade Association Secretariat (1998). "Interim Agreement between the European Free Trade Association (EFTA) States and Palestine Liberation Organization (PLO) for the Benefit of the Palestinian Authority", available on the Internet (http://secretariat.efta.int). [Note added by the editor.]

3.   No restrictive measures shall apply to transfers related to investments and in particular to the repatriation of amounts invested or reinvested and of any kind of revenues stemming therefrom.

ARTICLE 14
Public procurement

1.   The Parties to this Agreement consider the effective liberalization of their respective public procurement markets, on the basis of non-discrimination and reciprocity, as an integral objective of this Agreement.

2.   To this effect, the Parties shall co-operate within the framework of the Joint Committee.

ARTICLE 15
Protection of intellectual property

1.   The Parties shall grant and ensure adequate and effective protection of intellectual property rights in accordance with the highest international standards. They shall adopt and take adequate and effective measures for the enforcement of such rights against infringement thereof, in particular against counterfeiting and piracy.

2.   The Parties shall co-operate in matters of intellectual property in accordance with Article 26 (Technical assistance) of this Agreement.

3.   The implementation of this Article shall be regularly reviewed by the Parties. If problems which affect trade arise in connection with intellectual property rights, urgent consultations shall be undertaken within the framework of the Joint Committee, at the request of any Party, with a view to reaching mutually satisfactory solutions.

ARTICLE 16
Rules of competition concerning undertakings

1.   The following are incompatible with the proper functioning of this Agreement in so far as they may affect trade between an EFTA State and the West Bank and the Gaza Strip:

   (a)   all agreements between undertakings, decisions by associations of undertakings and concerted practices between undertakings which have as their object or effect the prevention, restriction or distortion of competition;

   (b)   abuse by one or more undertakings of a dominant position in the territories of the Parties to this Agreement as a whole or in a substantial part thereof.

2.   The provisions of paragraph 1 shall also apply to the activities of public undertakings, and undertakings for which the Parties to this Agreement grant special or exclusive rights, in so far as the application of these provisions does not obstruct the performance, in law or in fact, of the particular public tasks assigned to them.

3.   If a Party to this Agreement considers that a given practice is incompatible with the provisions of paragraphs 1 and 2, it may take appropriate measures under the conditions and in

accordance with the procedures laid down in Article 23 (Procedure for the application of safeguard measures).

ARTICLE 22
Balance of payments difficulties

1.   The Parties to this Agreement shall endeavour to avoid the imposition of restrictive measures for balance of payments purposes.

2.   A Party in serious balance of payments difficulties, or under imminent threat thereof, may, in accordance with the conditions established under the General Agreement on Tariffs and Trade 1994 and the Understanding on the Balance-of-Payments Provisions of the General Agreement on Tariffs and Trade 1994, adopt trade restrictive measures, which shall be of limited duration and non-discriminatory, and may not go beyond what is necessary to remedy the balance of payments situation. Preference shall be given to price-based measures which shall be progressively relaxed as balance of payments conditions improve and eliminated when conditions no longer justify their maintenance. The Party introducing such restrictive measures, shall inform the other Parties to this Agreement and the Joint Committee forthwith, if possible, prior to their introduction and shall provide a time schedule for their removal. The Joint Committee shall, upon the request of any other Party, examine the need for maintaining the measures taken.

ARTICLE 25
Services and Investments

1.   The Parties recognize the growing importance of services and investments. In their efforts to gradually develop and broaden their co-operation, the Parties will co-operate with the aim of further promoting investments and achieving a gradual liberalization and mutual opening of markets for trade in services.

2.   The Parties will discuss this co-operation in the Joint Committee with the aim of developing and deepening their relations under this Agreement.

ARTICLE 26
Technical assistance

In order to facilitate the implementation of this Agreement the Parties shall agree upon appropriate modalities for technical assistance and co-operation of their respective authorities in trade-related matters. To this end, they shall co-ordinate efforts with relevant international organizations.

ARTICLE 27
The Joint Committee

1.   The implementation of this Agreement shall be supervised and administered by a Joint Committee.

2.   For the purpose of the proper implementation of this Agreement, the Parties to this Agreement shall exchange information and, at the request of any Party to this Agreement, shall hold consultations within the Joint Committee. The Joint Committee shall keep under review the

possibility of further removal of the obstacles to trade between the EFTA States and the West Bank and the Gaza Strip.

3.   The Joint Committee may take decisions in the cases provided for in this Agreement.

On other matters the Joint Committee may make recommendations.

*

FREE TRADE AGREEMENT BETWEEN TURKEY AND POLAND[*]
[excerpts]

> The Free Trade Agreement between Turkey and Poland was signed in October 1999. It entered into force on 1 May 2000.

CHAPTER III

Article 19
Payments

1.   Payments in freely convertible currencies relating to commercial transactions between the Parties within the framework of this Agreement and the transfer of such payments to the territory of the Party where the creditor resides shall be free from any restrictions.

2.   The Parties shall refrain from any exchange or administrative restrictions, other than those existing in their current legislation, on the grant, repayment or acceptance of short and medium term credits covering commercial transactions within the framework of this Agreement in which their residents participate.

3.   Notwithstanding the provisions of paragraph 2, any measures concerning current payments connected with the movement of goods shall be in conformity with the conditions laid down under Article VIII of the Articles of Agreement of the International Monetary Fund.

Article 20
Rules of competition concerning undertakings

1.   The following are incompatible with the proper functioning of this Agreement, in so far as they may affect trade between the Parties:

(a)   all agreements between undertakings, decisions by associations of undertakings and concerted practices between undertakings which have as their object or effect the prevention, restriction or distortion of competition;

(b)   abuse by one or more undertakings of a dominant position in the territories of the Parties as a whole or in a substantial part thereof.

2.   The provisions of paragraph 1 shall apply to the activities of all undertakings including public undertakings and undertakings to which the Parties grant special or exclusive rights. Undertakings entrusted with the operation of services of general economic interest or having the character of a revenue producing monopoly, shall be subject to provisions of paragraph 1 in so

---

[*] *Source*: World Trade Organization (1999). "Free Trade Agreement between Turkey and Poland", World Trade Organization, WT/REG107/1, 19 July 2000; available also on the Internet (http://www.wto.org/). [Note added by the editor.]

far as the application of these provisions does not obstruct the performance, in law or fact, of the particular public tasks assigned to them.

3.   With regard to products covered by Chapter II the provisions in paragraph 1(a) shall not apply to such agreements, decisions and practices which form an integral part of a national market organization.

4.   If a Party considers that a given practice is incompatible with this Article and if such practice causes or threatens to cause serious prejudice to the interest of that Party or material injury to its domestic industry, it may take appropriate measures under the conditions and in accordance with the procedure laid down in Article 30.

5.   Subject to its laws, regulations and policies, each Party will accord fair and equitable treatment to the individuals, companies, government agencies and other entities of the other Party engaged in the pursuit of activities under this Agreement.

Article 22
Public procurement

1.   The Parties consider the liberalization of their respective public procurement markets as an objective of this Agreement.

2.   The Parties shall progressively develop their respective regulations for public procurement with a view to grant suppliers of the other Party, access to contract award procedures on their respective public procurement markets according to the provisions of the Agreement on Government Procurement concluded in the framework of the WTO and the Parties' undertakings therein.

3.   The Joint Committee shall examine developments related to the achievement of the objectives of this Article and may recommend practical modalities of implementing the provisions of paragraph 2 so as to ensure free access, transparency and a mutual opening of their respective public procurement markets.

4.   During the examination referred to in paragraph 3, the Joint Committee may consider, especially in the light of development in this area in international relations, the possibility of expanding the coverage of the market opening provided for in paragraph 2.

5.   The Parties shall endeavour to accede to the relevant agreements negotiated under the auspices of the World Trade Organization.

Article 25
Protection of intellectual property

1.   The Parties shall grant and ensure adequate, effective and non-discriminatory protection of intellectual property rights including measures for the grant and the enforcement of such rights. The Parties confirm their will to respect Conventions on protection of intellectual property, which are specified in Annex IV to this Agreement.

2.   For the purpose of this Agreement "intellectual property" includes, in particular, copyright and neighbouring rights, trade marks, geographical indications, industrial designs,

utility models, patents, topographies of integrated circuits, undisclosed information including "know-how" and new varieties of plants.

3. The Parties shall co-operate in matters of intellectual property. They shall hold, upon request of each Party, expert consultations on these matters, in particular, on activities relating to the existing or to future international conventions on harmonization, administration and enforcement of intellectual property and on activities in international organizations, such as the World Trade Organization, the World Intellectual Property Organization, as well as relations of the Parties with other countries on matters concerning intellectual property.

Article 31
Balance-of-payments difficulties

1. The Parties shall endeavour to avoid the imposition of restrictive measures including measures relating to imports for balance of payment purposes.

2. When one of the Parties is in serious balance of payment difficulties, or under imminent threat thereof, the Party concerned may in accordance with the conditions established under the WTO/GATT 1994, and with Article VIII of the Articles of Agreement of International Monetary Fund adopt restrictive measures, including measures related to imports, which shall be of limited duration and may not go beyond what is necessary to remedy the balance of payments situation. The measures shall be progressively relaxed as balance of payments conditions improve and they shall be eliminated when conditions no longer justify their maintenance. The Party concerned shall inform the other Party forthwith of their introduction and, whenever practicable, of a time schedule of their removal.

Article 33
The Joint Committee

1. A Joint Committee is hereby established and shall be composed of the representatives of the Parties.

2. The Joint Committee shall be responsible for the administration of this Agreement and shall ensure its proper implementation. It shall examine any major issue arising within the framework of this Agreement and any other trade or economic issues of mutual interest. The Joint Committee shall keep under review the possibility of further removal of the obstacles to trade between the Parties.

3. For the purpose of the proper implementation of this Agreement, the Parties shall exchange information and, at the request of each Party, shall hold consultations within the Joint Committee.

4. The Joint Committee may take decisions in the cases provided for in this Agreement. These decisions shall be implemented by the Parties in accordance with their internal legislation. The Joint Committee may also make recommendations on any other trade and economic matter of mutual interest to the Parties.

Article 35
Services and investments

1.   The Parties to this Agreement recognize the growing importance of certain areas, such as services and investments. In their efforts to gradually develop and broaden their co-operation, in particular in the context of the European integration, they will co-operate with the aim of achieving a progressive liberalization and mutual opening of their markets for investments and trade in services, taking into account relevant provisions of the General Agreement on Trade and Services.

2.   The Parties will discuss in the Joint Committee the possibilities to extend their trade relations to the fields of foreign direct investment and trade in services.

ANNEX IV
referred to in paragraph 1 of Article 25

ON INTELLECTUAL PROPERTY

The multilateral Agreements mentioned in paragraph 1 of Article 25 are the following:

- Paris Convention of 20 March 1883 for the Protection of Industrial Property (Stockholm Act, 1967, as amended in 1979);

- Bern Convention of 9 September 1886 for the Protection of Literary and Artistic Works (Paris Act, 1971);

- International Convention of 26 October 1961 for the Protection of Performers, Producers of Phonograms and Broadcasting Organizations (Rome Convention);

- Agreement on Trade Related Aspects of Intellectual Property Rights of 15 April 1994;

- Budapest Treaty of the International Recognition of the Deposit of Microorganisms for the Purposes of Patent Procedure (1977, as amended in 1980);

- Patent Cooperation Treaty (Washington 1970, amended in 1979 and modified in 1984);

- Nice Agreement Concerning the International Classification of Goods and Services for the Purposes of the Registration of Marks (Stockholm 1967);

- International Convention for the Protection of New Varieties of Plants (UPOV) (Geneva Act 1991).

*

COOPERATION AGREEMENT BETWEEN THE EUROPEAN COMMUNITY AND THE PEOPLE'S REPUBLIC OF BANGLADESH ON PARTNERSHIP AND DEVELOPMENT *
[excerpts]

The Cooperation Agreement between the European Community and the People's Republic of Bangladesh on Partnership and Development was signed on 22 May 2000. The member States of the European Communities are: Austria, Belgium, Denmark, Finland, France, Germany, Greece, Ireland, Italy, Luxembourg, the Netherlands, Portugal, Spain, Sweden and the United Kingdom.

…

HAVING REGARD to the need to create favourable conditions for direct investment and economic cooperation between the Parties,

…

Article 2
Objectives

The principal objectives of this Agreement are to enhance and develop the various aspects of cooperation between the Parties in the areas which fall within the bounds of their respective competences, with the following aims:

…

3.   to promote investment and economic, technical and cultural links in their mutual interest;

…

Article 6
Economic cooperation

1.   In accordance with their respective policies and objectives and to the extent of their available resources, the Parties undertake to foster economic cooperation for mutual benefit. They will determine together, to their mutual advantage and within the limits of their respective competences, the areas and priorities for economic cooperation programmes and activities in the context of a clear cooperation strategy.

2.   The Parties agree to cooperate in the following broad fields:

(a)   developing a creative competitive economic environment in Bangladesh by facilitating the use of know-how and technology from the Community, including,

---

* *Source*: European Communities (2001)."Cooperation Agreement between the European Community and the People's Republic of Bangladesh on Partnership and Development", *Official Journal of the European Communities*, L 118, 27 April 2001, pp. 48 - 56; available also on the Internet (http://europa.eu.int). [Note added by the editor.]

in the fields of design, packaging, standards, such as consumer and environmental standards, new materials and products;

(b)   facilitating contacts between economic operators and other measures designed to promote commercial exchanges and investments;

(c)   facilitating exchanges of information on policies relating to enterprise and to small and medium-sized enterprises (SMEs), particularly with a view to improving the business and investment environment and encouraging closer contacts between SMEs, in order to promote trade and increase industrial cooperation opportunities;

(d)   strengthening management training in Bangladesh with a view to developing business operators who are able to interact effectively with the European business environment;

(e)   promoting dialogue between Bangladesh and the Community in the fields of energy policy and transfer of technology.

3.   Within the limits of their respective competences, the Parties undertake to encourage an increase in mutually beneficial investment by establishing a more favourable climate for private investments through better conditions for the transfer of capital and by supporting, where appropriate, the conclusion of conventions on the promotion and protection of investments between the Member States of the Community and Bangladesh.

Article 8
Cooperation in science and technology

The Parties in accordance with their respective policies and competences, will promote scientific and technological cooperation in areas of common interest. This shall include cooperation on standards and quality control.

Article 12
Joint Commission

1.   The Parties agree to set up a Joint Commission whose tasks shall be to:

(a)   ensure the proper functioning and implementation of the Agreement;

(b)   set priorities in relation to the aims of the Agreement;

(c)   make recommendations for promoting the objectives of the Agreement.

Provisions will be laid down on the frequency and venue of the meetings, chairmanship and the setting up of subgroups.

2.   The Joint Commission shall be composed of representatives of both sides, at the senior official level. The Joint Commission shall normally meet every other year, alternately in Brussels and in Dhaka, on a date to be fixed by mutual agreement. Extraordinary meetings may also be convened by agreement between the Parties.

3.   The Joint Commission may set up specialised subgroups to assist in the performance of its tasks and to coordinate the formulation and implementation of projects and programmes in the framework of the Agreement.

4.   The agenda for meetings of the Joint Commission shall be determined by agreement between the Parties.

5.   The Parties agree that it shall also be the task of the Joint Commission to ensure the proper functioning of any sectoral agreements concluded or which may be concluded between the Community and Bangladesh.

ANNEX I
Joint Declaration on Article 4(5) of the Agreement

Under the Agreement, the Parties agree that "intellectual, industrial and commercial property" comprises, in particular, copyright, including copyright in computer programs, and neighbouring rights, trademarks, service marks and geographical indications, including designation of origin, industrial designs and models, patents, configuration plans (topographies) of integrated circuits, sui generis protection of databases, protection of undisclosed information and protection against unfair competition.

ANNEX II

International conventions on intellectual, industrial and commercial property protection referred to in Article 4(5)

1.   Article 4(5)(b) concerns the following multilateral conventions:

- Berne Convention for the Protection of Literary and Artistic Work as last revised at Paris (Paris Act 1971).

- Madrid Agreement Concerning the International Registration of Marks as last revised at Stockholm (Stockholm Act 1967).

- Protocol Relating to the Madrid Agreement Concerning the International Registration of Marks (1989).

- International Convention for the Protection of Performers, Producers of Phonograms and Broadcasting Organisations (Rome Convention 1961).

- Patent Cooperation Treaty (PCT Union) as modified in 1984.

- Trademark Law Treaty (1994).

2.   Article 4(5)(c) concerns the following multilateral conventions:

- Nice Agreement Concerning the International Classification of Goods and Services for the Purposes of the Registration of Marks as revised at Geneva (Geneva Act 1977).

- Budapest Treaty on the International Recognition of the Deposit of Micro-organisms for the Purposes of Patent Procedure (1977).

- International Convention for the Protection of New Varieties of Plants (UPOV) as revised at Geneva (Geneva Act 1991).

- WIPO Copyright Treaty (Geneva 1996).

- WIPO Performances and Phonograms Treaty (Geneva 1996).

3.   The Joint Commission may decide that Article 4(5)(b) and (c) shall apply to other

*

FREE TRADE AGREEMENT BETWEEN CROATIA AND HUNGARY *
[excerpts]

The Free Trade Agreement between Croatia and Hungary was signed in 2001.

Article 20
Rules of Competition concerning Undertakings

1.   The following are incompatible with the proper functioning of this Agreement in so far as they may affect trade between the Parties:

(a)   all agreements between undertakings, decisions by associations of undertakings and concerted practices between undertakings which have as their object or effect the prevention, restriction or distortion of competition;

(b)   abuse by one or more undertakings of a dominant position in the territories of the Parties as a whole or in substantial part thereof.

2.   The provisions of paragraph 1 shall apply to the activities of all undertakings including public undertakings and undertakings to which the Parties grant special or exclusive rights. Undertakings entrusted with the operation of services of general economic interest or having the character of a revenue-producing monopoly, shall be subject to provisions of paragraph 1 insofar as the application of these provisions does not obstruct the performance, in law or fact, of the particular public tasks assigned to them.

3.   With regard to products referred to in Chapter II to this Agreement the provisions stipulated in paragraph 1(a) shall not apply to such agreements, decisions and practices which form an integral part of a national market organization.

4.   If a Party considers that a given practice is incompatible with paragraphs 1, 2 and 3 of this Article or if such practice causes or threatens to cause serious prejudice to the interest of that Party or material injury to its domestic industry, the Party concerned may take appropriate measures under the conditions and in accordance with the procedure laid down in Article 28 to this Agreement.

Article 22
Public Procurement

1.   The Parties consider the liberalization of their respective public procurement markets as an objective of this Agreement.

---

* *Source*: World Trade Organization (2001). "Free Trade Agreement between Croatia and Hungary ", World Trade Organization, WT/REG130/1, 15 November 2001, available on the Internet (http://www.wto.org). [Note added by the editor.]

2.   The Parties shall progressively develop their respective regulations for public procurement with a view to grant suppliers of the other Party access to contract award procedures on their respective public procurement markets.

3.   The Joint Committee shall examine developments related to the achievement of the objectives of this Article and may recommend practical modalities of implementing the provisions of paragraph 2 so as to ensure free access, transparency, full balance of rights and obligations and mutual opening of their respective public procurement markets.

Article 23
Protection of Intellectual Property

1.   The Parties shall grant and ensure the protection of intellectual property rights on a non-discriminatory basis, including measures for granting and enforcing such rights. The protection shall be improved to a level corresponding to the substantive standards of the multilateral agreements which are specified in Annex III to this Agreement by the date of entry into force of this Agreement.

2.   For the purpose of this Agreement the term "intellectual property protection" includes, in particular, protection of copyright and related rights, including computer programs, data bases, trade marks for goods and services, geographical indications including mark of origin, patents, industrial designs, new varieties of plants, topographies of integrated circuits, as well as undisclosed information on know-how.

3.   The Parties shall co-operate in matters of intellectual property. They shall hold, upon request of any Party, expert consultations on these matters, in particular, on activities relating to the existing or future international conventions on harmonisation, administration and enforcement of intellectual property and on activities in international organizations, such as the World Trade Organization and the World Intellectual Property Organization, as well as relations of the Parties with any third country on matters concerning intellectual property.

Article 29
Balance-of-Payments Difficulties

1.   The Parties shall endeavour to avoid the imposition of restrictive measures including measures relating to imports for balance of payments purposes.

2.   Where one of the Parties is in serious balance-of-payments difficulties, or under imminent threat thereof, the Party concerned may, in accordance with the conditions established under the GATT 1994 and the WTO adopt restrictive measures, including measures related to imports, which shall be of limited duration and may not go beyond what is necessary to remedy the balance of payments situation. The measures shall be progressively relaxed as balance of payments conditions improve and they shall be eliminated when conditions no longer justify their maintenance. The Party shall inform the other Party forthwith of their introduction and, whenever practicable, of a time schedule for their removal.

Article 31
The Joint Committee

1.   A Joint Committee is hereby established and shall be composed of representatives of the Parties.

2.   The implementation of this Agreement shall be supervised and administered by the Joint Committee.

3.   For the purpose of the proper implementation of this Agreement, the Parties shall exchange information and, at the request of any Party, shall hold consultations within the Joint Committee. The Joint Committee shall keep under review the possibility of further removal of the obstacles to trade between the Parties.

4.   The Joint Committee may take decisions in cases provided for in this Agreement. On other matters the Joint Committee may make recommendations.

Article 33
Services and Investment

1.   The Parties recognize the growing importance of certain areas such as services and investments. In their efforts to gradually develop and broaden their cooperation, in particular in the context of the European integration, they will co-operate with the aim of achieving a progressive liberalization and mutual opening of their markets for investments and trade in services, taking into account relevant provisions of the General Agreement on Trade in Services.

2.   The Parties will discuss in the Joint Committee the possibilities to extend their trade relations to the fields of foreign direct investment and trade in services.

ANNEX III
(referred to in paragraph 1 of Article 23)

ON INTELLECTUAL PROPERTY

1.   Paragraph 1 of Article 23 concerns the following multilateral conventions:

-       WTO Agreement on Trade Related Aspects of Intellectual Property Rights of 15 April 1994 (TRIPS Agreement);

-       International Convention for the Protection of Performers, Producers of Phonograms and Broadcasting Organizations of 26 October 1961 (Rome Convention);

-       Nice Agreement concerning the International Classification of Goods and Services for the purposes of the Registration of Marks (Geneva, 1977 and amended in 1979);

-       Protocol relating to the Madrid Agreement concerning the International Registration of Marks (Madrid, 1989);

- Budapest Treaty on the International Recognition of the Deposit of Microorganisms for the purpose of Patent Procedures (Budapest, 1977);

- International Convention for the Protection of New Varieties of Plants (UPOV, Geneva Act, 1991).

The Joint Committee may decide that the paragraph 1 of Article 23 shall apply to other multilateral conventions.

2.   The Parties confirm the importance they attach to the obligations arising from the following multilateral conventions:

- Bern Convention for the Protection of Literary and Artistic Works of 9 September 1971 (Paris Act, 1971);

- Paris Convention for the Protection of Industrial Property of 20 March 1996 (Stockholm Act, 1967 and amended in 1979);

- Patent Co-operation Treaty (Washington, 1970, amended in 1979 and modified in 1984).

*

INTERIM AGREEMENT ON TRADE AND TRADE-RELATED MATTERS BETWEEN THE EUROPEAN COMMUNITY, OF THE ONE PART, AND THE REPUBLIC OF CROATIA, OF THE OTHER PART *
[excerpts]

> The Interim Agreement on Trade and Trade-related Matters between the European Community, of the One Part, and the Republic of Croatia, of the Other Part was signed on 29 October 2001. The member States of the European Communities are: Austria, Belgium, Denmark, Finland, France, Germany, Greece, Ireland, Italy, Luxembourg, the Netherlands, Portugal, Spain, Sweden and the United Kingdom.

TITLE III

PAYMENTS, COMPETITION AND OTHER ECONOMIC PROVISIONS

Article 33 (SAA Article 59)

The Parties undertake to authorise, in freely convertible currency, in accordance with the provisions of Article VIII of the Articles of the Agreement of the International Monetary Fund, any payments and transfers on the current account of balance of payments between the Community and Croatia.

Article 34 (SAA Article 66)

1.   The Parties shall endeavour wherever possible to avoid the imposition of restrictive measures, including measures relating to imports, for balance of payments purposes. A Party adopting such measures shall present as soon as possible to the other Party a timetable for their removal.

2.   Where one or more Member States of the European Union or Croatia is in serious balance of payments difficulties, or under imminent threat thereof, the Community or Croatia, as the case may be, may, in accordance with the conditions established under the WTO Agreement, adopt restrictive measures, including measures relating to imports, which shall be of limited duration and may not go beyond what is strictly necessary to remedy the balance of payments situation. The Community or Croatia, as the case may be, shall inform the other Party forthwith.

3.   Any restrictive measures shall not apply to transfers related to investment and in particular to the repatriation of amounts invested or reinvested or any kind of revenues stemming therefrom.

---

* *Source*: European Communities (2001). "Interim Agreement on Trade and Trade-related Matters between the European Community, of the One Part, and the Republic of Croatia, of the Other Part", *Official Journal of the European Communities*, R 330 L, 14 December 2001 pp. 3 - 210; available also on the Internet (http://europa.eu.int). [Note added by the editor.]

Article 35 (SAA Article 70)

Competition and other economic provisions

1.   The following are incompatible with the proper functioning of the Agreement, in so far as they may affect trade between the Community and Croatia:

    (i)   all agreements between undertakings, decisions by associations of undertakings and concerted practices between undertakings which have as their object or effect the prevention, restriction or distortion of competition;

    (ii)   abuse by one or more undertakings of a dominant position in the territories of the Community or of Croatia as a whole or in a substantial part thereof;

    (iii)   any state aid which distorts or threatens to distort competition by favouring certain undertakings or certain products.

2.   Any practices contrary to this Article shall be assessed on the basis of criteria arising from the application of the competition rules applicable in the Community, in particular from Articles 81, 82, 86 and 87 of the Treaty establishing the European Community and interpretative instruments adopted by the Community institutions.

3.   The Parties shall ensure that an operationally independent public body is entrusted with the powers necessary for the full application of paragraph 1(i) and (ii) of this Article, regarding private and public undertakings and undertakings to which special rights have been granted.

4.   Croatia shall establish an operationally independent authority which is entrusted with the powers necessary for the full application of paragraph 1(iii) of this Article within one year from the date of entry into force of this Agreement. This authority shall have, inter alia, the powers to authorise state aid schemes and individual aid grants in conformity with paragraph 2 of this Article, as well as the powers to order the recovery of state aid that has been unlawfully granted.

5.   Each Party shall ensure transparency in the area of state aid, inter alia by providing to the other Party a regular annual report, or equivalent, following the methodology and the presentation of the Community survey on state aid. Upon request by one Party, the other Party shall provide information on particular individual cases of public aid.

6.   Croatia shall establish a comprehensive inventory of aid schemes instituted before the establishment of the authority referred to in paragraph 4 and shall align such aid schemes with the criteria referred to in paragraph 2 of this Article within a period of no more than four years from the entry into force of this Agreement.

7.   (a)   For the purposes of applying the provisions of paragraph 1(iii), the Parties recognise that during the first four years after the entry into force of this Agreement, any public aid granted by Croatia shall be assessed taking into account the fact that Croatia shall be regarded as an area identical to those areas of the Community described in Article 87(3)(a) of the Treaty establishing the European Community.

(b)   Within three years from the entry into force of this Agreement, Croatia shall submit to the Commission of the European Communities its GDP per capita figures harmonised at NUTS II level. The authority referred to in paragraph 4 and the Commission of the European Communities shall then jointly evaluate the eligibility of the regions of Croatia as well as the maximum aid intensities in relation thereto in order to draw up the regional aid map on the basis of the relevant Community guidelines.

8.   With regard to products referred to in Chapter II of Title II:

- paragraph 1(iii) shall not apply,

- any practices contrary to paragraph 1(i) shall be assessed according to the criteria established by the Community on the basis of Articles 36 and 37 of the Treaty establishing the European Community and specific Community instruments adopted on this basis.

9.   If one of the Parties considers that a particular practice is incompatible with the terms of paragraph 1 of this Article, it may take appropriate measures after consultation within the Interim Committee or after 30 working days following referral for such consultation.

Nothing in this Article shall prejudice or affect in any way the taking, by either Party, of anti-dumping or countervailing measures in accordance with the relevant Articles of GATT 1994 and WTO Agreement on Subsidies and Countervailing Measures or related internal legislation.

Article 36 (SAA Article 71)
Intellectual, industrial and commercial property

1.   Pursuant to the provisions of this Article and Annex VI, the Parties confirm the importance that they attach to ensure adequate and effective protection and enforcement of intellectual, industrial and commercial property rights.

2.   Croatia shall take the necessary measures in order to guarantee no later than three years after entry into force of this Agreement a level of protection of intellectual, industrial and commercial property rights similar to that existing in the Community, including effective means of enforcing such rights.

3.   The Interim Committee may decide to oblige Croatia to accede to specific multilateral Conventions in this area.

4.   If problems in the area of intellectual, industrial and commercial property affecting trading conditions occur, they shall be referred urgently to the Interim Committee, at the request of either Party, with a view to reaching mutually satisfactory solutions.

TITLE IV

INSTITUTIONAL, GENERAL AND FINAL PROVISIONS

Article 38

An Interim Committee is hereby established which shall supervise the application and implementation of this Agreement. It shall hold meetings at regular intervals and when circumstances require.

ANNEX VI

INTELLECTUAL, INDUSTRIAL AND COMMERCIAL PROPERTY RIGHTS
(referred to in Article 36)

1.   The Parties confirm the importance they attach to the obligations arising from the following Multilateral Conventions:

- International Convention for the Protection of Performers, Producers of Phonograms and Broadcasting Organizations (Rome, 1961),

- Paris Convention for the Protection of Industrial Property (Stockholm Act, 1967 and amended in 1979),

- Madrid Agreement concerning the International Registration of Marks (Stockholm Act, 1967 and amended in 1979),

- Patent Cooperation Treaty (Washington, 1970, amended in 1979 and modified in 1984),

- Convention for the Protection of Producers of Phonograms against Unauthorised Duplications of their Phonograms (Geneva 1971),

- Berne Convention for the Protection of Literary and Artistic Works (Paris Act, 1971),

- Nice Agreement concerning the International Classification of Goods and Services for the purposes of the Registration of Marks (Geneva, 1977 and amended in 1979),

- WIPO Copyright Treaty (Geneva, 1996),

- WIPO Performances and Phonograms Treaty (Geneva, 1996).

2.   From the entry into force of this Agreement, the Parties shall grant, in accordance with the TRIPS Agreement, to each others companies and nationals, in respect of the recognition and protection of intellectual, industrial and commercial property, treatment no less favourable than that granted by them to any third country under bilateral agreements.

*

FREE TRADE AGREEMENT BETWEEN THE REPUBLIC OF SLOVENIA AND BOSNIA AND HERZEGOVINA *
[excerpts]

The Free Trade Agreement between the Republic of Slovenia and Bosnia and Herzegovina was signed at Zenica on 3 October 2001. It entered into force on 1 January 2002.

The Republic of Slovenia and Bosnia and Herzegovina (hereinafter "the Parties"),

…

Considering the importance of the links existing between the Parties, their desire to strengthen those links and to further extend the relations established previously, in particular through the Agreement on Economic Co-operation between the Republic of Slovenia and Bosnia and Herzegovina signed on 7 November 1997, which entered into force on 22 November 1999;

Convinced that this Agreement will create a new climate for economic relations between the Parties and above all for the development of trade and investment;

…

Have agreed as follows:

Article 17
Rules of competition concerning undertakings

1.   The following are incompatible with the proper functioning of this Agreement insofar as they may affect trade between the Parties:

(a)   all agreements between undertakings, decisions by associations of undertakings and concerted practices between undertakings which have as their object or effect the prevention, restriction or distortion of competition;

(b)   abuse by one or more undertakings of a dominant position in the territories of the Parties as a whole or in a substantial part thereof.

2.   The provisions of paragraph 1 of this Article shall apply to the activities of all undertakings including public undertakings and undertakings to which the Parties grant special or exclusive rights. Undertakings entrusted with the operation of services of general economic interest or having the character of a revenue-producing monopoly, shall be subject to provisions of paragraph 1 of this Article insofar as the application of these provisions does not obstruct the performance, in law or in fact, of the particular public tasks assigned to them.

---

* *Source*: World Trade Organization (2002). "Free Trade Agreement between the Republic of Slovenia and Bosnia and Herzegovina"; World Trade Organization, WT/REG131/1, 30 April 2002; also available on the Internet (http://www.wto.org). [Note added by the editor.]

3.   With regard to agricultural products the provisions of paragraph 1 a. of this Article shall not apply to such agreements, decisions and practices which form an integral part of a national market organisation.

4.   If a Party considers that a given practice is incompatible with paragraphs 1, 2 and 3 of this Article and if such practice causes or threatens to cause serious prejudice to the interest of that Party or material injury to its domestic industry, it may take appropriate measures under the conditions and in accordance with the procedure laid down in Article 26 of this Agreement.

Article 19
Public procurement

1.   The Parties consider the liberalization of their respective public procurement markets as an objective of this Agreement.

2.   The Parties shall progressively adjust their respective rules, conditions and practices with a view to grant suppliers of the other Party access to contract award procedures on their respective public procurement markets.

3.   The Joint Committee shall examine developments related to the achievement of the objectives of this Article and may recommend practical modalities of implementing the provisions of paragraph 2 of this Article so as to ensure free access, transparency and mutual opening of their respective public procurement markets.

4.   The Parties shall endeavour to accede to the relevant Agreements negotiated under the auspices of the GATT 1994 and the WTO.

Article 20
Protection of intellectual property

1.   The Parties shall in accordance with their national legislation grant and ensure protection of intellectual property rights (industrial property rights and protection of copyright and related rights) to the nationals, companies and institutions of the other Party as well as to their legal successors under the same conditions applicable for the domestic nationals, companies and institutions.

2.   In addition, the Parties agree to respect mutually in accordance with their national legislation the intellectual property rights (industrial property rights and protection of copyright and related rights) of their nationals, companies and institutions in accordance with the standards of protection, which shall not be lower than that arising from the Bern Convention, Rome Convention and Paris Convention.

Article 27
Balance of payments difficulties

1.   The Parties shall endeavour to avoid the imposition of restrictive measures including measures relating to imports for balance of payments difficulties.

2.   Where one of the Parties is in serious balance of payments difficulties, or under imminent threat thereof, the Party concerned may, in accordance with the conditions established under the

GATT 1994 and the WTO, adopt restrictive measures, including measures related to imports, which shall be of limited duration and may not go beyond what is necessary to remedy the balance of payments situation. The measures shall be progressively relaxed as balance of payments conditions improve and they shall be eliminated when conditions no longer justify their maintenance. The Party concerned shall inform the other Party forthwith of their introduction and, whenever practicable, of a time schedule for their removal.

Article 29
Joint Committee

1.   A Joint Committee is hereby established and shall be composed of the representatives of the Parties.

2.   The implementation of this Agreement shall be supervised and administered by the Joint Committee.

3.   For the purpose of the proper implementation of this Agreement, the Parties shall exchange information and, at the request of a Party, shall hold consultations within the Joint Committee. The Joint Committee shall keep under review the possibility of further removal of the obstacles to trade between the Parties.

4.   The Joint Committee may take decisions in the cases provided for in this Agreement. On other matters the Joint Committee may make recommendations.

Article 31
Services and investments

1.   The Parties recognise the growing importance of certain areas, such as services and investments. In their efforts to gradually develop and broaden their co-operation, in particular in the context of the European integration, they will co-operate with the aim of achieving a progressive liberalisation and mutual opening of markets for investments and trade in services, taking into account relevant provisions of the General Agreement on Trade in Services.

2.   The Parties shall examine within the Joint Committee the possibilities to extend their relations to the fields of foreign direct investment and trade in services by separate agreements.

*

EURO-MEDITERRANEAN ASSOCIATION AGREEMENT BETWEEN THE EUROPEAN COMMUNITY AND ITS MEMBER STATES OF THE ONE PART, AND THE REPUBLIC OF LEBANON, OF THE OTHER PART *
[excerpts]

The Euro-Mediterranean Association Agreement between the European Community and Its Member States of the One Part, and the Republic of Lebanon, of the Other Part was signed on 17 June 2002. The member States of the European Communities are: Austria, Belgium, Denmark, Finland, France, Germany, Greece, Ireland, Italy, Luxembourg, the Netherlands, Portugal, Spain, Sweden and the United Kingdom.

ARTICLE 1

1.   An association is hereby established between the Community and its Member States, of the one part, and Lebanon, of the other part.

2.   The aims of this Agreement are to:

(a)   provide an appropriate framework for political dialogue between the Parties, allowing the development of close relations in all areas they consider relevant to such dialogue,

(b)   establish the conditions for the gradual liberalisation of trade in goods, services and capital,

...

TITLE III

RIGHT OF ESTABLISHMENT AND SUPPLY OF SERVICES

ARTICLE 30

1.   Treatment granted by either Party to the other with respect to the right of establishment and the supply of services shall be based on each Party's commitments and other obligations under the General Agreement on Trade in Services (GATS). This provision shall take effect from the date of the final accession of Lebanon to the WTO.

2.   Lebanon undertakes to provide a schedule of specific commitments on services, prepared in accordance with Article XX of the GATS, to the European Community and their Member States as soon as it is finalised.

---

* *Source*: European Communities (2002)."The Euro-Mediterranean Association Agreement between the European Community and Its Member States of the One Part, and the Republic of Lebanon, of the Other Part", *Council of the European Union*, Brussels, 7293/02 RL 4L, 18 April 2002; available also on the Internet (http://www.dellbn.cec.eu.int/english/text/7293-en.pdf). [Note added by the editor.]

3.   The Parties undertake to consider development of the above provisions with a view to the establishment of an "economic integration agreement" as defined in Article V of the GATS.

4.   The objective provided for in paragraph 3 shall be subject to a first examination by the Association Council one year after the entry into force of this Agreement.

5.   The Parties shall not, between the date of entry into force of this Agreement and Lebanon's accession to the WTO, take any measures or actions which render the conditions for the supply of services by Community or Lebanese service suppliers more discriminatory than those existing on the date of entry into force of this Agreement.

6.   For the purposes of this Title:

   (a)   "service suppliers" of a Party means any juridical or natural person that seeks to provide or provides a service;

   (b)   a "juridical person" means a company or a subsidiary, set up in accordance with the laws either of a Member State of the Community or of Lebanon and having its registered office, central administration or principal place of business in the territory either of the Community or of Lebanon. Should the juridical person have only its registered office or central administration in the territory either of the Community or of Lebanon, it shall not be considered as either a Community or a Lebanese juridical person, unless its operations possess a real and continuous link with the economy either of the Community or Lebanon;

   (c)   "subsidiary" means a juridical person which is effectively controlled by another juridical person;

   (d)   "natural person" means a person who is a national either of a Member State of the Community or of Lebanon according to their respective national legislations.

TITLE IV

PAYMENTS, CAPITAL, COMPETITION AND OTHER ECONOMIC PROVISIONS

CHAPTER 1

CURRENT PAYMENTS AND MOVEMENT OF CAPITAL

ARTICLE 31

Within the framework of the provisions of this Agreement, and subject to the provisions of Articles 33 and 34, there shall be no restrictions between the Community of the one part, and Lebanon of the other part, on the movement of capital and no discrimination based on the nationality or on the place of residence of their nationals or on the place where such capital is invested.

ARTICLE 32

Current payments connected with the movement of goods, persons, services or capital within the framework of this Agreement shall be free of all restrictions.

ARTICLE 33

1.   Subject to other provisions in this Agreement and other international obligations of the Community and Lebanon, the provisions of Articles 31 and 32 shall be without prejudice to the application of any restriction which exists between them on the date of entry into force of this Agreement, in respect of the movement of capital between them involving direct investment, including in real estate, establishment, the provision of financial services or the admission of securities to capital markets.

2.   However, the transfer abroad of investments made in Lebanon by Community residents or in the Community by Lebanese residents and of any profit stemming therefrom shall not be affected.

ARTICLE 34

Where one or several Member States of the Community or Lebanon face or risk facing serious difficulties concerning balance of payments, the Community or Lebanon respectively may, in conformity with the conditions laid down within the framework of the GATT and Articles VIII and XIV of the Statutes of the International Monetary Fund, take restrictive measures with regard to current payments if such measures are strictly necessary. The Community or Lebanon, as appropriate, shall inform the other Party immediately thereof and shall provide as soon as possible a timetable for the removal of such measures.

CHAPTER 2

COMPETITION AND OTHER ECONOMIC MATTERS

ARTICLE 35

1.   The following are incompatible with the proper functioning of this Agreement, insofar as they may affect trade between the Community and Lebanon:

(a)   all agreements between undertakings, decisions by associations of undertakings and concerted practices between undertakings which have as their object or effect the prevention, restriction or distortion of competition, as defined by their respective legislation;

(b)   abuse by one or more undertakings of a dominant position in the territories of the Community or Lebanon as a whole or in a substantial part thereof, as defined by their respective legislation.

2.   The Parties will enforce their respective competition legislation and shall exchange information taking into account the limitations imposed by the requirements of confidentiality.

The necessary rules for cooperation in order to implement paragraph 1 shall be adopted by the Association Committee within five years of entry into force of this Agreement.

3.   If the Community or Lebanon considers that a particular practice is incompatible with the terms of paragraph 1 of this Article, and if such practice causes or threatens to cause serious prejudice to the other Party, it may take appropriate measures after consultation within the Association Committee or after thirty working days following referral for such consultation.

ARTICLE 36

The Member States and Lebanon shall progressively adjust, without prejudice to their commitments respectively taken or to be taken under the GATT, any State monopolies of a commercial character, so as to ensure that, by the end of the fifth year following the entry into force of this Agreement, no discrimination regarding the conditions under which goods are procured and marketed exists between nationals of the Member States and of Lebanon. The Association Committee will be informed about the measures adopted to implement this objective.

ARTICLE 37

With regard to public enterprises and enterprises to which special or exclusive rights have been granted, the Association Council shall ensure that as from the fifth year following the date of entry into force of this Agreement there is neither enacted nor maintained any measure distorting trade between the Community and Lebanon to an extent contrary to the Parties' interests. This provision should not obstruct the performance in law or in fact of the particular tasks assigned to these enterprises.

ARTICLE 38

1.   Pursuant to the provisions of this Article and of Annex 2, the Parties shall ensure adequate and effective protection of intellectual, industrial and commercial property rights in conformity with the highest international standards, including effective means of enforcing such rights.

2.   The implementation of this Article and of Annex 2 shall be regularly reviewed by the Parties. If problems in the area of intellectual property protection affecting trading conditions occur, urgent consultations shall be undertaken, at the request of either Party, with a view to reaching mutually satisfactory solutions.

ARTICLE 39

1.   The Parties shall take as their aim a reciprocal and gradual liberalisation of public procurement contracts.

2.   The Association Council shall take the steps necessary to implement paragraph 1.

TITLE V

ECONOMIC AND SECTOR COOPERATION

ARTICLE 40
Objectives

1.   The two Parties shall together establish the strategies and procedures needed to achieve cooperation in the fields covered by this Title.

2.   The Parties undertake to intensify economic cooperation in their mutual interest and in the spirit of partnership which is at the root of this Agreement.

3.   The aim of economic cooperation shall be to support Lebanon's own efforts to achieve sustainable economic and social development.

ARTICLE 41
Scope

1.   Cooperation shall be targeted first and foremost at areas of activity suffering the effects of internal constraints and difficulties or affected by the process of liberalising Lebanon's economy as a whole, and more particularly by the liberalisation of trade between Lebanon and the Community.

2.   Similarly, cooperation shall focus on areas likely to bring the economies of the Community and Lebanon closer together, particularly those which will generate growth and employment.

3.   Preservation of the environment and ecological balances shall constitute a central component of the various fields of economic cooperation

4.   The Parties may agree to extend the economic cooperation to other sectors not covered by the provisions of this Title.

ARTICLE 44
Scientific, technical and technological cooperation

The aim of cooperation shall be to:

(a)   encourage the establishment of permanent links between the Parties' scientific communities, notably by means of:

–   providing Lebanon with access to Community research and technological development programmes in accordance with Community rules governing non-Community countries' involvement in such programmes;

–   Lebanese participation in networks of decentralised cooperation;

–   promoting synergy between training and research;

(b)   improve Lebanon's research capabilities; and its technological development;

(c)   stimulate technological innovation and the transfer of new technology and dissemination of know-how;

(d)   study the ways Lebanon can participate in European framework programmes for research.

ARTICLE 46
Industrial cooperation

The aim of cooperation shall be to:

(a)   encourage cooperation between the Parties' economic operators, including cooperation in the context of access for Lebanon to Community business networks;

(b)   support the effort to modernise and restructure Lebanon's public and private sector industry (including the agri-food industry);

(c)   foster an environment which favours private initiative, with the aim of stimulating and diversifying output for the domestic and export markets;

(d)   enhance Lebanon's human resources and industrial potential through better use of policy in the fields of innovation and research and technological development;

(e)   facilitate access to capital markets to finance productive investment.

(f)   encourage the development of SMEs, particularly by:

–   promoting contacts between enterprises, partly by using Community networks and instruments for the promotion of industrial cooperation and partnership,

–   facilitating credit access for financing investment,

–   making information and support services available,

–   enhance human resources to encourage innovation, and setting up projects and economic activities.

ARTICLE 47
Promotion and protection of investment

1.   Cooperation shall aim at increasing the flow of capital, expertise and technology to Lebanon through, inter alia:

(a)   appropriate means of identifying investment opportunities and information channels on investment regulations;

(b)   providing information on European investment regimes (technical assistance, direct financial support, fiscal incentives, investment insurance, etc.) related to outward investment and enhancing the possibility of Lebanon to benefit from them;

(c) examining the creation of joint ventures (especially for small and medium-sized enterprises), and when appropriate the conclusion of agreements between the Member States and Lebanon;

(d) establishing mechanisms for encouraging and promoting investments;

(e) the development of a legal framework conducive to investment between the two Parties, through the conclusion by Lebanon and the Member States of investment protection agreements, where appropriate, and agreements preventing double taxation.

2. Cooperation may extend to the planning and implementation of projects demonstrating the effective acquisition and use of basic technologies, the use of standards, the development of human resources and the creation of jobs locally.

ARTICLE 49
Approximation of legislation

The Parties shall use their best endeavours to approximate their respective laws in order to facilitate the implementation of this Agreement.

ARTICLE 50
Financial services

The aim of cooperation shall be to achieve closer common rules and standards in areas including the following:

(a) developing the financial markets in Lebanon;

(b) improving accounting, auditing, supervision and regulation of financial services and financial monitoring in Lebanon.

ARTICLE 55
Tourism

Cooperation shall aim to:

(a) promote investment in tourism,

(b) improve the knowledge of the tourist industry and ensure greater consistency of policies affecting tourism,

(c) promote a good seasonal spread of tourism,

(d) highlight the importance of the cultural heritage for tourism,

(e) ensure that the interaction between tourism and the environment is suitably maintained,

(f)   make tourism more competitive through support for increased standards and professionalism,

(g)   enhance information flows,

(h)   intensify training activities in hotel management and administration, and training in other hotel trades,

(i)   organise exchanges of experience so as to ensure balanced, sustainable development of tourism, notably through exchanges of information, exhibitions, conventions and publications on tourism.

ARTICLE 84

In the fields covered by this Agreement, and without prejudice to any special provisions contained therein:

(a)   the arrangements applied by Lebanon in respect of the Community shall not give rise to any discrimination between the Member States, their nationals, or their companies or firms,

(b)   the arrangements applied by the Community in respect of Lebanon shall not give rise to any discrimination between Lebanese nationals or its companies or firms.

ARTICLE 74

1.   An Association Council is hereby established which shall meet at ministerial level when circumstances require, on the initiative of its Chairman and in accordance with the conditions laid down in its rules of procedure.

2.   The Association Council shall examine any major issues arising within the framework of this Agreement and any other bilateral or international issues of mutual interest.

ANNEX 2

INTELLECTUAL, INDUSTRIAL AND COMMERCIAL PROPERTY REFERRED TO IN ARTICLE 38

1.   By the end of the fifth year after the entry into force of this Agreement, Lebanon shall ratify the revisions to the following multilateral conventions on intellectual property, to which Member States and Lebanon are parties or which are de facto applied by Member States:

   –   Paris Convention for the protection of industrial property (Stockholm Act 1967 and amended in 1979),

   –   Berne Convention for the Protection of Literary and Artistic Works (revised at Paris in 1971 and amended in 1979),

–   Nice Agreement concerning the International Classification of Goods and Services for the purposes of the Registration of Marks (Geneva 1977, amended in 1979).

2.   By the end of the fifth year after the entry into force of this Agreement, Lebanon shall accede to the following multilateral conventions to which Member States are Parties or which are de facto applied by Member States:

–   Patent Cooperation Treaty (Washington, 1970, amended in 1979 and modified in 1984),

–   Budapest Treaty on the International Recognition of the deposit of Microorganisms for the Purposes of Patent Procedure (1977, modified in 1980),

–   Protocol to the Madrid Agreement concerning the international registration of marks (Madrid, 1989),

–   Trademark Law Treaty (Geneva, 1994),

–   International Convention for the Protection of New Varieties of Plants (UPOV) (Geneva Act of 1991),

–   Agreement on Trade-related Aspects of Intellectual Property, Annex 1C to the Agreement establishing the World Trade Organisation (TRIPs, Marrakesh 1994).

The Parties shall make every effort to ratify the following multilateral conventions at the earliest possible opportunity:

–   WIPO Copyright Treaty (Geneva, 1996),

–   WIPO Performances and Phonograms Treaty (Geneva, 1996).

3.   The Association Council may decide that paragraph 1 shall apply to other multilateral conventions in this field.

JOINT DECLARATION RELATING TO ARTICLE 35 OF THE AGREEMENT

The implementation of cooperation mentioned in Article 35 paragraph 2 is conditional upon the entry into force of a Lebanese competition law and of the taking up of the duties of the authority responsible for its application.

JOINT DECLARATION RELATING TO ARTICLE 38 OF THE AGREEMENT

The Parties agree that for the purpose of the Agreement, intellectual, industrial and commercial property includes in particular copyright, including the copyright in computer programmes, and neighbouring rights, the rights relating to databases, the rights relating to patents, industrial designs, geographical indications, including designations of origin, trademarks and service marks, topographies of integrated circuits, as well as protection against unfair competition as referred to in Article 10 Bis of the Paris Convention for the Protection of Industrial Property and protection of undisclosed information on know-how.

INTERIM AGREEMENT ON TRADE AND TRADE-RELATED MATTERS BETWEEN THE EUROPEAN COMMUNITY, OF THE ONE PART, AND THE REPUBLIC OF LEBANON, OF THE OTHER PART[*]
[excerpts]

The Interim Agreement on Trade and Trade-related Matters between the European Community, of the One Part, and the Republic of Lebanon, of the Other Part was signed on 17 June 2002. Pending the entry into force of the Euro-Mediterranean Agreement Establishing an Association between the European Community and Its Member States, of the One Part, and the Republic of Lebanon, of the Other Part, the Interim Agreement becomes applicable. The member States of the European Communities are: Austria, Belgium, Denmark, Finland, France, Germany, Greece, Ireland, Italy, Luxembourg, the Netherlands, Portugal, Spain, Sweden and the United Kingdom.

TITLE III

TRADE-RELATED PROVISIONS

CHAPTER 1

COMPETITION

ARTICLE 27 (AA35)

1.   The following are incompatible with the proper functioning of this Agreement, insofar as they may affect trade between the Community and Lebanon:

    (a)   all agreements between undertakings, decisions by associations of undertakings and concerted practices between undertakings which have as their object or effect the prevention, restriction or distortion of competition, as defined by their respective legislation;

    (b)   abuse by one or more undertakings of a dominant position in the territories of the Community or Lebanon as a whole or in a substantial part thereof, as defined by their respective legislation.

2.   The Parties will enforce their respective competition legislation and shall exchange information taking into account the limitations imposed by the requirements of confidentiality. The necessary rules for cooperation in order to implement paragraph 1 shall be adopted by the Cooperation Council within five years of entry into force of this Agreement.

---

[*] *Source*: European Communities (2002)."Interim Agreement on Trade and Trade-related Matters between the European Community, of the One Part, and the Republic of Lebanon, of the Other Part", *Council of the European Union, Brussels*, 7470/1/02 REV 1 RL 5, 11 June 2002; available also on the Internet (http://www.dellbn.cec.eu.int/english/text/7470-en.pdf). [Note added by the editor.]

3. If the Community or Lebanon considers that a particular practice is incompatible with the terms of paragraph 1 of this Article, and if such practice causes or threatens to cause serious prejudice to the other Party, it may take appropriate measures after consultation within the Cooperation Council or after thirty working days following referral for such consultation.

CHAPTER 2

INTELLECTUAL, INDUSTRIAL AND COMMERCIAL PROPERTY

ARTICLE 30 (AA38)

1. Pursuant to the provisions of this Article and of Annex 2, the Parties shall ensure adequate and effective protection of intellectual, industrial and commercial property rights in conformity with the highest international standards, including effective means of enforcing such rights.

2. The implementation of this Article and of Annex 2 shall be regularly reviewed by the Parties. If problems in the area of intellectual property protection affecting trading conditions occur, urgent consultations shall be undertaken, at the request of either Party, with a view to reaching mutually satisfactory solutions.

JOINT DECLARATION RELATING TO ARTICLE 30 OF THE INTERIM AGREEMENT (AA38)

The Parties agree that for the purpose of the Agreement, intellectual, industrial and commercial property includes in particular copyright, including the copyright in computer programmes, and neighbouring rights, the rights relating to databases, the rights relating to patents, industrial designs, geographical indications, including designations of origin, trademarks and service marks, topographies of integrated circuits, as well as protection against unfair competition as referred to in Article 10 Bis of the Paris Convention for the Protection of Industrial Property and protection of undisclosed information on know-how.

The provisions of Article 30 shall not be interpreted in a manner to oblige either Party to accede to international conventions other than those referred to in Annex 2.

The Community will grant technical assistance to the Lebanese Republic in its endeavour to comply with its obligations under Article 30.

*

FREE TRADE AGREEMENT BETWEEN THE EFTA STATES AND SINGAPORE[*]
[excerpts]

The Free Trade Agreement between the European Free Trade Association (EFTA) States and Singapore was signed on 26 June 2002. Annex VII and its corresponding appendices (1,2,3,4,5) containing the Parties' Schedules of specific commitments referred to in Article 27 not reprinted in this volume. The member States of European Free Trade Association are: Iceland, Liechtenstein, Norway and Switzeland.

The Republic of Iceland, the Principality of Liechtenstein, the Kingdom of Norway and the Swiss Confederation (hereinafter referred to as "the EFTA States"),

and

The Republic of Singapore (hereinafter referred to as "Singapore"),

hereinafter collectively referred to as the Parties,

CONSIDERING the important links existing between Singapore and the EFTA States, and wishing to strengthen these links through the creation of a free trade area, thus establishing close and lasting relations;

REAFFIRMING their commitment to the principles set out in the United Nations Charter and the Universal Declaration of Human Rights;

DESIROUS by way of the removal of obstacles to trade to contribute to the harmonious development and expansion of world trade and provide a catalyst to broader international co-operation, in particular between Europe and Asia;

DETERMINED to create an expanded and secure market for goods and services in their territories;

RESOLVED to ensure a stable and predictable environment for investment;

INTENDING to enhance the competitiveness of their firms in global markets;

AIMING to create new employment opportunities, improve living standards and ensure a large and steadily growing volume of real income in their respective territories through the expansion of trade and investment flows;

RECOGNIZING that the gains from trade liberalisation should not be offset by private, anti-competitive practices;

---

[*] *Source*: European Free Trade Association Secretariat (2002). "Free Trade Agreement between the EFTA States and Singapore", available on the Internet (http://secretariat.efta.int/library/legal/fta/singapore/dbafile23418.html). [Note added by the editor.]

CONVINCED that this Agreement will create conditions encouraging economic, trade and investment relations between them;

BUILDING on their respective rights and obligations under the Marrakesh Agreement Establishing the World Trade Organization and the other agreements negotiated thereunder and other multilateral and bilateral instruments of co-operation; and

RECOGNIZING that trade liberalisation should allow for the optimal use of the world's resources in accordance with the objective of sustainable development, seeking both to protect and preserve the environment;

HAVE AGREED, in pursuit of the above, to conclude the following Agreement (hereinafter referred to as "this Agreement"):

I GENERAL PROVISIONS

Article 1: Objectives

1.   The EFTA States and Singapore hereby establish a free-trade area in accordance with the provisions of this Agreement.

2.   The objectives of this Agreement, which is based on trade relations between market economies are:

    (a)   to achieve the liberalisation of trade in goods, in conformity with Article XXIV of the General Agreement on Tariffs and Trade (hereinafter referred to as "the GATT 1994");

    (b)   to promote competition in their economies, particularly as it relates to economic relations between the Parties;

    (c)   to achieve further liberalisation on a mutual basis of the government procurement markets of the Parties;

    (d)   to achieve the liberalisation of trade in services, in conformity with Article V of the General Agreement on Trade in Services (hereinafter referred to as "the GATS");

    (e)   to mutually enhance investment opportunities and accord constant protection for investors and investments;

    (f)   to ensure adequate and effective protection of intellectual property rights, in accordance with international standards; and

    (g)   to contribute in this way, by the removal of barriers to trade and investment, to the harmonious development and expansion of world trade.

III SERVICES

Article 21: Scope and Coverage

1.   This Chapter applies to measures affecting trade in services taken by central, regional or local governments and authorities as well as by non-governmental bodies in the exercise of powers delegated by central, regional or local governments or authorities.

2.   This Chapter applies to measures affecting trade in all services sectors with the exception of air services, including domestic and international air transportation services, whether scheduled or non-scheduled, and related services in support of air services, other than:

> (a)   aircraft repair and maintenance services;

> (b)   the selling and marketing of air transport services;

> (c)   computer reservation system (CRS) services[1].

3.   The EFTA States and Singapore agree to review developments in the air transport sector with a view to reassessing the need for further co-operation in this sector.

4.   Nothing in this Chapter shall be construed to impose any obligation with respect to government procurement.

Article 22: Definitions

For the purposes of this Chapter:

(a)   "measure" means any measure by a Party, whether in the form of a law, regulation, rule, procedure, decision, administrative action or any other form;

(b)   "supply of a service" includes the production, distribution, marketing, sale and delivery of a service;

(c) "measures by Parties affecting trade in services" include measures in respect of:

> (i)   the purchase, payment or use of a service;

> (ii)   the access to and use of, in connection with the supply of a service, services which are required by those Parties to be offered to the public generally;

> (iii)   the presence, including commercial presence, of persons of a Party for the supply of a service in the territory of another Party;

(d)   "commercial presence" means any type of business or professional establishment, including through:

---

[1]   The terms "aircraft repair and maintenance services", "selling and marketing of air transport services" and "computer reservation system (CRS) services" are as defined in paragraph 6 of the Annex on Air Transport Services to the GATS.

(i)   the constitution, acquisition or maintenance of a juridical person; or

(ii)   the creation or maintenance of a branch or a representative office;

within the territory of a Party for the purpose of supplying a service;

(e)   "sector" of a service means:

(i)   with reference to a specific commitment, one or more, or all, subsectors of that service, as specified in a Party's Schedule;

(ii)   otherwise, the whole of that service sector, including all of its subsectors;

(f)   "service supplier" means any person that seeks to supply or supplies a service[2];

(g)   "service consumer" means any person that receives or uses a service;

(h)   "service of another Party" means a service which is supplied:

(i)   from or in the territory of that other Party, or in the case of maritime transport, by a vessel registered under the laws of that other Party, or by a person of that other Party which supplies the service through the operation of a vessel and/or its use in whole or in part; or

(ii)   in the case of the supply of a service through commercial presence or through the presence of natural persons, by a service supplier of that other Party;

(i)   "person" means either a natural person or a juridical person;

(j)   "natural person of a Party" means a natural person who resides in the territory of that Party or elsewhere and who under the law of that Party:

(i)   is a national of that Party; or

(ii)   has the right of permanent residence in that Party and is accorded substantially the same treatment as nationals in respect of measures affecting trade in services;

(k)   "juridical person" means any legal entity duly constituted or otherwise organised under applicable law, whether for profit or otherwise, and whether privately-owned or governmentally-owned, including any corporation, trust, partnership, joint venture, sole proprietorship or association;

(l)   "juridical person of another Party" means a juridical person which is either:

---

[2]   Where the service is not supplied directly by a juridical person but through other forms of commercial presence such as a branch or a representative office, the service supplier (i.e. the juridical person) shall, nonetheless, through such presence be accorded the treatment provided for service suppliers under this Agreement. Such treatment shall be extended to the presence through which the service is supplied and need not be extended to any other parts of the supplier located outside the territory where the service is supplied.

(i)   constituted or otherwise organised under the law of that other Party, and is engaged in substantive business operations[3] in the territory of any Party; this includes a service supplier of a WTO member who is a non-Party that is a juridical person constituted under the laws of a Party, provided that it engages in substantive business operations in the territory of the Parties; or

(ii)   in the case of the supply of a service through commercial presence, owned or controlled by:

    1.   natural persons of that other Party; or

    2.   juridical persons identified under paragraph (l)(i);

(m)   a juridical person is:

(i)   "owned" by persons of a Party if more than 50 per cent of the equity interest in it is beneficially owned by persons of that Party;

(ii)   "controlled" by persons of a Party if such persons have the power to name a majority of its directors or otherwise to legally direct its actions;

(iii) "affiliated" with another person when it controls, or is controlled by, that other person; or when it and the other person are both controlled by the same person;

(n)   "monopoly supplier of a service" means any person, public or private, which in the relevant market of the territory of a Party is authorised or established formally or in effect by that Party as the sole supplier of that service;

(o)   "trade in services" means the supply of a service:

(i)   from the territory of a Party into the territory of another Party (hereinafter referred to as "cross-border supply");

(ii)   in the territory of a Party to the service consumer of another Party (hereinafter referred to as "consumption abroad");

(iii) by a service supplier of a Party, through commercial presence in the territory of another Party (hereinafter referred to as "commercial presence");

(iv)   by a service supplier of a Party, through presence of natural persons of that Party in the territory of another Party (hereinafter referred to as "presence of natural persons");

(p)   "services" includes any service in any sector except services supplied in the exercise of governmental authority;

---

[3]   This also includes juridical persons intending to engage in substantive business operations such as start-up companies.

(q)   "a service supplied in the exercise of governmental authority" means any service which is supplied neither on a commercial basis nor in competition with one or more service suppliers;

(r)   "direct taxes" comprise all taxes on total income, on total capital or on elements of income or of capital, including taxes on gains from the alienation of property, taxes on estates, inheritances and gifts, and taxes on the total amounts of wages or salaries paid by enterprises, as well as taxes on capital appreciation.

Article 23: Most-Favoured-Nation Treatment

1.   Subject to exceptions that may derive from harmonisation of regulations based on agreements concluded by a Party with a non-Party providing for mutual recognition in accordance with Article VII of the GATS, and except as provided in Annex VI, a Party shall accord immediately and unconditionally, with respect to any measure covered by this Chapter, to services and service suppliers of another Party treatment no less favourable than that it accords to like services and service suppliers of any non-Party.

2.   Treatment granted under other agreements concluded by one of the Parties with a non-Party which have been notified under Article V of the GATS shall not be subject to paragraph 1.

3.   If a Party enters into an agreement of the type referred to in paragraph 2, it shall, upon request from another Party, afford adequate opportunity to the other Parties to negotiate the benefits granted therein.

Article 24: Market Access

1.   With respect to market access through the modes of supply identified in Article 22 (o), each Party shall accord services and service suppliers of another Party treatment no less favourable than that provided for under the terms, limitations and conditions agreed and specified in its Schedule[4].

2.   In sectors where market access commitments are undertaken, the measures which a Party shall not maintain or adopt either on the basis of a regional sub-division or on the basis of its entire territory, unless otherwise specified in its Schedule, are defined as:

(a)   limitations on the number of service suppliers whether in the form of numerical quotas, monopolies, exclusive service suppliers or the requirements of an economic needs test;

(b)   limitations on the total value of service transactions or assets in the form of numerical quotas or the requirement of an economic needs test;

---

[4]   If a Party undertakes a market-access commitment in relation to the supply of a service through the mode of supply referred to in Article 22 (o) (i) and if the cross-border movement of capital is an essential part of the service itself, that Party is thereby committed to allow such movement of capital. If a Party undertakes a market-access commitment in relation to the supply of a service through the mode of supply referred to in Article 22 (o) (iii), it is thereby committed to allow related transfers of capital into its territory.

(c)   limitations on the total number of service operations or on the total quantity of service output expressed in terms of designated numerical units in the form of quotas or the requirement of an economic needs test[5];

(d)   limitations on the total number of natural persons that may be employed in a particular service sector or that a service supplier may employ and who are necessary for, and directly related to, the supply of a specific service in the form of numerical quotas or the requirement of an economic needs test;

(e)   measures which restrict or require specific types of legal entity or joint venture through which a service supplier may supply a service; and

(f)   limitations on the participation of foreign capital in terms of maximum percentage limit on foreign shareholding or the total value of individual or aggregate foreign investment.

Article 25: National Treatment

1.   In the sectors inscribed in its Schedule, and subject to any conditions and qualifications set out therein, each Party shall accord to services and service suppliers of another Party, in respect of all measures affecting the supply of services, treatment no less favourable than that it accords to its own like services and service suppliers[6].

2.   A Party may meet the requirement in paragraph 1 by according to services and service suppliers of another Party either formally identical treatment or formally different treatment to that it accords to its own like services and service suppliers.

3.   Formally identical or formally different treatment shall be considered to be less favourable if it modifies the conditions of competition in favour of services or service suppliers of a Party compared to like services or service suppliers of another Party.

Article 26: Additional Commitments

The Parties may negotiate commitments with respect to measures affecting trade in services not subject to scheduling under Articles 24 and 25 above, including those regarding qualifications, standards or licensing matters. Such commitments shall be entered in a Party's Schedule.

Article 27: Trade Liberalisation/Schedule of Specific Commitments

1.   The Parties shall liberalise trade in services between themselves, in conformity with Article V of the GATS.

2.   Each Party shall set out in a Schedule the specific commitments it undertakes under Articles 24, 25 and 26. With respect to sectors where such commitments are undertaken, each Schedule shall specify:

---

[5]   Paragraph 2 (c) does not cover measures of a Party which limit inputs for the supply of services.

[6]   Specific commitments assumed under this Article shall not be construed to require any Party to compensate for any inherent competitive disadvantages which result from the foreign character of the relevant services or services suppliers.

(a)   terms, limitations and conditions on market access;

(b)   conditions and qualifications on national treatment;

(c)   undertakings relating to additional commitments; and

(d)   where appropriate, the time-frame for implementation of such commitments.

3.   Measures inconsistent with both Articles 24 and 25 shall be inscribed in the column relating to Article 24. In this case, the inscription will be considered to provide a condition or qualification to Article 25 as well.

4.   The Parties' Schedules of specific commitments are set out in Annex VII, and form an integral part of this Chapter.

5.   The Parties undertake to review their Schedules of specific commitments at least every two years, but earlier if so agreed, with a view to provide for the elimination of substantially all remaining discrimination between the Parties with regard to trade in services covered in this Chapter at the end of a transitional period of ten years from the date of entry into force of this Agreement. Such review shall continue if substantially all remaining discrimination has not been eliminated at the end of this transitional period. This paragraph is not subject to dispute settlement pursuant to Chapter IX.

Article 28: Domestic Regulation

1.   In sectors where specific commitments are undertaken, each Party shall ensure that all measures of general application affecting trade in services are administered in a reasonable, objective and impartial manner.

2.   Each Party shall maintain or institute as soon as practicable judicial, arbitral or administrative tribunals or procedures which provide, at the request of an affected service supplier of another Party, for the prompt review of, and where justified, appropriate remedies for, administrative decisions affecting trade in services. Where such procedures are not independent of the agency entrusted with the administrative decision concerned, the Party shall ensure that the procedures in fact provide for an objective and impartial review.

3.   Where authorisation is required for the supply of a service on which a specific commitment has been made, the competent authorities of a Party shall promptly, after the submission of an application considered complete under domestic laws and regulations, inform the applicant of the decision concerning the application. At the request of the applicant, the competent authorities of the Party shall provide, without undue delay, information concerning the status of the application.

4.   The Parties shall jointly review the results of the negotiations on disciplines for certain regulations, including qualification requirements and procedures, technical standards and licensing requirements, pursuant to Article VI.4 of the GATS, with a view to their incorporation into this Agreement. The Parties note that such disciplines aim to ensure that such requirements are inter alia:

(a)   based on objective and transparent criteria, such as competence and the ability to supply the service;

(b)   not more burdensome than necessary to ensure the quality of the service;

(c)   in the case of licensing procedures, not in themselves a restriction on the supply of the service.

5.   In sectors where a Party has undertaken specific commitments, subject to any terms, limitations, conditions or qualifications set out therein, pending the incorporation of disciplines developed pursuant to paragraph 4, a Party shall not apply licensing and qualification requirements and technical standards that nullify or impair such specific commitments in a manner which:

(a)   does not comply with the criteria outlined in paragraph 4 (a), (b) or (c) and

(b)   could not reasonably have been expected of that Party at the time the specific commitments in those sectors were made.

6.   Whenever a domestic regulation is prepared, adopted and applied in accordance with international standards of relevant international organisations[7] applied by a Party, there shall be a rebuttable presumption that it complies with the provisions of this Article.

7.   In sectors where specific commitments regarding professional services are undertaken, each Party shall provide for adequate procedures to verify the competence of professionals of another Party.

Article 29: Subsidies

A Party which considers that it is adversely affected by a subsidy of another Party may request consultations with that Party on such matters. Such requests shall be accorded sympathetic consideration.

Article 30: Recognition

1.   In principle no later than three years following the entry into force of this Agreement, the Joint Committee shall establish the necessary steps for the negotiation of agreements or arrangements providing for the mutual recognition of education or experience obtained, requirements, qualifications, licenses and other regulations, for the purpose of the fulfilment, in whole or in part, by service suppliers of the criteria applied by each Party for the authorisation, licensing, operation and certification of service suppliers.

2.   Any such recognition conferred by a Party shall be in conformity with the relevant provisions of the WTO and, in particular, Article VII of the GATS.

3.   Where a Party recognises, by agreement or arrangement, the education or experience obtained, requirements met or licenses or certifications granted in the territory of a non-Party,

---

[7]   The term "relevant international organisations" refers to international bodies whose membership is open to the relevant bodies of the Parties.

that Party shall accord another Party, upon request, adequate opportunity to negotiate its accession to such an agreement or arrangement or to negotiate comparable ones with it. Where a Party accords recognition autonomously, it shall afford adequate opportunity for another Party to demonstrate that the education or experience obtained, requirements met or licenses or certifications granted in the territory of that other Party should also be recognised.

Article 31: Monopolies and Exclusive Service Suppliers

1.   Each Party shall ensure that any monopoly supplier of a service in its territory does not, in the supply of the monopoly service in the relevant market, act in a manner inconsistent with the Party's obligations under its specific commitments.

2.   Where a Party's monopoly supplier competes, either directly or through an affiliated company, in the supply of a service outside the scope of its monopoly rights and which is subject to that Party's obligations under its specific commitments, the Party shall ensure that such a supplier does not abuse its monopoly position to act in its territory in a manner inconsistent with such commitments.

3.   If a Party has reason to believe that a monopoly supplier of a service of another Party is acting in a manner inconsistent with paragraph 1 or 2, it may request that other Party to provide specific information concerning the relevant operations.

4.   The provisions of this Article shall also apply to cases of exclusive service suppliers, where a Party, formally or in effect, (a) authorises or establishes a small number of service suppliers and (b) substantially prevents competition among those suppliers in its territory.

Article 32: Movement of Natural Persons

1.   This Chapter applies to measures affecting natural persons who are service suppliers of a Party, and natural persons of a Party who are employed by a service supplier of a Party, in respect of the supply of a service. Natural persons covered by a Party's specific commitments shall be allowed to supply the service in accordance with the terms of those commitments.

2.   This Chapter shall not apply to measures affecting natural persons seeking access to the employment market of a Party, nor shall it apply to measures regarding citizenship, residence or employment on a permanent basis.

3.   This Chapter shall not prevent a Party from applying measures to regulate the entry of natural persons of another Party into, or their temporary stay in, its territory, including those measures necessary to protect the integrity of, and to ensure the orderly movement of natural persons across, its borders, provided that such measures are not applied in a manner so as to nullify or impair the benefits accruing to a Party under the terms of a specific commitment[8].

Article 33: General Exceptions

Subject to the requirement that such measures are not applied in a manner which would constitute a means of arbitrary or unjustifiable discrimination between countries where like

---

[8]   The sole fact of requiring a visa for natural persons of a certain nationality and not for those of others shall not be regarded as nullifying or impairing benefits under a specific commitment.

conditions prevail, or a disguised restriction on trade in services, nothing in this Chapter shall be construed to prevent the adoption or enforcement by any Party of measures:

(a)   necessary to protect public morals or to maintain public order[9];

(b)   necessary to protect human, animal or plant life or health;

(c)   necessary to secure compliance with laws or regulations which are not inconsistent with the provisions of this Chapter including those relating to:

    (i)   the prevention of deceptive and fraudulent practices or to deal with the effects of a default on services contracts;

    (ii)   the protection of the privacy of individuals in relation to the processing and dissemination of personal data and the protection of confidentiality of individual records and accounts;

    (iii)   safety;

(d)   inconsistent with Article 25, provided that the difference in treatment is aimed at ensuring the equitable or effective[10] imposition or collection of direct taxes in respect of services or service suppliers of another Party;

(e)   inconsistent with Article 23, provided that the difference in treatment is the result of an agreement on the avoidance of double taxation or provisions on the avoidance of double taxation in any other international agreement or arrangement by which a Party is bound.

Article 34: Security Exceptions

Nothing in this Agreement shall be construed:

(a)   to require a Party to furnish or allow access to information the disclosure of which it considers contrary to its essential security interests;

---

[9] The public order exception may be invoked only where a genuine and sufficiently serious threat is posed to one of the fundamental interests of society.

[10] Measures that are aimed at ensuring the equitable or effective imposition or collection of direct taxes include measures taken by a Party under its taxation system which:

    (i)   apply to non-resident service suppliers in recognition of the fact that the tax obligation of non-residents is determined with respect to taxable items sourced or located in the Party's territory; or

    (ii)   apply to non-residents in order to ensure the imposition or collection of taxes in the Party's territory; or

    (iii)   apply to non-residents or residents in order to prevent the avoidance or evasion of taxes, including compliance measures; or

    (iv)   apply to consumers of services supplied in or from the territory of another Party in order to ensure the imposition or collection of taxes on such consumers derived from sources in the Party's territory; or

    (v)   distinguish service suppliers subject to tax on worldwide taxable items from other service suppliers, in recognition of the difference in the nature of the tax base between them; or

    (vi)   determine, allocate or apportion income, profit, gain, loss, deduction or credit of resident persons or branches, or between related persons or branches of the same person, in order to safeguard the Member's tax base.

    Tax terms or concepts in Article 33 (d) and in this footnote are determined according to tax definitions and concepts, or equivalent or similar definitions and concepts, under the domestic law of the Party taking the measure.

(b)   to prevent a Party from taking any action which it considers necessary for the protection of its essential security interests:

      (i)   relating to the supply of services as carried out directly or indirectly for the purpose of provisioning a military establishment;

      (ii)   relating to fissionable and fusionable materials or the materials from which they are derived;

      (iii)   taken in time of war or other emergency in international relations; or

(c)   to prevent a Party from taking any action in pursuance of its obligations under the United Nations Charter for the maintenance of international peace and security.

Article 35: Restrictions to Safeguard the Balance-of-Payments

1.   The Parties shall endeavour to avoid the imposition of restrictive measures for balance-of-payments purposes.

2.   Articles XI and XII of the GATS shall apply to payments and transfers, and to restrictions to safeguard the balance-of-payments relating to trade in services.

3.   A Party adopting or maintaining a measure under this Article shall promptly notify the other Parties and the Joint Committee thereof.

IV INVESTMENT

Article 37: Definitions

For the purposes of this Chapter:

(a)   "company" means any entity constituted or organized under the applicable law, whether or not for profit, and whether private or government owned or controlled, including any corporation, trust, partnership, sole proprietorship, joint venture or other association;

(b)   "investment" means any kind of asset and particularly:

      (i)   movable and immovable property as well as any other rights in rem, such as mortgages, liens, and pledges;

      (ii)   shares, bonds and debentures or any other forms of participation in a company;

      (iii)   claims to money or to any performance associated with a company having an economic value;

      (iv)   intellectual property rights, technical know-how and goodwill;

      (v)   business concessions conferred by law or under contract, including any concession to search for, cultivate, extract or exploit natural resources;

(c) "investment of an investor of a Party" means an investment that is owned or controlled, either directly or indirectly, by an investor of that Party;

(d) "investor of a Party" means:

  (i) a natural person having the nationality of that Party or having the right of permanent residence of that Party in accordance with its applicable laws;

  (ii) a company constituted or organized under the applicable law of that Party and carrying out substantial business activities there;

making or having made an investment in the territory of another Party.

Article 38: Scope and Coverage

1. This Chapter shall apply to investors of a Party, and to their investments whether made before or after the entry into force of this Agreement.

2. Article 40 (1) shall not apply to measures affecting trade in services whether or not a sector concerned is scheduled in Chapter III.

3. Article 40 (1) shall also not apply to investors of a Party in services sectors and their investments in such sectors. This provision is subject to review after a period of ten years from the date of entry into force of this Agreement, with a view to examining its continued need.

4. The provisions of this Chapter shall be without prejudice to the rights and obligations of the Parties under other international agreements relating to investment.

Article 39: Promotion and Protection

1. Each Party shall, in accordance with the provisions of this Chapter, create and maintain stable, equitable, favourable and transparent conditions for investors of the other Parties to make investments in its territory.

2. Such conditions shall include a commitment to accord at all times to investments of investors of another Party fair and equitable treatment. Such investments shall also enjoy the most constant protection and security.

Article 40: National Treatment and Most-Favoured-Nation Treatment

1. Each Party shall accord to investors and investments of investors of another Party, in relation to the establishment, acquisition, expansion, management, conduct, operation and disposal of investments, treatment that is no less favourable than that which it accords in like situations to its own investors and their investments or to investors and their investments of any other State, whichever is more favourable.

2. If a Party accords more favourable treatment to investors of any other State or their investments by virtue of a free trade agreement, customs union or similar agreement that also provides for substantial liberalisation of investments, it shall not be obliged to accord such

treatment to investors of another Party or their investments. However, upon request from another Party, it shall afford adequate opportunity to negotiate the benefits granted therein.

3.   The standard of national treatment as provided for in paragraph 1 shall not apply to subsidies based on a Party's social policy or its economic development policy, even if such subsidies, directly or indirectly, favour local enterprises or entrepreneurs. If another Party considers that such subsidies, in a particular case, have a seriously distortive effect on the investment opportunities of its own investors, it may request consultations on such matters. Such requests shall be accorded sympathetic consideration.

4.   The standard of national treatment as provided for in paragraph 1, means, with respect to a sub-national entity, treatment no less favourable than the most favourable treatment accorded, in like situations, by that entity to investors, and to investments of investors, of the Party of which it forms a part.

Article 41: Taxation

1.   Except as otherwise provided for in this Article, nothing in this Chapter shall create rights or impose obligations with respect to taxation measures.

2.   Article 40 shall apply to taxation measures subject to deviations from national treatment that are necessary for the equitable or effective imposition or collection of direct taxes[11].

3.   If a Party accords special advantages to investors and their investments of any other State by virtue of an agreement for the avoidance of double taxation, it shall not be obliged to accord such advantages to investors of another Party and their investments.

Article 42: Dispossession, Compensation

1.   None of the Parties shall take, either de jure or de facto, measures of expropriation or nationalisation against investments of investors of another Party, unless such measures are in the public interest; non-discriminatory; carried out under due process of law; and accompanied by the payment of compensation. The amount of compensation shall be settled in a freely convertible currency and paid without delay to the person entitled thereto without regard to its residence or domicile.

2.   Investors of a Party whose investments in the territory of another Party have suffered losses due to armed conflict or civil strife in the territory of the latter Party, shall benefit from treatment in accordance with Article 40 as regards restitution, indemnification, compensation or any other settlement it adopts or maintains relating to such losses.

Article 43: Domestic Regulation

Nothing in this Chapter shall be construed to prevent a Party from adopting, maintaining or enforcing any measure consistent with this Chapter that is in the public interest, such as measures to meet health, safety or environmental concerns.

---

[11]   Footnote 10 under Article 19 of Chapter III on Services shall also apply mutatis mutandis to this Chapter.

Article 44: Transfers

1.   Each Party shall allow payments relating to an investment in its territory of an investor of another Party to be freely transferred into and out of its territory without delay. Such transfers shall include, in particular, though not exclusively:

(a)   profits, interest, dividends, capital gains, royalties and fees as well as any other amounts yielded by an investment;

(b)   payments made under a contract including a loan agreement;

(c)   additional amounts to maintain or increase an investment;

(d)   proceeds from the sale or liquidation of all or any part of an investment; and

(e)   earnings and other remuneration of personnel engaged from abroad in connection with an investment.

2.   A transfer shall be deemed to have been made "without delay" if effected within such a period as is normally required for the completion of transfer formalities, including reports of currency transfers.

3.   Each Party shall permit such transfers to be made in a freely convertible currency. "Freely convertible currency" means a currency that is widely traded in international foreign exchange markets and widely used in international transactions.

4.   It is understood that paragraphs 1 to 3 above are without prejudice to the equitable, non-discriminatory and good faith application of laws relating to:

(a)   bankruptcy, insolvency or the protection of the rights of creditors;

(b)   the issuing, trading or dealing in securities;

(c)   criminal or penal offences, and the recovery of proceeds of crimes;

(d)   ensuring the satisfaction of judgments in adjudicatory proceedings.

5.   It is also understood that paragraphs 1 to 3 above are without prejudice to obligations under tax laws or social security and public retirement schemes.

Article 45: Key Personnel

1.   The Parties shall, subject to their laws and regulations relating to the entry, stay and work of natural persons, grant investors of another Party, and key personnel (executives, managers and specialists, as defined by the granting Party as "Intra-corporate transferees" in the horizontal commitments of its respective Appendix of Annex VII) who are employed by such investors or investments of such investors, temporary entry, stay and authorisation to work in their territories to engage in activities connected with the establishment, management, maintenance, use, enjoyment, expansion or disposal of relevant investments.

2.   The Parties shall, subject to their laws and regulations, permit investors of another Party which have investments in their territories, and investments of such investors, to employ any key personnel of the investor's or the investment's choice regardless of nationality and citizenship provided that such key personnel has been permitted to enter, stay and work in the territory of the other Party and that the employment concerned conforms to the terms, conditions and time limits of the permission granted to such key personnel.

3.   The Parties are encouraged to grant, subject to their laws and regulations, temporary entry and stay to the spouse and minor children of an investor of another Party or of key personnel employed by such investors, who has been granted temporary entry, stay and authorisation to work.

Article 46: Reservations

1.   Article 40 (1), shall not apply to:

(a)   any reservation that is listed by a Party in Annex XI;

(b)   an amendment to a reservation covered by sub-paragraph (a) to the extent that the amendment does not decrease the conformity of the reservation with Article 40;

(c)   any new reservation adopted by a Party, and incorporated into Annex XI provided that such reservation does not affect the overall level of commitments of that Party under this Chapter;

to the extent that such reservation is inconsistent with the above-mentioned Article.

2.   The Parties undertake to review at least every two years the status of the reservations set out in Annex XI with a view to reducing the reservations or removing them.

3.   A Party may, at any time, either upon the request of another Party or unilaterally, remove in whole or in part reservations set out in Annex XI by written notification to the other Parties.

4.   A Party may, at any time, incorporate a new reservation into Annex XI in accordance with paragraph 1 (c) of this Article by written notification to the other Parties. On receiving such notification, the other Parties may request consultations regarding the reservation. On receiving the request for consultations, the Party incorporating the new reservation shall enter into consultations with the other Parties.

Article 47: Subrogation

In the event that a Party (or any agency, institution, statutory body or corporation designated by it), as a result of an indemnity it has given in respect of an investment or any part thereof, makes a payment to its own investors in respect of any of their claims under this Chapter, the other Party acknowledges that the former Party (or any agency, institution, statutory body or corporation designated by it) is entitled by virtue of subrogation to exercise the rights and assert the claims of its own investors. The subrogated rights or claims shall not be greater than the original rights or claims of such investors.

Article 48: Disputes Between an Investor and a Party

1.   If an investor of a Party considers that a measure applied by another Party is inconsistent with an obligation of this Chapter, thus causing loss or damage to him or his investment, he may request consultations with a view to solving the matter amicably.

2.   Any such matter which has not been settled within a period of six months from the date of request for consultations may be referred to the courts or administrative tribunals of the Party concerned or, if both parties to the dispute agree, be submitted to one of the following:

    a)   arbitration under the Convention on the Settlement of Investment Disputes between States and Nationals of other States (the "ICSID Convention"), if this Convention is available;

    b)   conciliation or arbitration under the Additional Facility Rules of the International Centre for the Settlement of Investment Disputes;

    c)   arbitration under the Arbitration Rules of the United Nations Commission on International Trade Law.

3.   A Party may conclude contractual agreements with investors of another Party giving its unconditional and irrevocable consent to the submission of all or certain types of disputes to international conciliation or arbitration in accordance with paragraph 2 above. Such agreements may be notified to the Depositary of this Agreement.

Article 49: Exceptions

The following provisions shall apply, mutatis mutandis, to this Chapter:

Articles 33, 34 and 35, as well as Article 19 (e), (f) and (g).

V COMPETITION

Article 50: Competition

1.   The Parties recognise that certain business practices, such as anti-competitive agreements or concerted practices, and abuse of a dominant position, may restrict trade between the Parties.

2.   A Party shall, at the request of another Party, enter into consultations with a view to eliminating practices referred to in paragraph 1. The Party addressed shall accord full and sympathetic consideration to such a request and shall co-operate through the supply of publicly available non-confidential information of relevance to the matter in question. Subject to its domestic law and the conclusion of a satisfactory agreement safeguarding confidentiality of information, the Party addressed shall also provide any other information available to the requesting Party.

3.   No Party may have recourse to arbitration under Chapter IX with respect to matters arising under this Chapter.

VI GOVERNMENT PROCUREMENT

Article 51: Scope and Coverage

1.   The rights and obligations of the Parties to this Agreement in respect of public procurement shall be governed by the WTO Agreement on Government Procurement.

2.   The Parties agree to co-operate in the Joint Committee with the aim of increasing the understanding of their respective public procurement systems, and achieving further liberalisation and mutual opening up of public procurement markets.

Article 52: Exchange of Information

The Parties shall exchange the names and addresses of "contact points" responsible for providing information on the rules and regulations in the field of public procurement.

Article 53: Further Negotiations

If a Party grants to a non-Party, after the entry into force of this Agreement, additional benefits with regard to the access to their public procurement markets, it shall agree to enter into negotiations with a view to extending these benefits to another Party on a reciprocal basis.

VII PROTECTION OF INTELLECTUAL PROPERTY

Article 54: Protection of Intellectual Property

1.   The Parties shall grant and ensure adequate and effective protection of intellectual property rights, and provide for measures for the enforcement of such rights against infringement thereof, counterfeiting and piracy, in accordance with the provisions of this Article, Annex XII and the international agreements referred to therein.

2.   The Parties shall accord to each other's nationals treatment no less favourable than that they accord to their own nationals. Exemptions from this obligation must be in accordance with the substantive provisions of the WTO Agreement on Trade-Related Aspects of Intellectual Property Rights (hereinafter referred to as "the TRIPS Agreement"), in particular Articles 3 and 5 thereof.

3.   The Parties shall accord to each other's nationals treatment no less favourable than that they accord to nationals of any other State. Exemptions from this obligation must be in accordance with the substantive provisions of the TRIPS Agreement, in particular Articles 4 and 5 thereof.

4.   The Parties agree, upon request of any Party to the Joint Committee and subject to its consensus, to review the provisions on the protection of intellectual property rights contained in the present Article and in Annex XII, with a view to further improving the levels of protection and to avoiding or remedying trade distortions caused by actual levels of protection of intellectual property rights.

Article 55: The Joint Committee

1.   The Parties hereby establish the EFTA-Singapore Joint Committee comprising representatives of each Party. It shall be co-chaired by Ministers or by senior officials delegated by them for this purpose.

2.   The Joint Committee shall:

(a)   supervise the implementation of this Agreement;

(b)   keep under review the possibility of further removal of barriers to trade and other restrictive measures concerning commerce between the EFTA States and Singapore;

(c)   oversee the further elaboration of this Agreement;

(d)   supervise the work of all sub-committees and working groups established under this Agreement;

(e)   endeavour to resolve disputes that may arise regarding the interpretation or application of this Agreement; and

(f)   consider any other matter that may affect the operation of this Agreement.

3.   The Joint Committee may decide to set up such sub-committees and working groups as it considers necessary to assist it in accomplishing its tasks. Except where specifically provided for in this Agreement, the sub-committees and working groups shall work under a mandate established by the Joint Committee.

4.   The Joint Committee may take decisions as provided for in this Agreement. On other matters the Joint Committee may make recommendations.

5.   The Joint Committee shall take decisions and make recommendations by consensus.

6.   The Joint Committee shall meet whenever necessary but normally once every two years. The regular meetings of the Joint Committee shall be chaired jointly by one of the EFTA States and Singapore. The Joint Committee shall establish its rules of procedure.

7.   Each Party may request at any time, through a notice in writing to the other Parties, that a special meeting of the Joint Committee be held. Such a meeting shall take place within 30 days of receipt of the request, unless the Parties agree otherwise.

8.   The Joint Committee may decide to amend the Annexes and Appendices to this Agreement. Subject to paragraph 9, it may set a date for the entry into force of such decisions.

9.   If a representative of a Party in the Joint Committee has accepted a decision subject to the fulfillment of constitutional requirements, the decision shall enter into force on the date that the last Party notifies that its internal requirements have been fulfilled, unless the decision itself specifies a later date. The Joint Committee may decide that the decision shall enter into force for those Parties that have fulfilled their internal requirements, provided that Singapore is one of

those Parties. A Party may apply a decision of the Joint Committee provisionally until such decision enters into force, subject to its constitutional requirements.

Article 56: Scope and Coverage

1.   The provisions of this Chapter shall apply with respect to the avoidance or the settlement of all disputes arising from this Agreement between any one or more of the EFTA States and Singapore.

2.   Disputes on the same matter arising under both this Agreement and the WTO Agreement, or any agreement negotiated thereunder, to which the Parties are party, may be settled in either forum at the discretion of the complaining Party. The forum thus selected shall be used to the exclusion of the other.

3.   Before a Party initiates a dispute settlement proceedings under the WTO Agreement against another Party or Parties or, vice–versa, that Party shall notify all other Parties of its intention.

Article 57: Good Offices, Conciliation or Mediation

1.   Good offices, conciliation and mediation are procedures that are undertaken voluntarily if the Parties involved so agree. They may begin at any time and be terminated at any time.

2.   Proceedings involving good offices, conciliation and mediation shall be confidential and without prejudice to their rights in any other proceedings.

Article 58: Consultations

1.   The Parties shall at all times endeavour to agree on the interpretation and application of this Agreement, and shall make every attempt through co-operation and consultations to arrive at a mutually satisfactory resolution of any matter that might affect its operation.

2.   Any one or more of the EFTA States may request in writing consultations with Singapore, and vice-versa whenever a Party considers that a measure applied by the Party or Parties to which the request is made is inconsistent with this Agreement or that any benefit accruing to it directly or indirectly under this Agreement is impaired by such measure[12].The Party requesting consultations shall at the same time notify the other Parties in writing thereof. Consultations shall take place before the Joint Committee unless the Party or Parties making or receiving the request for consultations disagree.

3.   Consultations shall be held within 30 days from the date of receipt of the request for consultations. Consultations on urgent matters, including those on perishable agricultural goods, shall commence within 15 days from the receipt of the request for consultations.

4.   The Parties involved in the consultations shall provide sufficient information to enable a full examination of how the measure or other matter might affect the operation of this Agreement and treat any confidential or proprietary information exchanged in the course of consultations in the same manner as the Party providing the information.

---

[12]   The word "such" refers to "a measure applied by the Party or Parties to which the request is made".

5.   The consultations shall be confidential and without prejudice to the rights of the Parties involved in any further proceedings.

6.   The Parties involved in the consultations shall inform the other Parties of any mutually agreed resolution of the matter.

Article 59: Establishment of Arbitration Panel

1.   If the matter has not been resolved within 60 days, or 30 days in relation to a matter of urgency, after the date of receipt of the request for consultations, it may be referred to arbitration by one or more of the Parties involved by means of a written notification addressed to the Party or Parties complained against. A copy of this notification shall also be communicated to all Parties so that each Party may determine whether to participate in the dispute.

2.   Where more than one Party requests the establishment of an arbitration panel relating to the same matter, a single arbitration panel should be established to examine these complaints whenever feasible.

3.   A request for arbitration shall give the reason for the complaint including the identification of the measure at issue and an indication of the legal basis of the complaint.

Article 60: Arbitration Panel

1.   The arbitration panel shall comprise three members.

2.   In the written notification pursuant to Article 59, the Party or the Parties referring the dispute to arbitration shall designate one member of the arbitration panel.

3.   Within 15 days of the receipt of the notification referred to in paragraph 2, the Party or Parties to which it was addressed to shall designate one member of the arbitration panel.

4.   The Parties to the dispute shall agree on the appointment of the third arbitrator within 30 days of the appointment of the second arbitrator. The member thus appointed shall chair the arbitration panel.

5.   If all 3 members have not been designated or appointed within 45 days from the date of receipt of the notification referred to in paragraph 2, the necessary designations shall be made at the request of any Party to the dispute by the Director-General of the World Trade Organization within a further 30 days.

6.   The Chair of the arbitration panel shall not be a national of any of the Parties, nor have his or her usual place of residence in the territory of any of the Parties, nor be employed or previously have been employed by any of the Parties, nor have dealt with the case in any capacity.

7.   If an arbitrator dies, withdraws or is removed, a replacement shall be selected within 15 days in accordance with the selection procedure followed to select him or her. In such a case, any time period applicable to the arbitration panel proceedings shall be suspended for a period beginning on the date the arbitrator dies, withdraws or is removed and ending on the date the replacement is selected.

8.   The date of establishment of the arbitration panel shall be the date on which the Chair is appointed.

Article 61: Procedures of the Arbitration Panel

1.   Unless the Parties to the dispute agree otherwise, the arbitration panel proceedings shall be conducted in accordance with the Model Rules of Procedure that shall be adopted at the first meeting of the Joint Committee. Pending the adoption of such rules, the arbitration panel shall regulate its own procedures, unless the Parties to the dispute agree otherwise.

2.   Notwithstanding paragraph 1, for all arbitration panel proceedings the procedures shall ensure that:

(a)   the Parties to the dispute have the right to at least one hearing before the arbitration panel as well as the opportunity to provide initial and rebuttal written submissions;

(b)   the Parties to the dispute shall be invited to all the hearings held by the arbitration panel;

(c)   all submissions and comments made to the arbitration panel be available to the Parties to the dispute, subject to any requirements on confidentiality; and

(d)   hearings, deliberations and initial report and all written submissions to and communications with the arbitration panel be confidential.

3.   Unless the Parties to the dispute otherwise agree within 20 days from the date of delivery of the request for the establishment of the arbitration panel, the terms of reference shall be:

"To examine, in the light of the relevant provisions of the Agreement, the matter referred to in the request for the establishment of an arbitration panel pursuant to Article 59 and to make findings of law and fact together with the reasons therefore as well as recommendations, if any, for the resolution of the dispute."

4.   At the request of a Party to the dispute or on its own initiative, the arbitration panel may seek scientific information and technical advice from experts as it deems appropriate.

5.   The arbitration panel shall make its award based on the provisions of this Agreement, applied and interpreted in accordance with the rules of interpretation of public international law.

6.   Decisions of the arbitration panel shall be taken by a majority of its members. Panellists may furnish separate opinions on matters not unanimously agreed. No arbitration panel may disclose which panellists are associated with majority or minority opinions.

7.   The expenses of the arbitration panel, including the remuneration of its members, shall be borne by the Parties to the dispute in equal shares.

Article 62: Initial Report

1.   The arbitration panel shall within 90 days from the date of the establishment of the arbitration panel present to the Parties to the dispute an initial report.

2.   The arbitration panel shall base its report on the submissions and arguments of the Parties to the dispute and on any scientific information and technical advice pursuant to paragraph 4 of Article 61.

3.   A Party to the dispute may submit written comments to the arbitration panel on its initial report within 14 days of presentation of the report.

4.   In such an event, and after considering such written comments, the arbitration panel, on its own initiative or at the request of any of the Parties to the dispute, may:

(a)   request the views of any of the Parties to the dispute;

(b)   reconsider its report; and

(c)   make any further examination that it considers appropriate.

Article 63: Final Report

1.   The arbitration panel shall present to the Parties to the dispute a final report, containing the matters referred to in paragraph 2 of Article 62, including any separate opinions on matters not unanimously agreed, within 30 days of presentation of the initial report.

2.   Unless the Parties to the dispute decide otherwise, the final report shall be published 15 days after it is presented to them.

Article 64: Termination of Arbitration Panel Proceedings

A complaining Party may withdraw its complaint at any time before the initial report has been issued. Such withdrawal is without prejudice to its right to introduce a new complaint regarding the same issue at a later point in time.

Article 65: Implementation of Arbitration Panel Reports

1.   The final report shall be final and binding on the Parties to the dispute. Each Party to the dispute shall be bound to take the measures involved in carrying out the final report referred to in Article 63.

2.   The Party or Parties concerned shall inform the other Party or Parties to the dispute within 30 days after the final report has been issued of its intentions in respect of its implementation.

3.   The Parties to the dispute shall endeavour to agree on the specific measures that are required for implementing the final report. Wherever possible, the resolution shall be the removal of a measure not conforming to this Agreement, or failing such a resolution, compensation.

4.   The Party or Parties concerned shall promptly comply with the final report. If it is impracticable to comply immediately, the Parties to the dispute shall endeavour to agree on a reasonable period of time to do so. In the absence of such agreement, any Party to the dispute may request the original arbitration panel to determine the length of the reasonable period of time, in light of the particular circumstances of the case. The ruling of the arbitration panel shall be given within 15 days from that request.

5.   The Party or Parties concerned shall notify to the other Party or Parties to the dispute the measures adopted in order to implement the final report before the expiry of the reasonable period of time determined in accordance with paragraph 4. Upon that notification, any Party to the dispute may request the original arbitration panel to rule on the conformity of those measures with the final report. The ruling of the arbitration panel shall be given within 60 days from that request.

6.   If the Party or Parties concerned fails to notify the implementing measures before the expiry of the reasonable period of time determined in accordance with paragraph 4, or if the arbitration panel rules that the implementing measures notified by the Party or Parties concerned are inconsistent with the final report, such Party or Parties shall, if so requested by the complaining Party or Parties, enter into consultations with a view to agree on a mutually acceptable compensation. If no such agreement has been reached within 20 days from the request, the complaining Party or Parties shall be entitled to suspend only the application of benefits granted under this Agreement equivalent to those affected by the measure found to violate this Agreement.

7.   In considering what benefits to suspend, the complaining Party or Parties should first seek to suspend benefits in the same sector or sectors as that affected by the measure that the arbitration panel has found to violate this Agreement. The complaining Party or Parties that consider it is not practicable or effective to suspend benefits in the same sector or sectors may suspend benefits in other sectors.

8.   The complaining Party or Parties shall notify the other Party or Parties of the benefits which it intends to suspend no later than 60 days before the date on which the suspension is due to take effect. Within 15 days from that notification, any of the Parties to the dispute may request the original arbitration panel to rule on whether the benefits which the complaining Party or Parties intend to suspend are equivalent to those affected by the measure found to violate this Agreement, and whether the proposed suspension is in accordance with paragraphs 6 and 7. The ruling of the arbitration panel shall be given within 45 days from that request. Benefits shall not be suspended until the arbitration panel has issued its ruling.

9.   The suspension of benefits shall be temporary and shall only be applied by the complaining Party or Parties until the measure found to violate this Agreement has been withdrawn or amended so as to bring it into conformity with this Agreement, or the Parties to the dispute have reached agreement on a resolution of the dispute.

10.   At the request of any of the Parties to the dispute, the original arbitration panel shall rule on the conformity with the final report of any implementing measures adopted after the suspension of benefits and, in light of such ruling, whether the suspension of benefits should be terminated or modified. The ruling of the arbitration panel shall be given within 30 days from the date of that request.

11.   The rulings provided for in paragraphs 4, 5, 8 and 10 shall be binding.

Article 66: Other Provisions

Any time period mentioned in this Chapter may be extended by mutual agreement of the Parties involved.

ANNEX VI

REFERRED TO IN ARTICLE 23
MOST-FAVOURED-NATION TREATMENT

1.   A Party may maintain measures inconsistent with Article 23 (1) provided that such measures have been listed in and meet the conditions in the Annex on Article II Exemptions to the GATS.

2.   Treatment granted under agreements concluded by one of the Parties with a non-Party which have been notified under Article V bis of the GATS shall not be subject to Article 23.

ANNEX VIII
REFERRED TO IN ARTICLE 36

FINANCIAL SERVICES

Article 1
Definitions

For the purposes of Chapter III and this Annex:

I.   "financial service" means any service of a financial nature offered by a financial service supplier of a Party. Financial services include the following activities:

   A.   Insurance and insurance-related services:

      1.   direct insurance (including co-insurance):

         (a)   life;

         (b)   non-life;

      2.   reinsurance and retrocession;

      3.   insurance inter-mediation, such as brokerage and agency;

      4.   services auxiliary to insurance, such as consultancy, actuarial, risk assessment and claim settlement services.

   B.   Banking and other financial services (excluding insurance):

1.   acceptance of deposits and other repayable funds from the public;

2.   lending of all types, including consumer credit, mortgage credit, factoring and financing of commercial transaction;

3.   financial leasing;

4.   all payment and money transmission services, including credit, charge and debit cards, travellers cheques and bankers drafts;

5.   guarantees and commitments;

6.   trading for own account or for account of customers, whether on an exchange, in an over-the-counter market or otherwise, the following:

     (a)   money market instruments (including cheques, bills, certificates of deposits);

     (b)   foreign exchange;

     (c)   derivative products including, but not limited to, futures and options;

     (d)   exchange rate and interest rate instruments, including products such as swaps, forward rate agreements;

     (e)   transferable securities;

     (f)   other negotiable instruments and financial assets, including bullion;

7.   participation in issues of all kinds of securities, including underwriting and placement as agent (whether publicly or privately) and provision of services related to such issues;

8.   money broking;

9.   asset management, such as cash or portfolio management, all forms of collective investment management, pension fund management, custodial, depository and trust services;

10.   settlement and clearing services for financial assets, including securities, derivative products, and other negotiable instruments;

11.   provision and transfer of financial information, and financial data processing and related software by suppliers of other financial services;

12.   advisory, intermediation and other auxiliary financial services on all the activities listed in subparagraphs (1) through (11), including credit

reference and analysis, investment and portfolio research and advice, advice on acquisitions and on corporate restructuring and strategy.

II.   "financial service supplier" means any natural or juridical person of a Party wishing to supply or supplying financial services but the term "financial service supplier" does not include a public entity.

III.   "public entity" means:

(i)   a government, a central bank or a monetary authority, of a Party, or an entity owned or controlled by a Party, that is principally engaged in carrying out governmental functions or activities for governmental purposes, not including an entity principally engaged in supplying financial services on commercial terms; or

(ii)   a private entity, performing functions normally performed by a central bank or monetary authority, when exercising those functions.

IV.   For the purpose of scheduling market access commitments in financial services, the mode of supply referred to in Article 22 (o) (i) of this Agreement means the supply of financial services by non-resident suppliers of financial services into the territory of a Party; a "non-resident supplier of financial services" is a financial service supplier of a Party which supplies a financial service into the territory of another Party from an establishment located in the territory of a GATS Member, regardless of whether such a financial service supplier has or has not a commercial presence in the territory of the Party in which the financial service is supplied.

Article 2
National Treatment

1.   Under terms and conditions that accord national treatment, each Party shall grant to financial service suppliers of another Party established in its territory access to payment and clearing systems operated by public entities, and to official funding and refinancing facilities available in the normal course of ordinary business. This paragraph is not intended to confer access to the Party's lender of last resort facilities.

2.   When membership or participation in, or access to, any self-regulatory body, securities or futures exchange or market, clearing agency, or any other organisation or association, is required by a Party in order for financial service suppliers of any other Party to supply financial services on an equal basis with financial service suppliers of the Party, or when the Party provides directly or indirectly such entities, privileges or advantages in supplying financial services, the Party shall ensure that such entities accord national treatment to financial service suppliers of any other Party resident in the territory of the Party.

Article 3
Prudential Measures

1.   Nothing in Chapter III and its Annexes shall be construed to prevent a Party from adopting or maintaining reasonable measures for prudential reasons, such as:

(a)   the protection of investors, depositors, policy-holders, policy-claimants, persons to whom a fiduciary duty is owed by a financial service supplier, or any similar financial market participants; or

(b)   the maintenance of the safety, soundness, integrity or financial responsibility of financial service suppliers; or

(c)   ensuring the integrity and stability of a Party's financial system.

2.   These measures shall not be more burdensome than necessary to achieve their aim, and shall not constitute a means of arbitrary or unjustifiable discrimination against financial service suppliers of another Party in comparison to its own like financial service suppliers, or a disguised restriction on trade in services.

3.   Nothing in Chapter III and its Annexes shall be construed to require a Party to disclose information relating to the affairs and accounts of individual consumers or any confidential or proprietary information in the possession of public entities.

4.   Each Party shall make its best endeavours to ensure that the Basle Committee's "Core Principles for Effective Banking Supervision", the standards and principles of the International Association of Insurance Supervisors and the International Organisation of Securities Commissions' "Objectives and Principles of Securities Regulation" are implemented and applied in its territory.

Article 4
Recognition

1.   A Party may recognise prudential measures of any other country in determining how the Party's measures relating to financial services shall be applied. Such recognition, which may be achieved through harmonisation or otherwise, may be based on an agreement or arrangement with the country concerned or may be accorded autonomously.

2.   A Party that is a party to such an agreement or arrangement referred to in paragraph 1, whether future or existing, shall afford adequate opportunity for another Party to negotiate their accession to such agreements or arrangements, or to negotiate comparable ones with it, under circumstances in which there would be equivalent regulation, oversight, implementation of such regulation, and, if appropriate, procedures concerning the sharing of information between the parties to the agreement or arrangement. Where a Party accords recognition autonomously, it shall afford adequate opportunity for another Party to demonstrate that such circumstances exist.

Article 5
Data Processing

1.   Each Party shall permit a financial service supplier of another Party to transfer information in electronic or other form, into and out of its territory, for data processing where such processing is required in the ordinary course of business of such financial service supplier.

2.   As far as the transfer of data obtained in the course of the supply of financial services is concerned, each Party shall adopt or maintain adequate safeguards on the protection of the

confidentiality and integrity of such records, and to that end Parties may have consultations whenever necessary.

3.   Nothing in this Article restricts the right of a Party to protect personal data, personal privacy and the confidentiality of individual records and accounts so long as such right is not used to circumvent the provisions of this Agreement.

Article 6
Specific Exceptions

1.   Nothing in Chapter III and its Annexes shall be construed to prevent a Party, including its public entities, from exclusively conducting activities or supplying services in its territory forming part of a public retirement plan or statutory system of social security.

2.   Nothing in Chapter III and its Annexes shall be construed to prevent a Party, including its public entities, from exclusively conducting activities or supplying services in its territory for the account or with the guarantee or using the financial resources of the Party, or its public entities.

3.   If a Party allows any of the activities or services referred to in paragraphs 1 or 2 to be conducted or supplied by its financial service suppliers in competition with a public entity or a financial service supplier, "services" shall include such activities.

4.   Nothing in Chapter III and its Annexes shall apply to activities conducted or services supplied by a central bank or monetary authority or by any other public entity, in pursuit of monetary or exchange rate policies.

Article 7
Modification of Schedules

1.   A Party may propose to introduce or amend limitations contained in a specific commitment referred to in the financial services section of its Schedule, to the extent that such amendments do not decrease the level of commitment undertaken by the Party and provided that the proposed amendments do not reduce the opportunities of the service suppliers of another Party affected by the amendments compared to the situation prevailing immediately before the amendments.

2.   The amending Party shall notify its intent to amend a commitment to the other Parties at least three months before the intended date of implementation of the amendment. On receiving such written notification, the other Parties may request consultations regarding the proposed amendment. If agreement is not reached by consultations, the matter shall be dealt with in accordance with Chapter IX.

ANNEX IX
REFERRED TO IN ARTICLE 36

TELECOMMUNICATIONS SERVICES

Article 1
Definitions

1.   For the purposes of this Annex:

a)   "Supplier" refers to a telecommunications operator that supplies or intends to supply telecommunications services.

b)   "Dominant Supplier" is a Supplier who, on its own or, together with other Suppliers based on an agreement or otherwise, has the ability to materially affect the terms of participation (having regard to price and supply) in the relevant market for a specific telecommunications service as a result of:

i)   control over essential facilities; or

ii)   use of its position in the market.

c)   "Essential facilities" mean facilities of a public telecommunications network or service that

i)   are exclusively or predominantly provided by a single or limited number of suppliers; and

ii)   cannot feasibly be economically or technically substituted in order to provide a service.

Article 2
General Principles

1.   Competition and Reliance on Market Forces

With a view to ensure the supply of cost-effective, high quality telecommunications services, the Parties shall adopt or maintain appropriate measures to prevent anti-competitive practices of Suppliers. There shall be primary reliance on private negotiations and industry self-regulation, subject to requirements designed to prevent anti-competitive conduct.

2.   Regulatory Principles

Measures and their application shall be objective, impartial and non-discriminatory. They shall, to the extent feasible, be technology-neutral.

3.   Transparency

Regulatory requirements shall be applied in a transparent manner. Unless there is an overriding public or private interest not to do so, the regulatory authorities shall make interconnection agreements publicly available.

4.   Avoidance of Unnecessary Delay

Recognising the need to respond rapidly to changing market forces, all decisions and directions pertaining to the regulatory measures outlined in this Annex, including decisions regarding appeals, shall be implemented by the relevant authorities as quickly as reasonably possible.

5.   Right to appeal

A Supplier affected by a decision of a regulatory authority shall have recourse to appeal to an independent administrative body and/or a court, in accordance with domestic legislation.

Article 3
Licensing Procedures

1.   Where a licence is required, all the licensing criteria and the period of time normally required to reach a decision concerning an application for a licence shall be made publicly available.

2.   The granting of the license shall be based on the licensing criteria referred to in paragraph 1.

3.   The period of time normally required to reach a decision concerning an application for a licence shall be reasonable.

4.   Where a licence has been denied to an applicant, the reasons for the denial shall be made known to the applicant upon request.

Article 4
Allocation and Use of Scarce Resources

Any procedures for the allocation and use of scarce resources, including frequencies, numbers and rights of way, shall be carried out in an objective, timely, transparent and non-discriminatory manner. The current state of allocated frequency bands shall be made publicly available.

Article 5
Competitive Safeguards

1.   The Parties shall provide for measures to prevent anti-competitive conduct by Dominant Suppliers, acting singly or collectively, which frustrate the benefits of this Agreement as it relates to telecommunications services.

2.   With regard to Dominant Suppliers, the anti-competitive practices, referred to in paragraph 1, shall include in particular:

a)   engaging in anti-competitive pricing or cross-subsidisation;

b)   using information obtained from competitors with anti-competitive results;

c)   not making available to other Suppliers on a timely basis technical information about essential facilities and commercially relevant information which are necessary for them to provide services; and

d)   not offering to other Suppliers, on a non-discriminatory basis, access to essential facilities and commercially relevant information which are necessary for them to provide services.

Article 6
Minimum Interconnection Obligations

1.   Obligation to Interconnect with Other Suppliers

Suppliers offering a public switched telephone service shall interconnect either directly or indirectly with other Suppliers.

2.   Disclose Technical and Commercial Conditions

A Supplier shall be required to make publicly available, in a clear format and in sufficient detail, any technical and commercial conditions concerning interconnection.

3.   Protection of Confidential Information

According to domestic laws and regulations, Suppliers shall protect from disclosure any confidential or proprietary information obtained from another Supplier in the course of negotiating or implementing an interconnection agreement. Suppliers may use such information only for the provision of the specific Interconnection Related Services (IRS) requested.

4.   Duty to Prevent Technical Harm to the Network

A Supplier that interconnects with another Supplier shall only use telecommunications installations that do not cause physical or technical harm to the other Supplier's network.

5.   Comply with Mandatory Technical Standards

Suppliers shall be required to comply with any applicable mandatory technical standard adopted. The telecommunications industry shall be consulted with regard to efforts to determine which technical standards should be made mandatory.

6.   Facilitate Change of Suppliers

Suppliers shall be required to take any reasonable action necessary to allow an end user that chooses to obtain service from a different Supplier to do so with minimum difficulty. This includes the duty, where technically feasible, to allow the end user to retain the same telephone number or network address and to continue to receive service using the same local loop.

7.   Duty to Provide Billing Information

Unless they agree otherwise, the interconnecting Suppliers shall be required to exchange information that is necessary to provide accurate and timely billing to themselves, their affiliates or other Suppliers.

Article 7
Interconnection with Dominant Suppliers

1.   A Dominant Supplier shall grant interconnection to other Suppliers without discrimination and in accordance with the principles of transparent and cost oriented price policy. The provisions of Article 6, paragraphs 2 to 7 shall also apply.

2.   Interconnection with a Dominant Supplier shall be ensured at any technically feasible point in the network. Such interconnection shall be provided:

   a)   under non-discriminatory terms, conditions (including technical standards and specifications) and rates and of a quality no less favourable than that provided for its own like services or for like services of non-affiliated Suppliers or for its subsidiaries or other affiliates;

   b)   in a timely fashion, on terms, conditions (including technical standards and specifications) and cost-oriented rates that are transparent, reasonable, having regard to economic feasibility, and sufficiently unbundled so that Suppliers need not pay for network components or facilities they do not require for the service to be provided;

   c)   upon request, at points in addition to the network termination points offered to the majority of users, subject to charges that reflect the cost of construction of necessary additional facilities.

3.   A Supplier that seeks to interconnect with a Dominant Supplier shall be able to do so pursuant to the terms of a Reference Interconnection Offer (RIO) extended by the Dominant Supplier. The RIO shall contain written statements of the prices, terms and conditions on which a Dominant Supplier will provide interconnection services to a Supplier seeking interconnection. The RIO shall be required to contain the following:

   a)   A list and description of the IRS offered, the terms and conditions for such services, the commercial and technical requirements;

   b)   A list of cost-based prices for the IRS where the Supplier has a dominant position. The Dominant Supplier shall use an established methodology based on long-run average incremental costs (LRAIC) or any other forward-looking methodology better reflecting the relevant costs.

4.   The RIO must be modular, allowing a Supplier seeking interconnection to purchase only those IRS that it wants to obtain. The RIO must be sufficiently detailed to enable a Supplier that is willing to accept its prices, terms and conditions to obtain IRS without having to engage in negotiations with the Dominant Supplier. If a Supplier accepts the RIO, further discussions will be limited to implementing the accepted prices, terms and conditions.

Article 8
Interconnection Dispute Resolution

Where Suppliers are unable to resolve disputes regarding the negotiation of an Interconnection Agreement with Dominant Suppliers within a stipulated time, they shall have recourse to assistance from the relevant regulatory authorities to resolve disputes regarding appropriate terms, conditions and rates for interconnection within a reasonable time frame. The relevant regulatory authority shall fix the conditions for the interconnection in accordance with the normal principles governing the market and the sector in question and in accordance with the principles of Article 2, Article 6 and Article 7. Domestic legislation may provide for special conciliation proceedings.

Article 9
Independent Regulators

The regulatory authority shall be separate from, and not accountable to, any Supplier of basic telecommunications services.

Article 10
Universal Service

Domestic regulation may define the kind of universal service obligation that should be maintained. Such obligations will not be regarded as anti-competitive per se, provided they are administered in a transparent, non-discriminatory and competitively neutral manner and are not more burdensome than necessary for the kind of universal service defined by domestic regulation.

ANNEX XI

REFERRED TO IN ARTICLE 46

INVESTMENT RESERVATIONS

The reservations referred to in Article 46 are set out in the Appendices attached to this Annex.

APPENDIX 4 TO ANNEX XI
RESERVATIONS BY ICELAND

ICELAND

Sector: All sectors

Sub-sector: Company Law

Obligation or article in respect
of which the reservation is taken: National Treatment and Most-Favoured-Nation Treatment

Level of Government:	National
Legal source or authority of the measure:	Law No. 138/1994 Respecting Private Limited Companies, Law No. 2/1995 Respecting Public Limited Companies, Law No. 34/1991 on Investment by Non-Residents in Business Enterprises
Succinct description of the measure:	The majority of the founders of a private limited company or a public limited company must be resident in Iceland or another EEA[1] member state. The Minister of Commerce can grant exemptions from these restrictions on grounds of an applications. The manager/-s and at least half the board of directors of a private limited company or a public limited company must be resident in Iceland or another EEA member state. The Minister of Commerce can grant exemptions from these restrictions on grounds of an applications
Purpose or motivation of the measure:	To secure that the legal venue of the majority of the board of directors and managers is within Icelandic jurisdiction
Sector:	All sectors
Sub-sector:	Real estate
Obligation or article in respect of which the reservation is taken:	National Treatment and Most-Favoured-Nation Treatment
Level of Government:	National
Legal source or authority of the measure:	Law No. 19/1966 on the Right to Own and Use Real Estate, Law No. 34/1991 on Investment by Non-Residents in Business Enterprises
Succinct description of the measure:	Only Icelandic citizens and Icelandic legal entities and citizens and legal entities from another EEA[2] member state are allowed to own real estate in Iceland unless the ownership and use is linked to an investment in real estate pertaining to the business activity of the investor. The same applies to the

---

[1] European Economic Area
[2] European Economic Area

255

hiring of a real estate if the duration of the lease lasts for more than 3 years. These restriction do not apply to a non-EEA citizen who has been residing in Iceland for at least five years. The Minister of Justice can grant exemptions from these restrictions on grounds of an applications

Purpose or motivation of the measure:	Fluctuations in real estate prices due to possible excess foreign demand can adversely affect the domestic market for housing and summer houses (secondary homes)
Sector:	Fisheries
Sub-sector:	Fishing, whaling
Obligation or article in respect of which the reservation is taken:	National Treatment
Level of Government:	National
Legal source or authority of the measure:	Law No. 13/1992 on the Right to Conduct Fishing in Iceland's Economic Zone, Law No. 34/1991 on Investment by Non-Residents in Business Enterprises, Law No. 26/1949 on Whaling
Succinct description of the measure:	Only Icelandic citizens and Icelandic legal entities under Icelandic control are allowed to fish in the Icelandic economic zone. The same applies to whaling
Purpose or motivation of the measure:	The relative economic importance of the fishing industry for Iceland, with fish and fish products constituting around half of the country's foreign earnings, as well as Iceland's determination to maintain a sustained yield from its fishing stocks. Iceland believes that it is in a better position to preserve its fishing stocks if those that harvest those stocks come under Icelandic jurisdiction
Sector:	Fisheries
Sub-sector:	Fish Processing
Obligation or article in respect of which the reservation is taken:	National Treatment
Level of Government:	National

Legal source or authority of the measure:

Law No. 34/1991 on Investment by Non-Residents in Business Enterprises

Succinct description of the measure:

Only Icelandic citizens and Icelandic legal entities are allowed to own and manage enterprises engaged in fish processing in Iceland. Fish processing in this context is freezing, salting, drying and any other process used to initially preserve fish and fish products, including melting and meal processing. This reservation does not apply to secondary fish processing

Purpose or motivation of the measure:

See 1. The reservation on fish processing is an integral part of retaining such controls in the field of fishing and whaling. The relative economic importance of the fishing industry for Iceland, with fish and fish products constituting around half of the country's foreign earnings, as well as Iceland's determination to maintain a sustained yield from its fishing stocks. Iceland believes that it is in a better position to preserve its fishing stocks if those that harvest those stocks come under Icelandic jurisdictionas described in 1

Sector:

Fisheries

Subsector:

Fish Auctioning

Obligation or Article in respect of which the reservation is taken:

National Treatment

Level of Government:

National

Legal source or authority of the measure:

Law No. 123/1989 on the Auctioning of Fish

Succinct description of the measure:

Only Icelandic citizens and Icelandic legal entities are allowed to own and manage enterprises engaged in fish auctioning in Iceland

Purpose or motivation of the measure:

See 1. The reservation on fish auctioning is an integral part of retaining such controls as described in 1 in the field of fishing and whaling. The relative economic importance of the fishing industry for Iceland, with fish and fish products constituting around half of the country's foreign earnings, as well as Iceland's determination to maintain a sustained yield from its fishing stocks. Iceland believes that it is in a better position to preserve its fishing stocks if those that harvest those stocks come under Icelandic jurisdiction

APPENDIX 5 TO ANNEX XI
RESERVATIONS BY LIECHTENSTEIN

LIECHTENSTEIN

Sector:	All sectors
Sub-sector:	--
Obligation or article in respect of which the reservation is taken:	National Treatment
Level of Government:	National
Legal source or authority of the measure:	Gewerbegesetz vom 10. Dezember 1969 (Act on Commercial Law of 10 December 1969), LR (Systematic Collection of Liechtenstein Law) 930.1 and the relevant laws with regard to categories mentioned in Article 2 Paragraph 1 of that Act as well as relevant Parliament or Government decisions
Succinct description of the measure:	The establishment of a commercial presence by a juridical person (including branches) is subject to the requirement that no objection for reasons of national economy (balanced proportion of national and foreign capital; balanced ratio of foreigners in comparison with the number of resident population; balanced ratio of total number of jobs in the economy in comparison with the number of the resident population; balanced geographic situation; balanced development of the national economy, between and within the sectors) exists
Purpose or motivation of the measure:	To ensure a balanced development of the national economy
Sector:	All sectors
Sub-sector:	--
Obligation or article in respect of which the reservation is taken:	National Treatment
Level of Government:	National
Legal source or authority of the measure:	Gewerbegesetz vom 10. Dezember 1969 (Commercial Law Act) Personen-und Gesellschaftsrecht vom 20. Januar 1926 (Company Law), LR 216.0

Succinct description of the measure:	The establishment of a commercial presence by an individual is subject to the requirement of prior residence during a certain period of time and of permanent domicile in Liechtenstein. He/she must possess sector specific government-recognized professional qualifications
	The establishment of a commercial presence by a juridical person (including branches) is subject to the following requirements: At least one of the managers has to fulfil the requirements of prior residence during a certain period of time and of permanent domicile in Liechtenstein. He must possess sector specific government-recognized professional qualifications. The majority of the administrators (authorized to manage and represent the juridical person) must be resident in Liechtenstein and have either to be Liechtenstein citizens or have prior residence during a certain period of time in Liechtenstein. The general and the limited partnership have to fulfil the same conditions as corporations with limited liability (juridical person). In addition the majority of the associates have to be Liechtenstein citizens or to have prior residence during a certain period of time in LiechtensteinThe Liechtenstein company law does not prohibit joint stock companies from foreseeing in their articles of incorporation the preclusion or limitation of the transfer of registered shares
Purpose or motivation of the measure:	To facilitate judicial proceedings
Sector:	All sectors
Subsector:	--
Obligation or article in respect of Which the reservation is taken:	National Treatment
Level of Government:	National
Legal source or authority of the measure:	Agreement on the European Economic Area of 2 May 1992 (EEA Agreement)
Succinct description of the measure:	Treatment accorded to subsidiaries of third-country companies formed in accordance with the law of an EEA Member State and having registered office, central administration or principal place of business within an EEA Member State is not extended to

branches or agencies established in an EEA Member State by a third-country company Treatment less favourable may be accorded to subsidiaries of third countries having only their registered office in the territory of an EEA Member State unless they show that they possess an effective and continuous link with the economy of one of the EEA Member States

Purpose or motivation of the measure:	To ensure that benefits from the EEA Agreement are not automatically accorded to third countries
Sector:	All sectors
Subsector:	--
Obligation or article in respect of which the reservation is taken:	National Treatment
Level of Government National and Sub-national Legal source or authority of the measure:	Grundverkehrsgesetz vom 9 Dezember 1992 (Law on the acquisition of real estate of 9 December 1992), LR 214.11
Succinct description of the measure:	All acquisitions of real estate are subject to authorization. Such authorization is granted only if an actual and proven requirement for living or business purposes is given and a certain period of residence has been completed. Non-residents are excluded from the acquisition of real estate
Purpose or motivation of the measure:	Extreme scarcity of available land. Preservation of access to real estate for the resident population and maintenance of a balanced geographic situation

APPENDIX 6 TO ANNEX XI

RESERVATIONS BY NORWAY

NORWAY

Sector:	All sectors
Sub-sector:	--
Obligation or article in respect of which the reservation is taken:	National Treatment and Most Favoured Nation Treatment

Level of Government:	National
Legal source or authority of the measure:	Companies Act of 13 June 1997 No 44 (aksjeloven) and Joint Stock Public Companies Act of 13 June 1997 No 45 (allmennaksjeselskapsloven)
Succinct description of the measure:	Manager and at least one half of the members of the board must be domiciled in Norway. The residency criteria do not apply to nationals of an EEA State who are permanent residents of one of these States. The Ministry of Trade and Industry may grant exemptions from this provision
Purpose or motivation of the measure:	The resident criteria are based on reasons of jurisdiction, in order to ensure that the persons responsible for the company's affairs are accessible
Sector:	Real estate
Sub-sector:	Secondary residences
Obligation or article in respect of which the reservation is taken:	National Treatment
Level of Government:	National
Legal source or authority of the measure:	Concessions Act of 31 May 1974 No. 19
Succinct description of the measure:	Acquisition or leasing of secondary residences by non-residents is subject to a concession
Purpose or motivation of the measure:	To prevent that prices in the market for secondary residences are adversely affected due to possible increases in demand from non-residents
Sector:	Fishing and fish processing
Subsector:	--
Obligation or Article in respect of which the reservation is taken:	National Treatment
Level of Government: Legal source or authority of the measure:	Regulation of Participation in Fishing Act of 16 June 1972 No 57 Economic Zone Act of 17 December 1976 No 91 The Fishing Limit Act of 17 June 1966 No 19
Succinct description of the measure:	A concession to acquire a fishing vessel or share in a company which owns such vessels can only be

given to a Norwegian citizen or a body that can be defined as a Norwegian citizen. A company is regarded as having equal rights with a Norwegian citizen when its main office is situated in Norway and the majority of the Board, including the Chair of the Board, are Norwegian citizens and have stayed in the country the last two years. Norwegian citizens also have to own a minimum of 60% of the shares and have to be authorised to vote for at least 60% of the votesOwnership to the fishing fleet shall be reserved for professional fishermen. To obtain the right to own a fishing vessel, one has to have a record of active, professional fishing on a Norwegian fishing boat for at least three of the last five yearsIt is prohibited for those persons than Norwegian nationals or companies, as defined above, to process, pack or transship fish, crustaceans and mollusc or parts and products of these inside the fishing limits of the Norwegian Economic zone. This applies to catches from both Norwegian and foreign vessels. Exceptions are granted under special circumstances

Purpose or motivation of the measure:	Resource conservation and management

APPENDIX 7 TO ANNEX XI

RESERVATIONS BY SWITZERLAND

SWITZERLAND

Sector:	All sectors
Sub-sector:	--
Obligation or article in respect of which the reservation is taken:	National Treatment
Level of Government:	National
Legal source or authority of the measure:	Federal Act of 30 March 1911 (Code of Obligations) supplementing the Swiss Civil Code (Systematic Collection of Federal Laws and Regulations [RS] No. 220)
Succinct description of the measure:	- The vast majority of companies in Switzerland are organized as **corporations** (Société anonyme [SA]-Aktiengesellschaft [AG]), featuring a predetermined capital and shareholders' liability

limited to the nominal capital invested. Of the members of the board of directors of a Swiss corporation, the majority must be Swiss citizens residing in Switzerland. Exceptions are possible in the case of holding companies

-       **Limited liability companies** (Société à responsabilité limité [Sàrl]-Gesellschaft mit beschränkter Haftung [GmbH]) are characterized by a limited capital divided into quotas. In a limited liability company, at least one managing officer must be residing in Switzerland

-       A foreign company may also establish one or several **branch offices** in Switzerland. At least one representative of a branch office must be residing in Switzerland

Purpose or motivation of the measure:	To facilitate judicial proceedings
Sector:	All sectors
Sub-sector:	Real estate
Obligation or article in respect of which the reservation is taken:	National Treatment
Level of Government:	National and Sub-national
Legal source or authority of the measure:	Federal Act of 16 December 1983 on the acquisition of real estate by persons abroad (RS 211.412.41)
Succinct description of the measure:	Foreign nationals not residing in Switzerland and companies established or controlled from abroad are not allowed to invest in the residential property market (except for residential property directly linked to a business presence) and in agricultural real estate. For the acquisition of vacation homes, a cantonal permit is required
Purpose or motivation of the measure:	Scarcity of available land

APPENDIX 3 TO ANNEX XI

RESERVATIONS BY SINGAPORE

SINGAPORE

A.	All sectors
Obligation Concerned:	National Treatment
Legal Citation:	Companies Act, Cap 50 (1994) Business Registration Act, Cap 32 (2001) Business Registration Act, Cap 32 (2001)
Description:	Compliance by Foreign Companies and Foreigners with the Companies Act and Business Registration Act requirements as to the establishment of a branch/business firm/company and the filing of accounts (where applicable).

a) Commercial presence, right of establishment and movement of juridical persons are subject to compliance with the following provisions:

   i) a foreigner who wishes to register a business firm must have a local manager who should be:

   A) a Singapore citizen;

   B) a Singapore permanent resident; or

   C) a Singapore employment pass holder. However, a foreigner who is a Singapore permanent resident or a Singapore employment pass holder can register a business without appointing a local manager;

   ii) for establishing a company, at least 1 director of the company must be locally resident;

   iii) all branches of foreign companies registered in Singapore must have at least 2 locally resident agents. (To qualify as locally resident, a person should be either a Singapore citizen or Singapore permanent resident or Singapore employment pass holder.)

b) establishment of the branch of a foreign company is subject to the filing of the prescribed documents.

Purpose or motivation of the measure:	To facilitate judicial proceedings
B.	All sectors
Obligation Concerned:	National Treatment
Legal Citation:	Residential Property Act, Cap 274 (1985) Housing & Development Act, Cap 129 (1997) Executive Condominium Housing Scheme Act, Cap 99A (1997) Banking Act, Cap 19 Finance Companies Act, Cap 108 MAS Act, Cap 186

Description:

1 Ownership of land:

    a) non-citizens cannot own residential land.

2 Ownership of property:

    a) non-citizens are restricted from purchasing lande property and residential property in a building of less than 6 levels;

    b) there are also restrictions on non-citizens owning residential properties under government public housing schemes;

3 Housing loans: Measures may be imposed to restrict financial institutions from extending S$ loans to non-Singapore citizens and non-Singapore companies for the purchase of residential property in Singapore.

Purpose or motivation of the measure: Scarcity of available land

C.   All Sectors

Obligation Concerned: National Treatment

Legal Citation: Banking Act, Cap. 19, MAS Notice 757 to Banks Securities Industry Act, Cap. 289, MAS Notice 1201 to Securities Dealers Finance Companies Act, Cap 108, MAS Notice 816 to Finance Companies Insurance Act, Cap 142, MAS Notice 109 to InsurersMAS Act, Cap 186, MAS Notice 1105 to Merchant Banks

Description: 1   Where amounts exceed S$5 million per entity[1], non-residents may obtain from banks[2] S$ credit facilities for any purpose in Singapore or overseas, subject to the following conditions:

                                        a.   For S$ investments in financial assets and real estate, banks are required to ensure that the S$ credit facilities extended are withdrawn when the investments, or part thereof, are in any way converted into S$ cash proceeds.

                                        b.   Where the S$ proceeds are to be used or invested offshore, non-residents are required to swap these proceeds into foreign currency upon draw-down. In this instance, banks are not allowed to convert the S$ proceeds into foreign currency via the spot or forward market. For S$ equity listings and bond issues by non-residents wishing to tap S$ markets to finance their activities offshore, non-residents are required to swap or convert the S$ proceeds into foreign currency for use offshore.

                                   2   Banks should not extend S$ credit facilities to non-residents for speculative activities in the S$ currency market.

---

[1]   For financial institutions seeking to obtain S$ credit facilities, each subsidiary is considered a separate entity while the Head Office and all overseas branches are collectively regarded as one entity.

[2]   The restrictions in this Reservation describe the measures in MAS' Notice 757 to Banks. Similar measures are set out in MAS Notice 1201 to Securities Dealers, MAS Notice 816 to Finance Companies, MAS Notice 109 to Insurers, and MAS Notice 1105 to Merchant Banks.

3   Banks may lend S$-denominated securities in any amount to non-residents as long as it is fully collateralised with S$ cash or other S$ assets upon the extension of the S$-denominated securities loan.

4   Banks may transact with non-residents S$ currency options as long as there is a requirement to hedge the S$ exchange rate risks arising from trade with, or economic and financial activities in, Singapore. There must be documentary evidence of the non-resident's need to hedge its trade with, or its economic and financial activities in Singapore. (The above reservation shall not be construed as causing a delay in transfers as defined in Article 44).

Purpose or motivation of the measure:	Measures with regards to the internationalisation of the Singapore currency
D.	Printing and Publishing Sector
Obligation Concerned:	National Treatment and Most-Favoured-Nation Treatment
Legal Source or Authority:	Newspaper and Printing Presses Act, Cap 206 (1991 Revised Edition) Ministry of Information, Communications and the Arts Ministry of Information, Communications and the Arts
Description:	National Treatment and Most-Favoured-Nation Treatment shall not apply to the printing and publishing sector
Purpose or motivation of the measure:	National social policy and national interest
E.	Arms and Explosives Sector
Obligation Concerned:	National Treatment and Most-Favoured-Nation Treatment
Legal Citation:	Arms and Explosives Act, Cap 13 (1985)
Description:	National Treatment and Most-Favoured-Nation Treatment shall not apply to the arms and explosives sector. The manufacture, use, sale, storage, transport, importation, exportation and possession of arms and explosives are regulated for protection of vital security interests.

Purpose or motivation of the measure: Protection of security interests

F.   Privatisation

Obligation Concerned: National Treatment and Most-Favoured-Nation Treatment

Legal Citation: Not applicable

Description: National Treatment and Most-Favoured-Nation Treatment shall not apply to the privatisation or divestment of corporate entities or assets currently in Government ownership

Purpose or motivation of the measure: Government Policy

G.   Manufacturing Sector

Obligation Concerned: National Treatment and Most-Favoured-Nation Treatment

Legal Citation: Control of Manufacture Act, Cap 57 (2001)

Description: For various reasons relating to public interest in certain manufacturing activities, National Treatment and Most-Favoured-Nation Treatment may not apply with regards to statutory licensing requirements and conditions imposed for the manufacture of the following:

a)   air-conditioners;

b)   beer and stout;

c)   cigars;

d)   drawn steel products;

e)   firecrackers;

f)   pig iron and sponge iron;

g)   refrigerators;

h)   rolled steel products;

i)   steel ingots, billets, blooms and slabs;

j)   chewing gum, bubble gum, dental chewing gum or any like substance;

k) CD (compact disc), CD-ROM (compact disc-read only memory), VCD (video compact disc);

l) DVD (digital video disc), DVD-ROM (digital video disc-read only memory);m) cigarettes;n) matches;

Purpose or motivation of the measure:	Public interest in certain manufacturing activities

APPENDIX 2 TO ANNEX XI
RESERVATIONS BY THE EFTA STATES

Sector:	All sectors
Sub-sector:	--
Obligation or article in respect of which the reservation is taken:	National Treatment and Most-Favoured-Nation Treatment
Level of Government:	National and Sub-national
Legal source or authority of the measure:	Not applicable
Succinct description of the measure:	Collective copyright or neighbouring rights' management systems; royalties, levies, grants and funds, designed to preserve and promote linguistic and cultural diversity
Purpose or motivation of the measure:	National cultural policy

APPENDIX 1 TO ANNEX XI
RESERVATIONS BY ALL PARTIES

Sector:	Power and Energy sectorRepair of Transport Equipment sector
Sub-sector:	--
Obligation or article in respect of which the reservation is taken:	National Treatment and Most-Favoured-Nation Treatment
Level of Government:	National and Sub-national
Legal source or authority of the measure:	Not Applicable

Succinct description of the measure: All activities in the power and energy sector as well as in the repair of transport equipment sector shall be treated as services under this Agreement

Purpose or motivation of the measure: To take into account the ambiguity of whether these sectors are considered manufacturing or services

ANNEX XII
REFERRED TO IN ARTICLE 54

PROTECTION OF INTELLECTUAL PROPERTY

Article 1
Intellectual Property

"Intellectual property" comprises in particular copyright, including computer programmes and databases[1], as well as neighbouring rights, trademarks for goods and services, geographical indications, including appellations of origin[2], industrial designs, patents, plant varieties, topographies of integrated circuits, as well as undisclosed information.

Article 2
International Conventions

1.   The Parties reaffirm their obligations set out in the international agreements to which they are parties, in particular the following multilateral agreements:

-     WTO Agreement of 15 April 1994 on Trade-Related Aspects of Intellectual Property Rights (TRIPS Agreement);

-     Paris Convention of 20 March 1883 for the Protection of Industrial Property (Stockholm Act, 1967); and

-     Berne Convention of 9 September 1886 for the Protection of Literary and Artistic Works (Paris Act, 1971).

2.   The Parties which are not party to one or more of the agreements listed below shall undertake to obtain their adherence to the following multilateral agreements on or before 1 January 2005.

-     the Geneva Act (1999) of the Hague Agreement concerning the International Registration of Industrial Designs;

-     the WIPO Copyright Treaty (Geneva 1996);

-     the WIPO Performances and Phonogram Treaty (Geneva 1996);

---

[1]   Databases are understood to be compilations of data or other material, in any form, which by reason of selection or arrangement of their contents constitute intellectual creations.

[2]   Appellations of origin are understood to be one form of geographical indications.

3.   The Parties agree to hold, without undue delay, expert consultations, upon request of any Party, on activities relating to the identified or to future international conventions on harmonisation, administration and enforcement of intellectual property rights and on activities in international organizations, such as the WTO and the World Intellectual Property Organization (WIPO), as well as on relations of the Parties with third countries on matters concerning intellectual property.

Article 3
Patents

The Parties shall ensure in their national laws at least the following:

(a)   adequate and effective patent protection for inventions in all fields of technology. For Liechtenstein and Switzerland, this means protection on a level corresponding to the one in the European Patent Convention of 5 October 1973, as implemented in their national law. For Iceland and Norway, this means protection on a level corresponding to the one in the Agreement on the European Economic Area of 2 May 1992, as implemented in their national law. For Singapore this means protection on a level corresponding to Articles 52 through 57 of the European Patent Convention as revised at the diplomatic Conference of November 2000 and as reflected under the Singapore Patents Act in force on 7 November 2001. Nothing in this provision shall preclude the Parties from affording higher levels of patent protection;

(b)

(i)   with respect to pharmaceutical and plant protection products that are subject to patent protection, an extension of the patent term to compensate the patentee for curtailment of the patent term as a result of the marketing approval process[3], subject to a maximum of 5 years. The overall term of patent protection, including any extension, shall not exceed 25 years from the filing date of the patent application. This compensatory extension will only apply when the marketing approval process takes more than 5 years;

(ii)   the implementation of paragraph (i) before or on 1 January 2005 and in accordance with well established and recognised national or regional standards[4].

Article 4
Designs

The Parties shall ensure in their national laws adequate and effective protection of industrial designs by providing in particular a period of protection of five years from the date of application with a possibility of renewal for at least two consecutive periods of five years each.

---

[3]   Marketing approval process is understood to encompass the period between the filing date of the patent application and the date of the first market authorisation of the product in the territory of the Party granting this authorisation. Singapore reserves the right to depart from the definition of the marketing approval process if it is found to be inconsistent with well established and recognised national or regional standards.

[4]   Singapore reserves the right to adopt the US regime.

Article 5
Geographical Indications

1.   The Parties shall provide legal means to protect geographical indications, including appellations of origin, with regard to all products and services.

2.   The Parties may provide different legal means[5] to prevent the misleading use of geographical indications in relation to services than that provided for the protection of geographical indications for products and shall be deemed to be in full compliance with the obligations under paragraph 1.

Article 6
Well-Known Marks

The Parties who have not given effect to the WIPO Joint Resolution on Well-Known Marks[6] shall undertake to do so on or before 1 January 2005.

Article 7
Acquisition and Maintenance of Intellectual Property Rights

Where the acquisition of an intellectual property right is subject to the right being granted or registered, the Parties shall ensure that the procedures for grant or registration are of the same level as that provided in the TRIPS Agreement, in particular Article 62.

Article 8
Enforcement of Intellectual Property Rights

The Parties shall provide for enforcement provisions under their national laws of the same level as that provided in the TRIPS Agreement, in particular Articles 41 to 61.

Article 9
Technical Co-Operation

The Parties shall agree upon appropriate modalities for technical assistance and co-operation of the respective authorities of the Parties. To this end, they shall co-ordinate efforts with relevant international organisations.

*

---

[5]   In accordance with the TRIPS Agreement.
[6]   As adopted by WIPO in September 1999.

PART TWO

PROTOTYPE INSTRUMENTS

ACUERDO ENTRE EL GOBIERNO DE LA REPÚBLICA DEL _____ Y EL GOBIERNO DE BOLIVIA SOBRE PROMOCION A PROTECCIÓN RECIPROCA DE INVERSIONES[*]

El Gobierno de la República de_____ y el Gobierno de la República de Bolivia en adelante denominadas "PARTES CONTRATANTES".

DESEANDO intensificar la integración económica en beneficio mutuo de ambos Estados;

CON INTENCION de crear y de mantener condiciones favorables a las inversiones de inversores de una Parte Contratante en el territorio de la otra Parte Contratante;

RECONOCIENDO que la promoción y protección de esas inversiones mediante un Acuerdo pueden servir de estímulo a la iniciativa económica privada e incrementar el bienestar de ambos Estados;

HAN ACORDADO LO SIGUIENTE:

ARTICULO 1
DEFINICIONES

Para los efectos del presente Acuerdo serán aplicables las siguientes definiciones para los términos consignados a continuación:

1.   "Inversión" designa una transferencia de capital o toda clase de activo que sea propiedad o esté controlado directa o indirectamente por un inversionista de una de las Partes Contratantes en el territorio de otra Parte Contratante, a tenor de la legislación de ésta última. Esta definición comprende las inversiones que adopten las siguientes formas o consistan en ellas:

El término designa en particular, aunque no exclusivamente:

    a.   sociedades;

    b.   propiedad tangible: que comprende los bienes raíces, y la propiedad intangible, que comprende los arriendos, las hipotecas, los privilegios de acreedor y las prendas, usufructos y derechos similares;

    c.   valores bursátiles, acciones, títulos, bonos y obligaciones u otra forma de participación en el capital de una sociedad;

    d.   dinero, acreencias y derechos al cobro de cualquier obligación basada en un contrato que represente un valor financiero;

    e.   Derechos derivados de todo tipo de aportaciones realizadas con el propósito de crear valor económico, los créditos que estén directamente relacionados con la

---

[*]   *Source*: The Government of Bolivia, Ministry of Foreign Affairs. [Note added by the editor.]

inversión, entre matriz y filial (tales como las aportaciones suplementarias de capital).

f.   plusvalía mercantil;

g.   derechos de propiedad intelectual e industrial, que comprende en forma ilustrativa y no exhaustiva:

- Derecho de autor y derechos conexos
- patentes;
- modelos de utilidad;
- diseños industriales;
- secretos empresariales;
- marcas;
- lemas;
- procedimientos tecnológicos;
- know-how;
- valor llave;
- denominaciones de origen;
- circuitos integrados;
- variedades vegetales.

h.   Derechos contractuales, incluyendo contratos de riesgo compartido y concesión, para ejecutar actividades económicas y/o comerciales, como los contratos de construcción, de administración, de producción, de exploración. de cultivo, de extracción y de explotación de recursos naturales.

i.   Los derechos conferidos conforme a la ley, como las licencias y los permisos.

Se considerará que una inversión está controlada por un inversionista, si el inversionista controla, directa o indirectamente, la empresa que es propietaria de la inversión.

La definición de inversión no comprende bienes raíces u otra propiedad, tangible o intangible, la que no es adquirida o utilizada con la perspectiva de obtener un beneficio económico y otros fines comerciales contemplados en el presente acuerdo.

2.   "Inversionista" 'o "Inversor" designa:

a.   Toda persona física que sea nacional de una de las Partes Contratantes, de conformidad con su legislación.

b.   Toda persona jurídica constituida de conformidad con las leyes y reglamentaciones de una Parte Contratante y que tenga su sede en el territorio de dicha Parte Contratante.

c.   Las personas jurídicas establecida en el territorio donde se realiza la inversión, efectivamente controladas, directa o indirectamente por personas físicas o jurídicas definidas en 2- a. y b.

3.   "Inversión abarcada" ó "Inversión efectuada" designa la inversión realizada por un inversionista de una Parte Contratante en el territorio de la otra Parte Contratante.

4.   "Empresa" designa cualquier entidad o persona jurídica constituida u organizada a tenor de la legislación de la Parte Contratante pertinente, persiga o no fines de lucro, y sea de propiedad privada o estatal, incluyendo pero no limitativamente, a las corporaciones, sociedades anónimas, fideicomisos, sociedad de personas, propiedad de una sola persona, asociación de empresas en participación u otro tipo de asociación; y toda sucursal de cualquiera de dichas entidades.

5.   "Empresa Estatal" designa a una empresa cuya es del gobierno o que esté controlada por un gobierno, en virtud de sus intereses en dicha empresa.

6.   "Nacionales" designa: respecto a cada Parte Contratante:

   a.   Personas físicas que posean la nacionalidad de esa Parte Contratante de acuerdo con su legislación;

   b.   Las sociedades constituidas de acuerdo con la legislación de esa Parte Contratante o que estén controladas, directa o indirectamente, por nacionales de la misma.

7.   "Persona natural de una Parte Contratante" designa a todo individuo que tenga la nacionalidad de esa Parte Contratante de conformidad con su legislación.

8.   "Persona jurídica de una Parte Contratante" designa a toda entidad jurídica, colectiva, pública o privada, con o sin fines de lucro, constituida de conformidad con la legislación de esa Parte Contratante.

9.   El término "Territorio" designa:

   a.   En relación con la República de Bolivia, se refiere al territorio geográfico que está bajo la soberanía y jurisdicción del Estado Boliviano, dentro del cual circulan libremente personas, bienes y capitales,conforme a su respectiva legislación y al derecho internacional.

   b.   En relación con la República de ...., se refiere ....

10.   "Estado receptor" designa el Estado en cuyo territorio se realiza la inversión.

11.   "Autorización de inversión" designa la autorización concedida por la autoridad competente en materia de inversiones extranjeras de una Parte Contratante a una inversión abarcada, a un nacional o sociedad de la otra Parte Contratante.

12.   "Autoridad competente" designa a la institución encargada de vigilar el cumplimiento de las normas legales que otorgan garantías y facilidades a la inversión.

13.   "Acuerdo de inversión" designa al Acuerdo suscrito entre las autoridades nacionales de una Parte Contratante y una inversión efectuada, nacional o de la otra Parte Contratante, por el

que se conceden derechos sobre los recursos naturales u otros bienes que controlen las autoridades nacionales, y del que dependen la inversión o el inversionista para lograr una inversión abarcada.

14.   "Convenio del CIADI" designa al Convenio sobre Arreglo de Diferencias Relativas a Inversiones entre Estados y Nacionales de Otros Estados, suscrito en Washington el 18 de marzo de 1965.

15.   "Centro" designa al Centro Internacional de Arreglo de Diferencias Relativas a Inversiones, creado por el Convenio del CIADI.

16.   "Normas de arbitraje de la CNUDMI." designa a las normas de arbitraje de la Comisión de las Naciones Unidas para el Derecho Mercantil Internacional.

17.   "Disposición" designa a toda ley, reglamento, procedimiento, requisito, o práctica de cada una de las Partes Contratantes.

18.   "Disposición vigente" designa a toda disposición existente en el momento en que este Acuerdo entre en vigor.

19.   "Beneficios (o ganancias)" designa a los excedentes, originados en los ingresos, descontados los costos de una inversión, especialmente, aunque no exclusivamente, las ganancias de capital, dividendos, regalías, intereses, rentas netas y cualquier otro excedente de explotación.

ARTICULO 2
AMBITO DE APLICACIÓN

1.   El presente Acuerdo será aplicado a las inversiones en el territorio de una de las Partes Contratantes, realizadas de conformidad con su legislación, antes o después de la entrada en vigencia de este Acuerdo. Sin embargo, el presente Acuerdo no será aplicado a ninguna controversia que se origine en hechos, reclamo o actos ocurridos que se hubiese originado con anterioridad a su entrada en vigencia incluso si sus efectos perduran después de ésta.

ARTICULO 3
PROMOCION DE INVERSIONES

1.   Cada Parte Contratante promoverá y garantizaráen su territorio, las inversiones de inversores de la otra Parte Contratante y admitirá tales inversiones conforme a sus leyes y reglamentos.

2.   La Parte Contratante que haya admitido una inversión en su territorio, otorgará los permisos necesarios con relación a dicha inversión, incluyendo la ejecución de contratos de licencia y asistencia técnica, comercial o administrativa. Cada Parte Contratante facilitará, cuando así se requiera, los permisos necesarios para las actividades de consultores o de otras personas calificadas de nacionalidad extranjera conforme a la legislación y disposiciones relativas a la entrada y estadía de los mismos, incluyendo los permisos necesarios para la entrada y permanencia en el territorio de los integrantes de su familia, conforme a sus leyes y reglamentos.

3.   Las inversiones realizadas en el territorio de una de las Partes Contratantes se registrarán e inscribirán de acuerdo con las leyes del Estado receptor.

ARTICULO 4
PROTECCION DE INVERSIONES
TRATAMIENTO NACIONAL Y DE LA NACION MAS FAVORECIDA

1.   Con respecto a la fundación, la adquisición, la expansión, la dirección, la explotación, funcionamiento, venta u otra enajenación o transferencia de las inversiones abarcadas, cada Parte Contratante otorgará un trato no menos favorable que el que otorga, en iguales circunstancias, a las inversiones en su territorio de sus propios nacionales o empresas (en adelante, "trato nacional") o a las inversiones en su territorio de los nacionales o las empresas de terceros países (en adelante, "trato de la nación más favorecida"), cualquiera que sea el más favorable (en adelante, "trato nacional y de la nación más favorecida").

2.   El Acuerdo convenido no excederá a los beneficios y ventajas que una de las Partes Contratantes conceda a los nacionales de terceros Estados en virtud de su participación, o asociación, presente o futura a una zona de libre comercio, a una unión aduanera, a un mercado común, unión económica o acuerdos internacionales similares celebrados con terceros Estados para la asistencia económica mutua u otras formas de cooperación regional.

3.   El Acuerdo convenido no excederá a los beneficios y ventajas que una de las Partes Contratantes conceda a los nacionales de terceros Estados como consecuencia de la celebración de Convenios o Acuerdos, para evitar la doble imposición u otros Acuerdos en materia impositiva.

4.   Las obligaciones contraídas conforme al numeral 1 no se aplicarán a los procedimientos previstos en los acuerdos multilaterales concertados bajo los auspicios de la Organización Mundial de la Propiedad Intelectual, relativos a la adquisición o conservación de los derechos de propiedad intelectual.

ARTICULO 5
TRATO JUSTO Y EQUITATIVO

1.   En todo momento, cada Parte Contratante otorgará a las inversiones abarcadas un trato justo y equitativo y en ningún caso les otorgará un trato menos favorable que el que exige el derecho internacional.

2.   Cada Parte Contratante protegerá en su territorio las inversiones efectuadas por los inversores de la otra Parte Contratante, conforme a sus leyes y reglamentos y no obstaculizará, con medidas discriminatorias la gestión, el mantenimiento, la utilización, el disfrute, el crecimiento, la explotación, la venta y, si fuera el caso, la liquidación, de dichas inversiones u otra enajenación de las inversiones abarcadas.

3.   Cada Parte Contratante se encargará que su ordenamiento jurídico, sus prácticas y procedimientos administrativos de carácter general, así como sus decisiones judiciales, cuando se refieran a las inversiones abarcadas o las afecten, se publiquen o pongan a disposición del público con prontitud.

4.   Ambas Partes Contratantes otorgarán a los inversionistas de la otra Parte Contratante, con respecto al disfrute, uso, administración, dirección, operación, expansión, explotación, venta u otro tipo de disposición de sus inversiones o beneficios, un trato no menos favorable al que, en iguales circunstancias, otorga a:

   a.   Los inversionistas de cualquier otro Estado;

   b.   Sus propios inversionistas.

ARTICULO 6
TRANSFERENCIA

1.   Cada Parte Contratante, en cuyo territorio inversores de la otra Parte Contratante hayan efectuado inversiones, garantizará a estos la libre transferencia de los pagos relacionados con esas inversiones, en particular aunque no exclusivamente de:

   a.   El capital de la inversión y las reinversiones

   b.   Los pagos, regalías, beneficios y dividendos

   c.   El producto de la venta o liquidación total o parcial de la inversión

   d.   Las indemnizaciones, compensaciones o resarcimientos resultantes de arreglo de controversias.

2.   Las transferencias arriba mencionadas serán efectuadas sin demora, en moneda libremente convertible a la tasa de cambio aplicable a la fecha de la transferencia, de conformidad con las reglamentaciones del régimen de divisas vigente de la Parte Contratante en cuyo territorio se realizó la inversión.

3.   Sin perjuicio de las disposiciones de los párrafos 1 y 2, cada Parte Contratante podrá impedir una transferencia a objeto de proteger los derechos de acreedores o asegurar el cumplimiento de decisiones firmes emitidas en procesos judiciales o arbitrales, a través de una aplicación equitativa, imparcial, no discriminatoria y de buena fe de sus leyes y reglamentaciones, incluyendo en particular aunque no exclusivamente:

   a.   Quiebra o insolvencia;
   b.   infracciones penales;
   c.   garantía del cumplimiento de los mandamientos o fallos en actuaciones judiciales;
   d.   incumplimiento de obligaciones laborales.

4.   En caso de existencia o inminencia de desequilibrio grave de su balanza de pagos y de conformidad con las normas internacionales existentes en esta materia, una Parte Contratante afectada, podrá aplicar las medidas correctivas que considere necesarias, de conformidad con los siguientes criterios:

   a.   No deberán ser medidas discriminatorias

b.   Deberán ser eliminadas progresivamente a medida que mejore la situación que las motivó.

c.   No excederán lo necesario para hacer frente a las circunstancias nacionales.

d.   Deberán ser compatibles con el Convenio Consultivo del Fondo Monetario Internacional.

ARTICULO 7
EXPROPIACION E INDEMINIZACION

1.   Las inversiones o los beneficios de los inversionistas de cualesquiera de las Partes Contratantes no podrán ser nacionalizadas, expropiados o sujetos a disposiciones que produzcan un efecto equivalente a la nacionalización o expropiación (en lo sucesivo denominadas "expropiación") en el territorio de la otra Parte Contratante, excepto en caso de interés público, utilidad pública o seguridad nacional determinados en la legislación de cada Parte Contratante, sobre bases no discriminatorias, respetando el debido proceso legal y mediante indemnización justa, pronta y efectiva.

2.   La indemnización se basará en el valor justo del mercado de la inversión o de los beneficios expropiados inmediatamente antes de la expropiación o en el momento en que la expropiación propuesta se hizo de conocimiento público, dependiendo de lo que ocurra primero.

3.   La indemnización se pagará a partir de la fecha de la expropiación y devengará intereses hasta la fecha de su pago efectivo, con la aplicación de una tasa de interés comercial normal, y será enteramente realizable y libremente transferible. Los criterios de valoración incluirán el valor de la empresa, valor de los activos, incluido el avalúo catastral declarado de la propiedad tangible, y otros criterios que corresponda para determinar el valor justo de mercado.

El valor justo en el mercado no quedará afectado por ningún cambio de valor, aún cuando la acción expropiatoria llegue a conocerse antes de que esta se haga pública.

4.   En caso de que el valor justo en el mercado se exprese en una moneda que no sea libremente convertible, la indemnización pagadera (convertida en la moneda de pago al cambio que rija en el mercado en la fecha de pago) no será inferior a:

a)   El valor justo en el mercado en la fecha de expropiación, convertido en una moneda libremente convertible al cambio que rija en el mercado en esa fecha, más

b)   Los intereses a una tasa comercialmente justificada para dicha moneda libremente convertible, devengados desde la fecha de expropiación hasta la fecha de pago.

5.   El inversionista afectado tendrá derecho, en virtud de las leyes aplicables de la Parte Contratante que proceda a ejecutar la expropiación, al más pronto examen de su caso por una autoridad judicial u otra autoridad independiente de esa Parte Contratante y a la valoración de su inversión o beneficios de acuerdo con los principios establecidos en el tema de expropiación.

ARTICULO 8
COMPENSACIONES POR PERDIDAS

1.   Los inversores de una de las Partes Contratantes que sufran pérdidas en sus inversiones en el territorio de la otra Parte Contratante a consecuencia de guerra, conflicto armado, revolución, estado de crisis nacional, rebelión, insurrección o motín en el territorio de la otra Parte Contratante, recibirán, en lo que se refiere a restitución, indemnizaciones, compensación u otro resarcimiento, un tratamiento no menos favorable que lo acordado a sus propios inversores.

ARTICULO 9
SUBROGACION

1.   Cuando una Parte Contratante o una de sus agencias autorizadas haya acordado una garantía o segura para cubrir los riesgos no comerciales con relación a una inversión efectuada por uno de sus inversores en el territorio de la otra Parte Contratante, esta última Parte Contratante reconocerá la subrogación de la primera Parte Contratante o sus agencias autorizadas en los mismos derechos del inversor reconocidos por la ley de la parte receptora de la inversión, siempre y cuando la primera Parte Contratante haya efectuado un pago en virtud de dicha garantía.

ARTICULO 10
SOLUCION DE CONTROVERSIAS

ARREGLO DE DIFERENDOS ENTRE UNA PARTE CONTRATANTE Y UN NACIONAL DE LA OTRA PARTE CONTRATANTE

1.   Cualquier controversia entre una Parte Contratante y un inversionista de la otra Parte Contratante, relacionada con una reclamación del inversionista en que una disposición tomada, o no-tomada, por la primera Parte Contratante viola este Acuerdo, y que el inversionista ha incurrido pérdidas o daños como consecuencia o resultado de tal violación se resolverá, en la medida de lo posible, amistosamente entre las partes.

2.   Si una controversia no se hubiese resuelto amistosamente dentro de un período de seis meses contado a partir de la fecha de su inicio, el inversionista podrá someterla a arbitraje. A efectos de este párrafo, se considera que se ha iniciado una disputa cuando el inversionista de una Parte Contratante haya notificado por escrito a la otra Parte Contratante alegando que una medida tomada, o no tomada, por esta última viola este Acuerdo, y que el inversionista ha incurrido pérdidas o daños como consecuencia o resultantes de tal violación.

3.   Cualquier inversionista podrá someter a arbitraje una diferencia según se indica en el numeral (1) solamente sí:

    a.   El inversionista ha dado su consentimiento por escrito a dicho trámite;

    b.   El inversionista ha renunciado a su derecho a iniciar o continuar cualquier otro procedimiento relacionado con la disposición que se alega viola este Acuerdo ante las cortes o tribunales de la Parte Contratante interesada, o con cualquier procedimiento de solución de cualquier clase de diferencias.

4.   El inversionista puede someter la disputa o bien a la:

a. Jurisdicción nacional de la Parte Contratante, en cuyo territorio se realizó la inversión, o bien al:

b. arbitraje internacional. Es este último caso el inversionista tiene las siguientes opciones:

    a) El Centro Internacional de Arreglo de Diferencias relativas a Inversiones (CIADI), establecido en virtud del Convenio sobre Arreglo de Diferencias Relativas a Inversiones entre Estados y Nacionales de Otros Estados, que quedó abierto para su adhesión en Washington el 18 de marzo de 1965 (Convención del CIADI), siempre y cuando tanto la Parte Contratante en desacuerdo como la Parte Contratante del inversionista sean signatarias de la Convención del CIADI; o

    b) Los Reglamentos de los Mecanismos Complementarios del CIADI, a condición de que la Parte Contratante en desacuerdo o la Parte Contratante del inversionista, pero no ambas, sea parte de la Convención del CIADI; o

    c) Un árbitro internacional o un tribunal de arbitraje ad hoc establecido bajo las Reglas de Arbitraje de la Comisión de las Naciones Unidas para el Derecho Mercantil Internacional (UNCITRAL).

5. El laudo arbitral será definitivo, obligatorio y plenamente ejecutables por las Partes.

6. El idioma en el que se tramitará el Arbitraje, será el que las Partes Contratantes decidan.

CONTROVERSIAS EN TORNO A LA INTERPRETACIÓN DEL PRESENTE ACUERDO

1. Las controversias entre las Partes Contratantes respecto de la interpretación o cumplimiento del presente Acuerdo, se resolverán preferentemente por la vía diplomática.

2. Si dentro de los seis meses siguientes a la fecha en que se suscitó el conflicto, éste no hubiere sido resuelto por la vía diplomática, a solicitud de cualquiera de las partes será sometido a arbitraje, observando el siguiente procedimiento:

a. Cada Parte Contratante nombrará un árbitro para integrar el Tribunal Arbitral, y los dos árbitros así designados nombrarán de común acuerdo un tercer árbitro que será nacional de un tercer Estado y cumplirá las funciones de Presidente del Tribunal.

b. Si en los dos mese siguientes a la fecha en que se decidió someter las controversias a arbitraje, una Parte Contratante no hubiere efectuado la designación de su árbitro, la otra parte podrá solicitar al Presidente de la Corte Internacional de Justicia se efectúe la designación.

c. Si el Presidente de la Corte Internacional de Justicia estuviere por cualquier causa impedido de efectuar la designación, o si fuere nacional de una de las Partes Contratantes, la designación del árbitro será hecha por el Vicepresidente. Pero, si éste igualmente se encontrare impedido o si fuere nacional de una de las Partes

Contratantes, el nombramiento será hecho por el juez de mayor antigüedad de la Corte Internacional de Justicia que no esté impedido o sea nacional de una de las Partes Contratantes.

d. En el desempeño de su función, los árbitros deberán proceder con imparcialidad, independencia, competencia, diligencia y discreción.

e. El Tribunal estará facultado para decidir acerca de su propia competencia y de las excepciones relativas a la existencia y validez de la convención arbitral. El Tribunal podrá decidir las excepciones relativas a su competencia como cuestión previa, pero también podrá seguir adelante con sus actuaciones y reservar la decisión de éstas excepciones para el laudo.

f. El tribunal arbitral tomará sus decisiones por mayoría de votos. Sus decisiones serán obligatorias. Cada Parte Contratante sufragará los gastos ocasionados por la actividad de su árbitro, así como los gastos de su representación en el procedimiento arbitral. Los gastos del Presidente, así como los demás gastos, serán sufragados por partes iguales por las dos Partes Contratantes. El tribunal arbitral determinará su propio procedimiento.

g. Las Partes Contratantes decidirán de común acuerdo, el idioma en el que se desarrollará el Arbitraje.

3. Ninguna de las Partes Contratantes, deberá ofrecer protección diplomática o acogerse a una demanda internacional por un diferendo que uno de sus nacionales y la otra Parte Contratante hayan presentado a un tribunal competente del Estado receptor o a un competente tribunal internacional de arbitraje, a menos que la otra Parte Contratante no acate ni cumpla con la sentencia o laudo dispuestos,

4. El laudo será escrito, fundado y decidirá completamente el litigio, con carácter definitivo y obligatorio y plenamente ejecutables para las Partes.

ARTICULO 11
DISPOSICIONES COMPLEMENTARIAS

1. Cada Parte Contratante respetará en todo momento las obligaciones contraídas con respecto de las inversiones de los inversores de la otra Parte Contratante.

2. Toda expresión que no esté definida en el presente Acuerdotendrá el sentido utilizado en la legislación vigente en cada Parte Contratante.

ARTICULO 12
VIGENCIA, DURACIÓN Y TERMINACIÓN DEL ACUERDO

1. El presente Acuerdo entrará en vigor a los treinta días siguientes de la fecha de la última notificación en la cual las Partes Contratantes se hayan notificado recíprocamente por escrito, que se ha cumplido con los procedimientos constitucionales necesarios para su aprobación en sus respectivos países y permanecerá en vigencia por un periodo de 10 años.

2.   En el caso de que cualquiera de las Partes Contratantes decida dar por terminado este Acuerdo, deberá notificar por escrito de su decisión, a la otra Parte por lo menos con doce (12) meses antes de la fecha de expiración de su actual vigencia, De lo contrario, el presente Convenio se prorrogará por tiempo indefinido, en esa etapa las Partes podrán notificarse de la decisión de dar por terminado este Convenio. Se hará efectiva la terminación del Convenio doce (12) meses después de la notificación escrita.

3.   Con relación a aquellas inversiones hechas antes de la fecha de terminación de este Acuerdo, los Artículos 1 al 12, precedentes del mismo, continuarán en vigor por un periodo de 10 años a partir de esa fecha.

EN FE DE LO CUAL, los abajo firmantes debidamente autorizados al efecto por sus respectivos Gobiernos, han suscrito el presente Acuerdo.

Hecho en ...., el día .... en el idioma español siendo los dos textos igualmente auténticos.

POR EL GOBIERNO DE LA REPUBLICA DEL _____.

POR EL GOBIERNO DE LA REPUBLICA DE BOLIVIA _____.

*

ACCORD ENTRE LE GOUVERNEMENT DU BURKINA FASO ET LE GOUVERNEMENT DE _____ CONCERNANT LA PROMOTION ET LA PROTECTION RECIPROQUES DES INVESTISSEMENTS [*]

Le Gouvernement du Burkina Faso et _____ le Gouvernement de ci-après dénommés les "Parties Contractantes"

DESIREUX d'intensifier leur coopération économique en créant des conditions favorables á la réalisation des investissements par les investisseurs de l'úne des Parties Contractantes sur le territoire de l'autre Partie Contractante,

CONSIDERAT l'influence bénéfique que pourra exercer ún tel Accord pour amélior les contacts d'affaires et renforcer la confiance dans domaine des investments ;

RECONNAISSANT la nécessité d'encourager et de protéger les investissements étrangers en vue de stimuler l'initiative économique privée et de promouvoir la prospérité économique des deux Parties Contractantes ;

sont convenus de ce qui suit :

ARTICLE 1
DEFINITIONS

Aux sens du présent Accord :

1.   Le terme "investissements" désigne tout élément d'actif quelconque et tout apport direct ou indirect en numéraire, en nature ou en services, investi ou réinvesti dans tout secteur d'activité économique quel qu'il soit.

Sont considérés notamment, mais non exclusivement, comme des investissements au sens du présent Accord :

a)   les biens meubles et immeubles, ainsi que tous les autres droits réels tels qu'hypothèques, sûretés réelles, usufruits et droits similaires ;

b)   les actions, les parts sociales et toutes les autres formes de participation aux sociétés ;

c)   les droits de créance et tous les autres droits concernant des prestations ayant une valeur économique ;

d)   les droits de propriété intellectuelle tels que droits d'auteur, brevets d'invention, dessins et modèles industriels, marques de commerce ou de service, noms commerciaux, savoir-faire, clientèle et tous les autres droits similaires reconnus par les lois nationales de chaque Partie Contractante ;

---

[*]   *Source*: The Government of Burkina Faso, Ministry of Foreign Affairs. [Note added by the editor.]

    e)   les concessions de droit public, y compris les concessions relatives à la prospection, l'extraction ou l'exploitation des ressources naturelles, ainsi que tout autre droit accordé par la loi, par contrat ou par décision des autorités compétentes en application de la loi.

Aucune modification de la forme juridique dans laquelle les avoirs, capitaux et autres biens ont été investis ou réinvestis n'affecte leur caractère d' ''investissements''au sens du présent Accord.

Ces investissements doivent être effectués selon les lois et règlements en vigueur dans le pays hôte.

Si l'investissement est effectué par un investisseur par l'intermédiaire d'un organisme visé à la lettre c/ de l'alinéa 2 ci-dessous, dans lequel il détient une participation au capital, cet investisseur jouira des avantages du présent Accord dans la mesure de cette participation indirecte à condition, toutefois, que ces avantages ne lui reviennent pas s'il invoque le mécanisme de règlement des différents prévue par un autre accord de protection des investissements étrangers conclu par une Partie Contractante sur le territoire de laquelle est effectué l'investissement.

2.   Le terme ''investisseur '' désigne les sujets qui effectuent des investissements sur le territoire de l'Etat de l'autre Partie Contractante, conformément au présent Accord :

    a)   les personnes physique qui, selon la loi des deux (2) Etats contractants, sont considérées comme leurs citoyens ;

    b)   les personnes morales, y compris les sociétés, corporations associations d'affaires et autres organisations, qui sont constituées ou autrement organisées. conformément à la loi des deux (2) Parties Contractantes, et qui ont leur siège social et leurs activités économiques effectives sur le territoire de l'Etat de la même Partie Contractante ;

    c)   les entités juridiques établies, conformément à la législation d'un quelconque pays qui sont contrôlées, directement ou indirectement, par des nationaux d'une Partie Contractante ou par des entités juridiques ayant leur siège, en même temps que des activités économiques réelles, sur le territoire de cette Partie Contractante.

3.   Le terme "revenus" designe les montants nets d'impôts rapportés par un investissement, et notamment, mais non exclusivement les bénéfices, intérêts, dividendes et redevances de licence.

4.   Le terme "territoire" désigne:

    a)   en ce qui concene la Burkina Faso ; le territoire sous sa souveraineté y compris la mer territoriale ainsi que les zones sous-marines et les autres espaces aériens et maritimes sur lesquels cette partie continentale exerce en conformité avec le droit international, les droits souverains ou une juridiction.

    b)   en ce qui concerne la Republique _____.

5.   On entend par "sociétés":

Les personnes morales, firmes ou associations constituées ou créées en vertus de la législation en vigueur.

ARTICLE 2
PROMOTION ET ADMISSION

1.   Chaque Partie contractante promouvra, autant que possible, les invest issements effectués sur le territoire de son Etat par les investisseurs de l'autre Partie contractante et admettra ces investissements conformément à ses lois et règlements nationaux. Elle traitera les investissements dans chaque cas, de façon juste et équitable.

2.   Lorsqu'une Partie contractante a admis un investissement effectué sur le territoire de son Etat par des investisseurs de l'autre Partie contractante, elle accordera, conformément à ses lois et règlements nationaux, les autorisations nécessaires relatives à cet investissement, y compris celles concernant le recrutement du personnel de direction ou technique, à leur choix, sans tenir compte de sa citoyennetë. Pour cela, aucune des Parties contractantes ne devra entraver, moyennant des mesures arbitraires ou discriminatoires, l'administration, l'utilisation, l'usage ou la jouissance des investissements des ressortissants ou sociétés de l'autre Partie contractante sur son territoire.

3.   Les revenus de l'investissement et en cas de leur réinvestissement conformément à la législation d'une Partie Contractante, jouissent de la même protection que l'investissement intial.

ARTICLE 3
TRAITEMENT NATIONAL ET CLAUSE DE LA
NATION LA PLUS FAVORISEE

1.   Chaque Partie Contractante protégera sur le territoire de son Etat les investissements effectués par les investisseurs de l'autre Partie Contractante conformément à ses lois et règlements nationaux, et n'entravera pas, par des mesures injustifiées ou discriminatoires, la gestion, l'entretien, l'utilisation, la jouissance, l'accroissement, la vente ou la liquidation de tels investissements.

2.   Chaque Partie contractante assurera sur le territoire de son Etat un traitement juste et équitable aux investissements effectués par des investisseurs de l'autre Partie contractante. Ce traitement ne sera pas moins favorable que eélui accordé par chaque Partie contractante aux investissements effectués sur le territoire de son Etat par ses propres investisseur ou par les investisseurs de n'importe quel Etat tiers, si ce dernier traitement est plus favorable.

3.   le traitement ne s'étendra pas aux privilèges consentis par Line Partie contractante aux ressortissants ou sociétés d'Etats tiers, en raison soit de son appartenance à une Union Douanière ou Economique, un Marché Commun ou une Zone de Libre Echange, soit de son association avec l'un ou l'autre de ces derniers.

4.   Le traitement accordé par le présent article ne s'étendra pas aux avantages accordés par une Partie contractante aux ressortissants ou sociétés d'un Etats tiers en vertu dun accord sur la double imposition, de tout autre arrangement dans le domaine fiscal.

ARTICLE 4
LIBERTE DE TRANSFERT

1.   Chaque Partie Contractante, sur le territoire de laquelle des investissements ont été effectués par des investisseurs de l'autre Partie Contractante, garantit à ces investisseurs, après l'acquittement des obligations fiscales, le libre transfert en monnaie convertible des avoirs liquides afférents à ces investissements et notamment :

   a)   du capital et des fonds supplémentaires nécessaires pour l'entretien et l'extension de l'investissement ;

   b)   des revenus conformément à l'Article 1, paragraphe (3) de cet Accord ;

   c)   des sommes provenant d'emprunts contractés ou d'autres obligations contractuelles à assumer aux fins d'un investissernent ;

   d)   des sommes provenant de la vente totale ou partielle, de l'aliénation ou de la liquidation d'un investissement ;

   e)   de toute indemnité due à un investisseur conformément à 1' Article 5 de cet Accord.

Le transfert sera effectué sans délai au cours en vigueur.

2.   Si on n'a pas convenu différemment avec l'investisseur, les transfert seront effectués, conformément aux lois et règlements nationaux en vigueur de la Partie contractante sur le territoire de 1'Etat duquel a été effectué 1'investisscient, au taux de change officiellement applicable à la date du transfert.

3-   Les garanties prévues par le présent article sont au moins égales à celles accordées aux investisseur de la nation la plus favorisée qui se trouvent dans des situations similaires.

ARTICLE 5
INDEMNISATION POUR EXPROPRIATION ET PERTES

1.   Aucune des Parties contratantes ne prendra, soit directement soit indirectement, des mesures d'expropriation, de nationalisation ou d'autres mesures de ce genre ou au même effet contre les investissements des investisseurs de l'autre Partie Contractante, que si les mesures sont prises pour des raisons d'utilité publique, dûment établies par la loi, sans être discriminatoires et conformément à la procédure légale.

2.   La partie Contractante qui serait amnée à prendre de telles mesures versera à l'ayant-droit, sans retard injustifié, une indeminté juste et équitable dont le montant correspondra à la valeur du marché de l'investissement concerné à la veille du jour ou les mesures sont prises ou rendues publiques.

3.   Les dispositions pour la fixation et le paiement de l'indemnité devront être prises d'une manière prompte au plus tard au moment de l'expropriation. En cas de retard de paiement, l'indemnité portera intérêt aux conditions du marché à compter de la date de son exigibilité. L'indemnité sera payée aux investisseurs en monnaie convertible et librement transférable.

4.   Les investisseurs de l'une des Parties contractes dont les investissements subiraient des dommages ou pertes dues à la guerre ou à tout autre conflit armé, révolution, état d'urgence national, révolte, insurrection, ou tout autre événement similaire sur le territoire de l'autre Partie Contractante, bénéficieront de la part de cette dernière d'un traitement non discriminatoire et au moins égal à celui accordé à ses propres investisseurs ou aux investisseurs de la nation la plus favorisée en ce qui concerne les restitutions, indemnisations, compensations ou autres dédommagements, le traitement le plus favorable étant retenu.

ARTICLE 6
APPLICATION

Le présent Accord couvre également, en ce qui concerne son application future, les investissements effectués avant son entrée en vigueur, par les investisseurs de l'une des parties Contractantes sur le territoire de l'autre Partie Contractante, conformément à ses lois et règlements. Toutefois le présent Accord ne s'appliquera pas aux différendsqui pourraient survenir avant son entrée en vigueur.

ARTICLE 7
AUTRES OBLIGATIONS

Lorsqu'une question relative aux investissements est règie à la fois par le présent Accord et par législation nationale de l'une des Partie Contractante ou par des conventions internationales existantes ou souscrites par les parties dans l'avenir, les investisseurs de l'autre Partie Contractante peuvent se prévaloir des dispositions qui leur sont les plus favorables.

ARTICLE 8
SUBROGATION

1.   Lorsque Tune des Parties contractantes ou l'agence designee par celle-ci effectue des paiements à ses propres investisseurs en vertu dune garantie financière couvrant les risques non commerciaux en liaison avec un investissement sur le territoire de l'Etat de l'autre Partie contractante, cette dernière reconnaîtra, en vertu du principe de la subrogation, la cession de tout droit ou titre de cet investisseur envers la première Partie contractante ou l'agence désignée par elle. L'autre Partie contractante sera justfiée a déduire les taxes et autres obligations à caractère publique dues et payables par l'investisseur.

2.   Conformément à la garantie donnée pour l'investissement concerné, l'assureur est admis à faire valoir tous les droits que l'investisseur aurait pu exercer si l'assureur ne lui avait pas été subrogé.

3.   Tout différend entre une Partie Contractante et l'assureur d'un investissement de l'autre Partie Contractante sera réglé conformément aux dispositions de l'article 9 du présent Accord.

ARTICLE 9
REGLEMENT DES DIFFERENDS RELATIFS AUX INVESTISSEMENTS

1.   Tout différend relatif aux investissements entre une Partie Contractante et un investisseur de l'autre Partie Contractante sera réglé, autant que possible, à l'amable, par consulatations et négociations entre les parties au différend..

2.   A défaut de règlement à l'amiable par arrangement direct entre les parties au différend dans un délai de six mois, à compter de la date de sa notification écrite, le différend est soumis, au choix de l'investisseur :

   a)   soit au tribunal compétent de la Partie contractante sur le territoire de laquelle l'investissement a été effectué :

   b)   soit pour arbitrage par la Cour Commune de Justice et d'Arbitrage (CCJA) de l'OHADA

   c)   soit pour arbitrage au Centre International pour Règlement des Différends relatifs aux Investissements (C.I.R.D.I.), crée par la Convention pour le Règlement des différends relatifs aux investissements etre Etats et ressortissants d'autres Etats ouverte à la signature à Washington. Le 18 mars 1965.

   d)   soit un tribunal ad-hoc qui à défaut d'autre arrangement entre les parties au différend, sera constitué conformément aux règles d'arbitrage de la Commission des Nations Unies pour le Droit Commercial International (C.N.U.D.C.I.).

A cette fin, chacune des Parties contractantes donne son consentement irrévocable à ce que tout différend relatif aux investissements soit soumis à cette procédure d'arbitrage.

3.   Aucune des Parties Contractantes, partie à un différend ne peut soulever d'objection, à aucun stade de la procédure d'arbitrage ou de l'exécution d'une sentence arbtrale, du fait que l'investisseur, partie adverse au différend, ait perçu une indemnité couvrant tout ou partie de ses pertes en vertu d'une police d'assurance.

4.   Le Tribunal arbitral statuera sur base du droit national de la Partie Contractante, partie au différend, sur le territoire de laquelle l'investissement est situé, y compris les règles relatives aux conflits de lois, des dispositions du présent Accord, des termes des accords particuliers qui seraient conclus au sujet de l'investissement ainsi que des principes de droit international. .

5.   Les sentences arbitrales sont définitives et obligatoires pour les parties au différend. Chaque Partie Contractante s'engage à exécuter ces sentences en conformité avec sa législation nationale.

ARTICLE 10
REGLEMENT DES DIFFERENDS ENTRE LES PARTIES CONTRACTANTES

1.   Tout différends entre les Parties contractantes au sujet de l'interprétation ou de l'application du présent Accord sera réglé, autant que possible, entre les deux Parties Contractantes par la voie dîplomatique.

2.   A défaut, le différend est soumis à une commission mixte, composée des représentants des Parties ; celle-ci se réunit sans délai, à la demande de la Partie la plus diligente.

3.   Si la commission mixte ne peut régler le différend dans un délai de six mois à dater du commencement des négociations, il est soumis à un tribunal d'arbitrage, à la demande de l'une des Parties Contractantes.

4.   Ledit tribunal sera constitué de la manière suivante : Chaque Partie Contractante désigne un arbitre, et les deux arbitres désignent ensemble un troisième arbitre, qui sera ressortissant d'un Etat tiers, commme Président du tribunal. Les arbitres doivent être désignés dans un délai de trois mois, le Président dans un délai de cinq mois à compter de la date à laquelle l'une des Parties Contractantes à fait part à l'autre Partie Contractante de son intention de soumettre le différend a un tribunal d'arbitrage.

5.   Si les délais fixés au paragraphe (4) ci-dessus n'ont pas été observés, l'une ou l'autre Partie Contractante invitera le Président de la Cour Internationale de Justice à procéder aux désignations nécessaires. Si le Président de la Cour Internationale de Justice sera invité à procéder aux nominations nécessaires. Si le Vice-Président possède la nationalit de l'une des Parties Contractantes ou bien s'il est empêché d'exyercer son mandat, le membre le plus ancien de la Cour Internationale de Justice qui n'est ressortissant d'aucune des Parties Contractantes, sera invité à procéder aux dites nominations. .

6.   Le tribune arbitral statue sur la base des dispositions du présent Accord et des règles et principes du droit International. La décision du tribunal sera adoptée par la majorité des voix. Elle sera définitive et obligatoire pour les Parties Contractantes .

7.   Le tribunal fixe ses propres règles de procédure.

8.   Chaque Partie contractante supportera les frais de son arbitre et de sa représentation dans la procédure d'arbitrage. Les frais concernant le Président et les autres frais seront supportés, à parts égales, par les Parties contractantes.

ARTICLE 11.
ENTREE EN VIGUEUR, DUREE ET EXPIRATION

1.   Le present Accord sera soumis à ratification et entrera en viqueur 30 jours à compter de la date de la réception de la dernière des deux notifications relatives à l'accomplissement par les deux Parties Contractantes des procédures constitutionnelles dans leur pays respectifs.

Il restera en vigueur pour une période de dix ans. Il pourra être révisé par écrit à la demande de chacune des Parties Contractantes douze (12) mois après la notification à l'autre Partie Contractante. A que l'une des Parties Contractantes ne le dénonce au moins six mois avant l'expiration de sa période de validité, il est chaque fois reconduit tactement pour une nouvelle période de dix ans chaque Partie contractante se réservant le droit de la dénoncer par notification écrite au moins six mois avant la date d'expiration de la période de validation en cours.

2.   Les investissements effectués antérieurment à la date d'expiration du présent Accord llui restent soumis pour unne période de dix ans à compter de la date de ladite expiration.

EN FOI DE QUOI, les représentants soussignés, dûment autorisés par leurs Gouvernements respectifs, ont signé le présent Accord.

Fait à ....le ....

En deux originaux, chacun en langue française

POUR LE GOUVERNEMENT DE BURKINA FASO _____.

POUR LE GOUVERNEMENT DU_____.

*

AGREEMENT BETWEEN THE GOVERNMENT OF THE REPUBLIC OF MAURITIUS AND THE GOVERNMENT OF _____ FOR THE AVOIDANCE OF DOUBLE TAXATION WITH RESPECT TO TAXES ON INCOME *

The Government of the Republic of Mauritius and the Government of ....,

Desiring to conclude an Agreement for the avoidance of double taxation with respect to taxes on income,

Have agreed as follows:

ARTICLE 1
PERSONAL SCOPE

This Agreement shall apply to persons who are residents of one or both of the Contracting States.

ARTICLE 2
TAXES COVERED

1.   This Agreement shall apply to taxes on income imposed on behalf of a Contracting State or its political subdivisions.

2.   There shall be regarded as taxes on income all taxes imposed on total income or on elements of income.

3.   The existing taxes to which this Agreement shall apply are in particular:

   (a)   in Mauritius, the income tax;

   (hereinafter referred to as "Mauritius tax");

   (b)   in : ....

   (hereinafter referred to as ....).

4.   This Agreement shall also apply to any other taxes of a substantially similar character which are imposed by either Contracting State after the date of signature of this Agreement in addition to, or in place of, the existing taxes.

5.   The competent authorities of the Contracting States shall notify each other of changes which have been made in their respective taxation laws, and if it seems desirable to amend any Article of this Agreement, without affecting the general principles thereof, the necessary amendments may be made by mutual consent by means of an Exchange of Notes.

---

*   *Source*: The Government of Mauritius, Ministry of Foreign Affairs. [Note added by the editor.]

ARTICLE 3
GENERAL DEFINITIONS

1.   In this Agreement, unless the context otherwise requires:

(a)   (i)   the term "Mauritius" means the Republic of Mauritius and includes:

(ii)   all the territories and islands which, in accordance with the laws of Mauritius, constitute the State of Mauritius;

(iii) the territorial sea of Mauritius; and

(iv)   any area outside the territorial sea of Mauritius which in accordance with international law has been or may hereafter be designated, under the laws of Mauritius, as an area, including the Continental Shelf, within which the rights of Mauritius with respect to the sea, the sea-bed and sub-soil and their natural resources may be exercised;

(b)   the term "................." means ....

(c)   the terms "a Contracting State" and "the other Contracting State" mean Mauritius or .... as the context requires;

(d)   the term "company" means any body corporate or any entity which is treated as a body corporate for tax purposes;

(e)   the term "competent authority" means:

a)   in Mauritius, the Commissioner of Income Tax or his authorised representative; and

b)   in ....,

(f)   the terms "enterprise of a Contracting State" and "enterprise of the other Contracting State" mean respectively an enterprise carried on by a resident of a Contracting State and an enterprise carried on by a resident of the other Contracting State;

(g)   the term "international traffic" means any transport by a ship or aircraft operated by an enterprise which has its place of effective management in a Contracting State, except when the ship or aircraft is operated solely between places in the other Contracting State;

(h)   the term "national" means any individual having the citizenship of a Contracting State and any legal person, partnership (société) or association deriving its status as such from the laws in force in a Contracting State;

(i)   the term "person" includes an individual, a company, a trust and any other body of persons which is treated as an entity for tax purposes; and

(j)   the term "tax" means Mauritius tax or .... as the context requires.

2.   As regards the application of the Agreement at any time by a Contracting State, any term not defined therein shall, unless the context otherwise requires, have the meaning that it has at that time under the law of that State for the purposes of the taxes to which the Agreement applies, any meaning under the applicable tax laws of that State prevailing over a meaning given to the term under other laws of that State.

ARTICLE 4
RESIDENT

1.   For the purposes of this Agreement, the term "resident of a Contracting State" means any person who, under the laws of that State, is liable to tax therein by reason of his domicile, residence, place of management or any other criterion of a similar nature and also includes that State and any political subdivision or local authority thereof. This term, however, does not include any person who is liable to tax in that State in respect only of income from sources in that State.

2.   Where by reason of the provisions of paragraph 1 an individual is a resident of both Contracting States, then his status shall be determined in accordance with the following rules:

(a)   he shall be deemed to be a resident only of the State in which he has a permanent home available to him. If he has a permanent home available to him in both States, he shall be deemed to be a resident of the State with which his personal and economic relations are closer (centre of vital interests);

(b)   if the State in which he has his centre of vital interests cannot be determined, or if he does not have a permanent home available to him in either State, he shall be deemed to be a resident only of the State in which he has an habitual abode;

(c)   if he has an habitual abode in both States or in neither of them, he shall be deemed to be a resident only of the State of which he is a national;

(d)   if he is a national of both States or of neither of them, the competent authorities of the Contracting States shall settle the question by mutual agreement.

3.   Where by reason of the provisions of paragraph 1 a person other than an individual is a resident of both Contracting States, then it shall be deemed to be a resident only of the State in which its place of effective management is situated.

ARTICLE 5
PERMANENT ESTABLISHMENT

1.   For the purposes of this Agreement, the term "permanent establishment" means a fixed place of business through which the business of an enterprise is wholly or partly carried on.

2.   The term "permanent establishment" shall include:

(a)   a place of management;

    (b)   a branch;

    (c)   an office;

    (d)   a factory;

    (e)   a workshop;

    (f)   a warehouse, in relation to a person providing storage facilities for others;

    (g)   a mine, an oil or gas well, a quarry or any other place of extraction of natural resources; and

    (h)   an installation or structure used for the exploration of natural resources.

3.   The term "permanent establishment" likewise encompasses:

    (a)   a building site or construction, installation or assembly project, or supervisory activities in connection therewith only if the site, project or activity lasts more than ..... months.

    (b)   the furnishing of services including consultancy services by an enterprise of a Contracting State through employees or other personnel engaged in the other Contracting State, provided that such activities continue for the same or a connected project for a period or periods aggregating to more than .... months within any ...... month period.

4.   Notwithstanding the preceding provisions of this Article, the term "permanent establishment" shall be deemed not to include:

    (a)   the use of facilities solely for the purpose of storage, display or delivery of goods or merchandise belonging to the enterprise;

    (b)   the maintenance of a stock of goods or merchandise belonging to the enterprise solely for the purpose of storage, display or delivery;

    (c)   the maintenance of a stock of goods or merchandise belonging to the enterprise solely for the purpose of processing by another enterprise;

    (d)   the maintenance of a fixed place of business solely for the purpose of purchasing goods or merchandise, or for collecting information, for the enterprise;

    (e)   the maintenance of a fixed place of business solely for the purpose of advertising, for the supply of information, for scientific research or for similar activities which have a preparatory or auxiliary character, for the enterprise; and

    (f)   the maintenance of a fixed place of business solely for any combination of activities mentioned in subparagraphs (a) to (e), provided that the overall activity of the fixed place of business resulting from this combination is of a preparatory or auxiliary character.

5.   Notwithstanding the provisions of paragraphs 1 and 2, a person acting in a Contracting State on behalf of an enterprise of the other Contracting State (other than an agent of an independent status to whom paragraph 6 of this Article applies) notwithstanding that he has no fixed place of business in the first-mentioned State shall be deemed to be a permanent establishment in that State if he has, and habitually exercises, a general authority in the first-mentioned State to conclude contracts in the name of the enterprise, unless his activities are limited to the purchase of goods or merchandise for the enterprise.

6.   An enterprise shall not be deemed to have a permanent establishment in a Contracting State merely because it carries on business in that State through a broker, general commission agent or any other agent of an independent status, provided that such persons are acting in the ordinary course of their business.

7.   The fact that a company which is a resident of a Contracting State controls or is controlled by a company which is a resident of the other Contracting State, or which carries on business in that other State (whether through a permanent establishment or otherwise), shall not of itself constitute either company a permanent establishment of the other.

ARTICLE 6
INCOME FROM IMMOVABLE PROPERTY

1.   Income derived by a resident of a Contracting State from immovable property, including income from agriculture or forestry, is taxable in the Contracting State in which such property is situated.

2.   The term "immovable property" shall have the meaning which it has under the law of the Contracting State in which the property in question is situated. The term shall in any case include property accessory to immovable property, livestock and equipment used in agriculture and forestry, rights to which the provisions of general law respecting landed property apply, usufruct of immovable property and rights to variable or fixed payments as consideration for the working of, or the right to work, mineral deposits, sources and other natural resources. Ships, boats and aircraft shall not be regarded as immovable property.

3.   The provisions of paragraph 1 shall apply to income derived from the direct use, letting or use in any other form of immovable property.

4.   The provisions of paragraphs 1 and 3 shall also apply to the income from immovable property of an enterprise and to income from immovable property used for the performance of independent personal services.

ARTICLE 7
BUSINESS PROFITS

1.   The profits of an enterprise of a Contracting State shall be taxable only in that State unless the enterprise carries on business in the other Contracting State through a permanent establishment situated therein. If the enterprise carries on business as aforesaid, the profits of the enterprise may be taxed in the other State but only so much of them as is attributable to that permanent establishment.

2.   Subject to the provisions of paragraph 3, where an enterprise of a Contracting State carries on business in the other Contracting State through a permanent establishment situated therein, there shall in each Contracting State be attributed to that permanent establishment the profits which it might be expected to make if it were a distinct and separate enterprise engaged in the same or similar activities under the same or similar conditions and dealing wholly independently with the enterprise of which it is a permanent establishment.

3.   In determining the profits of a permanent establishment, there shall be allowed as deductions expenses which are incurred for the purposes of the permanent establishment including executive and general administrative expenses so incurred, whether in the State in which the permanent establishment is situated or elsewhere. However, no such deduction shall be allowed in respect of amounts, if any, paid (otherwise than towards reimbursement of actual expenses) by the permanent establishment to the head office of the enterprise or any of its other offices, by way of royalties, fees or other similar payments in return for the use of patents or other rights, or by way of commission, for specific services performed or for management, or, except in the case of a banking enterprise, by way of interest on moneys lent to the permanent establishment. Likewise, no account shall be taken, in determining the profits of a permanent establishment, of amounts charged (otherwise than towards reimbursement of actual expenses), by the permanent establishment to the head office of the enterprise or any of its other offices, by way of royalties, fees or other similar payments in return for the use of patents or other rights, or by way of commission for specific services performed or for management, or, except in the case of a banking enterprise, by way of interest on moneys lent to the head office of the enterprise or any of its other offices.

4.   In so far as it has been customary in a Contracting State to determine the profits to be attributed to a permanent establishment on the basis of an apportionment of the total profits of the enterprise to its various parts, nothing in paragraph 2 shall preclude that Contracting State from determining the profits to be taxed by such an apportionment as may be customary. The method of apportionment adopted shall, however, be such that the result shall be in accordance with the principles contained in this Article.

5.   No profits shall be attributed to a permanent establishment by reason of the mere purchase by that permanent establishment of goods or merchandise for the enterprise.

6.   For the purposes of the preceding paragraphs, the profits to be attributed to the permanent establishment shall be determined by the same method year by year unless there is good and sufficient reason to the contrary.

7.   Where profits include items of income which are dealt with separately in other Articles of this Agreement, then the provisions of those Articles shall not be affected by the provisions of this Article.

ARTICLE 8
SHIPPING AND AIR TRANSPORT

1.   Profits of an enterprise from the operation or rental of ships or aircraft in international traffic and the rental of containers and related equipment which is incidental to the operation of ships or aircraft in international traffic shall be taxable only in the Contracting State in which the place of effective management of the enterprise is situated.

2.   If the place of effective management of a shipping enterprise is aboard a ship or boat, then it shall be deemed to be situated in the Contracting State in which the home harbour of the ship or boat is situated, or, if there is no such home harbour, in the Contracting State of which the operator of the ship or boat is a resident.

3.   The provisions of paragraph 1 shall also apply to profits from the participation in a pool, a joint business or an international operating agency.

ARTICLE 9
ASSOCIATED ENTERPRISES

1.   Where:

(a)   an enterprise of a Contracting State participates directly or indirectly in the management, control or capital of an enterprise of the other Contracting State; or

(b)   the same persons participate directly or indirectly in the management, control or capital of an enterprise of a Contracting State and an enterprise of the other Contracting State,

and in either case conditions are made or imposed between the two enterprises in their commercial or financial relations which differ from those which would be made between independent enterprises, then any profits which would, but for those conditions, have accrued to one of the enterprises, but, by reason of those conditions, have not so accrued, may be included in the profits of that enterprise and taxed accordingly.

2.   Where a Contracting State includes in the profits of an enterprise of that State - and taxes accordingly - profits on which an enterprise of the other Contracting State has been charged to tax in that other State and the profits so included are profits which would have accrued to the enterprise of the first-mentioned State if the conditions made between the two enterprises had been those which would have been made between independent enterprises, then that other State shall make an appropriate adjustment to the amount of the tax charged therein on those profits. In determining such adjustment, due regard shall be had to the other provisions of this Agreement and the competent authorities of the Contracting States shall if necessary consult each other.

ARTICLE 10
DIVIDENDS

1.   Dividends paid by a company which is a resident of a Contracting State to a resident of the other Contracting State shall, if the recipient is the beneficial owner of the dividends, be taxable only in that other State.

2.   The term "dividends" as used in this Article means income from shares or other rights, not being debt claims, participating in profits, as well as income from other corporate rights which is subjected to the same taxation treatment as income from shares by the laws of the Contracting State of which the company making the distribution is a resident.

3.   The provisions of paragraph 1 shall not apply if the beneficial owner of the dividends, being a resident of a Contracting State, carries on business in the other Contracting State of

which the company paying the dividends is a resident, through a permanent establishment situated therein, or performs in that other State independent personal services from a fixed base situated therein, and the holding in respect of which the dividends are paid is effectively connected with such permanent establishment or fixed base. In such a case, the provisions of Article 7 or Article 14, as the case may be, shall apply.

4.   Where a company which is a resident of a Contracting State derives profits or income from the other Contracting State, that other State may not impose any tax on the dividends paid by the company except in so far as such dividends are paid to a resident of that other State or in so far as the holding in respect of which the dividends are paid is effectively connected with a permanent establishment or a fixed base situated in that other State, nor subject the company's undistributed profits to a tax on undistributed profits, even if the dividends paid or the undistributed profits consist wholly or partly of profits or income arising in such other State.

ARTICLE 11
INTEREST

1.   Interest arising in a Contracting State and paid to a resident of the other Contracting State shall, if the recipient is the beneficial owner of the interest, be taxable only in that other State.

2.   The term "interest" as used in this Article means income from debt-claims of every kind, whether or not secured by mortgage and whether or not carrying a right to participate in the debtor's profits, and in particular, income from government securities and income from bonds or debentures, including premiums and prizes attaching to such securities, bonds or debentures. Penalty charges for late payment shall not be regarded as interest for the purpose of this Article. The term "interest" shall not include any item which is treated as a dividend under the provisions of Article 10 of this Agreement.

3.   The provisions of paragraph 1 shall not apply if the beneficial owner of the interest, being a resident of a Contracting State, carries on business in the other Contracting State in which the interest arises, through a permanent establishment situated therein, or performs in that other State independent personal services from a fixed base situated therein, and the debt-claim in respect of which the interest is paid is effectively connected with such permanent establishment or fixed base. In such a case, the provisions of Article 7 or Article 14, as the case may be, shall apply.

4.   Interest shall be deemed to arise in a Contracting State when the payer is a resident of that State. Where, however, the person paying the interest, whether he is a resident of a Contracting State or not, has in a Contracting State a permanent establishment or a fixed base in connection with which the indebtedness on which the interest is paid was incurred, and such interest is borne by such permanent establishment or fixed base, then such interest shall be deemed to arise in the State in which the permanent establishment or fixed base is situated.

5.   Where, by reason of a special relationship between the payer and the beneficial owner or between both of them and some other person, the amount of the interest, having regard to the debt-claim for which it is paid, exceeds the amount which would have been agreed upon by the payer and the beneficial owner in the absence of such relationship, the provisions of this Article shall apply only to the last-mentioned amount. In such a case, the excess part of the payments shall remain taxable according to the laws of each Contracting State, due regard being had to the other provisions of this Agreement.

ARTICLE 12
ROYALTIES

1.   Royalties arising in a Contracting State and paid to a resident of the other Contracting State shall, if the recipient is the beneficial owner of the royalties, be taxable only in that other State.

2.   The term "royalties" as used in this Article means payments of any kind received as a consideration for the use of, or the right to use, any copyright of literary, artistic or scientific work (including cinematograph films and films, tapes or discs for radio or television broadcasting), any patent, trade mark, design or model, computer programme, plan, secret formula or process, or for information concerning industrial, commercial or scientific experience.

3.   The provisions of paragraph 1 shall not apply if the beneficial owner of the royalties, being a resident of a Contracting State, carries on business in the other Contracting State in which the royalties arise, through a permanent establishment situated therein, or performs in that other State independent personal services from a fixed base situated therein, and the right or property in respect of which the royalties are paid is effectively connected with such permanent establishment or fixed base. In such a case, the provisions of Article 7 or Article 14, as the case may be, shall apply.

4.   Royalties shall be deemed to arise in a Contracting State when the payer is a resident of that State. Where, however, the person paying the royalties, whether he is a resident of a Contracting State or not, has in a Contracting State a permanent establishment or a fixed base with which the right or property in respect of which the royalties are paid is effectively connected, and such royalties are borne by such permanent establishment or fixed base, then such royalties shall be deemed to arise in the State in which the permanent establishment or fixed base is situated.

5.   Where, by reason of a special relationship between the payer and the beneficial owner or between both of them and some other person, the amount of the royalties paid, having regard to the use, right or information for which they are paid, exceeds the amount which would have been agreed upon by the payer and the beneficial owner in the absence of such relationship, the provisions of this Article shall apply only to the last-mentioned amount. In such a case, the excess part of the payments shall remain taxable according to the laws of each Contracting State, due regard being had to the other provisions of this Agreement.

ARTICLE 13
CAPITAL GAINS

1.   Gains derived by a resident of a Contracting State from the alienation of immovable property referred to in Article 6 and situated in the other Contracting State may be taxed in that other State.

2.   Gains from the alienation of movable property forming part of the business property of a permanent establishment which an enterprise of a Contracting State has in the other Contracting State or of movable property pertaining to a fixed base available to a resident of a Contracting State in the other Contracting State for the purpose of performing independent personal services, including such gains from the alienation of such a permanent establishment (alone or with the whole enterprise) or of such fixed base, may be taxed in that other State.

3. Gains from the alienation of ships or aircraft operated in international traffic or movable property pertaining to the operation of such ships or aircraft shall be taxable only in the Contracting State in which the place of effective management of the enterprise is situated.

4. Gains from the alienation of any property other than that referred to in paragraphs 1, 2 and 3 shall be taxable only in the Contracting State of which the alienator is a resident.

ARTICLE 14
INDEPENDENT PERSONAL SERVICES

1. Income derived by a resident of a Contracting State in respect of professional services or other activities of an independent character shall be taxable only in that State unless he has a fixed base regularly available to him in the other Contracting State for the purpose of performing his activities. If he has such a fixed base, the income may be taxed in the other State but only so much of it as is attributable to that fixed base.

2. The term "professional services" includes especially independent scientific, literary, artistic, educational or teaching activities as well as the independent activities of physicians, lawyers, engineers, architects, dentists and accountants.

ARTICLE 15
DEPENDENT PERSONAL SERVICES

1. Subject to the provisions of Articles 16, 18, 19 and 20, salaries, wages and other similar remuneration derived by a resident of a Contracting State in respect of an employment shall be taxable only in that State unless the employment is exercised in the other Contracting State. If the employment is so exercised, such remuneration as is derived therefrom may be taxed in that other State.

2. Notwithstanding the provisions of paragraph 1, remuneration derived by a resident of a Contracting State in respect of an employment exercised in the other Contracting State shall be taxable only in the first-mentioned State if:

    (a) the recipient is present in the other State for a period or periods not exceeding in the aggregate 183 days in any 12-month period commencing or ending in the fiscal year concerned; and

    (b) the remuneration is paid by, or on behalf of an employer who is not a resident of the other State; and

    (c) the remuneration is not borne by a permanent establishment or a fixed base which the employer has in the other State.

3. Notwithstanding the preceding provisions of this Article, remuneration derived in respect of an employment exercised aboard a ship or aircraft operated in international traffic may be taxed in the Contracting State in which the place of effective management of the enterprise is situated.

ARTICLE 16
DIRECTORS' FEES

Directors' fees and other similar payments derived by a resident of a Contracting State in his capacity as a member of the board of directors of a company which is a resident of the other Contracting State may be taxed in that other State.

ARTICLE 17
ENTERTAINERS AND SPORTSMEN

1.   Notwithstanding the provisions of Articles 14 and 15, income derived by a resident of a Contracting State as an entertainer such as a theatre, motion picture, radio or television artiste, or a musician, or as a sportsman, from his personal activities as such exercised in the other Contracting State, may be taxed in that other State.

2.   Where income in respect of personal activities exercised by an entertainer or a sportsman in his capacity as such accrues not to the entertainer or sportsman himself but to another person, that income may, notwithstanding the provisions of Articles 7, 14 and 15, be taxed in the Contracting State in which the activities of the entertainer or sportsman are exercised.

3.   Notwithstanding the provisions of paragraphs 1 and 2, income derived from activities, referred to in paragraph 1, performed under a cultural agreement or arrangement between the Contracting States shall be exempt from tax in the Contracting State in which the activities are exercised if the visit to that State is wholly or substantially supported by funds of either Contracting State, a local authority or public institution thereof.

ARTICLE 18
PENSIONS

1.   Subject to the provisions of paragraph 2 of Article 19, pensions and other similar payments arising in a Contracting State and paid in consideration of past employment to a resident of the other Contracting State, shall be taxable only in that other State.

2.   Notwithstanding the provisions of paragraph 1, pensions paid and other payments made under a public scheme which is part of the social security system of a Contracting State or a political subdivision or a local authority thereof shall be taxable only in that State.

ARTICLE 19
GOVERNMENT SERVICE

1.   (a)   Salaries, wages, and other similar remuneration, other than a pension, paid by a Contracting State or a political subdivision, local authority or statutory body thereof to an individual in respect of services rendered to that State or subdivision, authority or body shall be taxable only in that State.

    (b)   However, such salaries, wages and other similar remuneration shall be taxable only in the other Contracting State if the services are rendered in that State and the individual is a resident of that State who:

        (i)   is a national of that State; or

(ii)   did not become a resident of that State solely for the purpose of rendering the services.

2.   (a)   Any pension paid by, or out of funds created by, a Contracting State or a political subdivision, local authority or statutory body thereof to an individual in respect of services rendered to that State or subdivision, authority or body shall be taxable only in that State.

       (b)   However, such pension shall be taxable only in the other Contracting State if the individual is a resident of, and a national of, that State.

3.   The provisions of Articles 15, 16, 17 and 18 shall apply to salaries, wages and other similar remuneration, and to pensions, in respect of services rendered in connection with a business carried on by a Contracting State, or a political subdivision, local authority or statutory body thereof.

ARTICLE 20
PROFESSORS AND TEACHERS

1.   Notwithstanding the provisions of Article 15, a professor or teacher who makes a temporary visit to one of the Contracting States for a period not exceeding two years for the purpose of teaching or carrying out research at a university, college, school or other educational institution in that State and who is, or immediately before such visit was, a resident of the other Contracting State shall, in respect of remuneration for such teaching or research, be exempt from tax in the first-mentioned State, provided that such remuneration is derived by him from outside that State.

2.   The provisions of this Article shall not apply to income from research if such research is undertaken not in the public interest but wholly or mainly for the private benefit of a specific person or persons.

ARTICLE 21
STUDENTS AND BUSINESS APPRENTICES

A student or business apprentice who is present in a Contracting State solely for the purpose of his education or training and who is, or immediately before being so present was, a resident of the other Contracting State, shall be exempt from tax in the first-mentioned State on payments received from outside that first-mentioned State for the purposes of his maintenance, education or training.

ARTICLE 22
OTHER INCOME

1.   Subject to the provisions of paragraph 2 of this Article, items of income of a resident of a Contracting State, wherever arising, not dealt with in the foregoing Articles of this Agreement shall be taxable only in that State.

2.   The provisions of paragraph 1 shall not apply to income if the recipient of such income, being a resident of a Contracting State, carries on business in the other Contracting State through a permanent establishment situated therein, or performs in that other State independent personal

services from a fixed base situated therein, and a right or property in respect of which the income is paid is effectively connected with such permanent establishment or fixed base. In such a case, the provisions of Article 7 or Article 14, as the case may be, shall apply.

ARTICLE 23
ELIMINATION OF DOUBLE TAXATION

Double taxation shall be eliminated as follows:

1.   In the case of Mauritius:

   (a)   Where a resident of a Contracting State derives income from .... the amount of tax on that income payable in .... in accordance with the provisions of this Agreement may be credited against the Mauritius tax imposed on that resident.

   (b)   Where a company which is a resident of .... pays a dividend to a resident of Mauritius who controls, directly or indirectly, at least 5% of the capital of the company paying the dividend, the credit shall take into account (in addition to any .... tax for which credit may be allowed under the provisions of subparagraphs (a) and (b) of this paragraph) the .... tax payable by the first-mentioned company in respect of the profits out of which such dividend is paid.

   (c)   Provided that any credit allowed under subparagraphs (a) and (b) shall not exceed the Mauritius tax (as computed before allowing any such credit), which is appropriate to the profits or income derived from sources within ....

2.   In the case of .... ;

   (a)   ....

3.   For the purposes of allowance as a credit the tax payable in Mauritius or .... as the context requires, shall be deemed to include the tax which is otherwise payable in either of the two Contracting States but has been reduced or waived by either State in order to promote its economic development.

ARTICLE 24
NON-DISCRIMINATION

1.   The nationals of a Contracting State shall not be subjected in the other Contracting State to any taxation or any requirement connected therewith which is other or more burdensome than the taxation and connected requirements to which nationals of that other State in the same circumstances in particular with respect to residence, are or may be subjected. This provision shall, notwithstanding the provisions of Article 1, also apply to persons who are not residents of one or both of the Contracting States.

2.   The taxation on a permanent establishment which an enterprise of a Contracting State has in the other Contracting State shall not be less favourably levied in that other State than the taxation levied on enterprises of that other State carrying on the same activities.

3.   Enterprises of a Contracting State, the capital of which is wholly or partly owned or controlled, directly or indirectly, by one or more residents of the other Contracting State, shall not be subjected in the first-mentioned State to any taxation or any requirement connected therewith which is other or more burdensome than the taxation and connected requirements to which other similar enterprises of that first-mentioned State are or may be subjected.

4.   Nothing in this Article shall be construed as obliging a Contracting State to grant to residents of the other Contracting State any personal allowances, reliefs and reductions for taxation purposes on account of civil status or family responsibilities which it grants to its own residents.

5.   In this Article the term "taxation" means taxes which are the subject of this Agreement.

ARTICLE 25
MUTUAL AGREEMENT PROCEDURE

1.   Where a person considers that the actions of one or both of the Contracting States result or will result for him in taxation not in accordance with the provisions of this Agreement, he may, irrespective of the remedies provided by the domestic law of those States, present his case to the competent authority of the Contracting State of which he is a resident or, if his case comes under paragraph 1 of Article 24, to that of the Contracting State of which he is a national. The case must be presented within three years from the first notification of the action resulting in taxation not in accordance with the provisions of this Agreement.

2.   The competent authority shall endeavour, if the objection appears to it to be justified and if it is not itself able to arrive at an appropriate solution, to resolve the case by mutual agreement with the competent authority of the other Contracting State, with a view to the avoidance of taxation which is not in accordance with the Agreement. Any agreement reached shall be implemented notwithstanding any time limits in the domestic law of the Contracting States.

3.   The competent authorities of the Contracting States shall endeavour to resolve by mutual agreement any difficulties or doubts arising as to the interpretation or application of this Agreement. They may also consult together for the elimination of double taxation in cases not provided for in this Agreement.

4.   The competent authorities of the Contracting States may communicate with each other directly, including through a joint commission consisting of themselves or their representatives, for the purpose of reaching an agreement in the sense of the preceding paragraphs.

ARTICLE 26
EXCHANGE OF INFORMATION

1.   The competent authorities of the Contracting States shall exchange such information as is necessary for carrying out the provisions of this Agreement or of the domestic laws of the Contracting States concerning taxes covered by this Agreement in so far as the taxation thereunder is not contrary to the Agreement. The exchange of information is not restricted by Article 1. Any information so exchanged shall be treated as secret in the same manner as information obtained under the domestic law of that State and shall be disclosed only to persons or authorities (including courts or administrative bodies) concerned with the assessment or collection of, the enforcement or prosecution in respect of, or the determination of appeals in

relation to, the taxes covered by this Agreement. Such persons or authorities shall use the information only for such purposes. They may disclose the information in public court proceedings or in judicial decisions.

2.   In no case shall the provisions of paragraph 1 be construed so as to impose on a Contracting State the obligation:

(a)   to carry out administrative measures at variance with the laws and administrative practice of that or of the other Contracting State;

(b)   to supply information which is not obtainable under the laws or in the normal course of the administration of that or of the other Contracting State;

(c)   to supply information which would disclose any trade, business, industrial, commercial or professional secret or trade process, or information, the disclosure of which would be contrary to public policy (ordre public).

ARTICLE 27
DIPLOMATIC AGENTS AND CONSULAR OFFICERS

Nothing in this Agreement shall affect the fiscal privileges of members of diplomatic missions or consular posts under the general rules of international law or under the provisions of special agreements.

ARTICLE 28
ENTRY INTO FORCE

1.   Each of the Contracting Parties shall notify to the other the completion of the procedures required by its law for the entering into force of this Agreement. The Agreement shall enter into force on the date of the later of these notifications.

2.   The provisions of this Agreement shall apply:

(a)   in Mauritius, on income for any income year beginning on or after the first day of July next following the date upon which this Agreement enters into force; and

(b)   in : ....

ARTICLE 29
TERMINATION

1.   This Agreement shall remain in force indefinitely but either of the Contracting States may terminate the Agreement through diplomatic channels, by giving to the other Contracting State written notice of termination not later than 30 June of any calendar year starting five years after the year in which the Agreement entered into force.

2.   In such event the Agreement shall cease to have effect:

(a)   in Mauritius, on income for any income year beginning on or after the first day of July next following the calendar year in which such notice is given; and (b)　　in : ....

IN WITNESS WHEREOF the undersigned, being duly authorised thereto, have signed this Agreement.

DONE at .... in duplicate, this .... day of .... of the year one thousand nine hundred and ninety ....

FOR THE GOVERNMENT OF　　　　　　　　FOR THE GOVERNMENT OF
REPUBLIC OF MAURITIUS　　　　　　　　　....................................

.

*

SELECTED UNCTAD PUBLICATIONS ON TRANSNATIONAL CORPORATIONS AND FOREIGN DIRECT INVESTMENT

(For more information, please visit www.unctad.org/en/pub on the web.)

A. Serial publications

World Investment Reports

World Investment Report 2002: Transnational Corporations and Export Competitiveness. 282 p. Sales No. E.02.II.D.4 $49. http://www.unctad.org/wir/contents/wir02content.en.htm.

World Investment Report 2002: Transnational Corporations and Export Competitiveness. An Overview.72 p. Free of charge. http://www.unctad.org/wir/contents/wir02content.en.htm.

World Investment Report 2001: Promoting Linkages. 356 p. Sales No. E.01.II.D.12 $49. http://www.unctad.org/wir/contents/wir01content.en.htm.

World Investment Report 2001: Promoting Linkage. An Overview.67 p.Free of charge. http://www.unctad.org/wir/contents/wir01content.en.htm.

Ten Years of World Investment Reports: The Challenges Ahead. Proceedings of an UNCTAD special event on future challenges in the area of FDI.UNCTAD/ITE/Misc.45. Free of charge. http://www.unctad.org/wir.

World Investment Report 2000: Cross-border Mergers and Acquisitions and Development. 368 p. Sales No. E.99.II.D.20. $49. http://www.unctad.org/wir/contents/wir00content.en.htm.

World Investment Report 2000: Cross-border Mergers and Acquisitions and Development. An Overview. 75 p. Free of charge. http://www.unctad.org/wir/contents/wir00content.en.htm.

World Investment Report 1999: Foreign Direct Investment and the Challenge of Development. 543 p. Sales No. E.99.II.D.3. $49. http://www.unctad.org/wir/contents/wir99content.en.htm.

World Investment Report 1999: Foreign Direct Investment and Challenge of Development. An Overview. 75 p. Free of charge. http://www.unctad.org/wir/contents/wir99content.en.htm.

World Investment Report 1998: Trends and Determinants. 432 p. Sales No. E.98.II.D.5. $45. http://www.unctad.org/wir/contents/wir98content.en.htm.

World Investment Report 1998: Trends and Determinants. An Overview. 67 p. Free of charge. http://www.unctad.org/wir/contents/wir98content.en.htm.

World Investment Report 1997: Transnational Corporations, Market Structure and Competition Policy. 384 p. Sales No. E.97.II.D.10. $45. http://www.unctad.org/wir/contents/wir97content.en.htm.

World Investment Report 1997: Transnational Corporations, Market Structure and

Competition Policy. An Overview. 70 p. Free of charge.
http://www.unctad.org/wir/contents/wir97content.en.htm.

World Investment Report 1996: Investment, Trade and International Policy Arrangements.
332 p. Sales No. E.96.II.A.14. $45. http://www.unctad.org/wir/contents/wir96content.en.htm.

***World Investment Report 1996: Investment, Trade and International Policy Arrangements. An
Overview.*** 51 p. Free of charge. http://www.unctad.org/wir/contents/wir96content.en.htm.

World Investment Report 1995: Transnational Corporations and Competitiveness. 491 p. Sales
No. E.95.II.A.9. $45. http://www.unctad.org/wir/contents/wir95content.en.htm.

***World Investment Report 1995: Transnational Corporations and Competitiveness. An
Overview.*** 51 p. Free of charge. http://www.unctad.org/wir/contents/wir95content.en.htm.

World Investment Report 1994: Transnational Corporations, Employment and the Workplace.
482 p. Sales No. E.94.II.A.14. $45. http://www.unctad.org/wir/contents/wir94content.en.htm.

***World Investment Report 1994: Transnational Corporations, Employment and the Workplace.
An Executive Summary.*** 34 p. http://www.unctad.org/wir/contents/wir94content.en.htm.

***World Investment Report 1993: Transnational Corporations and Integrated International
Production.*** 290 p. Sales No. E.93.II.A.14. $45.
http://www.unctad.org/wir/contents/wir93content.en.htm.

***World Investment Report 1993: Transnational Corporations and Integrated International
Production. An Executive Summary.*** 31 p. ST/CTC/159. Free of charge.
http://www.unctad.org/wir/contents/wir93content.en.htm.

World Investment Report 1992: Transnational Corporations as Engines of Growth. 356 p.
Sales No. E.92.II.A.19. $45. http://www.unctad.org/wir/contents/wir92content.en.htm.

***World Investment Report 1992: Transnational Corporations as Engines of Growth. An
Executive Summary.*** 30 p. Sales No. E.92.II.A.24. Free of charge.
http://www.unctad.org/wir/contents/wir92content.en.htm.

World Investment Report 1991: The Triad in Foreign Direct Investment. 108 p. Sales
No.E.91.II.A.12. $25. http://www.unctad.org/wir/contents/wir91content.en.htm.

World Investment Directories

***World Investment Directory1999: Asia and the Pacific. Vol. VII* (Parts I and II).** 332+638 p.
Sales No. E.00.II.D.21. $80.

World Investment Directory 1996: West Asia. Vol. VI.138 p. Sales No. E.97.II.A.2. $35.

World Investment Directory 1996: Africa. Vol. V. 461 p.Sales No. E.97.II.A.1. $75.

World Investment Directory 1994: Latin America and the Caribbean. Vol. IV. 478 p. Sales No. E.94.II.A.10. $65.

World Investment Directory 1992: Developed Countries. Vol. III. 532 p. Sales No. E.93.II.A.9. $75.

World Investment Directory 1992: Central and Eastern Europe. Vol. II. 432 p. Sales No. E.93.II.A.1. $65. (Joint publication with the United Nations Economic Commission for Europe.)

World Investment Directory 1992: Asia and the Pacific. Vol. I. 356 p. Sales No. E.92.II.A.11. $65.

Investment Policy Reviews

Investment Policy Review of the United Republic of Tanzania. 98 p. Sales No. 02.E.II.D.6 $ 20. http://www.unctad.org/en/docs/poiteipcm9.en.pdf.

Investment Policy Review of Ecuador. 117 p. Sales No. E.01.II D.31. $ 25.Summary available from http://www.unctad.org/en/docs/poiteipcm2sum.en.pdf.

Investment and Innovation Policy Review of Ethiopia. 115 p. UNCTAD/ITE/IPC/Misc.4. Free of charge. http://www.unctad.org/en/docs/poiteipcm4.en.pdf.

Investment Policy Review of Mauritius. 84 p. Sales No. E.01.II.D.11. $22. Summary available from http://www.unctad.org/en/pub/investpolicy.en.htm

Investment Policy Review of Peru. 108 p. Sales No. E.00.II.D. 7. $22. Summary available from http://www.unctad.org/en/docs/poiteiipm19sum.en.pdf.

Investment Policy Review of Uganda. 75 p. Sales No. E.99.II.D.24. $15. Summary available from http://www.unctad.org/en/docs/poiteiipm17sum.en.Pdf.

Investment Policy Review of Egypt. 113 p. Sales No. E.99.II.D.20. $19. Summary available from http://www.unctad.org/en/docs/poiteiipm11sum.en.Pdf.

Investment Policy Review of Uzbekistan. 64 p. UNCTAD/ITE/IIP/Misc.13. Free of charge. http://www.unctad.org/en/docs/poiteiipm13.en.pdf.

International Investment Instruments

International Investment Instruments: A Compendium. Vol. IX. 353 p. Sales No. E.02.II.D.16. $60. http://www.unctad.org/en/docs/psdited3v9.en.pdf.

International Investment Instruments: A Compendium. Vol. VIII. 335 p. Sales No. E.02.II.D.15. $60. http://www.unctad.org/en/docs/psdited3v8.en.pdf.

International Investment Instruments: A Compendium. Vol. VII. 339 p. Sales No. E.02.II.D.14. $60. http://www.unctad.org/en/docs/psdited3v7.en.pdf.

International Investment Instruments: A Compendium. Vol. VI. 568 p. Sales No. E.01.II.D.34. $60. http://www.unctad.org/en/docs/ps1dited2v6_p1.en.pdf (part one).

International Investment Instruments: A Compendium. Vol. V. 505 p. Sales No. E.00.II.D.14. $55.

International Investment Instruments: A Compendium. Vol. IV. 319 p. Sales No. E.00.II.D.13. $55.

International Investment Instruments: A Compendium. Vol. I. 371 p. Sales No. E.96.II.A.9; *Vol. II.* 577 p. Sales No. E.96.II.A.10; *Vol. III.* 389 p. Sales No. E.96.II.A.11; the 3-volume set, Sales No. E.96.II.A.12. $125.

Bilateral Investment Treaties 1959-1999. 143 p. UNCTAD/ITE/IIA/2, Free of charge. Available only in electronic version from http://www.unctad.org/en/pub/poiteiiad2.en.htm.

Bilateral Investment Treaties in the Mid-1990s. 314 p. Sales No. E.98.II.D.8. $46.

LDC Investment Guides

*An Investment Guide to Mozambique: Opportunities and Conditions.*72 p. UNCTAD/ITE/IIA/4.http://www.unctad.org/en/pub/investguide.en.htm

*An Investment Guide to Uganda: Opportunities and Conditions.*76p. UNCTAD/ITE/IIT/Misc.30. http://www.unctad.org/en/docs/poiteiitm30.en.pdf.

An Investment Guide to Bangladesh: Opportunities and Conditions. 66 p. UNCTAD/ITE/IIT/Misc.29. http://www.unctad.org/en/docs/poiteiitm29.en.pdf.

Guide d'investissement au Mali. 108 p. UNCTAD/ITE/IIT/Misc.24. http://www.unctad.org/fr/docs/poiteiitm24.fr.pdf. (Joint publication with the International Chamber of Commerce, in association with PricewaterhouseCoopers.)

An Investment Guide to Ethiopia: Opportunities and Conditions. 69 p. UNCTAD/ITE/IIT/Misc.19. http://www.unctad.org/en/docs/poiteiitm19.en.pdf. (Joint publication with the International Chamber of Commerce, in association with PricewaterhouseCoopers.)

Issues in International Investment Agreements
(Executive summaries are available from http://www.unctad.org/iia.)

Transfer of Technology. 138p. Sales No. E.01.II.D.33. $18.

Illicit Payments. 108 p. Sales No. E.01.II.D.20. $13.

Home Country Measures. 96 p. Sales No.E.01.II.D.19. $12.

Host Country Operational Measures. 109 p. Sales No E.01.II.D.18. $15.

Social Responsibility. 91 p.Sales No. E.01.II.D.4. $15.

Environment. 105 p. Sales No. E.01.II.D.3. $15.

Transfer of Funds. 68 p. Sales No. E.00.II.D.27. $12.

Employment. 69 p. Sales No. E.00.II.D.15. $12.

Taxation. 111 p. Sales No. E.00.II.D.5. $12.

International Investment Agreements: Flexibility for Development. 185 p. Sales No. E.00.II.D.6. $12.

Taking of Property. 83 p. Sales No. E.00.II.D.4. $12.

Trends in International Investment Agreements: An Overview. 112 p. Sales No. E.99.II.D.23. $ 12.

Lessons from the MAI. 31 p. Sales No. E.99.II.D.26. $ 12.

National Treatment. 104 p. Sales No. E.99.II.D.16. $12.

Fair and Equitable Treatment. 64 p. Sales No. E.99.II.D.15. $12.

Investment-Related Trade Measures. 64 p. Sales No. E.99.II.D.12. $12.

Most-Favoured-Nation Treatment. 72 p. Sales No. E.99.II.D.11. $12.

Admission and Establishment. 72 p. Sales No. E.99.II.D.10. $12.

Scope and Definition. 96 p. Sales No. E.99.II.D.9. $12.

Transfer Pricing. 72 p. Sales No. E.99.II.D.8. $12.

Foreign Direct Investment and Development. 88 p. Sales No. E.98.II.D.15. $12.

B. Current Studies
Series A

No. 30. Incentives and Foreign Direct Investment. 98 p. Sales No. E.96.II.A.6. $30. [Out of print.]

No. 29. Foreign Direct Investment, Trade, Aid and Migration. 100 p. Sales No. E.96.II.A.8. $25. (Joint publication with the International Organization for Migration.)

No. 28. Foreign Direct Investment in Africa. 119 p. Sales No. E.95.II.A.6. $20.

ASIT Advisory Studies (Formerly Current Studies, Series B)

No. 17. The World of Investment Promotion at a Glance: A survey of investment promotion practices. UNCTAD/ITE/IPC/3. Free of charge.

No. 16. Tax Incentives and Foreign Direct Investment: A Global Survey. 180 p. Sales No. E.01.II.D.5. $23. Summary available from http://www.unctad.org/asit/resumé.htm.

No. 15. Investment Regimes in the Arab World: Issues and Policies. 232 p. Sales No. E/F.00.II.D.32.

No. 14. Handbook on Outward Investment Promotion Agencies and Institutions. 50 p. Sales No. E.99.II.D.22. $ 15.

No. 13. Survey of Best Practices in Investment Promotion. 71 p. Sales No. E.97.II.D.11. $ 35.

No. 12. Comparative Analysis of Petroleum Exploration Contracts. 80 p. Sales No. E.96.II.A.7. $35.

No. 11. Administration of Fiscal Regimes for Petroleum Exploration and Development. 45 p. Sales No. E.95.II.A.8.

C. Individual Studies

The Tradability of Consulting Services. 189 p. UNCTAD/ITE/IPC/Misc.8. http://www.unctad.org/en/docs/poiteipcm8.en.pdf.

Compendium of International Arrangements on Transfer of Technology: Selected Instruments. 308 p. Sales No. E.01.II.D.28. $45.

FDI in Least Developed Countries at a Glance. 150 p. UNCTAD/ITE/IIA/3. Free of charge. Also available from http://www.unctad.org/en/pub/poiteiiad3.en.htm.

Foreign Direct Investment in Africa: Performance and Potential. 89 p. UNCTAD/ITE/IIT/Misc.15. Free of charge. Also available from http://www.unctad.org/en/docs/poiteiitm15.pdf.

TNC-SME Linkages for Development: Issues-Experiences-Best Practices. Proceedings of the Special Round Table on TNCs, SMEs and Development, UNCTAD X, 15 February 2000, Bangkok, Thailand. 113 p. UNCTAD/ITE/TEB1. Free of charge.

Handbook on Foreign Direct Investment by Small and Medium-sized Enterprises: Lessons from Asia. 200 p. Sales No. E.98.II.D.4. $48.

Handbook on Foreign Direct Investment by Small and Medium-sized Enterprises: Lessons from Asia. Executive Summary and Report of the Kunming Conference. 74 p. Free of charge.

Small and Medium-sized Transnational Corporations.Executive Summary and Report of the Osaka Conference. 60 p. Free of charge.

Small and Medium-sized Transnational Corporations: Role, Impact and Policy Implications. 242 p. Sales No. E.93.II.A.15. $35.

Measures of the Transnationalization of Economic Activity. 93 p. Sales No. E.01.II.D.2. $20.

The Competitiveness Challenge: Transnational Corporations and Industrial Restructuring in Developing Countries. 283p. Sales No. E.00.II.D.35. $42.

Integrating International and Financial Performance at the Enterprise Level. 116 p. Sales No. E.00.II.D.28. $18.

FDI Determinants and TNCs Strategies: The Case of Brazil. 195 p. Sales No. E.00.II.D.2. $35. Summary available from http://www.unctad.org/en/pub/psiteiitd14.en.htm.

The Social Responsibility of Transnational Corporations. 75 p. UNCTAD/ITE/IIT/Misc. 21. Free-of- charge. [Out of stock.] Available from http://www.unctad.org/en/docs/poiteiitm21.en.pdf.

Conclusions on Accounting and Reporting by Transnational Corporations. 47 p. Sales No. E.94.II.A.9. $25.

Accounting, Valuation and Privatization. 190 p. Sales No. E.94.II.A.3. $25.

Environmental Management in Transnational Corporations: Report on the Benchmark Corporate Environment Survey. 278 p. Sales No. E.94.II.A.2. $29.95.

Management Consulting: A Survey of the Industry and Its Largest Firms. 100 p. Sales No. E.93.II.A.17. $25.

Transnational Corporations: A Selective Bibliography, 1991-1992. 736 p. Sales No. E.93.II.A.16. $75.

Foreign Investment and Trade Linkages in Developing Countries. 108 p. Sales No. E.93.II.A.12. $18.

Transnational Corporations from Developing Countries: Impact on Their Home Countries. 116 p. Sales No. E.93.II.A.8. $15.

Debt-Equity Swaps and Development. 150 p. Sales No. E.93.II.A.7. $35.

From the Common Market to EC 92: Regional Economic Integration in the European Community and Transnational Corporations. 134 p. Sales No. E.93.II.A.2. $25.

The East-West Business Directory 1991/1992. 570 p. Sales No. E.92.II.A.20. $65.

Climate Change and Transnational Corporations: Analysis and Trends. 110 p. Sales No. E.92.II.A.7. $16.50.

Foreign Direct Investment and Transfer of Technology in India. 150 p. Sales No. E.92.II.A.3. $20.

The Determinants of Foreign Direct Investment: A Survey of the Evidence. 84 p. Sales No. E.92.II.A.2. $12.50.

Transnational Corporations and Industrial Hazards Disclosure. 98 p. Sales No. E.91.II.A.18. $17.50.

Transnational Business Information: A Manual of Needs and Sources. 216 p. Sales No. E.91.II.A.13. $45.

The Financial Crisis in Asia and Foreign Direct Investment: An Assessment. 101 p. Sales No. GV.E.98.0.29. $20.

Sharing Asia's Dynamism: Asian Direct Investment in the European Union. 192 p. Sales No. E.97.II.D.1. $26.

Investing in Asia's Dynamism: European Union Direct Investment in Asia. 124 p. ISBN 92-827-7675-1. ECU 14. (Joint publication with the European Commission.)

International Investment towards the Year 2002. 166 p. Sales No. GV.E.98.0.15. $29. (Joint publication with Invest in France Mission and Arthur Andersen, in collaboration with DATAR.)

International Investment towards the Year 2001. 81 p. Sales No. GV.E.97.0.5. $35. (Joint publication with Invest in France Mission and Arthur Andersen, in collaboration with DATAR.)

D. Journals

Transnational Corporations Journal (formerly **The CTC Reporter**).
Published three times a year. Annual subscription price: $45; individual issues $20.
http://www.unctad.org/en/subsites/dite/1_itncs/1_tncs.htm

United Nations publications may be obtained from bookstores and distributors throughout the world.

Please consult your bookstore or write to:

For Africa, Asia and Europe to:

Sales Section
United Nations Office at Geneva
Palais des Nations
CH-1211 Geneva 10
Switzerland
Tel: (41-22) 917-1234
Fax: (41-22) 917-0123
E-mail: unpubli@unog.ch

For Asia and the Pacific, the Caribbean, Latin America and North America to:

Sales Section
Room DC2-0853
United Nations Secretariat
New York, NY 10017
U.S.A.
Tel: (1-212) 963-8302 or (800) 253-9646
Fax: (1-212) 963-3489
E-mail: publications@un.org

All prices are quoted in United States dollars.

For further information on the work of the Division on Investment, Technology and Enterprise Development, UNCTAD, please address inquiries to:

United Nations Conference on Trade and Development
Division on Investment, Technology and Enterprise Development
Palais des Nations, Room E-10054
CH-1211 Geneva 10, Switzerland
Telephone: (41-22) 907-5651
Telefax: (41-22) 907-0498
E-mail: natalia.guerra@unctad.org
http://www.unctad.org

QUESTIONNAIRE

International Investment Instruments: A Compendium

Volume X

In order to improve the quality and relevance of the work of the UNCTAD Division on Investment, Technology and Enterprise Development, it would be useful to receive the views of readers on this publication. It would therefore be greatly appreciated if you could complete the following questionnaire and return it to:

Readership Survey
UNCTAD Division on Investment, Technology and Enterprise Development
United Nations Office in Geneva
Palais des Nations
Room E-9123
CH-1211 Geneva 10
Switzerland
Fax: 41-22-907-0194

1. Name and address of respondent (optional):

_____

_____

2. Which of the following best describes your area of work?

Government	○	Public enterprise ○
Private enterprise	○	Academic or research institution ○
International organization	○	Media ○
Not-for-profit organization	○	Other (specify) _____

3. In which country do you work? _____

4. What is your assessment of the contents of this publication?

Excellent	○	Adequate ○
Good	○	Poor ○

5. How useful is this publication to your work?

Very useful ○   Of some use ○   Irrelevant ○

6. Please indicate the three things you liked best about this publication:

_____

_____

_____

7. Please indicate the three things you liked least about this publication:

_____

_____

_____

8. Are you a regular recipient of **Transnational Corporations** (formerly **The CTC Reporter**), UNCTAD-DITE's tri-annual refereed journal?

Yes   ○   No   ○

If not, please check here if you would like to receive
a sample copy sent to the name and address you have
given above   ○

*